Haeger® POTTERIES

THROUGH THE YEARS

By David D. Dilley

A Price Guide

© 1997

2nd Printing
September 2001

L-W Book Sales
P.O. Box 69
Gas City, IN 46933

ISBN #: 0-89538-083-8

Published by: L-W BOOK SALES
            P. O. Box 69
            Gas City, IN 46933

Please write for our free catalog.

TABLE OF CONTENTS

Acknowledgments 4
Pricing Information 4
History 5-6, 10-13
Story of Haeger 6-9
Haeger Leaflet 1996 14-15
Designers 16-17
Introduction 18
Labels 19-20
1930 Catalog Pages 21-23
1938 Catalog Pages 24-27
1938-40 Catalog Pages 28-31
1939 Catalog Pages 32-33
1940 Catalog Pages 34-38
1941 Catalog Pages 39-41
1942 Catalog Pages 42-49
1946 Catalog Pages 50-62
1949 Catalog Pages 63-67
1950 Catalog Pages 68-76
1953 Catalog Pages 77-78
1954 Catalog Pages 79-86
1955 Catalog Pages .... 87-88 & 94
1957 Catalog Pages 95-103
1958 Catalog Pages 104-110
1959 Catalog Pages 111-119
1960 Catalog Pages 120-127
1961 Catalog Pages 128-131
1962 Catalog Pages .... 102 & 132-137
1963 Catalog Pages 138
1964 Catalog Pages 139-141
1965 Catalog Pages 89-93
1967 Catalog Pages 142-149
1971 Catalog Pages 150-159
1973/74 Catalog Pages 159-163
1974/75 Catalog Pages 164-166
1976 Catalog Pages 167-171
Original Ads 172-174
Ashtrays & Lighters 175-186
Bookends 187-188
Bowls & Dishes 189-202
Candle Holders 203-208
Candy Bowls & Dishes 209-210
Coordinating Pieces 211
Coordinating Sets 212-222
Cookie Jars 223
Figural Pieces 224-242
Flower Frogs 243-244
Lamps 245-252
Lavabo's 253
Miscellaneous 254-263
Pitchers & Utilitarian 264-268
Figural Planters 269-289
Planters 290-295
Signs 296
Figural Vases 297-312
Vases 313-338
Wall Pockets 339-340
Photo Index 341-351
Price Guide 352-372

ACKNOWLEDGMENTS

I would like to thank the following people for contributing or helping me in making this book possible: Lee Garmon & Doris Frizzell, Angie Miller, Heather Wray, John R. Magon, Rick Risser, Don Barker, Cellar Door Antiques, Doug Kirk, Keith Kuperman, Eileen Snyder, Bobby Farris and Burdell & Doris Hall - authors of Morton Potteries. A special thanks to Haeger Potteries (A Division of Haeger Industries, Inc.), Alexandra Haeger Estes & Nevina M. Zarbock without their help this book would have been harder to accomplish. Nevina Zarbock went above and beyond in helping me accomplish this book. Nevina has been employed with Haeger for quite a few years. She wanted to see that the history and the pottery lived on in this book. Also, last but not least, I would like to thank Pat & Georgia Corvin for contributing many pieces of their collection and for their hospitality when I was there photographing.

PRICING INFORMATION

All items priced in this guide are for items in very good condition. Pieces that are stained, with holes, chipped or cracked are worth much less. Items in mint condition may bring a higher dollar amount. Items in common shapes, but with hard to find glazes may also bring more. Remember, this is only a guide. L-W Books nor Haeger Potteries nor the author assumes any liability because of loss or gain in using these prices. Prices may vary from region to region depending on availability, so keep in mind this is only a guide.

SPECIAL INFORMATION

All colors named by Haeger will be capitalized in quotes. Size abbreviations are as follows: L = Length, W = Wide, T = Tall.

A History from *The Bulletin of the American Ceramic Society, Vol. 24, No. 10. October 15, 1945*

In 1871, David H. Haeger arrived in Dundee, Illinois, to look about for a business that seemed to have a future. Shortly thereafter, he purchased an interest in the Dundee Brick Yard, which was making a fine sand-mold brick. The brick made there can still be seen in many of the large and prominent factories and homes of northern Illinois and southern Wisconsin.

He later added two other brick and tile factories which earned for him a comfortable fortune.

In 1900, Mr. Haeger passed away, and the management of the factories fell upon his sons. The building-material business was continued until 1912, when the company began to manufacture flowerpots for florists. The manufacture of glazed pottery followed along naturally in 1914.

Launching of Artware Line

A few days before the opening of World War I, the pottery launched its artware efforts with a designer and a moldmaker. A line was developed rapidly which was of interest to stores, and the first shipment was made to Marshall Field & Company of Chicago. Their acceptance of this new line helped greatly to interest other stores.

On July 16, 1919, Edmund H. Haeger, a member of The American Ceramic Society since 1916, purchased the pottery at Dundee from the family corporation and became president. The output of the pottery was immediately doubled by the construction of another kiln. Salesmen were added, and the output gradually increased as the years went by.

Employment of F.J.M. Koenig

In 1924, the company was fortunate in securing the services of Franz Josef Menko Koenig as superintendent and ceramic engineer.

Mr. Koenig, born in Vreeland, Netherlands, August 14, 1882, finished high school in Vreeland and attended the Art Institute of Haarlem, where he received his diploma; three and one-half years later he was graduated from the Ceramic School of Höhr-Grenzhausen, Germany. He was then for seven years assistant manager of the Delft Corporation, Hilversum, Netherlands. He owned his own pottery from 1912 to 1916.

In 1916, Mr. Koenig went to the Taastrup Faience factory in Copenhagen, Denmark, and later became assistant manager of a dinnerware factory in Wilhelmsburg near Vienna, Austria.

In 1918, the Bureau of Industries of the Netherlands sent him as ceramic consultant to Java, Dutch East Indies. To travel to Java, he had to go by way of America and Japan because of the first World War. Immediately after finishing his contract with the Netherlands Government, he returned to America to enter the employ of The Haeger Potteries.

Mr. Koenig, a member of The American Ceramic Society since 1923, has become one of the foremost art pottery men in the United States, and his development of new glazes and colors has played an important part in the success of the business.

Exhibit at Century of Progress

In 1934, Haeger Potteries occupied an important space at the Century of Progress in Chicago. A separate building housed a complete pottery plant. Indians were brought from New Mexico to demonstrate the handmade pottery, hand throwers made up special pieces for visitors, and a regular line of souvenirs was produced in the plant. About forty-two persons were employed during 1934 up until December 1. This exhibit was visited by more than four million persons and was of great advertising value.

In 1938, the pottery introduced a new, highly styled line which was known as Royal Haeger. The items in this line were largely of the very modern design and met with prompt acceptance by the trade.

In 1939, The Haeger Potteries, Inc., took over a pottery at Macomb, Illinois, which for many years had made a superior line of stoneware. With the growing demand for artware, it was necessary in 1941 to convert this plant into an art pottery exclusively.

In 1941, a second tunnel kiln was built at Dundee to take care of the market demand for pottery and pottery lamp bases. During the peak of this demand, the pottery made four thousand lamps a day in addition to its artware. A subsidiary company marketed an outstanding line of lamps and shades.

Sales have continued to climb as a result of having offices in New York, Chicago, Los Angeles, Portland, and Seattle. Salesmen cover the entire United States, and their customers include practically all of the larger stores. Plans are now under way to double the output at the Macomb pottery; a new kiln is being built.

The Working Force

J.F. Estes, before his enlistment in the Army Air Corps, was general manager and will later resume that position. The company is fortunate in having many experienced workmen who have come up through the ranks and who play such an important part in production. The normal working force of the company is 350 employees, whose welfare has the constant thought of the management. Mr. Haeger recently purchased a six-hundred-acre estate, part of which will be used for employees' recreational activities.

A Reprint from a 75th Anniversary Pamphlet (1946)

Our Anniversary Message

Since 1871 the Haeger trademark has been known for dependable quality and strikingly beautiful design from coast to coast. Royal Haeger and Regular Haeger Pottery in your store reflects your taste in presenting the finest pottery obtainable to customers who recognize and rely on the Haeger trademark.

Founded 75 years ago by D.H. Haeger with a group of talented craftsmen, Haeger combines the art of ancient pottery with the efficiency of modern American production methods. Yet the minute perfection of each piece remains the primary objective. Never has mass production and the call for more pottery and lamps caused Haeger to swerve from the top quality for which we are known.

Haeger is always striving to excel its glorious record in introducing designs that add to American living. At the end of three-quarters of a century, we stand rededicated to our belief in America's future and to full cooperation with all Haeger outlets. It has been our policy for seventy-five years to stand behind our products to the full satisfaction of all dealers. This fundamental principle continues unchanged.

A Reprint from a 75th Anniversary Brochure

Picture of a Pottery on its 75th Anniversary
The Haeger Pottery Story started 75 years ago...

> DEDICATED TO EDMUND H. HAEGER,
> PRESIDENT OF THE HAEGER POTTERIES, INC.
> • • •
> THIS BOOK COMMEMORATES
> SEVENTY-FIVE YEARS OF PROGRESS
> AND ACHIEVEMENT
> • • •
> Copyright, 1947, THE HAEGER POTTERIES, INC.
> DUNDEE, ILLINOIS

THE STORY

Typical street scene in 1871

The Haeger brick kilns in Dundee

It was 1871...Ulysses S. Grant was the President of the United States...the smoldering memory of the Civil War lay only six years behind a busy growing nation...with a rush of activity the country had turned its energies to the development of the great West...men were building railroads across the continent, linking the country from coast to coast...new factories, new enterprises were springing up throughout the East...new cities were building in the West.

During this active post-war era of 75 years ago, David H. Haeger came to Dundee in Illinois. It was a small, picturesque early-American village, surrounded by the famed natural splendor of a beautiful valley through whose wooded slopes and hillsides the Fox River slowly winds to the south. Here he began the manufacture of bricks made of clay dug from the river banks and nearby hills. At first a timeless method was employed–bricks were made by hand, dried in the sun, fired in huge kilns shaped like giant beehives. His business grew with the region, and when he died in 1900, the pioneer Haeger left a prosperous enterprise to his family.

One of the founder's sons was Edmund H. Haeger, and he had the perception to see that Haeger talents and equipment could be used to make new and equally useful objects from clay. Consequently, in 1912, the company started the manufacture of simple red flower pots. Two years later Edmund Haeger's plans had developed to the point where he could begin making glazed ware. Under his direction the first piece of Haeger Pottery was produced, and with his interested and careful supervision the Haeger line was created during the years that followed.

Pottery buyers for gift and department stores were immmediately interested in the new Haeger line. Soon thousands of customers were buying Haeger Pottery to enhance their homes. In order to handle the increasingly larger orders, the large four-story building–built by the Haeger family in 1908–was completely converted to pottery production. The new Haeger glazes and designs made such a public impression that, by 1920, the company was operating three bottle-type kilns in order to keep shops and stores supplied. And, by this time, Haeger Pottery was being sold by better stores from Detroit to Miami, from New York to San Francisco.

Edmund Haeger's decision to build a model pottery exhibit at the Century of Progress Exhibition in Chicago further introduced the Haeger line to Americans from every part of the country. This modern exhibit included a large display of Haeger Pottery, and a working production unit. As an interesting contrast to the Haeger operation, Indian potters were brought from New Mexico to demonstrate their primitive methods of making and firing ware. In 1934 more than four million people visited the educational exhibit and watched the making of Haeger Pottery.

Then, with the appointment of Joseph F. Estes as general manager, the Haeger third generation was associated with the family's enterprise. Following the tradition of the founder, the business pressed forward. A stoneware pottery in Macomb, Illinois, was purchased and converted to art pottery production. A new line, known as Royal Haeger Pottery, embodying lustrous new glazes and original design motifs, was created and successfully introduced. Royal Haeger Lamps were then designed and produced for a discerning trade. These Haeger-made lamp originals - acclaimed by homemakers for their beautiful pottery bases, highly stylized shades and perfection in every mechanical and design detail - have readily won sincere approval from discriminating buyers everywhere.

Now, in the midst of another expanding post-war period, The Haeger Potteries celebrate their 75th Anniversary...pausing to review the business that has grown from a simple hand-work operation in 1871 into the largest art pottery in the world...recognizing the important contributions made by employees who, like V. R. MacDonald, assistant treasurer, have been with the company for twenty-five years...looking forward, too, with confidence in the future...planning for new buildings in Dundee, initiating a working pottery exhibit at the Museum of Science and Industry in Chicago, developing an additional line of art pottery...and, above all, constantly adhering to the creative point-of-view that will result in ever-finer pottery bearing the Haeger seal.

Turning the first Haeger Pottery

HAEGER DESIGNERS

Haeger Pottery owes its principal charm to the talented artists who have created the original designs from which the pottery is made. The designers, who are specialists in their fields, contribute the ceramic forms that make Haeger Pottery distinctive and highly marketable.

Lee Sectrist, Art Director, heads the Haeger design group, anticipating trends and styles. His skill in this capacity and as a designer in his own right have been proved by the increasing popularity of Haeger Pottery.

Foremost among this Haeger design group is Franz Joseph Koenig, superintendent, ceramic artist and engineer at the Haeger Potteries, who has executed a number of notable designs, in addition to his developmental work on new glazes and colors.

Eric Olsen, a Norwegian artist formerly associated with England's famed Wedgwood and Spode, has designed an unusually interesting pottery series for Haeger. While his work with modern figures and forms was interrupted for service with the Norwegian Army during World War II, he has now returned to the field of contemporary ceramic design.

Martin I. Deutsch, New York sculptor and painter, whose work has been widely exhibited, has made a number of significant design contributions. In order to learn every phase of the medium, he set up his own small pottery and fired his own experimental pieces.

A variety of Haeger pieces have originated in the Larchmont, New York, studio of Joseph Pfanzelter, an alert arts and crafts designer. Not satisfied to work in a single medium, he has become adept with a number of materials, including wood, marble, metal and terra cotta.

Elaine Douglas Carlock is a Haeger designer who first won attention with her delightful sketches of her four little sons. Her creative work is modeled in clay on the fruit farm near Cincinnati, where she lives with her family.

Another Haeger contributor is the versatile designer, Maria Fuchs. In addition to designing silver, metal, plastic and glass objects, she creates new forms for Haegerware in her New York studio.

The Haeger plant in 1914

CLAY IS PREPARED

Haeger Pottery begins with the mixing of carefully selected materials: ball clay from Kentucky and Tennessee; kaolin–a pure white clay that endures fire without discoloring–from Florida and Georgia; whiting, or limestone from Illinois; and flint from Illinois and Wisconsin. These raw materials are washed, screened and purified to obtain the clay body suitable for Haeger glazes and the heat of the Haeger kilns. While the clays are being mixed, water is added to form a slurry, known to potters as "slip". It is this liquid slip which is poured into plaster-of-paris molds to form the pottery.

THE MOLD

After a Haeger designer completes the design for a new piece, expert molders carefully make a "mother", or original mold, from the designer's model. Plaster is used in making this original mold, and it must be carefully handled in order to obtain an exact duplicate, complete in every detail. Then a block and case is made and from it any number of plaster-of-paris copies may be made. It is these plaster-of-paris copy-molds–of which there are many for each design–that are used for casting Haeger Pottery.

CASTING

After the porous mold is filled with liquid slip, it is allowed to stand until a one-quarter-inch shell forms next to the mold. The mold is then turned upside down and the still-liquid slip drains from the center, leaving a hollow clay shell shaped to the form of the mold. The porous plaster-of-paris continues to absorb water until the clay has shrunk away and released itself from the mold.

FINISHING

When the pottery is sufficiently firm to handle, each piece is moved to the finishing section. Here, any seams or imperfections are removed by finishers, using knives, special wooden tools and a light sponging operation. After the finisher completes their work, each piece is rigidly inspected, and those that do not measure up to Haeger's high standard are further finished or discarded. A variety of original applique designs and techniques have been developed by Arnold Vogel, head of the casting departments.

APPLIQUE

Many Haeger designs are further enhanced by the addition of small handmade flowers and leaves, deftly fashioned by talented applique workers. These dextrous handcrafters also assemble other Haeger pieces, too complicated to be cast in one mold. The applique of separate, decorative designs is accomplished by moistening the contact points with liquid slip and carefully joining the pieces. Haeger's unusual applique techniques require a considerable amount of time as well as highly skilled handwork.

FIRING

The clay pottery–called "greenware" at this stage–is carefully placed on cars and moved into the kiln, where it is fired for 35 hours. A continuous kiln operation is used at the Haeger Potteries, permitting ware to enter one of the tunnel-shaped ovens at a low temperature and move some 225 feet. When the ware is removed from the kiln it has become a hard, white bisque.

HAEGER GLAZES

Haeger's famous glazes–frequently imitated but never successfully copied–are made by expert craftsmen with backgrounds of extensive training and experience. Two men are noted for their contributions to Haeger glaze making:

Franz Joseph Koenig has been associated with the Haeger Potteries for twenty-three years. He created the first Haeger matte glazes, and has constantly supervised and participated in the extensive experiments preceding the development of Haeger's many interesting colors and glazes.

Robert Heiden started his career at Haeger in 1913. He has known every phase of Haeger progress since he helped cast the first piece produced by the pottery. In charge of the kiln and glaze sections, his extensive knowledge of glaze-making and firing is relied upon when new glazes are being developed and tested.

Among the many glazes that will be featured during the 75th Anniversary year are:

Greenbriar–A rich mulberry agate highlighted by a white and green spray at the top.
Ciel–A soft mauve with a generous use of honey and blue–a delicate mauve-blue effect, highlighted with honey.
Yellow Drip–A Chinese (Ming) yellow body glaze with a honey drip highlighted by soft green.
Lime–A very lush, fresh green with either honey or yellow used as an accent and liner.
Chartreuse–A strikingly modern color, with slightly more yellow than Lime glaze.
Tomato–A deep rich henna tone, especially well-suited for modern pieces and decor.
Ox-Blood–A deep vibrant red, well-known as a glaze but not available for several years.
Honey Copen–A soft green-blue with a luxurious use of honey as a drip and liner.

Exhibit at the World's Fair

SPRAYING

When the first firing is completed, the bisqueware is then dipped or sprayed with Haeger glazes, famed for their matchless colors. These glazes must not crack or break during the final firing, and they must be hard and durable when the pottery is taken from the kiln. Above all, the color must always be clear and lustrous. Raw iron, copper and zinc oxides, sienna and manganese, together with other mineral products are used to create Haeger glazes. The next step is that of making "frit", the basis of every glaze and essentially a glass which gives the potter a wide color range. After the frit is broken up in grinding and ball mills, the liquid glaze may be prepared. In the final firing, the frit is fused and vitrified, making the clay watertight.

HAND PAINTING

A final handcraft operation is accomplished in Haeger's interesting hand painting section. Here a large and talented group of colorists add a variety of liquid glazes to the appliqued pottery. For many pieces of Royal Haeger Pottery the skill of the experienced hand painters means an added charm and appeal that could never be realized through purely mechanical pottery production methods. It is the truly individual manner in which these craftsmen use their brushes to apply colored glazes that achieves added character and interest for the finished Haeger pottery. When the hand painting is completed the pottery is taken to kilns for the final firing.

FINISHED HAEGERWARE

In terms of design, glazes, and construction, each piece of Haeger Pottery represents a useful and truly distinctive ceramic achievement. And tomorrow–as countless discriminating customers will agree–Haeger artist-craftsmen will continue to make the pottery that coming generations will collect and treasure.

WELCOME

Sometime soon, plan to travel out–through the beautiful Fox River Valley–to Dundee. You'll find a completely charming town, whose tree-lined streets are lined with authentic examples of early-American architecture. And, when you come, stop by and see the Haeger Potteries for yourself. Tours are conducted frequently–there are many interesting things to see. It's a standing invitation–so come as soon as you can!

You enter this doorway . . .

1871 / 1971

Haeger

the Craftsmen for a Century

THE STORY OF HAEGER'S FIRST ONE HUNDRED YEARS
THE HAEGER POTTERIES, INC., DUNDEE, ILLINOIS 60118

1912, the office of the Haeger Pottery.

The first bottle kiln in operation, 1916.

David H. Haeger

Edmund H. Haeger
Introduced Art Pottery
in 1914.

Haeger's present day facility at Dundee, Illinois.

To commemorate this centennial achievement, it's our pleasure to bring you a short pictorial story of Haeger. In it we shall attempt to acquaint you with our early history and, as well, outline the basic steps that constitute manufacture of fine artware and lamps. As you read on, it is our hope that you will come to realize the nature and substance of Haeger, in essence a commitment to the tradition of finely crafted quality.

The earliest existing photo of Haeger plant and grounds, 1908.

A century long heritage of craftsmanship

Few companies span a century. That Haeger Pottery has not merely survived, but truly thrived, is a tribute to leadership. Leadership shown by the four generations that headed the firm, and the leadership Haeger has demonstrated to the industry.

From founder David H. Haeger's Dundee Brick Yard in 1871, Haeger has progressed to its position today as a pace-setter in design and innovation. Haeger pottery is found anywhere in the world where selective good taste is evident.

One of David's sons, Edmund H. Haeger, assumed leadership of the Dundee factory and had the inspiration to begin the production of art pottery in 1914. He envisioned the use of lovely shapes in beautiful colors enhancing the homes of America (now international).

In 1934, he built a complete working ceramic factory at the Chicago World's Fair, showing both the ancient and the contemporary modes of production.

There is tradition here. Joseph F. Estes, named general manager in 1938, and president in 1954, is a third generation leader of Haeger Pottery. Expansion and diversification have been the fruits of his guidance. The Royal Haeger line of artware and lamp bases he introduced is one of the most respected in the field. In 1939, he was instrumental in starting the Macomb Pottery plant, which produces a complete line for florists.

The fourth generation is represented by a son, Nicholas Edmund Haeger Estes, General Manager of the Royal Haeger Lamp Company, Macomb division. This second plant, open-ed at Macomb, Illinois in 1969, is devoted exclusively to the manufacture of lamp bases and shades, augmenting the lamp company facilities at Dundee.

Though the company is a century old, its outlook is not. Our hundred years of experience is yours to benefit from. We are not looking back at the past century—only ahead to the next.

No company survives without the support of its customers and friends. And we pause during this benchmark in our history to offer our warmest thanks to those much appreciated friends. We pledge to each of you that we will do all possible to continue to lead, to innovate, to explore with just one goal in mind: to serve you much better with each passing year in our second century of growth.

Mr. Joseph F. Estes, President
Much of Haeger's substantial growth has occured under Mr. Estes' direction both while serving as General Manager and as President.

The Macomb, Illinois artware manufacturing facility, established 1939.

Haeger's lamp production plant in Macomb, in use since 1969.

Every single lamp or piece of artware goes through many steps from the time it originates as a fleeting idea in a designers mind. The following photos will outline briefly some of the major steps in manufacture. Certainly no photo essay can take the place of personal observation, and tours are available to give a first-hand view of this fascinating process.

Designs first develop as ideas on paper.

Three dimensional handworked models are made of promising design ideas.

Precise models have to be made for those pieces that will eventually be produced.

Glazes and surface treatments are constantly being explored and developed by Haeger personnel.

The block and case is being poured with plaster in order that production molds can be produced.

Slip, liquid clay, is pumped into production molds.

As a contrast, above is shown the early, slow process of carrying and pouring slip.

Through constant research and development, Haeger is continually developing new methods to help production and better the quality of Haeger.

After a certain thickness of wall has built up from solidified slip, the excess is poured out of the mold.

Haeger's new automatic mold filling operation.

After standing, the mold is opened and the delicate clay shell is removed from the mold.

Molds are dumped with no human hands touching them.

A jigger wheel is the outgrowth of a potter's wheel. Here we use a Plaster of Paris mold and a putty-like clay and form the piece of pottery according to the inside of the mold.

An automatic jigger wheel which produced automatically a piece of pottery according to the inside of the mold.

Certain hollow-ware designs can be made by a pressing process. Haeger uses this on certain items.

Highly developed glazes are applied by hand to each piece to assure fine quality.

All mold marks and any other slight imperfections are eliminated by hand finishing.

Each piece of Haeger ware is closely inspected and worked on as it progresses along its path toward completion.

Again, in contrast, earlier days saw no "shelves" on kiln cars. Each car in this case was loaded with round receptacles (saggers) which contained the ware, a slow tedious task.

When the glaze has dried, kiln cars are loaded with ware to be fired.

Much of today's ware is finished with features such as gold leaf for antiquing-all by skilled hands.

You're invited to come and see for yourself this fascinating process. You will notice the forward looking features of our operation, but even more, we're certain you'll be impressed by our attention to detail and the care which is taken to assure Haeger fine quality. It's a tradition! After all, we are the Craftsmen for a Century!

THE HAEGER POTTERIES, INC.
SEVEN MAIDEN LANE
DUNDEE, ILLINOIS 60118
(312) 426-3441

At the end of a 24 hour trip through Haeger's tunnel kilns, the ware is now fired and ready for final inspection.

**The Next Two Pages are a Reprint from Haeger 1996 Catalog.
125th Anniversary**

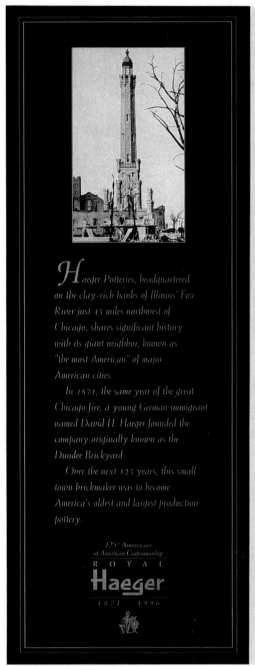

*H*aeger Potteries, headquartered on the clay-rich banks of Illinois' Fox River just 45 miles northwest of Chicago, shares significant history with its giant neighbor, known as "the most American" of major American cities.

In 1871, the same year of the great Chicago fire, a young German immigrant named David H. Haeger founded the company originally known as the Dundee Brickyard.

Over the next 125 years, this small town brickmaker was to become America's oldest and largest production pottery.

125th Anniversary of American Craftsmanship

ROYAL
Haeger
1871 – 1996

*T*he Chicago Fire destroyed more than 17,500 buildings and made tens of thousands suddenly homeless.

The Old Water Tower, completed just two years before David Haeger founded his

brick company, not only survived the flames, but remains a stirring memorial to the great fire of 1871.

*T*he company which David Haeger founded fired the first of millions of bricks needed to help rebuild the great midwest metropolis. In this way, the young company helped a city rise from the ashes of mass disaster and restore its faith in itself. The volume brickmaker was destined to secure a special place in American artware history.

For both Chicago and David Haeger's growing company, the late 19th century was a time of new confidence, energy and vision. Over the next 25 years the city's lakefront was rebuilt on the solid planning of Daniel Burnham, the legendary architect who laid the seeds for modern Chicago's magnificent shoreline, once laid low by the fire.

*A*t the same time, David Haeger, with the help of one of his sons, Edmund H. Haeger, began laying the groundwork for their company's transition from brickmakers to artisans. By 1900, the year of David H. Haeger's passing, the company was already making simple red clay flower pots for the florist trade. Edmund Haeger, with his artistic vision, was to complete the metamorphosis from Haeger Bricks to Haeger Potteries. In 1912 he introduced a more sophisticated line of glazed artware.

Chicago Historical Society. 1. Photograph, ICHi-02792, Water tower and waterworks after the fire of 1871, Chicago (Ill.), 1871, Photographer unknown. (The original photo has been altered by creating a duotone.)

Adam and Eve, from the lines first Artware collection, were of classic Greek style and symbolized the enduring qualities of fine design and craftsmanship for which Royal Haeger artware is known today.

1914

Haeger's famous glazes, frequently imitated but never successfully copied, have always been made by expert craftsmen. The glaze covering the artware must be perfectly mixed and blended, hard and durable when fired, without cracks. Above all, the color must be clear and lustrous. Careful dipping assures a uniform coating of the bisque.

Pottery designer J. Martin Stangl joined the company in 1914 to help Edmund Haeger develop a new line of commercial florist ware. Haeger's first "milk bottle" kiln was in operation by 1916.

At the Chicago's World's Fair of 1934, the histories of Haeger and "that most American city" came together once more — near the very shore laid waste by the fire 53 years before. For the year-long fair, "Century of Progress," Edmund Haeger built a complete working ceramic factory which demonstrated both ancient and modern modes of production. More than four million visited this remarkable exhibit, which featured a fascinating primitive demonstration by southwest Indian potters.

1935

*F*amily leadership continued at Haeger under son-in-law Joseph F. Estes, who became general manager in 1938. That same year, design genius Royal Hickman joined the company to introduce an extraordinary line of

artware, called Royal Haeger. Hickman's work was daringly intricate with smooth, flowing lines and highly original glazes. Public demand for Royal Haeger artware was immediate and strong. Royal Hickman's world-acclaimed designs included his famous black panther, a sleek elongated cat, first produced in 1941 and offered in three sizes.

1941

Another distinguished chief designer was Eric Olsen, whose career with Haeger spanned 25 years (1947-1972). Olsen's many contributions to the Royal Haeger line included his magnificent bull figure, produced in 1955. One year earlier, Joseph F. Estes was to become president of Haeger Potteries with the passing of Edmund H. Haeger. Early Royal Haeger artware, highly prized among serious

1955

collector's, was covered with a variety of original glazes. Gold Tweed was a unique glaze introduced in the 1960's.

The Royal Haeger ceramic lines continued to grow and evolve. At one time they included dinnerware,

but became especially known for vases, figurines, miniature animals, birds, flowers and lamps — as well as other unusual and useful accessories of exquisite taste. The broadest and best-selling lines in American artware.

Haeger Potteries in 1971 celebrated its 100th anniversary under Joseph F. Estes, who led the company through tremendous growth in his more than 50 years at the helm.

1970

In 1976 Haeger Potteries entered the Guiness Book of Records. An amazing vase, standing more than eight feet tall and weighing more than 650 pounds was created by Haeger Potteries. It rests in the museum at Haeger headquarters in Dundee, Illinois and according to the Guiness Book of Records, is the largest hand-thrown vase in the world.

*I*n 1979 Joseph F. Estes' daughter, Alexandra Haeger Estes (Great grand-daughter of the founder), became president of Haeger Potteries. In 1984, she became president of the parent company, Haeger Industries.

In the 1980's Royal Haeger represented broad lines of neoclassic and country designs, created for

1985

gracious living and covered with over 20 lustrous colored glazes.

Haeger Potteries, internationally known as the exclusive designers and craftsmen of Royal Haeger ceramic artware, produce the most collected accessories for the home – destined to continue into the 21st Century and beyond.

1990

*T*hank you for helping us celebrate Haeger Potteries' 125th Anniversary of American Craftsmanship.

"Through the decades, all Royal Haeger ceramic accessories have been graced with timeless design, color and texture. We hope you will discover that, like Royal Haeger lines of our proud past, the 1996 Royal Haeger line offers exceptional value for you, our customers.

"Four generations of family tradition stand behind David H. Haeger's original commitment to fine craftsmanship, consistent quality, service and value.

"As always, we pledge to please you."

Alexandra H Estes

Alexandra Haeger Estes

1996

THE Haeger® POTTERIES

Craftsmen for over a century

10. "The Merry Wanderer," a gift to Haeger on our 100th Anniversary (1971) from W. Goebel & Company, is a life-size copy of one of the most famous Hummel figurines, and was hand-made for the occasion. Visitors to our Ceramic Museum will see this unique work-of-art.

We are proud that the Haeger name is synonymous with quality and excellence in fine art pottery. Our history is as rich and enduring as the clay along the banks of the Fox River where it all began.

In 1871 founder David Haeger's Dundee Brickyard helped rebuild Chicago after its devastating Great Fire. Those early bricks were the solid foundation for what is now Haeger Potteries, the world's largest art pottery.

Today, under the direction of the fourth generation of the Haeger family, we still transform clay into art at our original location along the banks of the scenic and historic Fox River in Northwest Illinois.

The years have seen steady growth, creativity and innovation. With the intro-

duction of the first line of Haeger artware in 1914 to the present, Haeger quality has been accepted worldwide as the standard by which other pottery is judged.

Although thousands of Haeger pottery products are created each day, every single piece is handled with individual care by our dedicated and skilled craftsmen. We feel that is what makes Haeger Pottery so special. the unduplicated formula of an age-old process guided by talented, attentive hands.

Enjoy your trip to The Haeger Potteries Factory Outlet in Historic Dundee, Illinois. You will find an outstanding collection of Haeger ceramic accessories and original hand-turned pottery at Factory Direct Prices.

8. Colorful arrays of silk and dried florals and foliage are available the year around, as well as Custom or Ready-to-go Arrangements designed by our Floral Artists.

9. Located in the Haeger Museum is the World's Tallest Art Pottery Vase by Haeger. It is listed in the Guinness Book of Records and on display in the Factory Outlet Salesroom in Dundee.

Most Haeger pottery sold at our Haeger Factory Outlet are slightly imperfect, discontinued, or one-of-a-kind test pieces.

10

Haeger®

invites you to be our guest

Tour our Factory and Salesroom

in Historic Dundee, IL

THE Haeger® POTTERIES

a Division of Haeger Industries, Inc.
Seven Maiden Lane • Dundee, Illinois 60118-2397

The Next Two Pages are from a Leaflet on Visiting the Factory in Dundee, Illinois

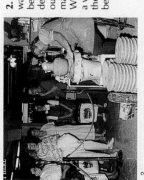

Enjoy Free Factory Tours

- Our Haeger Tour Guides lead visitors on a 40 minute walking tour of the world's largest art pottery.

- Tours are conducted Monday through Friday. Walk-ins are always welcome. Children must be four years or older to tour the factory. Schedules are subject to change without notice.

Call our Tour Office for tour schedules and group reservations

(847) 426-3441

The Haeger Factory Outlet is located on Van Buren St., two blocks south of Rt. 72 in Dundee.
Open Monday through Friday   10:00 a.m. to 6:00 p.m.
Saturday, Sunday and holidays   10:00 a.m. to 5:00 p.m.
CLOSED: New Year's Day, Easter, Thanksgiving and Christmas

Haeger®
Craftsmen for over a century

We invite you to discover the magical world of pottery. Follow the fascinating steps that change raw clay into works of art.

5. See the alternate methods used by skilled craftsmen in applying the beautiful glazes that bring an explosion of vibrant color to Haeger Pottery.

6. Walk into the Great Kiln Room where the block long kiln and round kiln are located.

7. Find a huge selection of Royal Haeger accessories to complement any decor.

1. Enter The Haeger Potteries Factory Outlet in Dundee and get ready for a memorable visit.

2. Your guided walking tour begins with a lively demonstration by our exceptional master potter. Watch as he spins a work of art on the potter's wheel before your eyes.

3. Learn the different skills required in forming raw clay into beautiful decorative ceramics. The process begins as slip (liquid clay) which is poured into molds.

4. Appreciate the care and meticulous attention our hand finishers give each piece of pottery as it comes from the mold. This vital process provides the necessary human touch to insure an exceptional product.

"**Haeger**. . . a fourth generation,
family-owned American business since 1871"

15

MARTIN J. STANGL

Martin J. Stangl left his employment with Fulper, where he was listed as the superintendent of the technical division of Fulper in 1911, to pursue developing a commercial artware line for Haeger. His employment, which started in 1914, lasted for five years, then he returned to Fulper in 1920 as general manager. He later started Stangl pottery, which is also a well known pottery throughout the collectible market. Sometimes pieces of Haeger will be signed by J. Stangl. The pieces that you do find are of value and of special interest to Stangl collectors also.

FRANZ JOSEPH KOENIG

Refer to A History from the bulletin of the American Ceramic Society on page 5.

ROBERT HEIDEN

Refer to A Reprint from the 75th Anniversary, Glazes section on page 8.

ROYAL ARDEN HICKMAN

None other than Royal Hickman comes to mind when reminiscing of Haeger's most talented designers. His passion for form and design led to a career of art pieces fashioned from not only pottery, but aluminum, crystal, paper, onyx, silver, and wood as well. Capable of both imagination and technique, he envisioned pieces which grew in his hands into free flowing inspirational sculptures.

Hickman was born in 1893 and raised in the little town of Willamette, Oregon. After developing his artistic ability throughout his youth, he left Oregon at the age of 19 to attend the Mark Hopkins Art Academy in San Francisco. Upon graduation, his first few years were spent laboring in Hawaii and Washington. The Depression led Hickman and his newly established construction company to the Panama Canal. Although a small business, they had managed to secure a job working on the Madden Dam. Unfortunately, laboring in the near-tropical heat brought a spell of severe sunstroke upon Hickman, bleaching his hair and leaving him partially paralyzed.

While recovering in California, his routine of therapy enabled him to play with and shape clay as much as he wished in order to strengthen his limbs and regain use of his digits, although this hardly seemed a monotonous task considering his talents. Honing his sculpting ability to a new level, he soon found himself designing dinnerware for the likes of Garden City Pottery and a pottery line called RaArt for S. & G. Gump Company- both of which are prestigious accomplishments.

The years to follow found Royal Hickman throughout the European region designing crystal for J.H. Vernon Company (based in New York City) and Kosta Glassbruck (in Sweden). He worked in Sweden, Denmark, Italy, and Czechoslovakia during the Nazi occupation, then left for New York City to continue his crystal designs for Kosta Crystal.

His mind began to wander considering mediums other than crystal into which he would inject his creativity. In 1938, he accepted the invitation to join with Haeger Potteries- later that year the Royal Haeger line (with Royal Hickman as Chief Designer) was released to immediate success. Haeger Potteries was forced to build a second tunnel kiln merely to keep up with the demand of their current lines. The next few years the company thrived and also formed the new Royal Haeger Lamp Company in 1939. One of his popular designs was the black panther that was many times imitated by other companies. The panther was only marked with a label so it is hard to identify without one. The Haeger panther has no holes for the eyes, no garnishing, no chains and no rhinestones. It does have a hooded eyelid over the curved mark of the eye. Also on the earliest version of the panther the tail reached out and did not touch the back of the leg on the curl up version. In 1944, Royal Hickman left Haeger to pursue other opportunities.

Throughout the 1940's Hickman worked solo and with a handful of companies all over the states, including the Heisey Glass Company, Vernon Potteries, Bruce Fox Aluminum and even his own Royal Hickman Industries in Chattanooga, TN, Tampa, FL and California.

Eventually, Royal Hickman made his home in Guadalajara, Mexico. Once again, Hickman returned to the fold with Haeger Potteries, designing and consulting on a freelance basis from the 1950's until his unfortunate passing on September 1st, 1969.

ERIC OLSEN

A Norwegian Artist, born in Drammen, Norway in 1903, that worked for Haeger for twenty-five years. As the chief designer, his work consisted of 90% of Haeger's artware and lamp production. He began his art training at the age of 11 with his academic study in Oslo, London and Paris. Before coming to Haeger he was also associated with England's famed Wedgwood in 1930 and Spode in 1932 until 1942. He was selected as National Register Designer in 1936 under the support of the English Board of Trade. In 1937 he gave a private exhibition in London that was opened by the Queen of Norway. One of Mr. Olsens more popular designs is the red bull, model # R-1510. This piece was also sold in ebony and I have also obtained one that is in the mandarin orange color, *(see photo in color section)*. He also enjoyed recognition in the art world for his busts of famous people including: Mahatma Ghandi, Winston Churchill and Carl Sandburg to name a few. A memorial bust of Edmund H. Haeger was also done by him and unveiled at the 100th anniversary of Haeger Pottery. The bust is now on display at the Macomb and Dundee, Illinois plants.

EDWIN K. KAELKE

Edwin Kaelke, an employee of Haeger for 50 years, was the executive vice-president and general manager who also did some of the designing and had suggestions on works by other artists.

MARTIN I. DEUTSCH

Martin Deutsch was a New York sculptor and painter who made design contributions.

LEE SECRIST

Mr. Secrist was hired to supervise and create designs for Haeger in 1946. He designed artware for Haeger and the lamp company in Macomb. He studied art at the Chicago Academy of Fine Arts, the Chicago Art Institute and the Yale School of Fine Arts. He also studied in Florence, Italy.

C. GLENN RICHARDSON

Director of design starting in 1971, Glenn studied at Wright Junior College and Illinois Institute of Design. While in the Marines he studied at San Diego Junior College, and also he had done design and artwork for Marine's Special Services.

SEBASTIANO MAGLIO

Sebastiano Maglio was a professor of art in Sicily. Being of a seventh generation of potters, his skills have been passed down. He started at Haeger in 1963. One of his great accomplishments was making the vase that is in the 1983 Guinness Book of Records for being the World's Largest art pottery vase. The vase is over 8' tall and used over 650 pounds of clay. The vase was completed in December 1971. See the flyer on visiting the Haeger plant for photo.

SASCHA BRASTOFF

Sascha Brastoff was a noted California designer. He was well known in the Hollywood community of stars and by wealthy collectors and admirers like the Rockefellers. He was talented in all forms of art including: dance, theatre, costume designing, fabrics, metals, sculpting, ceramics, painting and many more. His art can still be viewed in many of the major art museums or by purchasing pieces from his company in California. The best way to view his art is by viewing the 1971 line he designed called "Esplanade" and "Roman Bronze" for Haeger Potteries, which consisted of about 50 pieces. The pieces had Spanish or Florentine designs with silver or bronze metallic finish.

ALRUN OSTERBERG GUEST

Ceramic engineer currently with Haeger, Alrun Guest came to Haeger Potteries in 1969 from Berlin, Germany. A graduate of the ceramic school of Hohr-Grenzhausen, she has provided the Haeger companies with unique and lustrous glaze finishes as well as interesting shapes and designs. The painted scenes on the 1983 Guinness Book of Records Vase, on display in the Haeger Museum in Dundee, were done by Alrun and her design staff. The scenes on the vase are portraying potters at work.

OTHER DESIGNERS

Maria Fuchs, Elsa Ken Haeger, A.H. Estes, Don Lewis, Kevin Bradley, Kathryn DeSousa, Helen Conover, Helmut Bruchmann, Elaine Douglas Carlock, Joseph Pfanzelter, Ben Seibel and others.

After reading through all of the Haeger history, you probably now know plenty about Haeger Potteries Inc. I just want to make a few notes on certain lines and specialty items. As a general rule Haeger pottery was marked with a label, molded or stamped on the bottom. The pieces that were only marked with labels could be difficult to identify. I have seen wax markings on some pieces that did correspond to the correct model number, but this was not a Haeger practice. It could have been done by department stores or by dealers that were able to identify the mold number. Another thing I have noticed with most pieces is that the glaze flows over the bottom only leaving three unglazed dots. This happened when the pottery was fired on a triangular pedestal, called a "stilt", and then taken off after firing, leaving the three marks. Some pieces have been ground on the bottom according to the design (if it wouldn't stand on the triangular pedestal). This is not something to completely follow, but it will help if it is a combination of style, glaze color and texture which all seem to be Haeger.

Certain years and glazes have become more popular in the past few years. I don't know if it is just changing trends or the availability of the older items. The items from the 60's and the 70's have grown considerably more popular, while gaining in value. One example of this would be the Earth Graphic Wrap glazed items. Some of these will run higher than some 1930's and 40's pieces.

Some important dates: In 1939 the Buckeye Pottery Building was purchased in Macomb, IL for the florist trade items; In 1946 was the 75th Anniversary; In 1947 the Haeger Awards were developed; In 1969 the Western Stoneware factory was purchased in Macomb, IL for the Royal Haeger Lamp Company; In 1971 was the 100th Anniversary "Craftsmen for a Century"; In 1979 the Cherokee Indians built a pottery, Cherokee Nation Pottery, that was operated under Haeger's direction; In 1996 was the 125th Anniversary.

Haeger originated the Keebler Cookie Jar with the Keebler Co. This cookie jar was three dimensional on the Keebler logo and on Ernie the Keebler Elf. The three dimensional areas were hand painted with special detail, not decals like the McCoy version which came later. The reason for the switch in companies was because Keebler decided that Haeger was too expensive, so they sacrificed quality with a change for a cheaper cookie jar. We now see which one prevailed in the collectible market as the Haeger version is more desired by cookie jar collectors.

Ebony has been the most important color in the Haeger line for the past thirteen years. Some original designs have been re-released in this color but size changes have been made on most. The panther is a design which is still being made to this day. The original panther had a tail that did not do a loop-de-loop. The tail changed right away back in the 40's. They found in production that the tail was continually breaking off, so they redesigned it so that the tail was incorporated into the legs. The original version is very scarce.

Some early Haeger had sterling silver overlay on it that was applied in Mexico. These pieces are also hard to come by. Other items that are hard to find or are just down right scarce are: The model #R-766 Rudolph the Red-Nosed reindeer lamp base or planter; all Haeger portable fountains; Gold Parker Pen Holder; Eric Olsen's Bull; Lavabo's; wall pockets and sculptures; World's Fair items by Haeger; commemorative pieces; advertising pieces; Ezra Brooks Ceramic Decanters *(liquor bottles)* made by Haeger; Haeger pieces that have metal accessories (handles, baskets, bases); Musical Cradle; Musical Vase; Musical Madonna; 1947 Royal Haeger award pieces and Haeger clocks, which I have only seen three different designs. One design was a special piece for another company that is in the Haeger museum, another piece was owned by Lee Garmon and Doris Frizzell authors of the previous Haeger book, the other design owned by two different antique dealers in the Indiana region, and one that I own. The Harley-Davidson "Harley Hog" Piggy Bank was specifically designed and commissioned for the Harley-Davidson Motor Company, Inc. in the early 1980's.

When you start looking for model numbers, most of the early pieces did not have numbers molded on them, even though all pieces had model numbers. Numbers without the "R" prefix were from the regular Haeger line. Numbers with the "R" prefix were from the Royal Haeger line when they restarted the numbers with this line. Some pieces during the Royal Haeger line were also marked with "Royal Haeger by Royal Hickman". When a figure changed dimension becoming a lamp, planter or TV lamp, it would get a new model number. When a design had more than one size it would also have different numbers. Animal sets would have a number for the set in the catalogs and each piece would have its own individual number. Mantle sets would have a different number for each of the left and the right pieces. Animals that came in pairs that were in different positions would have separate numbers. Console sets would have different numbers for the main piece and a number for the side pieces.

Studio Haeger came along in 1947-48, designed by Helen Conover. Helen was a freelance artist hired by Haeger. The designs in the line were given an "S" prefix. Some pieces were later put into the Royal Haeger line and given the "R" prefix and new numbers.

When you find a piece that has the "RG" prefix it was part of the Royal Garden Flower-ware line. This line consisted of matte finishes including: sandalwood, soft yellow, moonstone white, dawn rose, cinna brown, patina green, charcoal and geranium green. This line was designed by Elsa Ken Haeger in 1954 and was in production until 1963. The slogan for this line was "rings like rare old porcelain". It wasn't thick and heavy like older pottery. When the line started it was given number 1 in its model numbering with the "RG" prefix.

In 1939 the Royal Haeger lamp company was formed in Dundee, IL until 1969 when it was moved to Macomb, IL. Royal Haeger figurines were used as a beginning to this line. They would have a matching finial and decorated shades that were custom designed for each lamp. In less than a year the lamp company was a success. Most lamps were only marked with a label and sometimes an "R" number would be on the lamp. Royal Hickman left the employment of Haeger during war time and started his own lamp company in Chattanooga, TN. The reason for this was that during the war there was a shortage of electrical supplies, so Haeger could not always fill the demand. Eric Olsen then filled the position of designer.

During the 1950's, TV lamps started to be produced by the Haeger company. This was brought on by the saying that "You should have a light on top of your TV so you wouldn't ruin your eyes". Some of the TV lamps would have molded model numbers on the bottom with the "R" prefix and others would have just been labeled. As in the beginning of the lamps, TV Lamps also were first based on the figurines in the Royal Haeger line. With all of that information out of the way, on to the book....

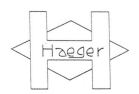

Early mark on pieces
until 1920's.
*Note: This mark has not
been found on any
pieces yet.*

This label was used
before the
Macomb, IL plant
was opened in
1939.

"Century of
Progress" label. Only
used on pieces sold at
the 1934 Chicago
World's Fair.

Labels used during the 75th Anniversary.

Examples of diamond mold stamp
used on pieces, circa 1933.

Handcrafted
Haeger Label.

Oval label.
Registration filed
on in 1941.
1914-1941+

100 yrs. label.
"Craftsmen for
a Century."

"Studio Haeger" label used on line
designed by Helen Conover

Crown foil label (large)
"Royal-Haeger by
Royal Hickman"

Crown foil label
"Royal-Haeger,
Dundee, Illinois"

Crown foil label
"Royal-Haeger
designed by Royal
Hickman"

Crown foil label
"Royal Haeger ®"

Crown printed foil
label "Royal-
Haeger ®, Dundee,
ILL."

Printed label "Terra Madre by
Haeger ®"

Printed Lamp Tag "A Royal Haeger Lamp"

Three versions of
Macomb, Il.
Labels.

Foil Label
"Haeger" in
H design.

Label from
Haeger outlet.

Foil Label
"Gardenhouse ™,
Haeger ® U.S.A."

Rectangular foil label "The Great
Name - Haeger ® - In American
Ceramics"

*Drawn labels were done by Patrick Campbell.

Oval foil label "Haeger ®, Gold Tweed Glaze, 22 K Gold"

Ink stamp "Haeger, Gold Tweed, 22 K Gold"

Rectangular foil label "Royal Haeger"

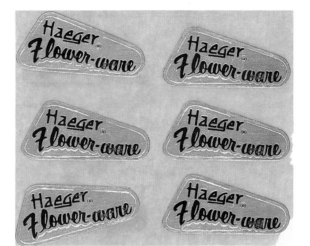

Foil Label "Haeger ®, Flower-ware"

Ink stamp "Royal, Haeger, USA ©"

Ink stamp "Haeger, USA ©"

Stamped felt bottom "Royal Haeger ®, U.S.A., The Haeger Potteries Inc. ©, Dundee, ILL"

Example of Molded bottom.

Label from 80's: "Royal Haeger ®, Handcrafted in America"

100th Anniversary label "Haeger, Ceramic Craftsmen For Over A Century"

125th Anniversary paper tag "125th Anniversary of American Craftsmanship, Royal Haeger ®, 1871-1996"

1990's Current Label

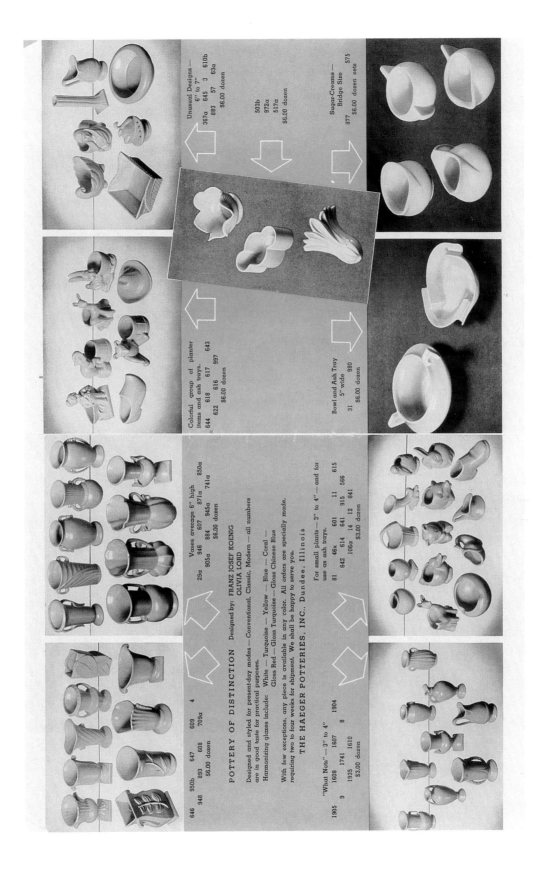

Unusual Designs —
6″ to 7″

367a   645   3   63a
618   617   610b
883   57   643

$6.00 dozen

503b
972a
517a
$6.00 dozen

Sugar-Creams —
Bridge Size

877   980   575

$6.00 dozen sets

Colorful group of planter
items and ash trays.

644   618   617   643
622   616   997

$6.00 dozen

Bowl and Ash Tray
5″ wide

31   980

$6.00 dozen

POTTERY OF DISTINCTION   Designed by: FRANZ JOSEF KOENIG
OLIVIA LORD

Designed and styled for present-day modes — Conventional, Classic, Modern — all numbers
are in good taste for practical purposes.

Harmonizing glazes include: White — Turquoise — Yellow — Blue — Coral —
Gloss Red — Gloss Turquoise — Gloss Chinese Blue

With few exceptions, any piece is available in any color. All orders are specially made,
requiring two to four weeks for shipment. We shall be happy to serve you.

THE HAEGER POTTERIES, INC., Dundee, Illinois

Vases average 6″ high

29a   946   607   871a   850a
905a   884   945a   741a

$6.00 dozen

For small plants — 3″ to 4″ — and for
use as ash trays.

81   46x   601   11   615
642   614   915   566
106a   14   12   841

$3.00 dozen

"What Nots" — 3″ to 4″

1905   1904
9   1608   1607   8
1741   1610
1935   1610

$3.00 dozen

950b   647   609   4
948   893   608   709a

$6.00 dozen

646

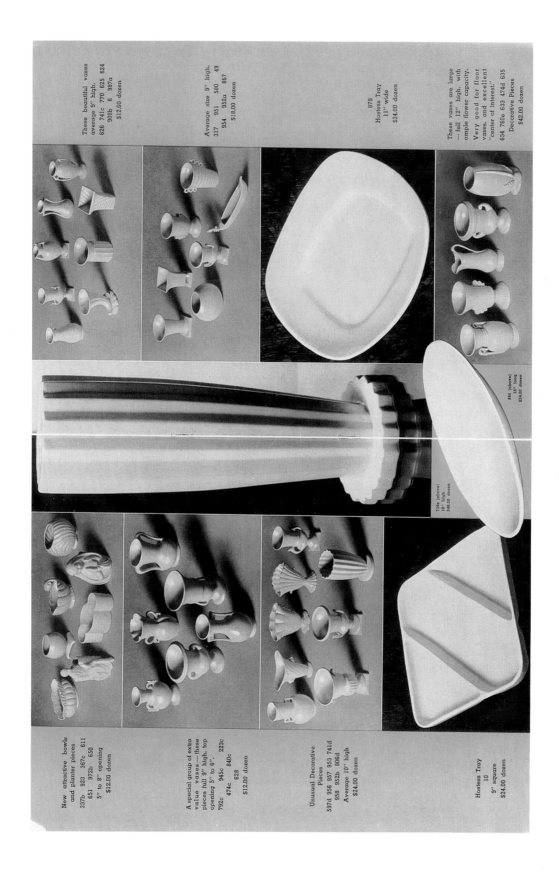

These beautiful vases average 9" high.
626 741c 770 625 624
900b 6 987a
$12.00 dozen

Average size 9" high.
317 951 580 49
954 952a 867
$18.00 dozen

879
Hostess Tray
11" wide
$24.00 dozen

These vases are large — full 12" high, with ample flower capacity.
Very good for floor vases, and excellent "center of interest."
634 760c 633 474d 635
Decorative Pieces
$42.00 dozen

New attractive bowls and planter pieces
337b 923 367c 611
651 972b 650
5" to 8" opening
$12.00 dozen

A special group of extra value vases — these pieces full 9" high, top opening 5" to 6".
792c 945c 223c
474c 628 840c
$12.00 dozen

Unusual Decorative Pieces
597d 956 957 953 741d
958 952b 906d
Average 10" high
$24.00 dozen

Hostess Tray
10
9" square
$24.00 dozen

850 (above)
15" long
$24.00 dozen

739e (above)
18" high
$48.00 dozen

Buffet or Dining Table

883 Set
5″ Bowl
$1.00

851 Set
8″ Bowl
$1.50

47a/243 Set
11″ Bowl
$3.50

We believe this is the finest line of Art Pottery ever offered. Correct in style and design, pleasing in tone colorings, and exquisite in every detail of workmanship, it is truly

POTTERY OF DISTINCTION

All pottery is sold f. o. b. Dundee, Illinois — terms on approved credit, 2/10 net 30.

A packing charge of 5% (minimum 50c) is added to orders less than $25.00.

THE HAEGER POTTERIES, INC., Dundee, Illinois

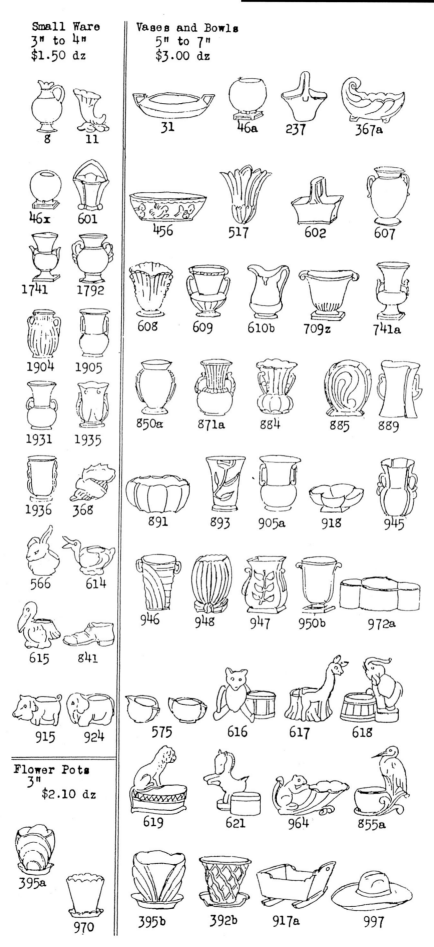

Small Ware
3" to 4"
$1.50 dz

8   11

46x   601

1741   1792

1904   1905

1931   1935

1936   368

566   614

615   841

915   924

Flower Pots
3"
$2.10 dz

395a

970

Vases and Bowls
5" to 7"
$3.00 dz

31   46a   237   367a

456   517   602   607

608   609   610b   709z   741a

850a   871a   884   885   889

891   893   905a   918   945

946   948   947   950b   972a

575   616   617   618

619   621   964   855a

395b   392b   917a   997

24

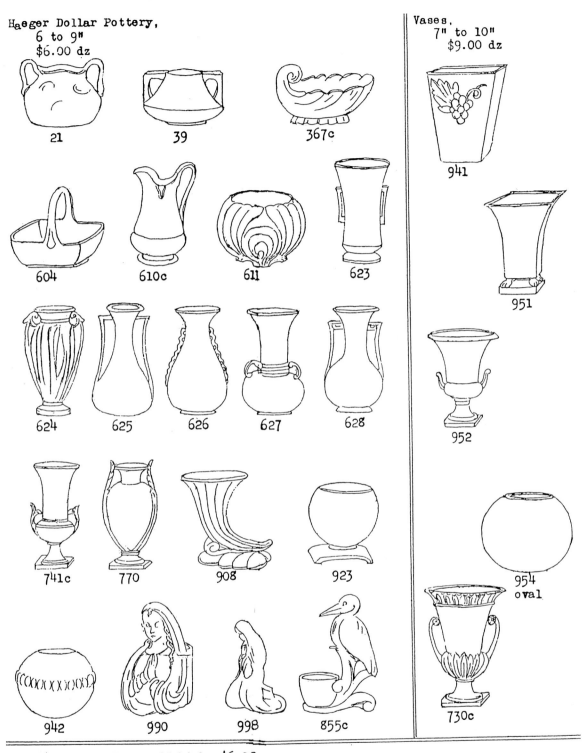

Haeger Dollar Pottery,
6 to 9"
$6.00 dz

21

39

367c

604

610c

611

623

624

625

626

627

628

741c

770

908

923

942

990

998

855c

Vases,
7" to 10"
$9.00 dz

941

951

952

954
oval

730c

Special Sale Vases, 9" high, $6.00 dz

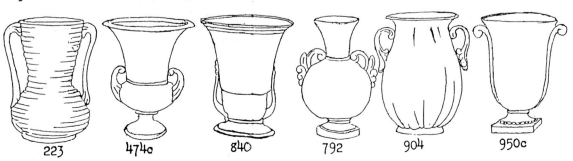

223

474c

840

792

904

950c

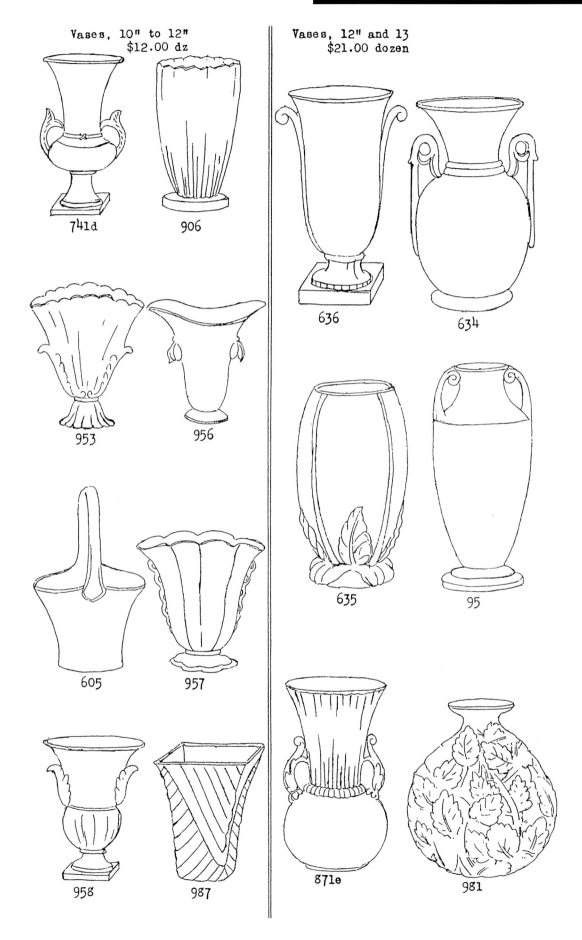

Vases, 10" to 12"
$12.00 dz

741d

906

953

956

605

957

958

987

Vases, 12" and 13
$21.00 dozen

636

634

635

95

871e

981

3-pc Console Sets -   supplied in Mat White only: priced per dozen sets.
Dimension given is diameter or length of bowl.

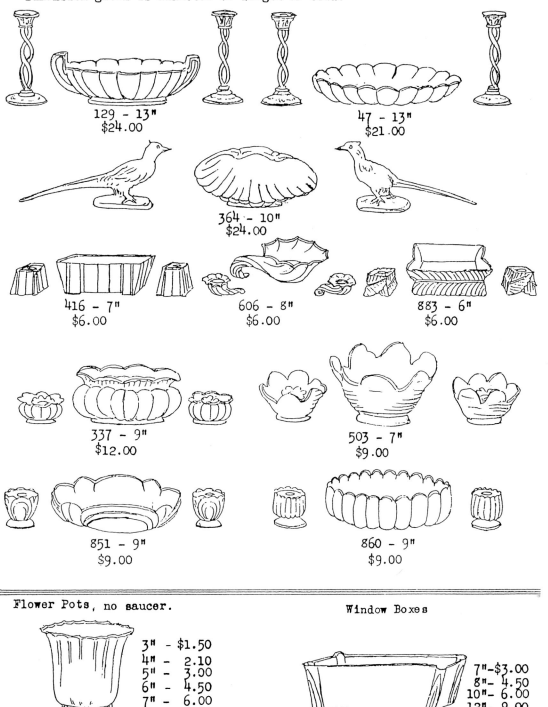

129 - 13"
$24.00

47 - 13"
$21.00

364 - 10"
$24.00

416 - 7"
$6.00

606 - 8"
$6.00

883 - 6"
$6.00

337 - 9"
$12.00

503 - 7"
$9.00

851 - 9"
$9.00

860 - 9"
$9.00

Flower Pots, no saucer.

852

3" - $1.50
4" -   2.10
5" -   3.00
6" -   4.50
7" -   6.00
8" -   9.00

Window Boxes

907

7"-$3.00
8"- 4.50
10"- 6.00
12"- 9.00

All Haeger Pottery, except Console Sets, is supplied in six soft, satin
matte glazes:
    White(eggshell) - Turquoise - Yellow - Blue - Green - Coral
Shipments f.o.b. Dundee, Illinois.   Terms strictly 2/10 net 30.
Packing charge 5% on orders under $50.00, with minimum charge 50¢.

THE HAEGER POTTERIES, Inc.   DUNDEE, ILLINOIS.

27

Below R-102
12 in. high

Below R-101
12 in. high

Right
R-195
R-196
R-243
R-114
12 in. high

D-1000
7 in. high

R-225
6 in. high

Above R-36
16 in.

Above R-182
8 in. high

Right
R-138
R-33
R-137
13½ in. high

Above R-246
15 in. wide

Center R-113, R-241   D-1021, R-229
15 in. high

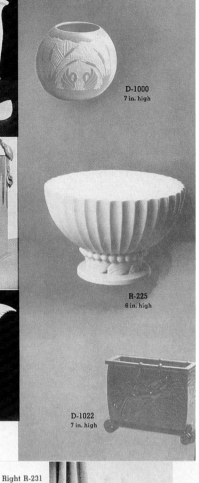

D-1022
7 in. high

Left
R-345 R-177 R-193
R-131 R-194
9 to 11 in. high

Right R-231
23 in. high

Above
R-117, R-347, R-238
8 to 13 in. high

Left
R-228
R-190
R-107
R-187
8½ to 12 in. high

Right R-31
14 in. high

Left R-144
20 in. high

THE ROYAL HAEGER LINE
introduced to you but a few months ago, is shown to you more completely now, in this presentation. As a really new idea, ROYAL-HAEGER has met with widespread and most enthusiastic acclaim. For as a crowning achievement of Royal Hickman, its designer, ROYAL-HAEGER has contributed much to a new depth of feeling in contemporary design. In the subtle contours and accents of these new ceramics of more than 200 designs are dynamic-poise, the fleetness of flight, symphonic combinations of curves and planes . . . and a vigorous idealism, delivered eloquently in the new romantic language of Today . . . and Tomorrow.

Left R-115
13 in. high

Right 1. R-116
12 in. wide

2. R-200
5 in. high

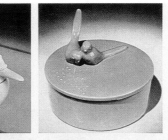

Right R-209
19 in. wide

Right 1. R-198
11½ in. wide

2. R-188
10 in. high

R-251
21 in. high

Left D-1023
13 in. high

Below R-184
11 in. high

Below D-1009
7½ in. wide

D-1019   D-1018   D-1020   D-1011   D-1017   D-1001
7½ in. high   9½ in. wide   15 in. high   10½ in. high   16 in. high   7½ in. high

Below R-235
12½ in. high

Right D-1004   D-1006
8 in. high   16 in. high

29

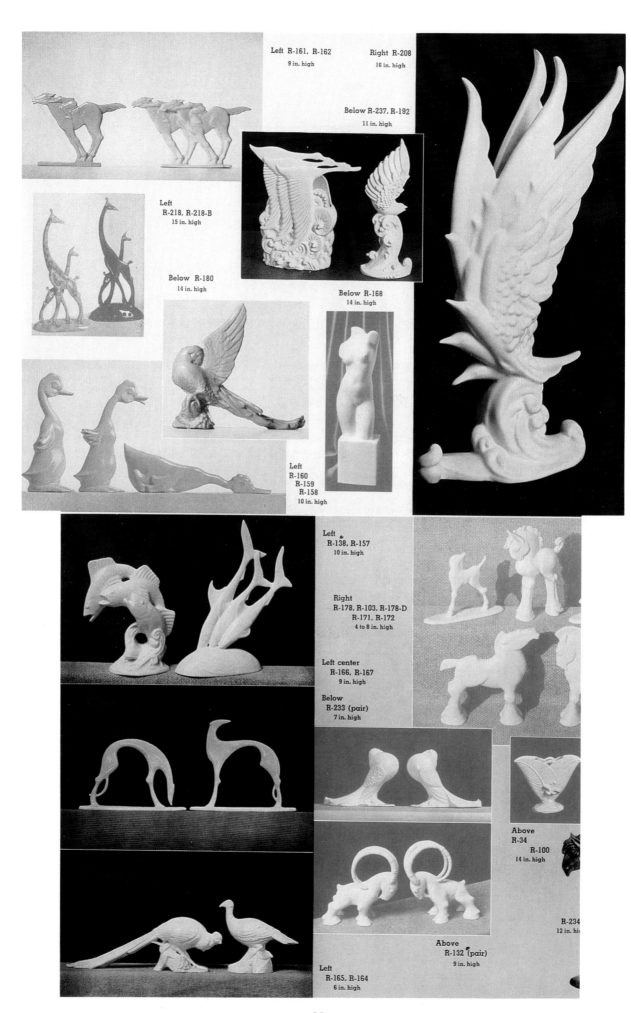

Left R-161, R-162
9 in. high

Right R-208
16 in. high

Below R-237, R-192
11 in. high

Left
R-218, R-218-B
15 in. high

Below R-180
14 in. high

Below R-168
14 in. high

Left
R-160
R-159
R-158
10 in. high

Left
R-138, R-157
10 in. high

Right
R-178, R-103, R-178-D
R-171, R-172
4 to 8 in. high

Left center
R-166, R-167
9 in. high

Below
R-233 (pair)
7 in. high

Above
R-34
R-100
14 in. high

R-234
12 in. high

Above
R-132 (pair)
9 in. high

Left
R-165, R-164
6 in. high

30

Left R-110
11½ in. high

Below, R-199
18 in. high

R-248
10½ in. high

Below
Hanging Basket and
Chain, R-179
9 in. high

Top R-205   206 (set)
6 and 7 in. high

Bottom R-155, 156, 157 (set)
5½, 6½ and 7½ in. high

R-252
7 in. wide

R-230
6 in. wide

THE HOUSE OF HAEGER

Your own experience with fine pottery will tell you that it is entirely natural that these new, refreshing creations of Royal Hickman should be brought to you by the House of Haeger.

For, with its progress and fame extending through three generations, the Haeger Potteries have nurtured freshness and sincerity in the design and production of decorative ceramics. Creative genius and mechanical skill have worked closely together at Haeger. And together they have made their contributions to the beauty and honest design of fine ceramics. They have created new colors, new textures, new glazes. As you inspect the items in this superb ROYAL-HAEGER line you will see how Haeger skill has supplemented the designs of the renowned Royal Hickman.

R-247
12½ in. high

Right
R-227
13 in. wide

R-223
7½ in. wide

Above R-210   D-1007
7½ in. wide   12½ in. wide

The Haeger Potteries
Incorporated
DUNDEE, ILLINOIS

Left
R-221
R-222
12 in. high

Above R-226
8 in. wide

Above R-181
14 in. high

Left R-242
13½ in. wide

Right R-232
8 in. high

Left R-134
11 in. high

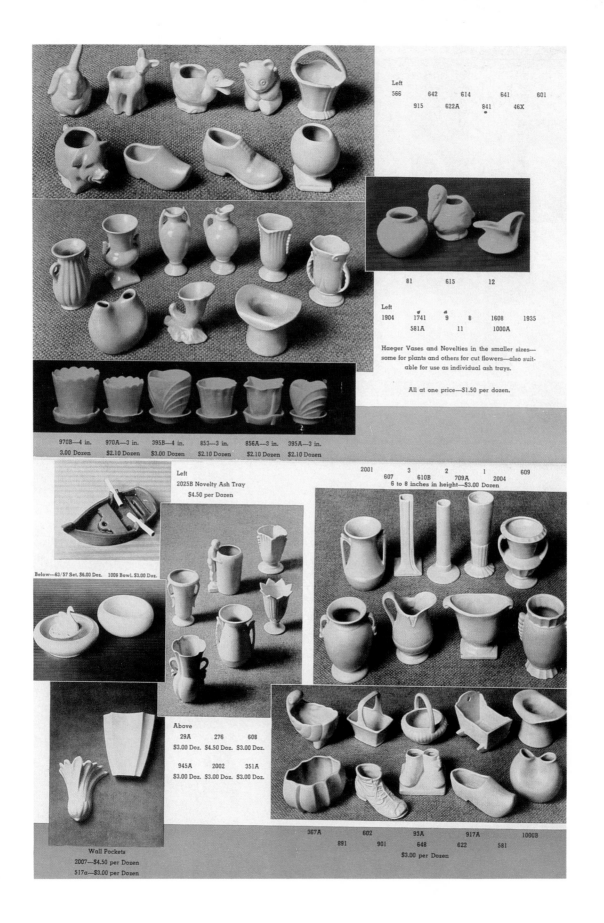

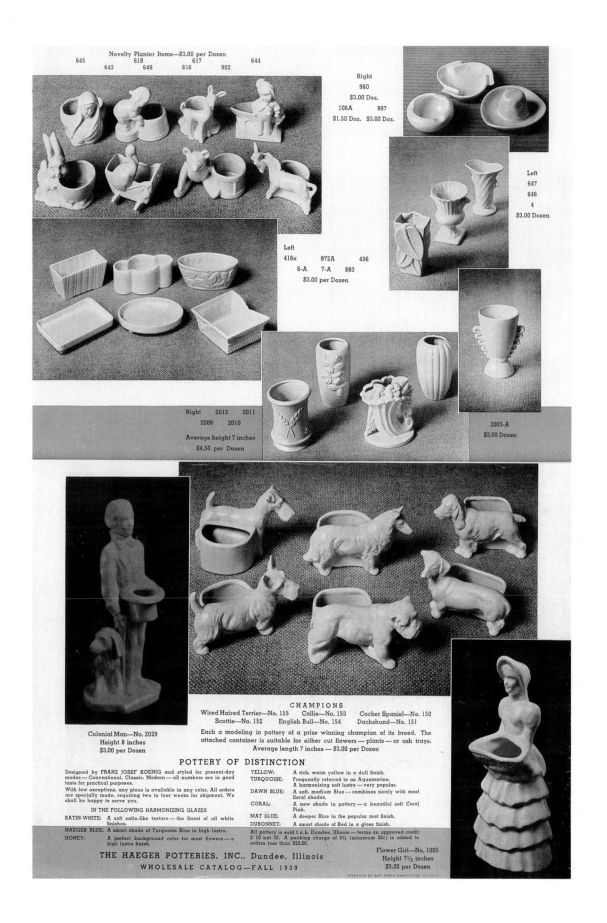

Novelty Planter Items—$3.00 per Dozen

| 645 | | 618 | | 617 | | 644 |
| | 643 | | 649 | 616 | 902 | |

Right
980
$3.00 Doz.
106A   997
$1.50 Doz. $3.00 Doz.

Left
647
646
4
$3.00 Dozen

Left
416x   972A   456
6-A   7-A   883
$3.00 per Dozen

Right   2012   2011
2009   2010
Average height 7 inches
$4.50 per Dozen

2003-A
$3.00 Dozen

CHAMPIONS

Wired Haired Terrier—No. 155   Collie—No. 153   Cocker Spaniel—No. 150
Scottie—No. 152   English Bull—No. 154   Dachshund—No. 151

Each a modeling in pottery of a prize winning champion of its breed. The attached container is suitable for either cut flowers — plants — or ash trays.
Average length 7 inches — $3.00 per Dozen

Colonial Man—No. 2029
Height 8 inches
$3.00 per Dozen

POTTERY OF DISTINCTION

Designed by FRANZ JOSEF KOENIG and styled for present-day modes — Conventional, Classic, Modern — all numbers are in good taste for practical purposes.

With few exceptions, any piece is available in any color. All orders are specially made, requiring two to four weeks for shipment. We shall be happy to serve you.

IN THE FOLLOWING HARMONIZING GLAZES

SATIN-WHITE: A soft satin-like texture — the finest of all white finishes.

HAEGER BLUE: A smart shade of Turquoise Blue in high lustre.

HONEY: A perfect background color for most flowers — a high lustre finish.

YELLOW: A rich, warm yellow in a dull finish.
TURQUOISE: Frequently referred to as Aquamarine. A harmonizing soft lustre — very popular.
DAWN BLUE: A soft, medium Blue — combines nicely with most floral shades.
CORAL: A new shade in pottery — a beautiful soft Coral Pink.
MAT BLUE: A deeper Blue in the popular mat finish.
DUBONNET: A smart shade of Red in a gloss finish.

All pottery is sold f.o.b. Dundee, Illinois — terms on approved credit 2/10 net 30. A packing charge of 5% (minimum 50c) is added to orders less than $25.00.

THE HAEGER POTTERIES, INC., Dundee, Illinois
WHOLESALE CATALOG—FALL 1939

Flower Girl—No. 1005
Height 7½ inches
$3.00 per Dozen

Haeger Fountains are available in the following finishes:

Satin White	Alice Blue
Turquoise	Honey
Green Agate	Gloss Green
Haeger Blue	Coffee
Peach Agate	Mulberry Agate

Decorative Fountains in Pottery, electrically operated, are a welcome addition to the Haeger line. As simple to operate as a table lamp—self-contained, no plumbing connections, water is used over and over again. Mechanical features are fully guaranteed for ninety days against electrical and mechanical defects.

Haeger Fountain No. 8010, Bowl Diameter 15″, Each **$7.50**

THE HAEGER POTTERIES, Inc.   · 2 ·   World's Largest Art Pottery

Haeger Fountain No. 8020, Bowl Diameter 17″, Each **$12.50**

Haeger Fountain No. 8015, Bowl Diameter 18″, Each **$8.75**

Dundee, Illinois   · 3 ·   THE HAEGER POTTERIES, Inc.

MINIATURE BOWLS and VASES $1.80 DOZ.

Bowl No. 106-B, 4¼ inch   Vase No. 44, 3¼ inch   Bowl No. 3002, 2¾″ x 5″   Bowl No. 1001-B, 3½″ x 6″
Vase No. 42, 4½ inch   Vase No. 1850, 4¼ inch   Vase No. 41, 5 inch   Vase No. 1792, 4½ inch   Vase No. 43, 4½ inch

Bowl No. 3047, 8½″x4¾″, Dozen **$4.50**   No. 15 Set, Dozen **$4.50**   No. 972-A, Length 8 inches, Dozen **$3.00**

LARGER BOWLS AND OUR POPULAR SUGAR AND CREAMER

Dundee, Illinois   · 5 ·   For List of Colors See Page 35

Vase No. 39, Height, 8½″
Dozen **$6.00**

Vase No. 40, Height 9″
Dozen **$6.00**

Vase No. 506, Height 10″, Dozen **$9.00**

THE HAEGER POTTERIES, Inc.   · 6 ·   World's Largest Art Pottery

Vase No. 3054, Height 8″,
Dozen **$7.50**

Sailor Boy No. 644, Length 6 inches, Dozen **$3.00**

Colonial Cradle
No. 917-A, 3½″x5″, Dozen **$3.00**
No. 917-C, 5¼″x7½″, Dozen **$6.00**

Flower Girl No. 1005, Height 7″,
Dozen **$3.00**

Booties No. 648, 4½″, Dozen **$3.00**

Dundee, Illinois　　　　　　　・7・　　　　　　For List of Colors See Page 35

No. 3057
Stork Vase, Height 13″, Doz. **$15.00**

Stork Vase No. 3045, Height 8¼″, Doz. **$6.00**

BABY ITEMS AVAILABLE IN
MAT WHITE—BABY BLUE
BABY PINK

Stork Vase No. 855-A, Height 6″, Doz. **$3.00**
Stork Vase No. 855-C, Height 9″, Doz. **$6.00**

THE HAEGER POTTERIES, Inc.　　　　・8・　　　　World's Largest Art Pottery

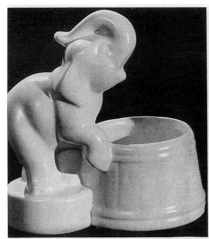

Elephant No. 618, Length 6 inches, Dozen **$3.00**

Donkey Vase No. 3053, Height 9½",
Dozen **$7.50**

Elephant Vase No. 3055, Height 10½", Dozen **$12.00**

VASES AND PLANTERS

Dundee, Illinois · 11 · For List of Colors See Page 35

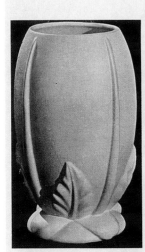

No. 635, Height 12", Dozen **$21.00**

No. 3030, Height 11", Dozen **$12.00**   No. 3022, Height 11", Dozen **$12.00**   No. 3023, Height 11", Dozen **$12.00**

No. 3025, Height 6", Dozen **$9.00**   No. 3026, Height 10", Dozen **$9.00**   No. 952-A, Height 8", Dozen **$9.00**

Dundee, Illinois · 23 · For List of Colors See Page 35

No. 3068
Diam. 12"
Dozen **$12.00**

No. 3069
5"x11½"
Dozen **$9.00**

No. 851, 3-Pc. Set, Dozen **$9.00**
Bowl No. 851, 9" Diam., Dozen **$6.00**

No. 3063, Set **$2.50**
Vase Opening, 3"x6¼"

CONSOLE

1940

THE HAEGER POTTERIES, Inc.   · 28 ·   World's Largest Art Pottery

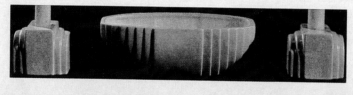

No. 3004, 3-Piece Set, Dozen **$6.00**
Bowl No. 3004, 8¼"x3¾", Dozen **$3.00**

No. 129, 3 Pieces
$2.50 Set
Bowl No. 129, 7"x11"
Each **$1.75**

No. 364/130, 3 pc. set,
Complete **$2.00**
Bowl No. 364, 8"x10", Each **1.00**
Pheasant No. 130 ...... Each   **50c**

SETS

No. 367-A, Length 6"

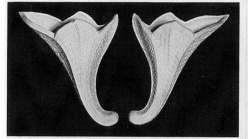

Wall Pocket No. 3112, 9½"x6½"

Cocker Spaniel No. 150, Length 7"

Patriotic Vase No. 67, Height 5½"

Wall Pocket
No. 50-A,
Diameter 8"

(Has pocket in rear
for either flowers
or plants)

Bowl No. 3033, 5"x8"

Basket No. 502, 7"x9"

No. 945-C, Height 9"

Ballet Girl No. 3105, Height 8"

No. F-6, Deer
Height 6¼"

No. F-7, Donkey
Height 6¼"

No. F-16, Wild Goose
Length 7"

No. 972-A, Length 8"

Bowl No. 860-B, Diameter 9"
(Matching Candlesticks Available, No. 860CK)

No. 68, Height 6"

No. 351-A, Height 6"

Ash Tray No. 980, Diam. 6½"

No. 645, Height 6"

No. 1020, Height 6¾"

Scottie No. 152, Length 7"

Bowl No. 63-A, Diameter 8"

Wall Pocket, No. 517-A, 7"

No. R-410, Wheat Sheaf Vase, Height 12"
Available in Antique Ivory Only

No. 2010, Height 6"

Oblong Vase No. 3106, 6" High x 12" Long

Elephant No. 69, Length 11"

No. 952-A, Height 8"

No. 2027, Height 3"   No. 2026, Height 2¾"
To be sold in Dozen Lots only

No. 3111, Length 4¾"
No. 3111 is available in all low bowl finishes (see page 21)

No. 3094, Vase, Height 4½"

No. F-11, Height 4"

No. 3089, Vase, Height 5"

No. F-9, Swan, Height 4"   No. F-4, Gander, Height 5"   No. F-5, Swan, Length 4"   No. F-2, Goose, Height 5"   No. F-10, Swan, Height 4"   No. F-3, Duck, Height 4½"

No. F-17, Wild Goose
Height 6½"

Candle Stick Holder
No. 3116, Height 4½"

No. 1018, Height 7¼"   No. 1019, Height 7"

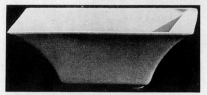

Bowl No. 3047, 8½"x4¾"

No. 709-A, Height 6"

No. R-310, Swan Bowl, Length 13", Width 9½", Height 6"
Available in colors 1, 2, 3, 4 and 11

Colonial Vase No. 3104, Height 8"

No. R-427, Height 11"
Available in Antique Ivory or
French Gray Only

No. R-390, South
American Girl
Height 11"

No. R-391, African Man with
Bananas, Height 12"

Available in Manganese Stain Only

THE HAEGER POTTERIES, INC.   • 2 •   **World's Largest Art Pottery**

No. R-361
Width 7", Height 4"

No. R-364
Height 13"

No. R-169B, Height 7"
Leaping Trout

No. R-392, Large Bull, Height 12", Length 18"
Available in Manganese with Gun Metal Base

No. R-402, Height 5"   No. R-400, Height 5"   No. R-401, Height 4"
Available in Musty Gray color

No. R-404, Height 12½"   No. R-403, Height 13½"
Available in Manganese Stain Only

No. R-335, Shell Bowl, Diameter 14", Depth 3½"
Available in colors 2, 3, 4, 5 and 11
No. R-363, Flower Block, Height 10", Length 5"
Available in colors 1 to 12

No. R-425
Cylinder with Parrot Vase
Height 16"
Available in Manganese and Mallow Only

Cradle No. 3245, Top 2"x3¼"   Pottee No. 3247, Diameter 3"   Boxing Glove No. 3253, Length 4"

See Page 22 for List of Colors Available

No. F-12 Fish, Height 4¾"   No. 646, Height 6"   Swan No. 3239, 4"   Bunny No. 3248, 3¾"

No. R-369, Shell Bowl, Height 14", Length 14"
Available in colors 2, 3, 5, 7, 10, 11 and 12

THE HAEGER POTTERIES, Inc.

Haeger Vase No. 3226, Ht. 11"   Candle Bud Vase No. 3201, Height 10"

Plume Vase No. 3020, Ht. 9½"

Figurines
No. 3235, Ht. 5"   No. 3237, Ht. 6"

Haeger Candle Vase No. 3215
Height 9½", Length 13", Width 3"

No. R-326, Round Fluted Bowl
Height 11"
Available in colors 1 to 12

No. R-117 Rooster Fish Vase, Height 10"
Available in colors 1 to 12

No. R-241, Yacha Vase
Height 16½"
Available in colors 1 to 12

No. R-416, Plain Urn
Height 13½"
Available in colors 15 and 16

No. R-303
Laurel Wreath Bow
Height 12"
Available in colors 2, 3, 4, 6,
11 and 12

No. R-281, Sphere & Three Plumes
Height 10"
Available in colors 2 and 3

No. R-290, Cut Out V Bowl, Height 10"
Available in colors 1, 2, 3, and 7

Haeger Vase No. 3220
Height 14", Length 7", Width 4"

No. R-327, Mantel Vase, Height 10"
Available in colors 2, 4, 5, 7 and 12

No. R-408, Double Racing Horses, Height 10"
Available in Mallow Only

No. R-409, Pillow Vase
Height 11½"
Available in Mallow Only
No. R-397, Candleholder
Length 8"
Available in colors 1 to 12

Haeger Pot with
Saucer attached
No. 391-A 3½"
No. 391-B 4½"

Haeger Victory Vase
No. 3205-A, Height 6"   No. 3205-B, Height 9"

No. R-305
Gazelle Head Vase
Height 19"

Available in colors 1 to 12

No. R-306, Plume Shell, Length 15", Width 8", Depth 4"
Available in colors 2, 3, 4, 7 and 11

No. R-271, Sail Fish Vase, Length 13", Height 8", Width 6"

Available in colors 1 to 12

No. F-5 Swan,
Length 4"

No. R-406 Calla Lily
Vase Height 13"

Available in Manganese
or Green Manganese
(Lilies in three pastel
shades of Turquoise, Coral
and Yellow)

**See Page 2 for List of
Colors Available in
Royal Haeger**

No. D-1011, Bird on Bee
Hive Vase, Height 10½"

Available in colors 1 to 12

Haeger Vase No. 3061, Top 3½"x12"

**FOR LIST OF COLORS
SEE PAGE 2**

R-432, Shell, 8½" x 9½"
Available in Colors 2, 3, 5, 6 and 11

R-445   R-436   R-445
Flower Pots, 3" x 4½" — 3½" x 7¾"
Available in Manganese/Stain Only

R-443, Coolie Hat Bowl, Diameter 16"
Available in Colors 2, 3, 5 and 7 at ....$3.25 Ea.
Gloss Honey/Decorated Flowers ....$4.00 Ea.

R-286, Leaf Plate, Length 12"
Available in Colors 2, 4, 5, 7, 11 and 12

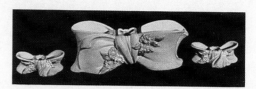

R-440   R-439   R-440
Bow Console Set, 1½" x 5" — 5" x 2½"
Available in Manganese/Stain or Alice Blue/Musty Gray

THE HAEGER POTTERIES, Inc.   World's Largest Art Pottery   **Page 3**

-295, Height 4"   R-248, Height 10"   R-295
Console Set, Plume Candelholders
Available in Colors 1 to 12

R-458, Small Triple Shell Candy Dish,
Length 6½"
Available in Colors 1 to 12

R-457, Triple Leaf Candy Dish,
Length 9½"
Available in Colors 1 to 12

R-459, Large Triple Candy Dish,
Length 9"
Available in Colors 1 to 12

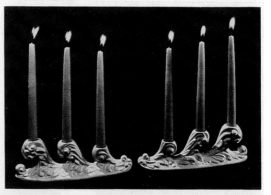

R-433, Triple Candelholders, Length 11½"
Available in Colors 1 to 12

R-438, 1" x 3½"   R-371, Length 13"   R-438
Console Set, Low Wave Bowl and Rosebud Candelholders
Bowl Available in Colors 1 to 12   Candleholders Available in Colors 1 to 12

R-437, 2½" x 5"   R-460, 5" x 12"   R-437
Console Set, Leaf Bowl and Leaf Candelholders
Bowl Available in Colors 2, 3, 4, 10 and 12   Candleholders Available in Colors 1 to 12

R-453, Small Peacock Vase, Height 10"
Available in Colors 2, 3, 7, 10 and 11

THE HAEGER POTTERIES, Inc.   World's Largest Art Pottery   **Page 5**

R-376B, Height 5½"　　　　　　　R-375B, Height 7"
R-376A, Height 2½"　　　　　　　R-375A, Height 3"
Bear Set, Available in Musty Gray Only

R-418, 6" x 9"　　　　R-421, 7" x 14"　　　　R-418
Console Set, Bowl Available in Colors 1 to 12 with exception of 11.
Candleholders Available in Colors 1 to 12 with exception of 10

R-442, Bowl, Length 18"
Available in Colors 1 to 12

R-373, Bowl, Length 19"
Available in Colors 2, 3, 5, 7, 10 and 12

THE HAEGER POTTERIES, Inc.　　　World's Largest Art Pottery　　　Page 7

R-122, Long Bowl with Handles, Length 27"
Available in Colors 1 to 12

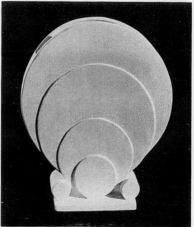

R-441, Modernistic Circle
Vase, Height 11½"
Available in Colors 1 to 12

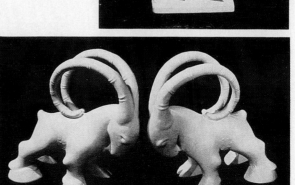

R-126A, Small Leaf Plate, 10" x 11"
R-126, Large Leaf Plate, 16" x 16"
Available in Colors 4, 5, 7, 11 and 12

R-132, Ram Bookends, 8" x 9"
Available in Colors 1 to 12

THE HAEGER POTTERIES, Inc.　　　World's Largest Art Pottery　　　Page 9

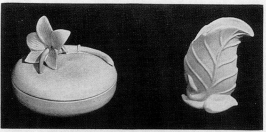

R-252, 7" x 7"   R-230, Diameter 7"   R-431,
Ash Trays   Lily Top
Available in Colors 1 to 12   Candy Box,
                                           Diameter 7¾"

Available in Colors, Mauve, Agate/Mauve Flower,
Mallow/Green Flower, Gloss White/Alice Blue
Flower, Honey Copenhagen/Gloss White Flower

R-444, Leaf Vase, Height 6½"
Available in Colors 1 to 12

R-422, Cornucopia Vase, Height 6"
Available in Colors 1 to 12

R-451, Horse and Colt, Height 10", Length 13½"
Available in Amber or Gun Metal Only

Page 10   World's Largest Art Pottery   THE HAEGER POTTERIES, Inc.

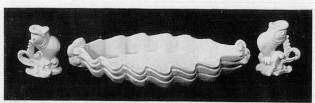

R-357, Bowl, 16" x 7"
Bowl Available in Colors 1, 2, 3, 4, 6 and 10

R-304, Candleholders, Height 4½"
Candleholders Available in Colors 1 to 12

R-322, Shell Cornucopia, Length 7½"
Available in Colors 1 to 12

**FOR LIST
OF COLORS
SEE PAGE 2**

R-337, Plain Vase, Height 11"
Available in Colors 4, 5, and 7

R-140, Deep Fluted Oval Bowl, Length 18"
Available in Colors 1 to 12

3286, Height 6"

3280, 3" x 6"

REGULAR HAEGER GLAZES

Satin White	Gloss Turquoise
Mat Turquoise	Gloss Honey
Mat Yellow	Mat Blue
Mat Coral	Willow Green
Dawn Blue	

3266, Height 6"

3282, Height 6½"

3285, Height 5"

3289, Height 7½"

Page 12   World's Largest Art Pottery   THE HAEGER POTTERIES, Inc.

3287, Height 10"

3291, Low Bowl, Length 10"

GLAZES AVAILABLE FOR LOW BOWL

Two Tone Colors	Single Tone Colors
White/Turquoise	White
White/Yellow	Turquoise
White/D. Blue	Yellow
White/Coral	D. Blue
White/Willow Green	Coral
Honey/Gl. Turq.	Gl. Turquoise
Honey/Apricot	Honey
	Willow Green

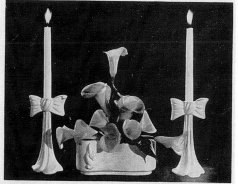

3261, 4" x 9½",   3277, Height 9"

3274P, Height 21"

3262, Height 13½"

3278, Height 13"

Page 16   World's Largest Art Pottery   THE HAEGER POTTERIES, Inc.

R-453—Small Peacock Vase, 10x10x3¼
In glazes 2, 7 & 10

R-210—Bowl with Birds, 7x6x7
In glazes 1 thru 12

R-220—Candleholder with Birds, 5½x5x5½
In glazes 1 thru 12

R-281—Sphere and Three Plumes
10x10¼x10, In glaze No. 2

R-437—3½x2¾x5   **R-460**—12x5x3½   **R-437**—3½x2¾x5
Console Set, Leaf Bowl and Leaf Candleholders
Bowl in glazes 2, 4, 10 & 12   Candleholders in glazes 1 thru 12

THE HAEGER POTTERIES, INC.   — 1 —   **WORLD'S LARGEST ART POTTERY**

R-446—Lily Vase
6¾x13¾x6¾
In glazes 4, 6 & 10

R-387—Tall Modern Vase
9½x16½x9¾, In glazes 2, 5, 7, 10 & 12
R-351—Squat Urn, 9¾x10¼x9¾
In glazes 2, 4, 5, 7 & 12

R-358—Footed Bowl, 5¾x3½x17½
In glazes 2, 4, 5, 7 & 10

R-445   **R-436**   **R-445**
R-445—Flower Pot, round, 4¾x3¼x4¾, In glaze combination 8 & 24
R-436—Flower Pot, oblong, 3x3½x7½, In glaze No. 24

R-443—Coolie Hat Bowl, 16½x3¾x16½
In glazes 2, 5 & 7
Not available decorated as pictured, but only in glazes listed.

DUNDEE, ILLINOIS   — 3 —   **THE HAEGER POTTERIES, INC.**

R-497—Roman Vase, 7¼x9½x7½
In glazes 2, 5, 7 & 12

R-489—Tropical Leaf Vase
4¾ x13¼ x4¾
In glazes 2, 5, 7 & 12

R-393—Bust of Pegasus Vase
3¾x11½x4¼
In glazes 4, 7 & 10

R-402—Dappled Horse,
2½x5½x5¾
In glaze No. 6

.R-132—Ram Bookends, 4¼x7¾x8, In glazes 1 thru 12

THE HAEGER POTTERIES, INC.   —4—   WORLD'S LARGEST ART POTTERY

R-115—Gazelle Head Vase, 4½x13x3
In glazes 1, 4, 5 & 7

R-373—Bowl with Floral Design, 8¾x20x6
In glazes 2, 5, 7, 10 & 12

R-499—Bowl, decorated, 8x2x8
In glazes 24, Comb. 5 & 20

R-36—Large Swan Vase, 10x15x5½
In glazes 1, 2, 4, 5, 7 & 8

R-456—Wrap-Around Spiral, 5¼x13x5¼
In glazes 4, 5, 7 & 12

R-454—Chinese Vase, 8x15½x8
In glazes 4 & 26

R-455—Tall Bow Vase, 5¼x14x15¼
In glaze comb. 1 & 8, 2 & 20, 12 & 22

Many of the pieces in this catalog have been fashioned into lamps. Ask for the Haeger Lamp Company catalog.

R-297—Oval Shell Bowl, 7½x3x4
In glazes 2, 5 & 7

R-450—Long Bowl, Floral Design,
7x6x23½. In glazes 2, 4 & 7

THE HAEGER POTTERIES, INC.   —6—   WORLD'S LARGEST ART POTTERY

R-335—Shell Bowl, 14x3¼x14
In glazes 2, 4 & 5

R-363—Nude on Fish Block, inset
4x10x4, In glazes 1 thru 12

R-279—Basket Vase, 9½x21x9, In glazes 1, 2, 4 & 7

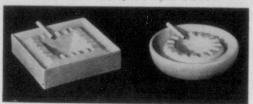

R-252—Ash Tray, 7x1¾x7,   Both in glazes 1-12   A-230—Ashtray, 7½x1½x7½

R-286—Leaf Plate, 8x2x12
In glazes 2, 4, 5, 7 & 12

THE HAEGER POTTERIES, INC.   —10—   WORLD'S LARGEST ART POTTERY

R-285—Swan Vase, 6x8¾x3¾
In glazes 1 thru 12

D-1001—Plain Oval Vase,
4¼x7¼x4¼
In glazes 1 thru 12

R-409—Pillow Vase with Flowers, 6x11¼x3¾
In glaze No. 10
R-397—Three Block Candleholder, 2¾x3x8¼
In glazes 1 thru 12

R-475
Calla Lily Bookends
3½x6x4¾, In glaze No. 13

R-323—Fluted Vase,
6½x9x6½
In glazes 1 thru 12

R-287—Wren House, 7½x9¼x4
In glazes 1 thru 12

R-208—Seagull Vase, 7¾x16x3¾
In glazes 2, 4, 6 & 7

R-295   R-248   R-295
Console Set, Plume & Candleholders
Plume, 4½x10x2½, Candleholders, 4x4¾x4
Both in glazes 1 thru 12

R-320—Elm Leaf Vase, 5½x12¾x5¼
In glazes 2, 4, 5, 7 & 12

R-414—Swan, 3½x10¼x12½
In glazes 1 thru 12

R-434, 435—Hen & Cock Pheasants, 4½x11½x12
In glazes 2, 5 & 8

R-432—Conch-Shell Bowl,
8½x4¾x9½. In glazes 2, 5 & 6

R-472—Russian Lady Vase,
3½x11¼x6, Glaze No. 6

R-441—Circular Vase, 10x11½x3¼
In glazes 1 thru 12

R-322—Shell Cornucopia, 10x6¼x3½
In glazes 1 thru 12

THE HAEGER POTTERIES, INC. — 14 — WORLD'S LARGEST ART POTTERY

R-492—Modernistic Horsehead Vase,
4x15½x5, In glaze No. 6

R-452—Morning Glory Vase, 9¾x16¼x4¾
In glazes 2, 4, 5, 10 & 12

R-332A—Cornucopia (Med.)   A-332B (Large)
3¼x7¼x3¼   4¼x11x4¼
In glazes 1 thru 12

R-448—Shell Ashtray (Small)   R-447—Shell Ashtray (Large)   R-449—Leaf Ashtray
3¼x1x3¼   4½x1¾x4½   3½x¾x5
All three in glazes 1 thru 12

R-278—Plume Dish (Large) R-277—Plume Dish (Small)
10¼x1¾x10¼   6¾x1x6¾
Both in glazes 1 thru 12

DUNDEE, ILLINOIS — 15 — THE HAEGER POTTERIES, INC.

54

R-364
Nude on Seal Block
5x12½x5
In glazes 1 thru 12

R-360—**Tropical Fish Block**
5¼x11¼x3¼

R-359—**Bird Block**
10x7¾x5

Both in glazes 1 thru 12

R-140—**Ruffled Oval Bowl,** 8½x3½x18
In glazes 1 thru 12

R-284—**Trout Flower Vase,** 9¾x7¼x4½
In glazes 1 thru 12

R-103—**Small Horse,**
2½x5½x5½
In glazes 1 thru 12

R-293—**Violin Bowl,** 5¼x1¾x16¼ In glazes 2, 5, 7 & 10

DUNDEE, ILLINOIS — 17 — **THE HAEGER POTTERIES, INC.**

R-418
Double Candleholder
4x5¾x8½
Glazes 1 thru 12,
except No. 10

R-421
Oval Bowl, Fruit Clusters
8¼x6x15
Glazes 1 thru 12

R-418
Double Candleholder
4x5¾x8½
Glazes 1 thru 12,
except No. 10

R-476—**Bowl with Beaded Sides,** 7¼x4½x15
In glazes 1 thru 12

R-271—**Sailfish Vase,** 2½x9x12
In glazes 1 thru 12

R-33—**Leaf Vase,** 15¾x13x5
In glazes 2, 4, 5 & 7

R-386—**Basket-Type Vase,** 13¼x8½x3¼
In glazes 2, 4 & 7

DUNDEE, ILLINOIS — 19 — **THE HAEGER POTTERIES, INC.**

55

R-442—Bowl with Floral Pattern, 7x18½x4¾
In glazes 1 thru 12

R-303—Laurel Wreath Bowl,
3x11¾x7, Glazes 2, 4, 6 & 12

R-298—Conch-Shell Cornucopia, 11x8¾x4¾
In glazes 2, 4, 5 & 6

R-475—Twin-Stalk Candleholders,
8¾x10¾x4, Glazes 1 thru 12

R-203—Flying Fish Candleholder,
3⅜x6x3⅜
Glazes 1 thru 12

R-474—Oblong Vase, Leaf Base,
5x9½x5, Glaze No. 24

R-363—Nude on Fish,
4x10x4
Glazes 1 thru 12

R-407—Wren House,
5½x6½x2
Glazes 1 thru 12

THE HAEGER POTTERIES, INC.   —20—   WORLD'S LARGEST ART POTTERY

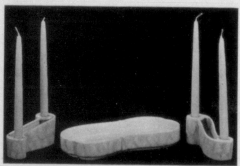

R-484—Miniature Garden Bowl, 6x2x13
R-485—Flower Candleholder, 2½x2¾x7½
Both in glazes 2, 4, 5, 7 & 12

R-494—Egyptian Cat (Head up)
2½x1¾x4¼

R-493 (Head down)
2½x6½x4

In glazes 13 & 18

R-498—Roman Vase, Bas-Relief Flowers
7½x9¼x7¼, Glazes 24, Comb. 5 & 20

R-496—Bud Vase, 3x8x3
Glazes 1 thru 12

R-500—Bee-Hive Vase, Grapes & Leaves
6x7½x6, Glazes 24, Comb. 5 & 20

R-491—Ramhead, Black Base
5½x12x6, Glaze No. 6

DUNDEE, ILLINOIS   —21—   THE HAEGER POTTERIES, INC.

R-490—Triangular Vase,
5½x15x5½, Glazes 2, 5, 7 & 12

R-483—Upright Shell, 11x10½x4½
In glazes 2, 4, 5 & 10

R-479—Prospector with Burros, 5x7x11½
In glazes 10 & 13

R-501—Bee-Hive Vase with Flowers, 6x7½x6
Glazes 24, Comb. 5 & 20

R-488—Pillow Vase, 5x7¾x2½
In glazes 1 thru 12

R-486—Square Bowl, 9½x2¾x9½
In glazes 2, 4, 5, 7 & 12

THE HAEGER POTTERIES, INC.   — 22 —   WORLD'S LARGEST ART POTTERY

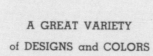

R-482—Large Plume, 10x14x4½
In glazes 1 thru 12

A GREAT VARIETY
of DESIGNS and COLORS

R-477—Modernistic Lady Head.
4x13½x3¼, Glazes 1 & 6

R-481—Sea-Shell on Base, 9¼x11¼x8¼
In glazes 1 thru 12

THE FINEST

in POTTERY

yet PRICED

to SELL

BACKED by

AMERICA'S

LARGEST

ART POTTERY

R-495—Black Panther, 4x5½x26
In glaze No. 18 only

DUNDEE, ILLINOIS   — 23 —   THE HAEGER POTTERIES, INC.

3200—Book Ends, 6½x4¼x3½

517-A—Wall Pocket, 6¼x7x2¾

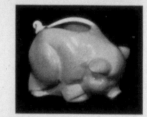

3295—Pig, 4¾x3¼x3

3208—Flying Fish Vase,
5¾x6x2½

3223—Vase, 4½x6x4½   3256—Leaf Vase, 4½x6x2½

3296—Donkey Cart, 2x3x5½

DUNDEE, ILLINOIS — 27 — **THE HAEGER POTTERIES, INC.**

3319—Lamb Planter,
6½x8½x3

3282—Girl & Buggy Vase, 3x6¼x5½

1018—Vase, 3x7¼x3

1005—Colonial Girl, 3½x7½x2½

3307—Madonna Planter, 4¾x5½x4

3280—Baby Carriage, 2½x4½x6

3005—Vase, 3½x4½x3½

DUNDEE, ILLINOIS — 29 — **THE HAEGER POTTERIES, INC.**

3234—Lamb Vase, 5¼x6x2¼

3315—Elephant Planter, 4½x6½x5½

3318—Colonial Girl, 6½x9x5

3254—Sugar Bowl & Creamer, 5x2x3½

3288—Lily Candlesticks, 4x2x4

3291—Low Bowl, 5¼x1¾x10¼

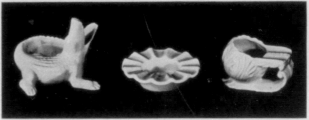

3075—Ash Tray, 6¼x4½x6¼   3257—Ash Tray, 5¼x1½x5¼   823—Ash Tray, 3x3¾x5

THE HAEGER POTTERIES, INC.   — 30 —   WORLD'S LARGEST ART POTTERY

3084—Bowl, 7¾x5½x4¼

Numerous designs and a wealth of color to appeal to every taste.

3266—Donkey Planter, 6x5¾x3

1013—Rabbit Planter, 4x4x7

3284—Oblong Planter, 3x3½x7½

3289—Crying Girl, 5x7½x4½

3270—Leaf Vase, 5¾x8¼x3

THE HAEGER POTTERIES, INC.   — 32 —   WORLD'S LARGEST ART POTTERY

2012—Vase, 4½x7¾x4½

3047—Bowl, 5x3¼x9

3085—Vase, 7½x5x3¾

1014—Baby Chicks, 4½x4¾x4½

3306—Horsehead Vase, 7x8¾x3¼

3311—Cat, 6x6½x4

3290—Madonna, 4½x9½x3½

DUNDEE, ILLINOIS   — 33 —   THE HAEGER POTTERIES, INC.

3015—Vase, 5¾x8½x5

3231—Vase, 5½x9x5½

3213—Vase, 7x8½x7

741-C—Vase, 4¾x9x4
741-D—Vase, 7x11¼x5½

3314—Horse Planter, 7½x6x3

3321—Girl & Baby Buggy, 2¾x7¼x9

3317—Scottie Planter, 8x6x3

3322—Stork Planter, 8x10x5¼

DUNDEE, ILLINOIS   — 35 —   THE HAEGER POTTERIES, INC.

444-A—Cornucopia, 8x7½x4

3202—Wall Pocket, 7½x9x2½

2030—Vase, 5¾x8¼x3½

3292—Bowl, 6x2x11½

3217—Bowl, 8¼x2x13½

THE HAEGER POTTERIES, INC.   — 36 —   WORLD'S LARGEST ART POTTERY

3118—Wall Pocket, 4x10x3

3105—Dancing Girl Vase, 5¼x8x5¼   3313—Madonna Vase, 6x9x6   3104—Colonial Girl, 5¾x7¾x3½

Observe the hand-wrought symmetry and clarity of detail on all Haeger pieces.

3309—Rabbit Vase, 7x7x3½

3224—Vase, 7x9x7

THE HAEGER POTTERIES, INC.   — 38 —   WORLD'S LARGEST ART POTTERY

3049—Triple-Girl Figure Vase, 9½x6½x5½

47—Bowl, 13x2½x13

3265—Donkey Cart, 5½x11

2021—Vase, 6x9½x4¾

1037—Vase, 6x9¼x6

DUNDEE, ILLINOIS   — 39 —   THE HAEGER POTTERIES, INC.

364/130 Console Set

130—Pheasant, 2¾x6x10½   364—Bowl, 10x4x10   130—Pheasant, 2¾x6x10½

3020—Feather Vase, 5x9¾x4

3088—Swan, 7x7½x4

1028—Vase, 6½x7¾x6½

THE HAEGER POTTERIES, INC.   — 40 —   WORLD'S LARGEST ART POTTERY

IT PAYS TO FEATURE ROYAL HAEGER VASES

R-430. SWAN VASE—3½ x 8 x 6. Mauve Agate, Cloudy Blue, Haze Blue, Ebony, Chartreuse and Honey .... $3.00 ea.

R-186. BIRD OF PARADISE—10½ x 13 x 4½. Mauve Agate, Cloudy Blue, Green Briar, Green Crystal, Green Agate .... $8.00 ea.

R-36. LARGE SWAN VASE—10 x 15 x 5½. Mauve Agate, Cloudy Blue, Green Briar, Gloss White .... $8.00 ea.

R-182. SWANS (L&R)—8 x 7¾ x 2¾. Mauve Agate, Cloudy Blue, Green Briar, Silver Spray and Chartreuse, Yellow. .... $2.50 ea.

R-456. WRAP AROUND SPIRAL—5¼ x 13 x 5¼. Green Briar, Silver Spray and Chartreuse, Yellow Drip, Chartreuse and Honey, Mere Green and White .... $5.00 ea.

R-453. SMALL PEACOCK—10 x 10 x 3¼. Mauve Agate, Cloudy Blue, Yellow Drip. .... $5.00 ea.

R-691. SQUARE VASE—6 x 15 x 8½. Pearl Grey Drip with White, Catseye Drip with White, Yellow with White, Chartreuse with White .... $8.00 ea.

R-452. MORNING GLORY VASE—9½ x 16¼ x 4¾. Mauve Agate, Green Briar, Silver Spray and Chartreuse, Chartreuse and Honey, Mere Green and White .... $9.00 ea.

R-693. WRAP AROUND VASE—5¼ x 18 x 6. Pearl Grey Drip with White, Catseye Drip with White, Chartreuse with White, Yellow with White. .... $9.00 ea

R-31. PEACOCK VASE—15¾ x 15 x 5¼—Mauve Agate, Cloudy Blue, Ebony, Chartreuse, Green Briar, Green Agate. .... $10.00 ea.

R-301. FAN VASE—9½ x 8¾ x 4. Green Agate, Mauve Agate, Cloudy Blue, Green Briar, Chartreuse and Honey, Green Crystal .... $3.50 ea.

R-446. LILY VASE—6¾ x 13¾ x 6¾. Silver Spray and Chartreuse, Mauve Agate, Mere Green and White .... $7.00 ea.

Nationally advertised by
Haeger of Dundee

ROYAL Haeger POTTERY

ALL PRICES SHOWN ARE LIST
Mail orders accepted subject to Company approval
THE ROYAL HAEGER POTTERIES
DUNDEE • ILLINOIS

CONSOLE SETS TO CREATE THAT PLUS VOLUME

R-679. ROUND BOWL—12 x 4 x 12. Romany Green, Antique Grey, Mere Green and White, Oxblood and White .... $6.00 ea.

R-680. ROUND CANDLEHOLDERS—5 x 2 x 5. Romany Green, Antique Grey, Mere Green, Oxblood .... $3.00 pr.

R-681. RECTANGULAR BOWL—7 x 2½ x 14¼. Romany Green, Antique Grey, Chartreuse and White, Oxblood and White .... $6.00 ea.

R-682. RECTANGULAR CANDLEHOLDERS—3¼ x 2 x 7. Romany Green, Antique Grey, Chartreuse, Oxblood. .... $4.00 pr.

R-309. RUCHING BOWL—8½ x 2½ x 14½. Mauve Agate, Cloudy Blue, Silver Spray and Chartreuse, Chartreuse and Yellow, Green Briar, Green Agate .... $6.00 ea.

R-360. TROPICAL FISH BLOCK—5¼ x 11¼ x 3¼. Mauve Agate, Cloudy Blue, Green Briar, Silver Spray, Hydrangea Pink, Chartreuse, Green Agate, Yellow-drip .... $4.00 ea.

R-486. SQUARE BOWL—9½ x 2¾ x 9½. Mauve Agate, Green Briar, Hydrangea Pink and White, Chartreuse and Yellow, Green Agate, Green Crystal .... $5.00 ea.

R-397. THREE BLOCK CANDLEHOLDER—2¾ x 3 x 8¼. Mauve Agate, Cloudy Blue, Green Briar, Silver Spray, Yellow, Hydrangea Pink, Ebony, Chartreuse, Green Agate, Green Crystal .... $5.00 pr.

R-621. CHINESE PLANTER—5 x 3⅞ x 8. Mere Green, Yellow, Ebony .... $2.00 ea.

R-622. CHINESE CANDLEHOLDERS—2¾ x 5 x 3¾. Mere Green, Yellow, Ebony .... $3.00 pr.

R-627. CHINESE BOWL—5½ x 1¾ x 10½. Yellow, Mere Green, Ebony .... $2.00 ea.

R-628. CHINESE LADY—2⅛ x 5¾ x 2⅛. Yellow, Mere Green, Ebony .... $1.00 ea.

R-629. CHINESE MAN—2⅛ x 5⅜ x 2⅛. Yellow, Mere Green, Ebony .... $1.00 ea.

R-312. CORNUCOPIA CANDLEHOLDER—5½ x 4¾ x 3. Mauve Agate, Cloudy Blue, Green Briar, Silver Spray, Yellow, Haze Blue, Hydrangea Pink, Chartreuse, Green Agate, Mere Green, Green Crystal. .... $2.50 pr.

R-476. BEADED BOWL—7¼ x 4½ x 15. Mauve Agate, Green Briar, Silver Spray and Chartreuse, Green Agate, Ebony and Chartreuse .... $5.00 ea.

R-561. DRAGON BOWL—10 x 5 x 10. Chartreuse and Yellow, Catseye .... $5.00 ea.

R-571. JEWELED LADY—5 x 15½ x 5. Yellow, Chartreuse, White .... $6.00 ea.

R-692. ROUND BOWL—12½ x 5 x 12½. Yellow, Chartreuse, Silver Spray, Persian Grey .... $5.00 ea.

R-692A. STAND FOR R-692—Ebony. .... $2.50 ea.

R-692B. ROUND BOWL AND STAND .... $7.50 set

ALL PRICES SHOWN ARE LIST
Mail orders accepted subject to Company approval
THE ROYAL HAEGER POTTERIES
DUNDEE • ILLINOIS

ROYAL Haeger POTTERY

Nationally advertised by
Haeger of Dundee

A WIDE RANGE OF UNIQUE POTTERY PIECES

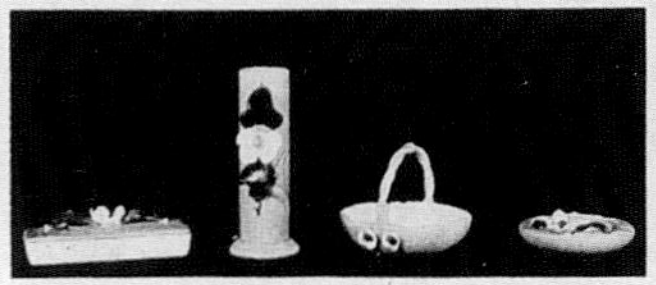

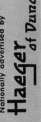

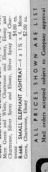

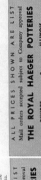

R-575. ROSE OF SHARON BASKET—6½ x 5¾ x 7. Yellow and White, Chartreuse and White ..... $5.00 ea.
R-577. ROSE OF SHARON CIGARETTE BOX—3½ x 2¾ x 8. Yellow and White, Chartreuse and White ..... $4.00 ea.
R-580. ROSE OF SHARON VASE—3⅜ x 9½ x 3⅜. Yellow and White, Chartreuse and White ..... $5.00 ea.
R-594. ROSE OF SHARON ASHTRAY—5¾ x 2¼ x 5¾. Yellow and White, Chartreuse and White ..... $3.00 ea.

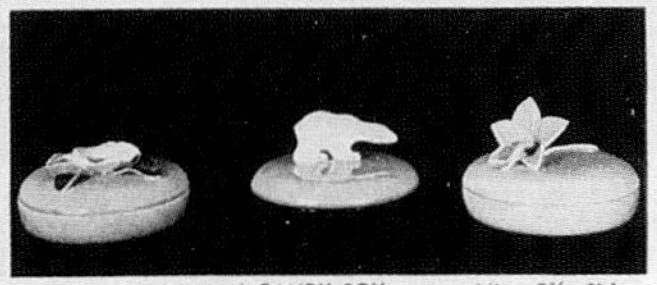

R-590. HAWAIIAN CANDY BOX—[illegible]¾ x 3¾ x 7¾. Yellow, White, Chartreuse (all decorated) ..... $5.00 ea.
R-664. POLAR BEAR CANDY BOX—7½ x 4¾ x 7½. Ebony and Chartreuse, Chartreuse and Ebony ..... $5.00 ea.
R-431. CALLA LILY BOWL—7½ x 5¼ x 7¼. Mauve Agate, Silver Spray and Chartreuse, Honeycopen, Chartreuse and Yellow ..... $5.00 ea.

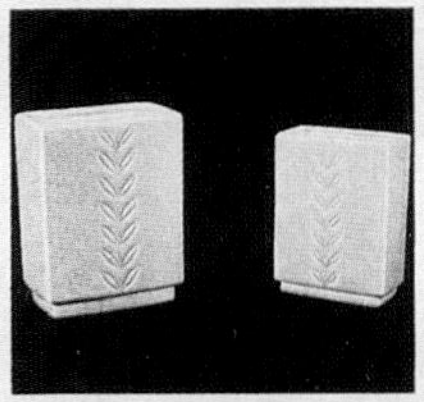

R-526. PILLOW VASE—4½ x 6¼ x 2½. Silver Spray and Chartreuse, Chartreuse and Yellow, Mission Marble and Gunmetal ..... $1.50 ea.
R-527. PILLOW VASE—5½ x 7¼ x 3⅛. Silver Spray and Chartreuse, Chartreuse and Yellow, Mission Marble and Gunmetal ..... $2.50 ea.

R-567. LEAF ASHTRAY (at right)—5 x 2½ x 8. Yellow, Chartreuse, Green Agate ..... $2.00 ea.

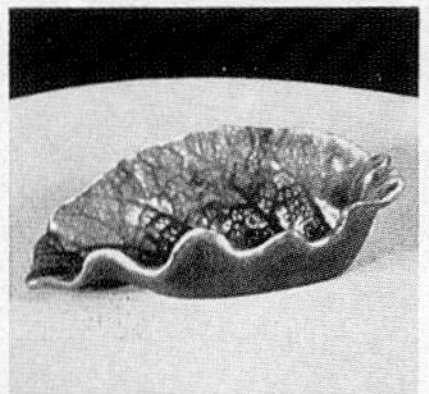

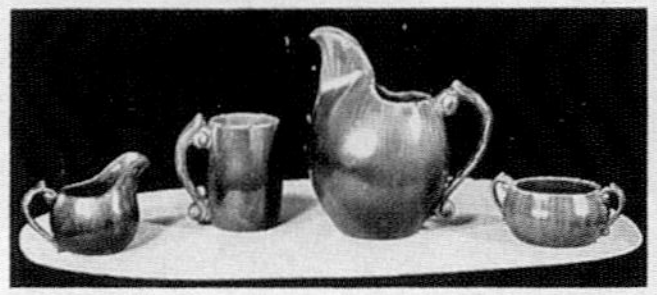

R-583. PITCHER—5½ x 8 x 7¾. Green Briar, Silver Spray and Chartreuse, Green Agate, Mere Green ..... $4.00 ea.
R-584. CREAMER—3¼ x 3½ x 5. Green Briar, Silver Spray and Chartreuse, Green Agate, Mere Green ..... $1.[illegible] ea.
R-585. SUGAR—4¼ x 2¾ x 5½. Green Briar, Silver Spray and Chartreuse, Green Agate, Mere Green ..... $1.50 ea.
R-586. MUG—2¾ x 2¾ x 4½. Green Briar, Green Agate, Chartreuse, Mere Green ..... $1.00 ea.

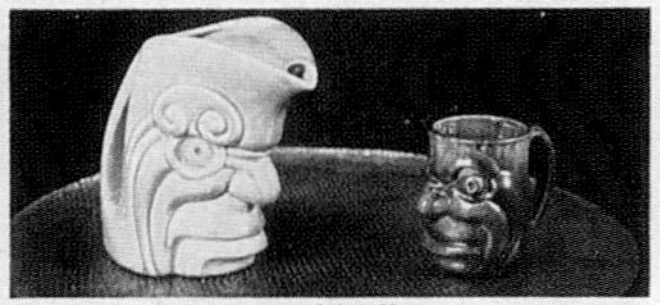

R-698. MEXICAN HEAD PITCHER—4½ x 7¼ x 7½. Green Agate, Green Briar, Chartreuse ..... $5.00 ea.
R-699. MEXICAN MUG—3 x 4¼ x 4¼. Green Agate, Green Briar, Chartreuse ..... $1.50 ea.

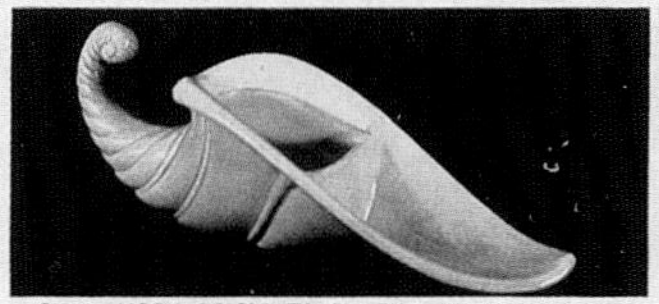

R-534. HORN OF PLENTY—7 x 7½ x 18. Mauve Agate, Green Briar, Green Agate, Chartreuse and Yellow ..... $12.00 ea.

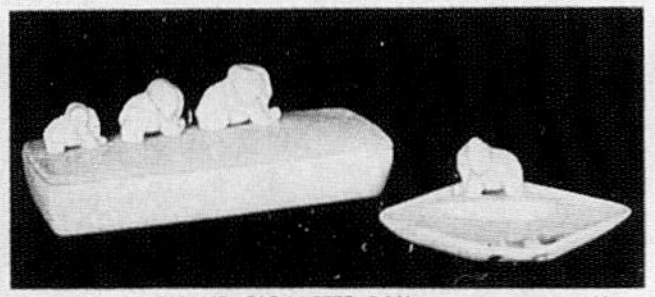

R-625. ELEPHANT CIGARETTE BOX—5½ x 3⅜ x 8¼. Mere Green and White, Chartreuse and Ebony, Ebony and Chartreuse, Silver Spray and Ebony, Silver Spray and Chartreuse ..... $4.00 ea.
R-668. SMALL ELEPHANT ASHTRAY—4 x 1¾ x 4. Mere Green, Chartreuse, Ebony ..... $2.00 ea.

Nationally advertised by
Haeger of Dundee

ROYAL Haeger POTTERY

ALL PRICES SHOWN ARE LIST
Mail orders accepted subject to Company approval
THE ROYAL HAEGER POTTERIES
DUNDEE • ILLINOIS

UNUSUAL VASES FOR ALL KINDS OF FLOWERS

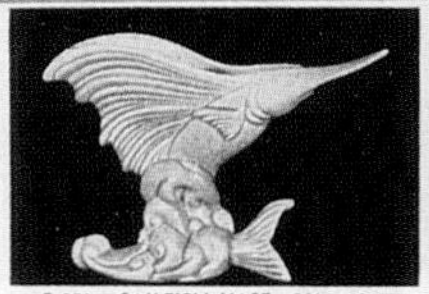

R-271. SAILFISH VASE—2½ x 9 x 12. Mauve Agate, Cloudy Blue, Silver Spray and Chartreuse, Green Agate, Chartreuse and Honey ..... $3.50 ea.

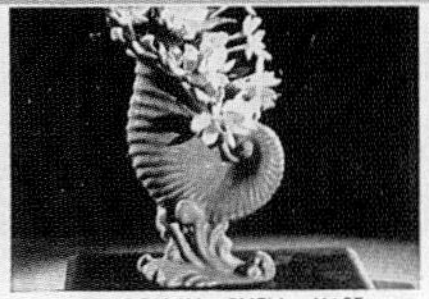

R-321. CONCH SHELL VASE—5½ x 7½ x 3½. Mauve Agate, Cloudy Blue, Green Briar, Chartreuse and Honey, Yellowdrip ..... $2.50 ea.

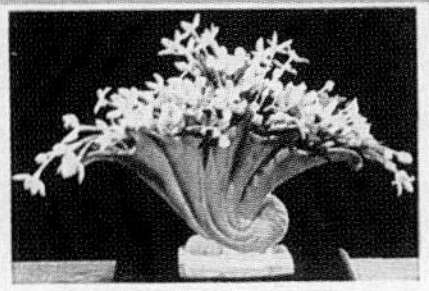

R-299. SNAIL SHELL BOWL—11½ x 7 x 3¼. Mauve Agate, Cloudy Blue, Green Briar, Silver Spray and Chartreuse, Yellow Drip, Green Agate. ..... $3.50 ea.

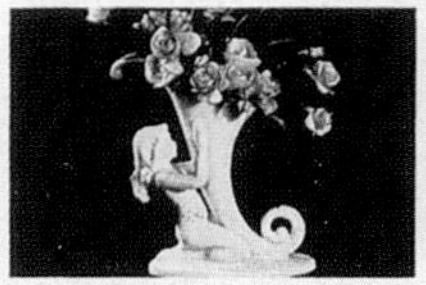

R-426. CORNUCOPIA WITH NUDE—2¾ x 8 x 7. Mauve Agate, Cloudy Blue, Silver Spray and Chartreuse, Chartreuse and Honey, Ebony $3.50

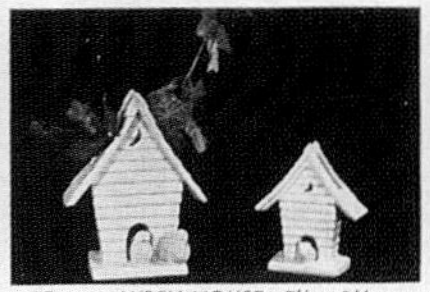

R-287. WREN HOUSE—7¼ x 9¼ x 4. Mauve Agate, Cloudy Blue, Green Agate, Green Briar, Yellow ..... $3.50 ea.
R-407. WREN HOUSE—5½ x 6½ x 2. Mauve Agate, Cloudy Blue, Green Briar, Yellow, Green Agate ..... $2.00 ea.

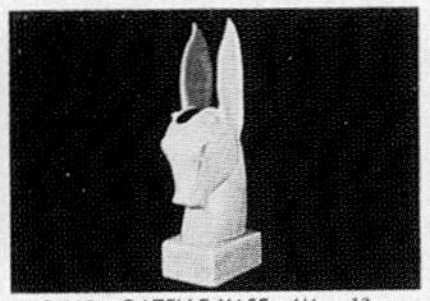

R-115. GAZELLE VASE—4½ x 13 x 3. Yellow, Chartreuse, Ebony. ..... $6.00 ea.

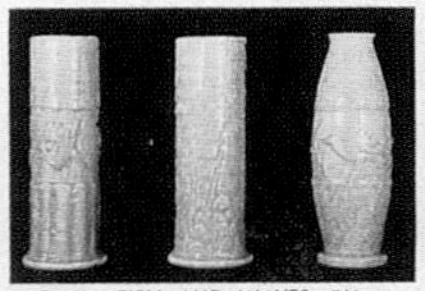

R-658. FISH AND WAVES—5½ x 14 x 5½. Romany Green, Chartreuse, Yellow ..... $6.00 ea.
R-659. ALLIGATOR VASE—5½ x 14¼ x 5½. Coconut Brown, Catseye, Silver Spray ..... $6.00 ea.
R-660. BIRDS AND SPRIGS—4¾ x 14 x 4¾. Antique Grey, Chartreuse, Yellow ..... $6.00 ea.

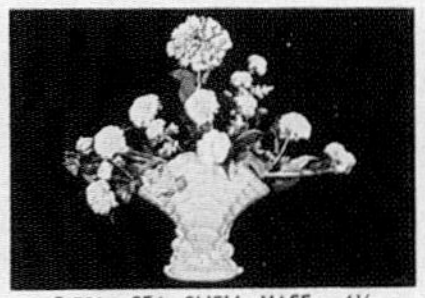

R-701. SEA SHELL VASE—4¼ x 10¼ x 11. Dark Green and White, Mulberry and White, Chartreuse and White, Silver Spray and White. ..... $5.00 ea.

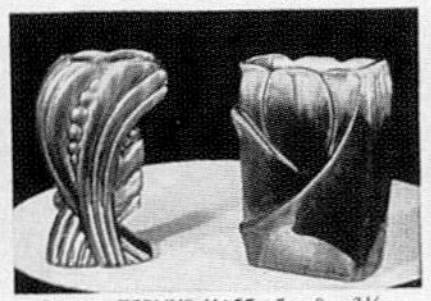

R-653. ZEPHYR VASE—5 x 8 x 3¼. Chinese Blue Drip, Ebony, Green Agate ..... $2.00 ea.
R-651. PILLOW VASE—5¾ x 7¾ x 3. Green Agate, Green Briar, Chartreuse and Honey ..... $2.00 ea.

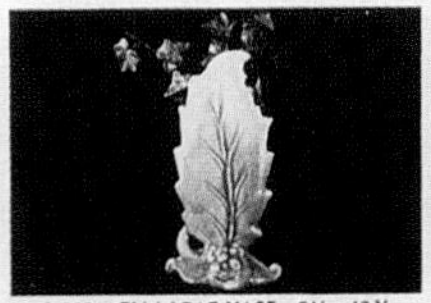

R-320. ELM LEAF VASE—5½ x 12¾ x 5¼. Mauve Agate, Cloudy Blue, Green Briar, Chartreuse and Honey, Green Agate ..... $4.00 ea.

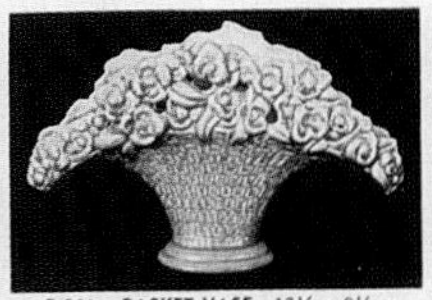

R-386. BASKET VASE—13¼ x 8½ x 3¼. Mauve Agate, Honeycopen, Yellow Drip, Chartreuse and Honey. ..... $5.00 ea.

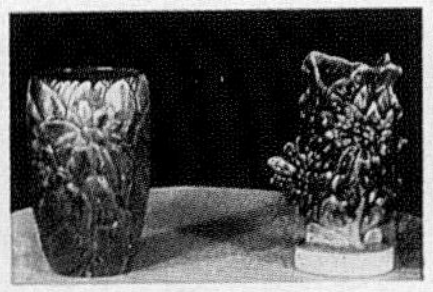

R-647. SUNFLOWER VASE—4¾ x 8 x 3¾. Yellow decorated, Gloss White decorated, Green Briar, Green Agate, Mauve Agate ..... $2.00 ea.
R-652. FLORAL VASE—4¼ x 7½ x 4¼. White decorated, Ebony, Green Crystal ..... $2.00 ea.

ALL PRICES SHOWN ARE LIST
Mail orders accepted subject to Company approval
THE ROYAL HAEGER POTTERIES
DUNDEE • ILLINOIS

ROYAL Haeger POTTERY

Nationally advertised by
Haeger of Dundee

FIGURINES FOR YEAR ROUND GIFT SELLING

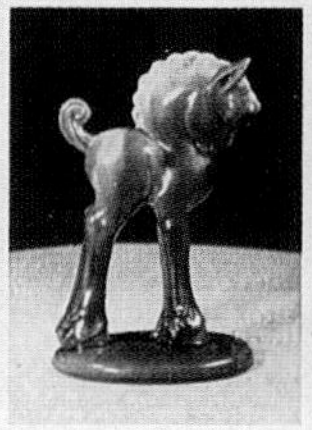

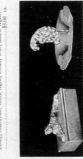

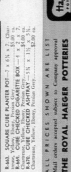

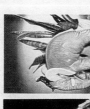

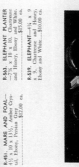

R-103. SMALL HORSE—2½ x 5½ x 5½. Mauve Agate, Green Briar, Ebony, Oxblood, Yellow .... $2.00 ea.

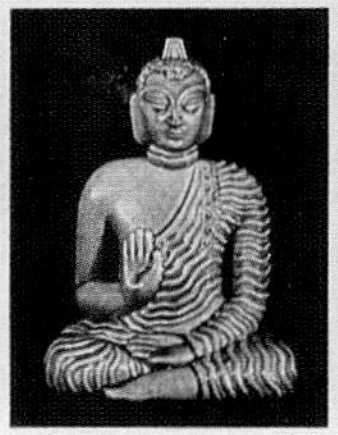

R-694. BUDDHA—7 x 10½ x 4. Ebony, Oxblood, Plain Catseye, Chartreuse .... $5.00 ea.

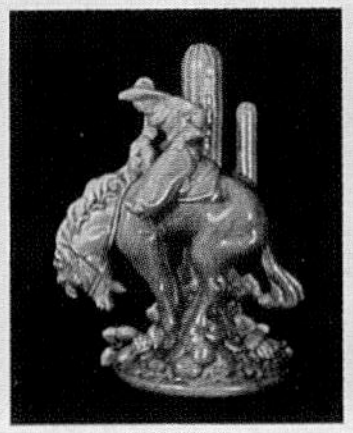

R-424. BUCKING BRONCO—6¼ x 13 x 8¼. Amber, Chartreuse, Persian Grey. .... $12.00 ea.

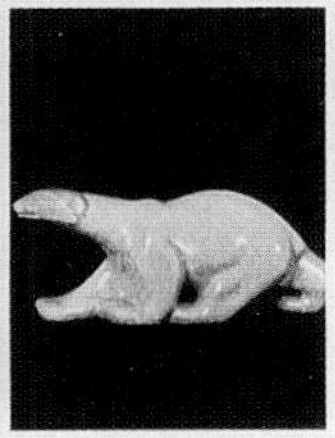

R-702. POLAR BEAR—3½ x 6¾ x 16. Silver Pebble, Pebble Black .... $5.00 ea.

STOCK THE COMPLETE HAEGER LINE FOR CONSISTENT VOLUME BUSINESS

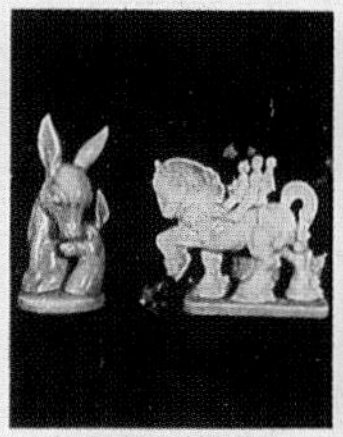

R-624. TWO DOES—7 x 14¾ x 7. Ebony, Oxblood, Chartreuse .... $15.00 ea.

R-596. BARNYARD RIDERS—13¾ x 12¾ x 7½. Silver Spray with Chartreuse Planter and Yellow Riders .... $25.00 ea.

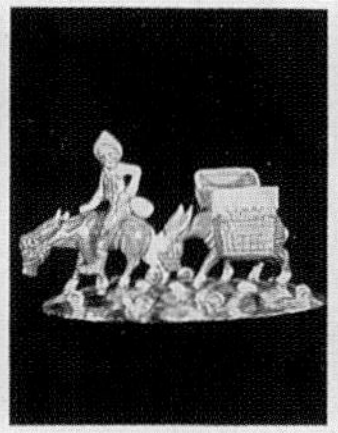

R-479. PROSPECTOR—4½ x 6⅞ x 10¼. Amber Crystal. .... $7.00 ea.

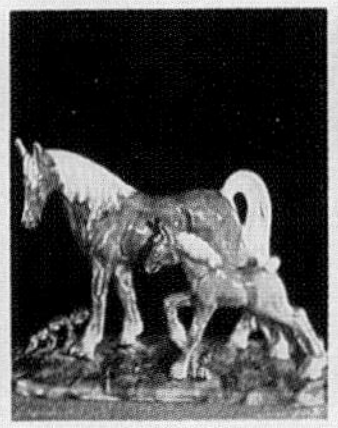

R-451. MARE AND FOAL—4½ x 10 x 13½. Amber Crystal, Ebony, Persian Grey .... $12.00 ea.

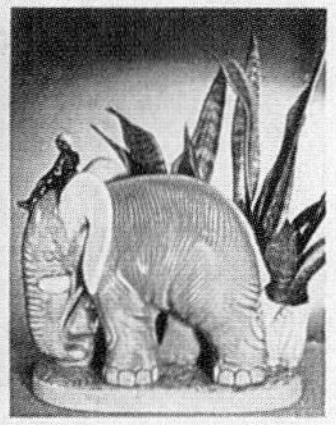

R-563. ELEPHANT PLANTER—7¼ x 10 x 10. Chartreuse and Honey, Ebony and White. .... $15.00 ea.

R-539. ELEPHANT—4¼ x 9 x 9. Chartreuse and Honey, Ebony and White .... $10.00 ea.

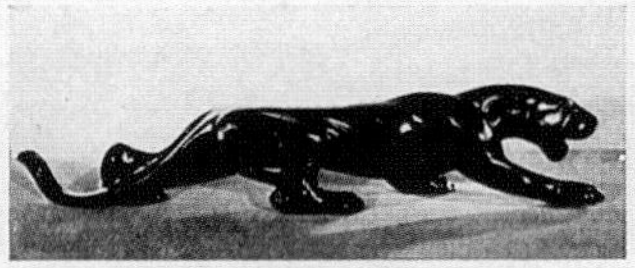

R-495. PANTHER—4 x 5½ x 26. Ebony, Amber Crystal. .... $15.00 ea.

R-683. SMALL PANTHER—3¾ x 4¾ x 17½. Ebony, Amber Spotted, Persian Grey .... $5.00 ea.

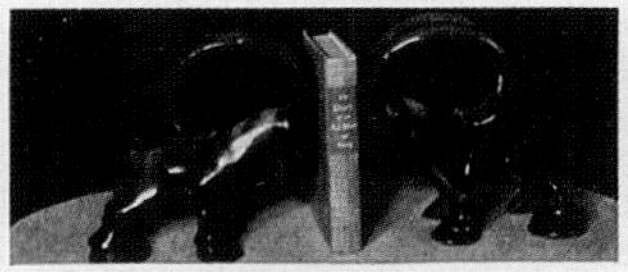

R-132. RAM BOOKENDS—4¾ x 7¾ x 8. Mauve Agate, Green Briar, Ebony, Silver Spray, Chartreuse .... $8.00 pr.

Nationally advertised by Haeger of Dundee

ALL PRICES SHOWN ARE LIST
Mail orders accepted subject to Company approval
THE ROYAL HAEGER POTTERIES
DUNDEE • ILLINOIS

PRACTICAL SMOKING ACCESSORIES BY HAEGER

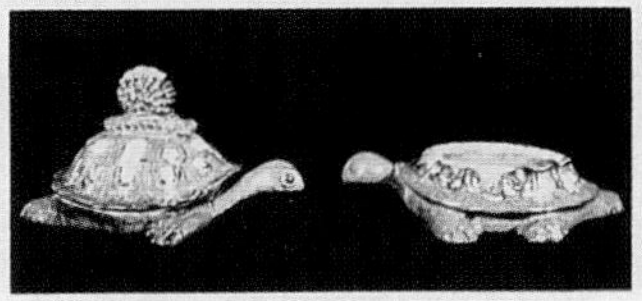

R-684. TURTLE CIGARETTE BOX—6½ x 4½ x 9¼. Green Crystal, Green Briar, Chartreuse .... $3.50 ea.

R-541. TURTLE ASHTRAY—5½ x 1⅞ x 7¾. Green Crystal, Green Briar, Chartreuse, Catseye .... $1.50 ea.

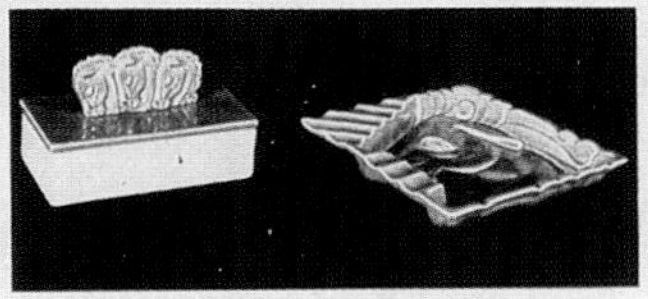

R-685. HORSEHEAD CIGARETTE BOX—4 x 4½ x 7. Ebony, Silver Spray, Chartreuse, Oxblood (interchangeable boxes). $4.00 ea.

R-686. HORSEHEAD ASHTRAY—8 x 1½ x 8. Ebony, Silver Spray, Chartreuse, Oxblood .... $2.50 ea.

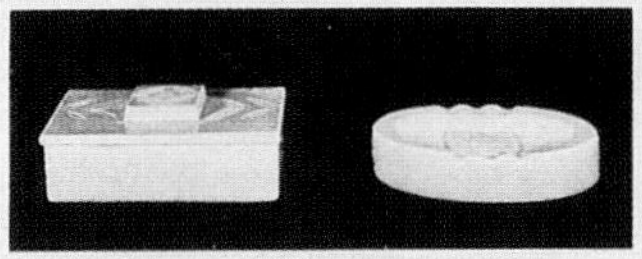

R-560. LAUREL CIGARETTE BOX—4 x 2⅜ x 7. Silver Spray and Chartreuse, Ebony, Chartreuse and Yellow, Silver Spray and Ebony .... $3.00 ea.

R-559. LAUREL ASHTRAY—4½ x 1½ x 6½. Silver Spray and Chartreuse, Ebony, Chartreuse and Yellow .... $1.30 ea.

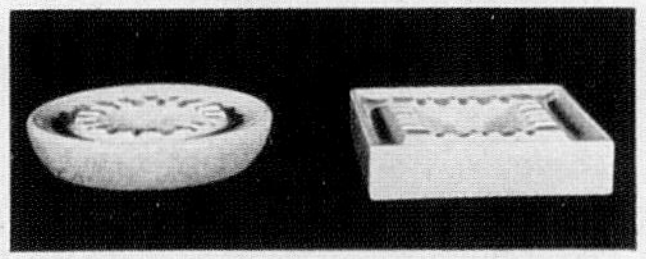

R-230. COG WHEEL ASHTRAY—7½ x 1½ x 7½. Green Briar, Haze Blue, Ebony, Chartreuse, Green Agate, Mauve Agate .... $3.00 ea.

R-252. SQUARE ASHTRAY—7 x 1¾ x 7. Green Briar, Ebony, Chartreuse, Green Agate, Cloudy Blue, Mauve Agate. .... $3.00 ea.

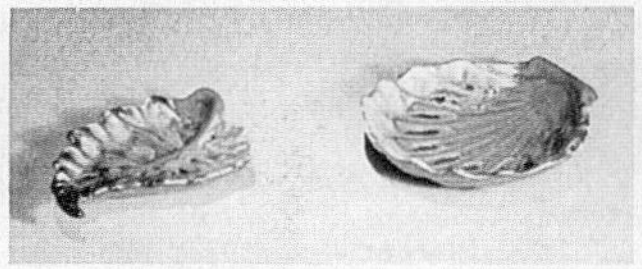

R-449. LEAF ASHTRAY—3½ x ¾ x 5. Green Agate, Green Briar, Mauve Agate, Chartreuse, Yellow, Green Crystal. .... $1.00 ea.

R-447. SHELL ASHTRAY—4½ x 1¾ x 4½. Green Agate, Green Briar, Mauve Agate, Chartreuse, Yellow, Green Crystal. .... $1.00 ea.

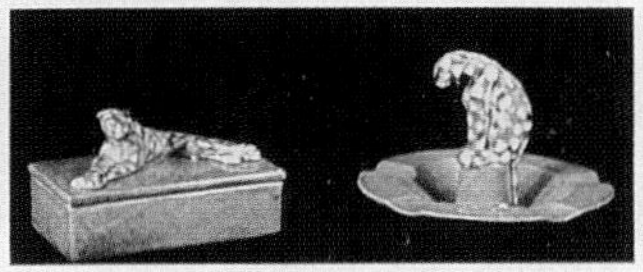

R-631. SMALL LEOPARD CIGARETTE BOX—4 x 4 x 7. Ebony, Amber .... $4.00 ea.

R-632. SMALL LEOPARD ASHTRAY—8¼ x 5½ x 8¼. Ebony, Amber .... $4.00 ea.

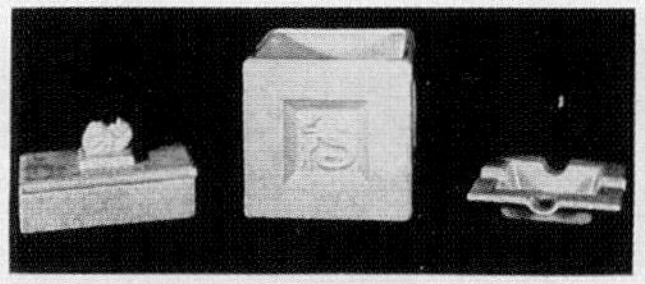

R-663. SQUARE CUBE PLANTER POT—7 x 6¾ x 7. Chartreuse, Yellow, Ebony, Persian Grey .... $5.00 ea.

R-669. CUBE CHECKED CIGARETTE BOX—4 x 2 x 7. Chartreuse, Yellow, Ebony, Persian Grey .... $4.00 ea.

R-670. CUBE CHECKED ASHTRAY—5¾ x 1½ x 5¾. Chartreuse, Yellow, Ebony, Persian Grey .... $2.00 ea.

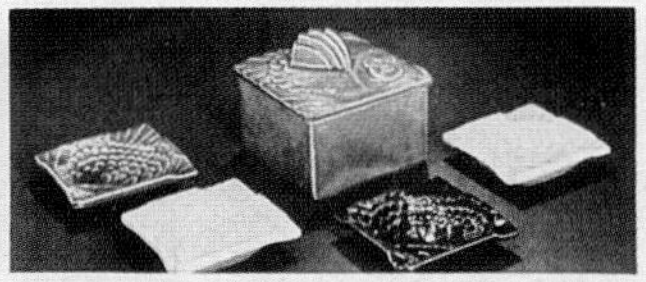

R-687. FISH CIGARETTE BOX—4½ x 4½ x 4½. Blue Black, Oxblood, Yellow, Mere Green (interchangeable boxes). .... $3.00 ea.

R-688. FISH ASHTRAY—4 x ½ x 4. Blue Black, Oxblood, Yellow, Mere Green .... $1.00 ea.

R-688X. FISH CIGARETTE BOX AND 2 ASHTRAYS ... $5.00 set

ALL PRICES SHOWN ARE LIST
Mail orders accepted subject to Company approval
THE ROYAL HAEGER POTTERIES
DUNDEE • ILLINOIS

Nationally advertised by Haeger of Dundee

FOR THOSE WHO SEEK SOMETHING DIFFERENT

R-633. IMPERIAL MONGOLIAN MAN—7 x 2¾ x 7. Mere Green decorated, Yellow decorated, Antique Grey—$40.00

R-634. IMPERIAL MONGOLIAN WOMAN—7 x 2¾ x 7. Mere Green decorated, Yellow decorated, Antique Grey—$40.00

R-700. LION HEAD BOOKEND—6¼ x 7½ x 4. Amber-Brown-White, Pebble Brown, Ebony—$5.00 pr.

R-475. CALLA LILY BOOKENDS—3½ x 6 x 2¾. Honeytopon, Amber Crystal—$5.00 pr.

R-540. TURTLE PLANTER—9½ x 4 x 13½. Green Crystal, Cateye—$6.00

R-455. FISH GLOBE STAND—12½ x 11¼ x 9. Cateye—$15.00 ea.

R-456. FISH GLOBE STAND—9¾ x 11½ x 6½. Cateye—$15.00 ea.

R-457. GONDOLIER PLANTER—19½ x 7½ x 5½. Chartreuse, Ebony, Oxblood—$15.00 ea.

R-570. PEI TUNG DRAGON—5 x 15¼ x 5. Yellow Drip, Chartreuse and Honey, Cateye—$6.00 ea.

R-363. NUDE ASTRIDE FISH BLOCK (at left)—4 x 10 x 4. Mauve Agate, Cloudy Blue, Green Briar, Silver Spray, Yellow, Chartreuse, Green Crystal—$4.00 ea.

R-672. MONGOLIAN MAN FLOWER BLOCK—3½ x 12½ x 3½. Dark Green, Mere Green, Yellow, Chartreuse—$3.50 ea.

R-673. MONGOLIAN WOMAN FLOWER BLOCK—3½ x 12½ x 3½. Dark Green, Mere Green, Yellow, Chartreuse—$3.50 ea.

R-641. STALLION BOOKEND PLANTER (at right)—3½ x 8¼ x 5. Gunmetal, Ebony, Chartreuse, Yellow—$5.00 pr.

ROYAL HAEGER BOWLS IN EXQUISITE GLAZES

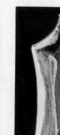

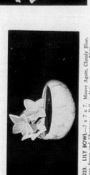

R-297. OVAL SHELL BOWL (at left)—7½ x 3 x 16. Mauve Agate, Green Briar, Chartreuse and Yellow, Silver Spray and Chartreuse, Green Agate, Green Crystal—$5.00 ea.

R-562. PEI TUNG BOWL (at right)—9½ x 4 x 9½. Silver Spray and Chartreuse, Ebony—$5.00 ea.

R-489. SQUARE SHALLOW BOWL—10½ x 2½ x 10¾. Green Crystal, Green Agate, Green Briar, Ebony (all white drip)—$5.00 ea.

R-373. BOWL WITH FLORAL DESIGN—8¾ x 20 x 6. Cloudy Blue, Green Briar, Mauve Agate—$9.00 ea.

R-223. LILY BOWL—7 x 7 x 7. Mauve Agate, Cloudy Blue, Silver Spray and Chartreuse, Yellow Drip—$5.00 ea.

R-568. OCTOPUS BOWL—16 x 2½ x 16. Silver Spray and Chartreuse, Mere Green, Romany Green—$10.00 ea.

R-140. LONG FLUTED BOWL—8½ x 17 x 3½. Yellow Drip, Green Briar, Mauve Agate—$7.00 ea.

R-358. FOOTED BOWL—5½ x 3½ x 17½. Green Briar, Mauve Agate, Persian Grey—$9.00 ea.

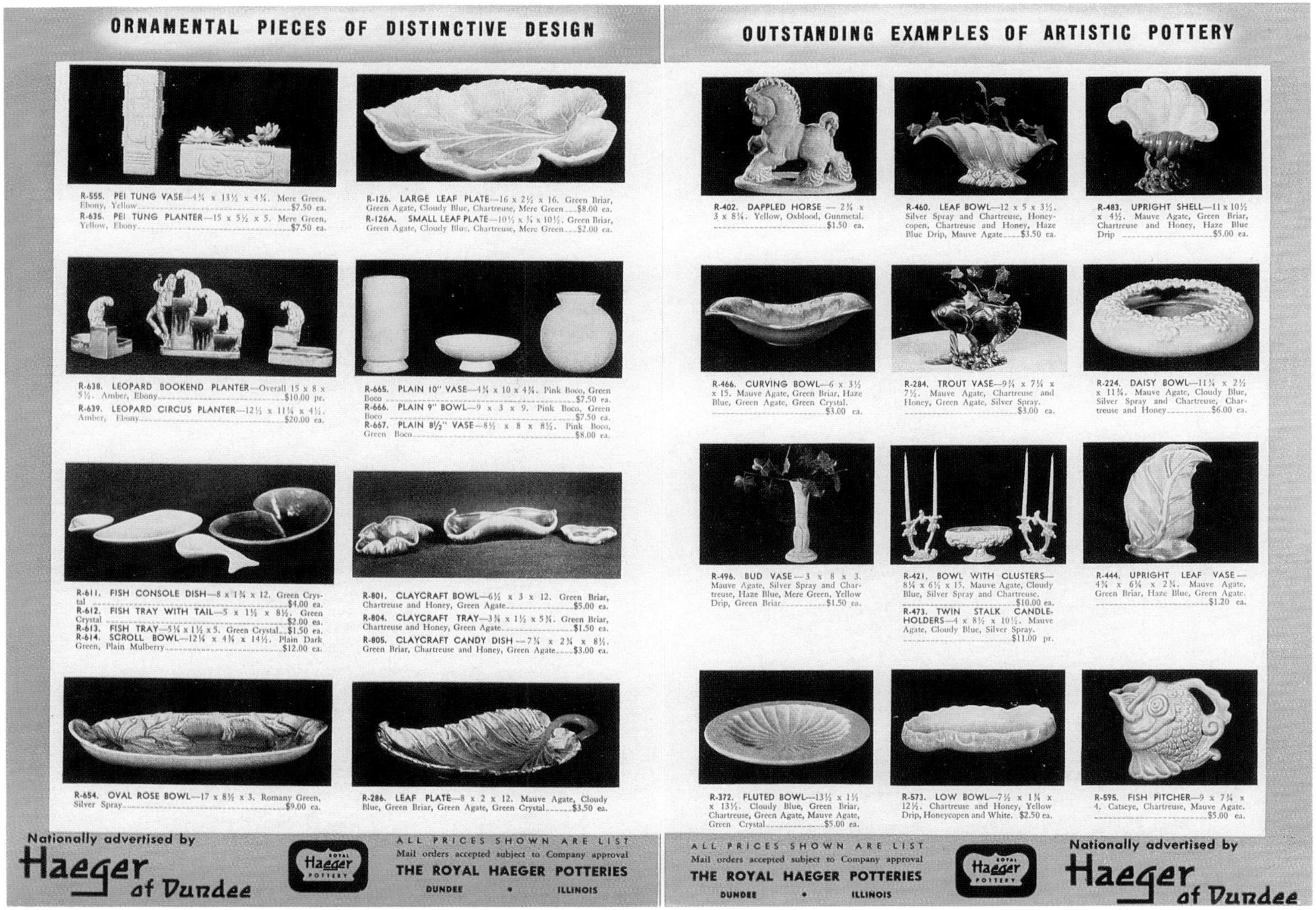

ORNAMENTAL PIECES OF DISTINCTIVE DESIGN

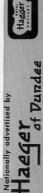

R-555. PEI TUNG VASE—4¾ x 13½ x 4¾. Mere Green, Ebony, Yellow .... $7.50 ea.
R-635. PEI TUNG PLANTER—15 x 5½ x 5. Mere Green, Yellow, Ebony .... $7.50 ea.

R-126. LARGE LEAF PLATE—16 x 2½ x 16. Green Briar, Green Agate, Cloudy Blue, Chartreuse, Mere Green .... $8.00 ea.
R-126A. SMALL LEAF PLATE—10½ x ¾ x 10½. Green Briar, Green Agate, Cloudy Blue, Chartreuse, Mere Green .... $2.00 ea.

R-638. LEOPARD BOOKEND PLANTER—Overall 15 x 8 x 5½. Amber, Ebony .... $10.00 pr.
R-639. LEOPARD CIRCUS PLANTER—12½ x 11¼ x 4½. Amber, Ebony .... $20.00 ea.

R-665. PLAIN 10" VASE—4¾ x 10 x 4¾. Pink Boco, Green Boco .... $7.50 ea.
R-666. PLAIN 9" BOWL—9 x 3 x 9. Pink Boco, Green Boco .... $7.50 ea.
R-667. PLAIN 8½" VASE—8½ x 8 x 8½. Pink Boco, Green Boco .... $8.00 ea.

R-611. FISH CONSOLE DISH—8 x 1¾ x 12. Green Crystal .... $4.00 ea.
R-612. FISH TRAY WITH TAIL—5 x 1½ x 8½. Green Crystal .... $2.00 ea.
R-613. FISH TRAY—5¼ x 1½ x 5. Green Crystal .... $1.50 ea.
R-614. SCROLL BOWL—12¼ x 4¾ x 14½. Plain Dark Green, Plain Mulberry .... $12.00 ea.

R-801. CLAYCRAFT BOWL—6½ x 3 x 12. Green Briar, Chartreuse and Honey, Green Agate .... $5.00 ea.
R-804. CLAYCRAFT TRAY—3¾ x 1½ x 5¾. Green Briar, Chartreuse and Honey, Green Agate .... $1.50 ea.
R-805. CLAYCRAFT CANDY DISH—7¾ x 2¼ x 8½. Green Briar, Chartreuse and Honey, Green Agate .... $3.00 ea.

R-654. OVAL ROSE BOWL—17 x 8½ x 3. Romany Green, Silver Spray .... $9.00 ea.

R-286. LEAF PLATE—8 x 2 x 12. Mauve Agate, Cloudy Blue, Green Briar, Green Agate, Green Crystal .... $3.50 ea.

Nationally advertised by
Haeger of Dundee

Royal Haeger Pottery

ALL PRICES SHOWN ARE LIST
Mail orders accepted subject to Company approval
THE ROYAL HAEGER POTTERIES
DUNDEE • ILLINOIS

OUTSTANDING EXAMPLES OF ARTISTIC POTTERY

R-402. DAPPLED HORSE — 2¾ x 3 x 8¼. Yellow, Oxblood, Gunmetal. .... $1.50 ea.

R-460. LEAF BOWL—12 x 5 x 3½. Silver Spray and Chartreuse, Honeycopen, Chartreuse and Honey, Haze Blue Drip, Mauve Agate .... $3.50 ea.

R-483. UPRIGHT SHELL—11 x 10½ x 4½. Mauve Agate, Green Briar, Chartreuse and Honey, Haze Blue Drip .... $5.00 ea.

R-466. CURVING BOWL—6 x 3½ x 15. Mauve Agate, Green Briar, Haze Blue, Green Agate, Green Crystal. .... $3.00 ea.

R-284. TROUT VASE—9¼ x 7¼ x 7½. Mauve Agate, Chartreuse and Honey, Green Agate, Silver Spray. .... $3.00 ea.

R-224. DAISY BOWL—11¼ x 2½ x 11¾. Mauve Agate, Cloudy Blue, Silver Spray and Chartreuse, Chartreuse and Honey .... $6.00 ea.

R-496. BUD VASE—3 x 8 x 3. Mauve Agate, Silver Spray and Chartreuse, Haze Blue, Mere Green, Yellow Drip, Green Briar .... $1.50 ea.

R-421. BOWL WITH CLUSTERS—8¼ x 6½ x 15. Mauve Agate, Cloudy Blue, Silver Spray and Chartreuse. .... $10.00 ea.
R-473. TWIN STALK CANDLEHOLDERS—4 x 8½ x 10½. Mauve Agate, Cloudy Blue, Silver Spray. .... $11.00 pr.

R-444. UPRIGHT LEAF VASE—4¾ x 6¼ x 2¾. Mauve Agate, Green Briar, Haze Blue, Green Agate. .... $1.20 ea.

R-372. FLUTED BOWL—13½ x 1½ x 13½. Cloudy Blue, Green Briar, Chartreuse, Green Agate, Mauve Agate, Green Crystal .... $5.00 ea.

R-573. LOW BOWL—7½ x 1¾ x 12½. Chartreuse and Honey, Yellow Drip, Honeycopen and White. $2.50 ea.

R-595. FISH PITCHER—9 x 7¾ x 4. Catseye, Chartreuse, Mauve Agate. .... $5.00 ea.

ALL PRICES SHOWN ARE LIST
Mail orders accepted subject to Company approval
THE ROYAL HAEGER POTTERIES
DUNDEE • ILLINOIS

Royal Haeger Pottery

Nationally advertised by
Haeger of Dundee

NEW ROYAL HAEGER CONSOLE SETS
MEET TODAY'S DECORATING AND SERVING TRENDS

R-727S HEXAGONAL BOWL, CANDLEHOLDERS, FLOWER BLOCK
Chartreuse and Yellow

R-727S PETUNIA BOWL AND CANDLEHOLDERS
Yellowdrip

R-755S MODERN FORM BOWL AND CANDLEHOLDERS
Ebony and Chartreuse

R-728S OVAL BOWL, CANDLEHOLDERS, FLOWER BLOCK
Silver Spray and Chartreuse

R-746S ROUND LEAF BOWL AND CANDLEHOLDERS
Mauve Agate

R-731 4-SECTIONAL TRAY
Green Agate, Green Briar,
Mauve Agate, Chartreuse

R-749 3-COMPARTMENT CLOVER DISH
Green Briar

Designed and Manufactured by
THE HAEGER POTTERIES, INC.
DUNDEE, ILLINOIS   MACOMB, ILLINOIS

Page 2
SECTION I
Issued Jan. 1950

THESE COMPLETE ROYAL HAEGER CONSOLE SETS
MEAN REPEAT SALES FOR YOU . . .

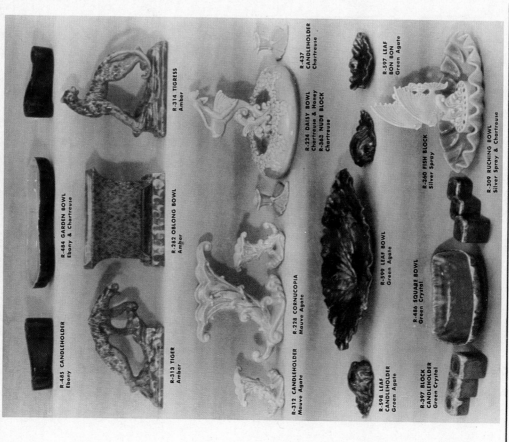

R-485 CANDLEHOLDER
Ebony

R-484 GARDEN BOWL
Ebony & Chartreuse

R-313 TIGER
Amber

R-314 TIGRESS
Amber

R-282 OBLONG BOWL
Amber

R-312 CANDLEHOLDER
Mauve Agate

R-228 CORNUCOPIA
Mauve Agate

R-224 DAISY BOWL
Chartreuse & Honey

R-363 NUDE BLOCK
Chartreuse

R-437 CANDLEHOLDER
Chartreuse

R-598 LEAF
CANDLEHOLDER
Green Agate

R-599 LEAF BOWL
Green Agate

R-597 LEAF
BON BON
Green Agate

R-397 BLOCK
CANDLEHOLDER
Green Crystal

R-486 SQUARE BOWL
Green Crystal

R-360 FISH BLOCK
Silver Spray

R-309 RUCHING BOWL
Silver Spray & Chartreuse

Designed and Manufactured by
THE HAEGER POTTERIES, INC.
DUNDEE, ILLINOIS   MACOMB, ILLINOIS

Page 1
SECTION I
Issued Jan. 1950

ROYAL HAEGER CONSOLES ARE IDEAL FOR MANTLE, BOOKCASE OR TABLE

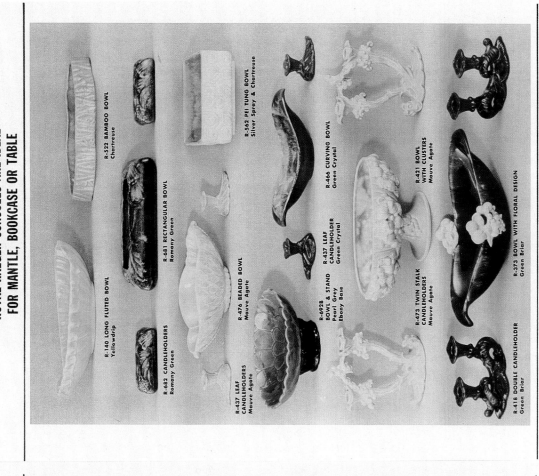

R-522 BAMBOO BOWL
Chartreuse

R-140 LONG FLUTED BOWL
Yellowdrip

R-681 RECTANGULAR BOWL
Romany Green

R-682 CANDLEHOLDERS
Romany Green

R-476 BEADD BOWL
Mauve Agate

R-437 LEAF CANDLEHOLDERS
Mauve Agate

R-692B BOWL & STAND
Pearl Grey
Ebony Base

R-562 PEI TUNG BOWL
Silver Spray & Chartreuse

R-466 CURVING BOWL
Green Crystal

R-437 LEAF CANDLEHOLDER
Green Crystal

R-473 TWIN STALK CANDLEHOLDERS
Mauve Agate

R-421 BOWL WITH CLUSTERS
Mauve Agate

R-373 BOWL WITH FLORAL DESIGN
Green Briar

R-418 DOUBLE CANDLEHOLDER
Green Briar

Designed and Manufactured by
THE HAEGER POTTERIES, INC.
DUNDEE, ILLINOIS   MACOMB, ILLINOIS

SECTION I
Page 4
Issued Jan. 1950

FEATURE THESE SALES TESTED CONSOLE SETS FOR ADDED TRAFFIC — FOR EXTRA VOLUME

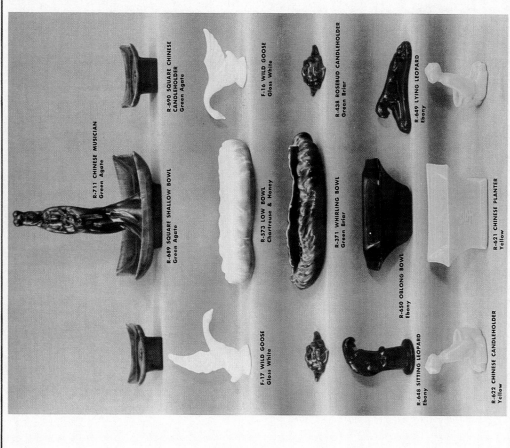

R-711 CHINESE MUSICIAN
Green Agate

R-690 SQUARE CHINESE CANDLEHOLDER
Green Agate

R-689 SQUARE SHALLOW BOWL
Green Agate

F-16 WILD GOOSE
Gloss White

F-17 WILD GOOSE
Gloss White

R-573 LOW BOWL
Chartreuse & Honey

R-371 WHIRLING BOWL
Green Briar

R-438 ROSEBUD CANDLEHOLDER
Green Briar

R-649 LYING LEOPARD
Ebony

R-648 SITTING LEOPARD
Ebony

R-650 OBLONG BOWL
Ebony

R-621 CHINESE PLANTER
Yellow

R-622 CHINESE CANDLEHOLDER
Yellow

Page 3
SECTION I
Issued Jan. 1950

Designed and Manufactured by
THE HAEGER POTTERIES, INC.
DUNDEE, ILLINOIS   MACOMB, ILLINOIS

SALES TESTED ROYAL HAEGER DESIGNS — TO PLEASE YOUR MOST EXACTING CUSTOMERS

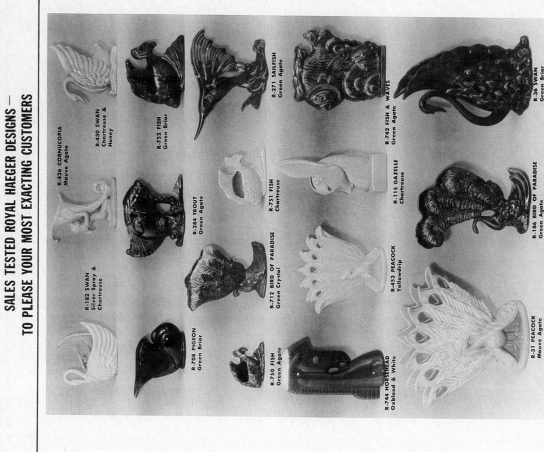

R-426 CORNUCOPIA
Mauve Agate

R-430 SWAN
Chartreuse &
Honey

R-752 FISH
Green Briar

R-271 SAILFISH
Green Agate

R-742 FISH & WAVES
Green Agate

R-30 SWAN
Green Briar

R-182 SWAN
Silver Spray &
Chartreuse

R-284 TROUT
Green Agate

R-751 FISH
Chartreuse

R-115 GAZELLE
Chartreuse

R-186 BIRD OF PARADISE
Green Agate

R-708 PIGEON
Green Briar

R-712 BIRD OF PARADISE
Green Crystal

R-453 PEACOCK
Yellowdrip

R-750 FISH
Green Agate

R-744 HORSEHEAD
Oxblood & White

R-31 PEACOCK
Mauve Agate

Designed and Manufactured by
THE HAEGER POTTERIES, INC.
DUNDEE, ILLINOIS   MACOMB, ILLINOIS

SECTION II
Page 2
Issued Jan. 1950

EXQUISITE NEW DESIGNS, SUPERB GLAZES TO PLEASE THE MOST DISCRIMINATING

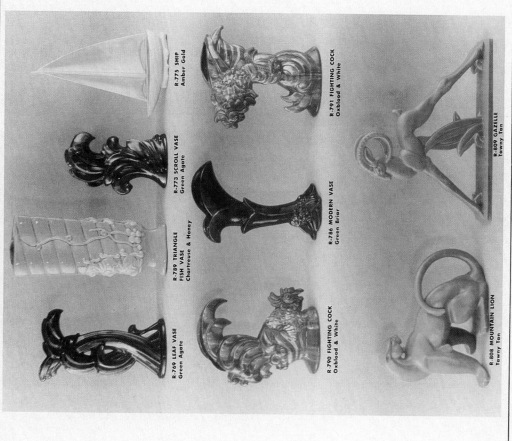

R-775 SHIP
Amber Gold

R-791 FIGHTING COCK
Oxblood & White

R-809 GAZELLE
Tawny Tan

R-773 SCROLL VASE
Green Agate

R-789 TRIANGLE
FISH VASE
Chartreuse & Honey

R-786 MODERN VASE
Green Briar

R-769 LEAF VASE
Green Agate

R-790 FIGHTING COCK
Oxblood & White

R-808 MOUNTAIN LION
Tawny Tan

Page 1
SECTION II
Issued Jan. 1950

Designed and Manufactured by
THE HAEGER POTTERIES, INC.
DUNDEE, ILLINOIS

EXQUISITE ROYAL HAEGER POTTERY VASES
FOR EVERY TYPE AND SIZE FLOWER . . .

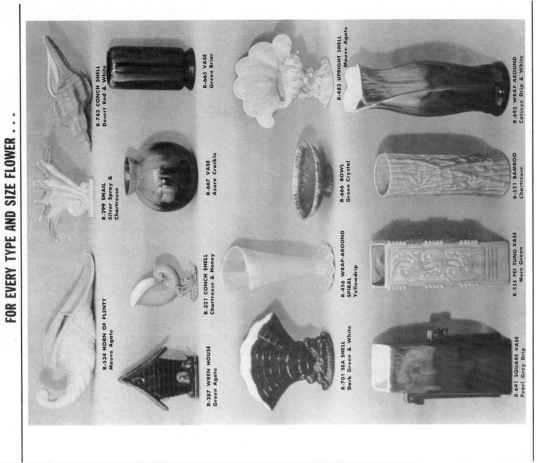

R-534 HORN OF PLENTY
Mauve Agate

R-743 CONCH SHELL
Desert Red & White

R-299 SNAIL
Silver Spray &
Chartreuse

R-665 VASE
Green Briar

R-287 WREN HOUSE
Green Agate

R-321 CONCH SHELL
Chartreuse & Honey

R-667 VASE
Azure Crackle

R-666 BOWL
Green Crystal

R-483 UPRIGHT SHELL
Mauve Agate

R-701 SEA SHELL
Dark Green & White

R-456 WRAP-AROUND
SPIRAL
Yellowdrip

R-521 BAMBOO
Chartreuse

R-693 WRAP-AROUND
Catseye Drip & White

R-691 SQUARE VASE
Pearl Grey Drip

R-555 PEI TUNG VASE
Mere Green

Designed and Manufactured by
THE HAEGER POTTERIES, INC.
DUNDEE, ILLINOIS

1950 HAEGER CATALOG

FAST SELLING ROYAL HAEGER DESIGNS
MAKE IDEAL YEAR-ROUND PROMOTION ITEMS

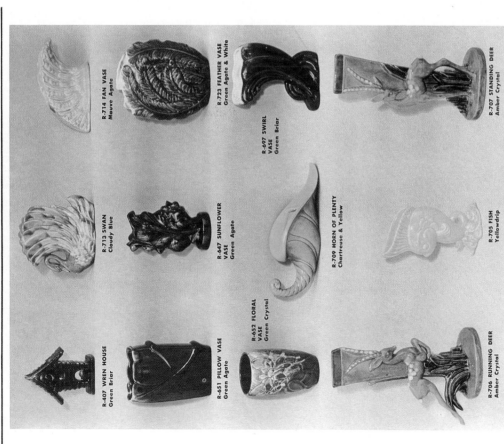

R-407 WREN HOUSE
Green Briar

R-714 FAN VASE
Mauve Agate

R-713 SWAN
Cloudy Blue

R-723 FEATHER VASE
Green Agate & White

R-651 PILLOW VASE
Green Agate

R-647 SUNFLOWER
VASE
Green Agate

R-652 FLORAL
VASE
Green Crystal

R-697 SWIRL
VASE
Green Briar

R-709 HORN OF PLENTY
Chartreuse & Yellow

R-707 STANDING DEER
Amber Crystal

R-705 FISH
Yellowdrip

R-706 RUNNING DEER
Amber Crystal

Designed and Manufactured by
THE HAEGER POTTERIES, INC.
DUNDEE, ILLINOIS

BEAUTIFUL ROYAL HAEGER LOW BOWLS ARE IDEAL FOR TODAY'S FLOWER ARRANGEMENTS

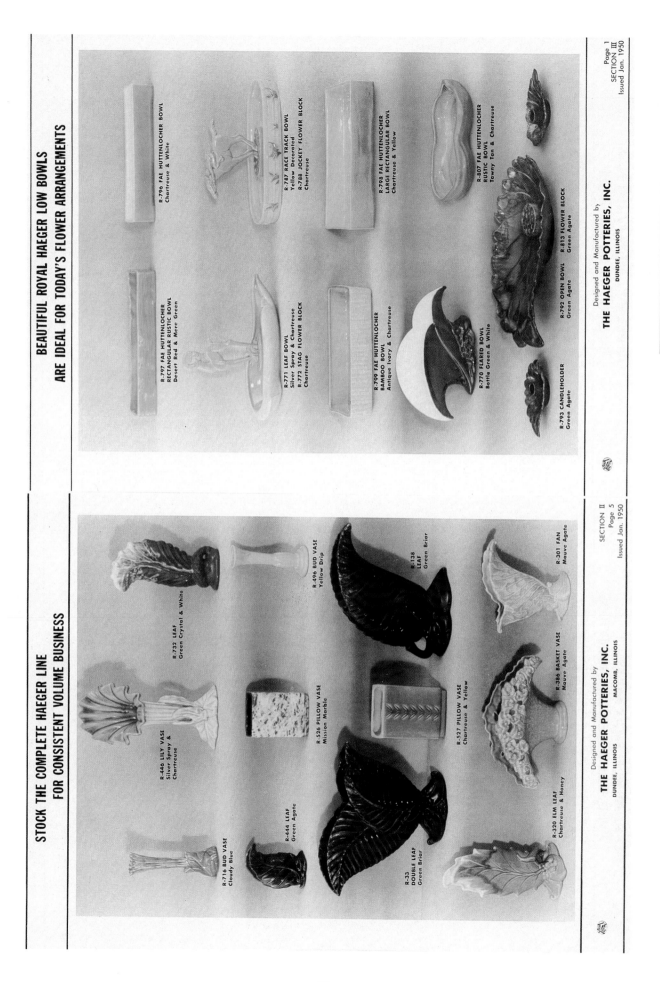

R-796 FAE HUTTENLOCHER BOWL
Chartreuse & White

R-787 RACE TRACK BOWL
Yellow Decorated

R-788 JOCKEY FLOWER BLOCK
Chartreuse

R-798 FAE HUTTENLOCHER
LARGE RECTANGULAR BOWL
Chartreuse & Yellow

R-807 FAE HUTTENLOCHER
RUSTIC BOWL
Tawny Tan & Chartreuse

R-813 FLOWER BLOCK
Green Agate

R-792 OPEN BOWL
Green Agate

R-797 FAE HUTTENLOCHER
RECTANGULAR RUSTIC BOWL
Desert Red & Mere Green

R-771 LEAF BOWL
Silver Spray & Chartreuse

R-772 STAG FLOWER BLOCK
Chartreuse

R-799 FAE HUTTENLOCHER
BAMBOO BOWL
Antique Ivory & Chartreuse

R-770 FLARED BOWL
Bottle Green & White

R-793 CANDLEHOLDER
Green Agate

Designed and Manufactured by
THE HAEGER POTTERIES, INC.
DUNDEE, ILLINOIS

Page 1
SECTION III
Issued Jan. 1950

STOCK THE COMPLETE HAEGER LINE FOR CONSISTENT VOLUME BUSINESS

R-732 LEAF
Green Crystal & White

R-496 BUD VASE
Yellow Drip

R-138 LEAF
Green Briar

R-301 FAN
Mauve Agate

R-446 LILY VASE
Silver Spray & Chartreuse

R-526 PILLOW VASE
Mission Marble

R-527 PILLOW VASE
Chartreuse & Yellow

R-386 BASKET VASE
Mauve Agate

R-716 BUD VASE
Cloudy Blue

R-444 LEAF
Green Agate

R-33 DOUBLE LEAF
Green Briar

R-320 ELM LEAF
Chartreuse & Honey

Designed and Manufactured by
THE HAEGER POTTERIES, INC.
DUNDEE, ILLINOIS   MACOMB, ILLINOIS

SECTION II
Page 5
Issued Jan. 1950

HAEGER OFFERS WIDE VARIETY FOR EVERY DECORATIVE PURPOSE

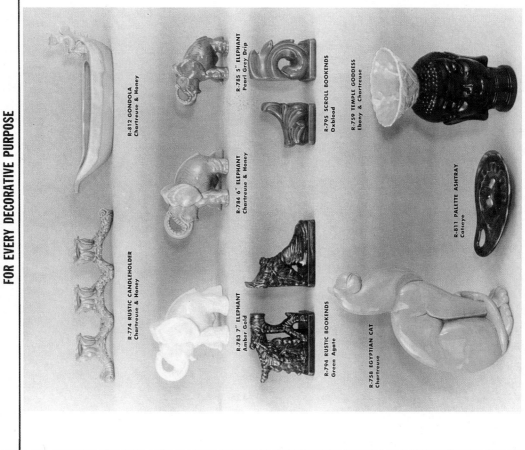

R-812 GONDOLA
Chartreuse & Honey

R-785 5" ELEPHANT
Pearl Grey Drip

R-795 SCROLL BOOKENDS
Oxblood

R-759 TEMPLE GODDESS
Ebony & Chartreuse

R-774 RUSTIC CANDLEHOLDER
Chartreuse & Honey

R-784 6" ELEPHANT
Chartreuse & Honey

R-783 7" ELEPHANT
Amber Gold

R-794 RUSTIC BOOKENDS
Green Agate

R-758 EGYPTIAN CAT
Chartreuse

R-811 PALETTE ASHTRAY
Catseye

Designed and Manufactured by
THE HAEGER POTTERIES, INC.
DUNDEE, ILLINOIS

SECTION IV
Page 3
Issued Jan. 1950

1950 HAEGER CATALOG

ROYAL HAEGER FIGURINES FOR EVERY TASTE — FOR EVERY HOME AND GIFT REQUIREMENT

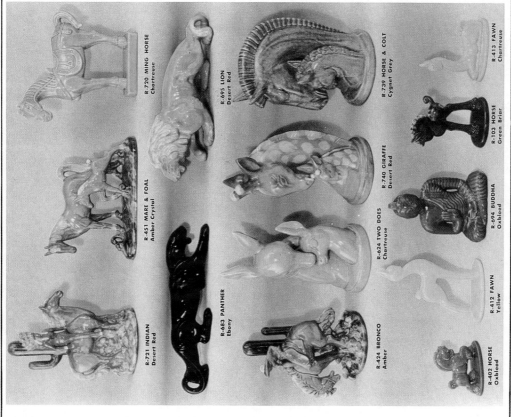

R-720 MING HORSE
Chartreuse

R-695 LION
Desert Red

R-739 HORSE & COLT
Cygnet Grey

R-413 FAWN
Chartreuse

R-451 MARE & FOAL
Amber Crystal

R-740 GIRAFFE
Desert Red

R-103 HORSE
Green Briar

R-721 INDIAN
Desert Red

R-683 PANTHER
Ebony

R-624 TWO DOES
Chartreuse

R-694 BUDDHA
Oxblood

R-424 BRONCO
Amber

R-412 FAWN
Yellow

R-402 HORSE
Oxblood

Designed and Manufactured by
THE HAEGER POTTERIES, INC.
DUNDEE, ILLINOIS   MACOMB, ILLINOIS

SECTION IV
Page 1
Issued Jan. 1950

73

UTILITY AND BEAUTY GO HAND IN HAND
IN THESE PRACTICAL POTTERY DESIGNS

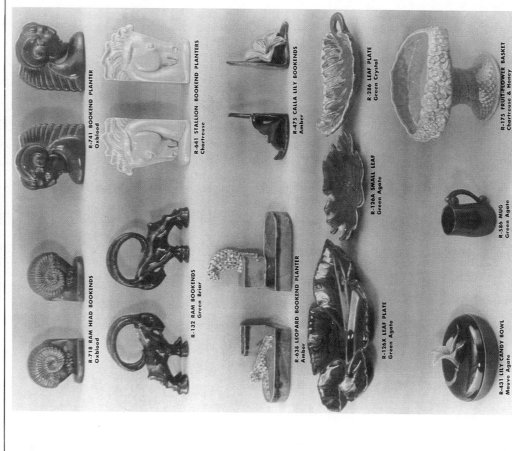

R-718 RAM HEAD BOOKENDS
Oxblood

R-741 BOOKEND PLANTER
Oxblood

R-132 RAM BOOKENDS
Green Briar

R-641 STALLION BOOKEND PLANTERS
Chartreuse

R-638 LEOPARD BOOKEND PLANTER
Amber

R-475 CALLA LILY BOOKENDS
Amber

R-126X LEAF PLATE
Green Agate

R-126A SMALL LEAF
Green Agate

R-286 LEAF PLATE
Green Crystal

R-431 LILY CANDY BOWL
Mauve Agate

R-586 MUG
Green Agate

R-175 FRUIT-FLOWER BASKET
Chartreuse & Honey

Designed and Manufactured by
THE HAEGER POTTERIES, INC.
DUNDEE, ILLINOIS

Page 5
SECTION IV
Issued Jan. 1950

NEW WALL POCKETS AND POTS
PRICED FOR VOLUME SELLING

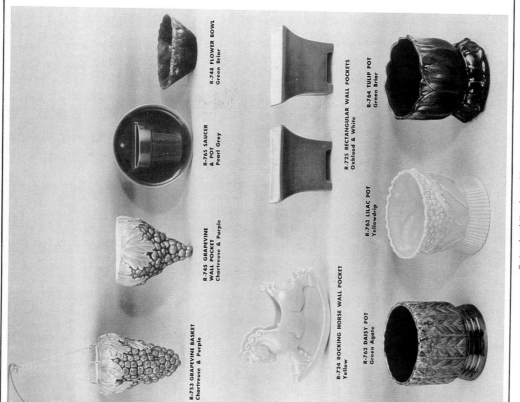

R-753 GRAPEVINE BASKET
Chartreuse & Purple

R-745 GRAPEVINE WALL POCKET
Chartreuse & Purple

R-765 SAUCER & POT
Pearl Grey

R-748 FLOWER BOWL
Green Briar

R-724 ROCKING HORSE WALL POCKET
Yellow

R-762 DAISY POT
Green Agate

R-763 LILAC POT
Yellowdrip

R-725 RECTANGULAR WALL POCKETS
Oxblood & White

R-764 TULIP POT
Green Briar

Designed and Manufactured by
THE HAEGER POTTERIES, INC.
DUNDEE, ILLINOIS

SECTION IV
Page 4
Issued Jan. 1950

LOVELY, PRACTICAL DESIGNS IN BON BON DISHES, ASHTRAYS AND CIGARETTE BOXES

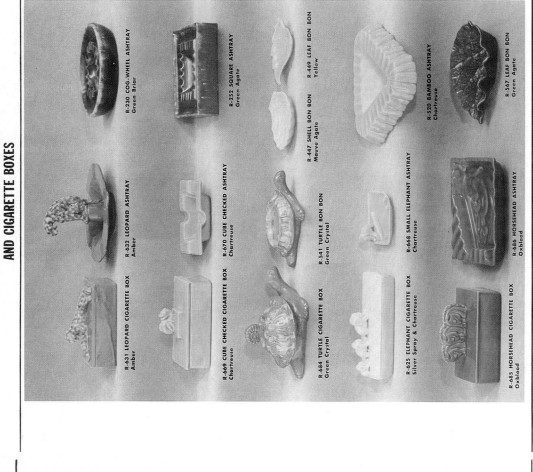

R-230 COG-WHEEL ASHTRAY
Green Briar

R-252 SQUARE ASHTRAY
Green Agate

R-447 SHELL BON BON
Mauve Agate

R-449 LEAF BON BON
Yellow

R-520 BAMBOO ASHTRAY
Chartreuse

R-567 LEAF BON BON
Green Agate

R-631 LEOPARD ASHTRAY
Amber

R-632 LEOPARD ASHTRAY
Amber

R-670 CUBE CHECKED ASHTRAY
Chartreuse

R-541 TURTLE BON BON
Green Crystal

R-668 SMALL ELEPHANT ASHTRAY
Chartreuse

R-686 HORSEHEAD ASHTRAY
Oxblood

R-631 LEOPARD CIGARETTE BOX
Amber

R-669 CUBE CHECKED CIGARETTE BOX
Chartreuse

R-684 TURTLE CIGARETTE BOX
Green Crystal

R-625 ELEPHANT CIGARETTE BOX
Silver Spray & Chartreuse

R-685 HORSEHEAD CIGARETTE BOX
Oxblood

Designed and Manufactured by
THE HAEGER POTTERIES, INC.
DUNDEE, ILLINOIS   MACOMB, ILLINOIS

Page 7
SECTION IV
Issued Jan. 1950

HAEGER'S WIDE SELECTION OF DISTINCTIVE POTTERY DESIGNS SATISFY EVERY TASTE

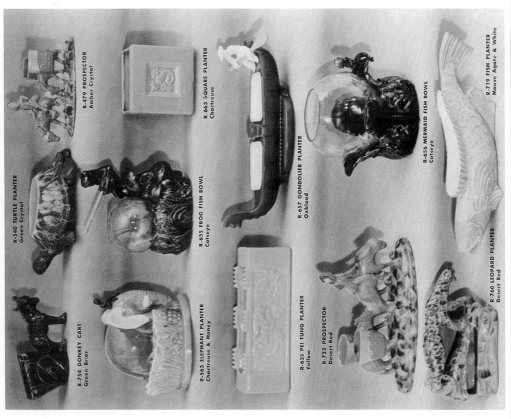

R-479 PROSPECTOR
Amber Crystal

R-663 SQUARE PLANTER
Chartreuse

R-719 FISH PLANTER
Mauve Agate & White

R-540 TURTLE PLANTER
Green Crystal

R-655 FROG FISH BOWL
Catseye

R-657 GONDOLIER PLANTER
Oxblood

R-656 MERMAID FISH BOWL
Catseye

R-754 DONKEY CART
Green Briar

R-563 ELEPHANT PLANTER
Chartreuse & Honey

R-635 PEI TUNG PLANTER
Yellow

R-722 PROSPECTOR
Desert Red

R-760 LEOPARD PLANTER
Desert Red

Designed and Manufactured by
THE HAEGER POTTERIES, INC.
DUNDEE, ILLINOIS   MACOMB, ILLINOIS

SECTION IV
Page 6
Issued Jan. 1950

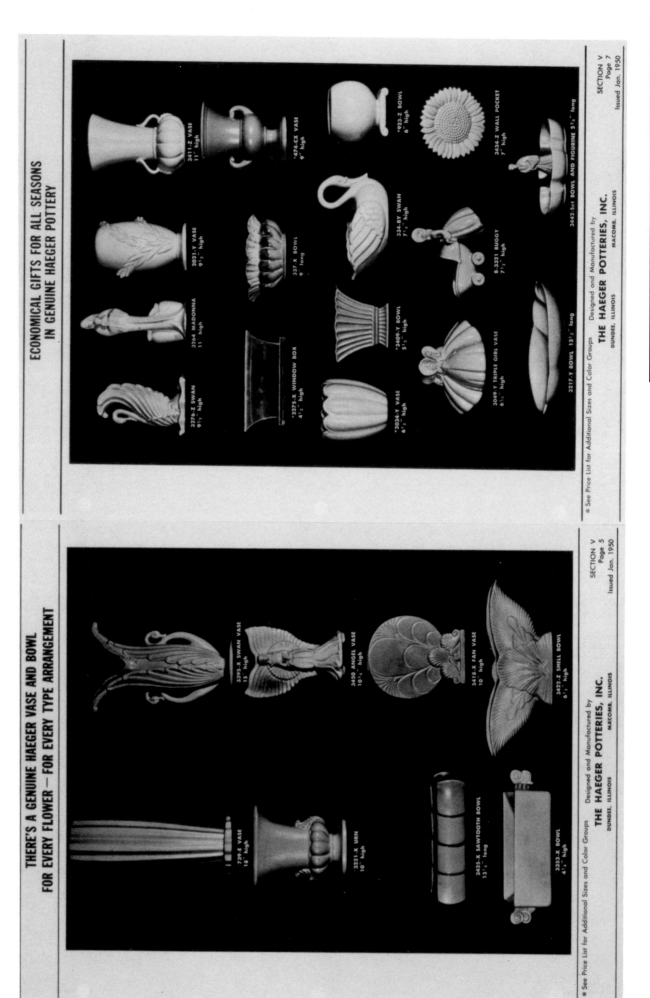

ECONOMICAL GIFTS FOR ALL SEASONS IN GENUINE HAEGER POTTERY

3376-Z SWAN 9½" high
3264 MADONNA 11" high
2021-Y VASE 9½" high
3491-Z VASE 11" high
*474-CX VASE 9" high
*3275-X WINDOW BOX 4½" high
337-X BOWL 9" long
*993-Z BOWL 6" high
3434-Z WALL POCKET 7" high
*3034-X VASE 6½" high
*3400-Y BOWL 5½" high
334-BY SWAN 7¼" high
8-3321 BUGGY 7½" high
3049-Y TRIPLE GIRL VASE 6½" high
3217-Y BOWL 13½" long
3442-Set BOWL AND FIGURINE 5¾" long

* See Price List for Additional Sizes and Color Groups   Designed and Manufactured by

THE HAEGER POTTERIES, INC.
DUNDEE, ILLINOIS   MACOMB, ILLINOIS

SECTION V
Page 7
Issued Jan. 1950

THERE'S A GENUINE HAEGER VASE AND BOWL FOR EVERY FLOWER — FOR EVERY TYPE ARRANGEMENT

3395-X SWAN VASE 15" high
3450 ANGEL VASE 10¾" high
3418-X FAN VASE 10" high
3422-Z SHELL BOWL 6½" high
*730-X VASE 18" high
*3321-X URN 10" high
3425-X SAWTOOTH BOWL 13¼" long
3353-X BOWL 4½" high

* See Price List for Additional Sizes and Color Groups   Designed and Manufactured by

THE HAEGER POTTERIES, INC.
DUNDEE, ILLINOIS   MACOMB, ILLINOIS

SECTION V
Page 5
Issued Jan. 1950

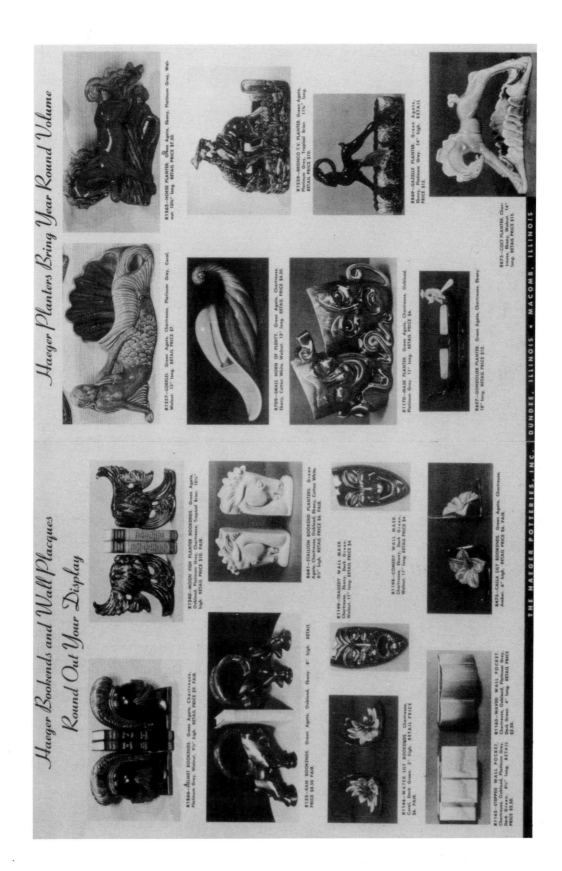

Haeger Planters Bring Year Round Volume

R1257—LORELEI. Green Agate, Chartreuse, Platinum Grey, Coral, Walnut. 13" long. RETAIL PRICE $7.

R1265—HORSE PLANTER. Green Agate, Ebony, Platinum Grey, Walnut. 10¼" long. RETAIL PRICE $7.50.

R1239—BRONCO T.V. PLANTER. Green Agate, Platinum Grey, Tropical Briar. 11¼" long. RETAIL PRICE $10.

R649—GAZELLE PLANTER. Green Agate, Ebony, Platinum Grey. 14" high. RETAIL PRICE $15.

R709—SMALL HORN OF PLENTY. Green Agate, Chartreuse, Ebony, Cotton White, Walnut. 13" long. RETAIL PRICE $4.50.

R1170—MASK PLANTER. Green Agate, Chartreuse, Oakleaf, Platinum Grey. 11" long. RETAIL PRICE $6.

R657—GONDOLIER PLANTER. Green Agate, Chartreuse, Ebony. 19" long. RETAIL PRICE $12.

R675—COLT PLANTER. Chartreuse, Ebony, Walnut. 14" long. RETAIL PRICE $15.

Haeger Bookends and Wall Placques
Round Out Your Display

R1860—PLUME BOOKENDS. Green Agate, Chartreuse, Platinum Grey, Walnut. 9½" high. RETAIL PRICE $9. PAIR.

R1240—MOON FISH PLANTER BOOKENDS. Green Agate, Oakleaf, Platinum Grey, Chartreuse, Tropical Briar. 10½" high. RETAIL PRICE $10. PAIR.

R461—STALLION BOOKEND PLANTERS. Green Agate, Chartreuse, Oakleaf, Ebony, Cotton White. 11" high. RETAIL PRICE $6. PAIR.

R1199—TRAGEDY WALL MASK. Chartreuse, Ebony, Dark Green, Walnut. 11" long. RETAIL PRICE $4.

R1198—COMEDY WALL MASK. Chartreuse, Ebony, Dark Green, Walnut. 11" long. RETAIL PRICE $4.

R475—CASSA LILY BOOKENDS. Green Agate, Chartreuse, Amber. 6" high. RETAIL PRICE $6. PAIR.

R125—RAM BOOKENDS. Green Agate, Oakleaf, Chartreuse, Ebony. 8" high. RETAIL PRICE $8.50. PAIR.

R1146—WATER LILY BOOKENDS. Chartreuse, Coral, Dark Green. 5" high. RETAIL PRICE $6. PAIR.

R1103—STEPPED WALL POCKET. Chartreuse, Oakleaf, Platinum Grey, Dark Green. 8½" long. RETAIL PRICE $3.50.

R1163—WAVED WALL POCKET. Chartreuse, Oakleaf, Platinum Grey, Dark Green. 6" long. RETAIL PRICE $2.50.

THE HAEGER POTTERIES, INC. DUNDEE, ILLINOIS • MACOMB, ILLINOIS

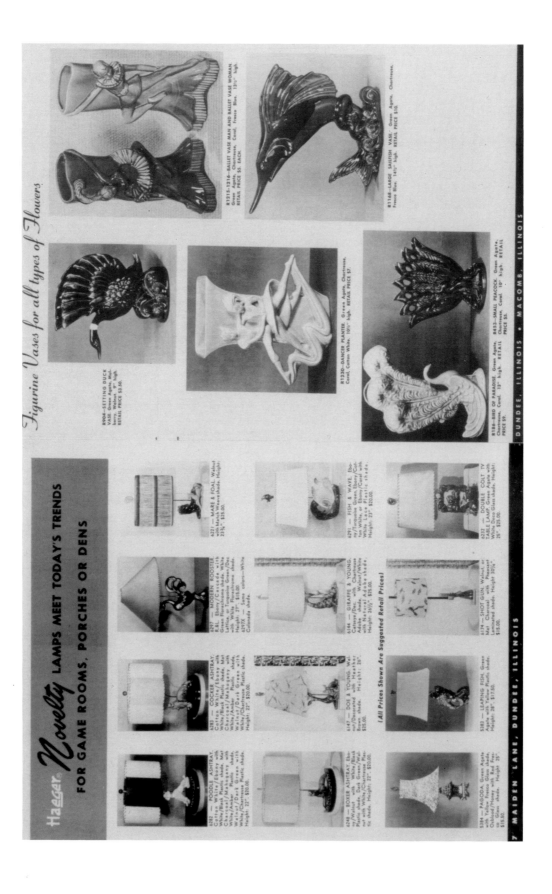

Figurine Vases for all types of Flowers

YOUR *Haeger* Television Section WILL PAY HANDSOME PROFITS WITH THESE DRAMATIC DESIGNS

(All Prices Shown Are Suggested Retail Prices)

Outstanding Haeger "PICTURE WINDOW LAMPS" TURN WINDOW SHOPPERS INTO CUSTOMERS

(All Prices Shown Are Suggested Retail Prices)

ROYAL HAEGER LAMP COMPANY, INC.

6234—THUNDER & LIGHTNING. Ebony/Decorated with White Chromespun shade, Tropical Briar with White Chromespun shade, Absinth Green with Green Chromespun shade. Height: 30½". RETAIL PRICE: $45.00.

5353—PETAL LOUVRE. Chartreuse/ Honey, Green Agate, Oxblood/ Honey, Cotton White, Walnut. Height: 11½". RETAIL PRICE: $12.00.

6198—GONDOLA TV. Green Agate with Chartreuse Plastic Shield, Ebony with Red Plastic Shield. Height: 7¼". RETAIL PRICE: $15.00.

6204—STALLION HEAD. Absinth Green Confetti with Gold Foil shade, Rust Marble with Gold Foil shade, Slate Marble with Gold Foil shade, Ebony with Gold Foil shade. Height: 30". RETAIL PRICE: $20.00.

6193 — COLT TV PLANTER. Ebony, Mahogany/White, Catseye, Walnut/White. Height: 13½". RETAIL PRICE: $13.50.

ubject to Customary Discount

6044—PRANCING HORSE TV. Chartreuse, Green Agate. Height: 11". RETAIL PRICE: $13.50.

5398—MERMAID ON SHELL. Platinum Grey/Green Agate with Yellow Synspun shade, Platinum Grey/Oxblood with Red Synspun shade, Platinum Grey/Tropical Briar with Yellow Synspun shade. Height: 23". RETAIL PRICE: $25.00.

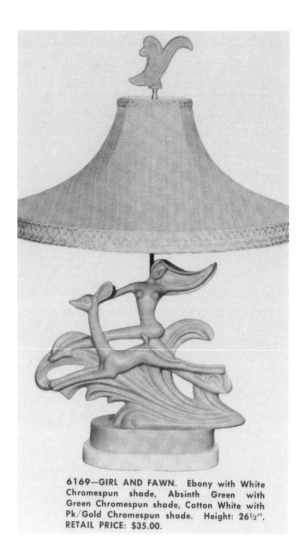

6169—GIRL AND FAWN. Ebony with White Chromespun shade, Absinth Green with Green Chromespun shade, Cotton White with Pk/Gold Chromespun shade. Height: 26½". RETAIL PRICE: $35.00.

6195—FISH & SEA GULL. Catseye with Golden Web White Handsewn Silk shade, Cotton White with Golden Web White Handsewn Silk shade, Ebony with Golden Web White Handsewn Silk shade. Height: 30½". RETAIL PRICE: $30.00.

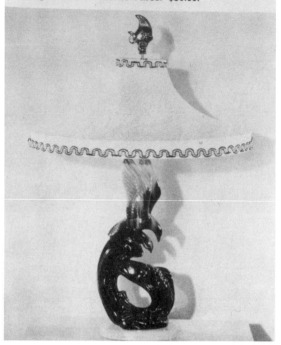

5205—GIRL ON TURTLE. Platinum Grey/Green Crystal with Chartreuse Glasschop shade, Tropical Briar/White with Chartreuse Glasschop shade. Height: 30". RETAIL PRICE: $55.00.

5383—LEAPING FISH. Green Agate with Yellow Plastic shade, Mahogany/White with Yellow Plastic shade. Height: 28". RETAIL PRICE: $17.50.

Haeger Wall Placques and Bookends Round Out Your Display

R1364—ROCOCO BOOKENDS R & L. Tropical Brier, Oxblood. Height: 6". RETAIL PRICE: $6.00 pr.

R641—STALLION BOOKEND PLANTERS. Green Agate, Chartreuse, Ebony, Cotton White. Height: 8½" RETAIL PRICE $6.00 pr.

R475—CALLA LILY BOOKENDS. Green Agate, Chartreuse, Tropical Brier. Height: 6" RETAIL PRICE $6.00 pr.

R1324—HORSEHEAD WALL POCKET. Ebony, Platinum Grey, Walnut, Cateye. Length: 13". RETAIL PRICE $3.00.

R1199—TRAGEDY WALL MASK. Chartreuse, Ebony, Mahogany, Dark Green. Height: 11" RETAIL PRICE $4.00.

R1198—COMEDY WALL MASK. Chartreuse, Ebony, Mahogany, Dark Green. Height: 11". RETAIL PRICE $4.00.

R1365—HORSEHEAD FIGURINE OR BOOKENDS. Cateye, Ebony, Walnut. Height: 7". RETAIL PRICE: $6.00 ea.

R1325—DOE HEAD WALL POCKET. Ebony, Walnut, Cateye. Height: 10". RETAIL PRICE $3.50.

R1316—DOUBLE LEAF WALL POCKET. Green Agate, Oxblood, Platinum Grey, Tropical Brier. Width: 11½". RETAIL PRICE $2.50.

All Prices Subject to Customary Discount

Royal Haeger Ashtrays Bring Extra Traffic

R860—ASHTRAY. Chartreuse, Oxblood, Ebony, Mahogany, Platinum Grey, Dark Green. Length: 7½" RETAIL PRICE $2.00.

R873—FREE FORM ASH BOWL. Green Agate, Chartreuse, Oxblood, Ebony, Mahogany, Platinum Grey. Length: 8½". RETAIL PRICE $4.00.

R811—PALLET ASHTRAY. Chartreuse, Oxblood, Ebony, Platinum Grey, Dark Green. Length: 9½". RETAIL PRICE $2.00.

R1359—PEAR SHAPED ASHTRAY. Green Agate, Cotton White, Tropical Brier. Length: 7". RETAIL PRICE $1.50.

R1403—8" RECTANGULAR ASHTRAY. Ebony, Dark Green, Mahogany. Length: 8". RETAIL PRICE: $2.50

R1287—TRIPLE TRIO ASHTRAY. Chartreuse, Ebony, Platinum Grey, Dark Green, Walnut. Diameter: 7½". RETAIL PRICE $2.00.

R1148—ROUND CUP ASH BOWL. Green Agate, Chartreuse, Oxblood, Mahogany, Platinum Grey. Width: 5". RETAIL PRICE $2.50.

R670—CUBE CHECKED ASHTRAY. Green Agate, Chartreuse, Ebony, Platinum Grey. 6" Square. RETAIL PRICE $2.00.

R1408—SANDS OF TIME ASHTRAY. Walnut, Chartreuse. Length: 12". RETAIL PRICE $3.00

R1357—SQUARE RIDGED ASHTRAY. Green Agate, Cotton White, Tropical Brier. 6" Square. RETAIL PRICE: $2.50.

THE HAEGER POTTERIES INC.,

Console Sets for All Occasions

R1413 - R1414 — ROUND BOWL AND CANDLEHOLDERS. Tropical Brier, Green Agate, Ebony, Aqua. Diameter of Bowl 10½", Diameter of Candleholders: 4¼". RETAIL PRICE: Bowl $5.00—Cdls. $4.00 pr.

R1338 - R1339—MODERN BOWL AND CANDLEHOLDERS. Green Agate, Chartreuse, Ebony, Walnut. Length of Bowl 13", Length of Cdls. 5½". RETAIL PRICE: Bowl $4.00, Cdls. $3.50 pr.

R312—CORNUCOPIA CANDLEHOLDERS. Green Agate, Chartreuse, Ebony, Platinum Grey, Cotton White, Tropical Brier. Height: 5". RETAIL PRICE: $3.00 pr.

R309—RUCHING BOWL. Green Agate, Tropical Brier, Chartreuse, Ebony. Length: 14½". RETAIL PRICE: $4.00.

R437—LEAF CANDLEHOLDER. Green Agate, Chartreuse, Ebony, Platinum Grey, Cotton White, Tropical Brier. Length: 5". RETAIL PRICE: $3.00 pr.

R1352 - R1354—LEAF EDGED CONSOLE BOWL AND CANDLEHOLDERS. Chartreuse, Ebony, Mahogany, Fresco Blue, Catseye. Length of Bowl: 11", Height of Cdls.: 3½". RETAIL PRICE: Bowl $3.00, Cdls. $2.50 pr.

R1268 - R1269—OVAL CONSOLE BOWL AND CANDLEHOLDERS. Green Agate, Oxblood, Chartreuse, Fresco Blue, Tropical Brier. Length of Bowl: 15", Height of Cdls.: 3½". RETAIL PRICE: Bowl $5.50, Cdls. $4.50 pr.

R363—NUDE ASTRIDE FISH BLOCK. Green Agate, Chartreuse, Platinum Grey, Tropical Brier. Height: 10". RETAIL PRICE: $4.00.

R224 — DAISY BOWL. Green Agate, Chartreuse, Platinum Grey. Width: 12". RETAIL PRICE: $6.00.

ROYAL Haeger POTTERY

All Prices Subject to Customary Discount

DUNDEE, ILL., MACOMB, ILL.

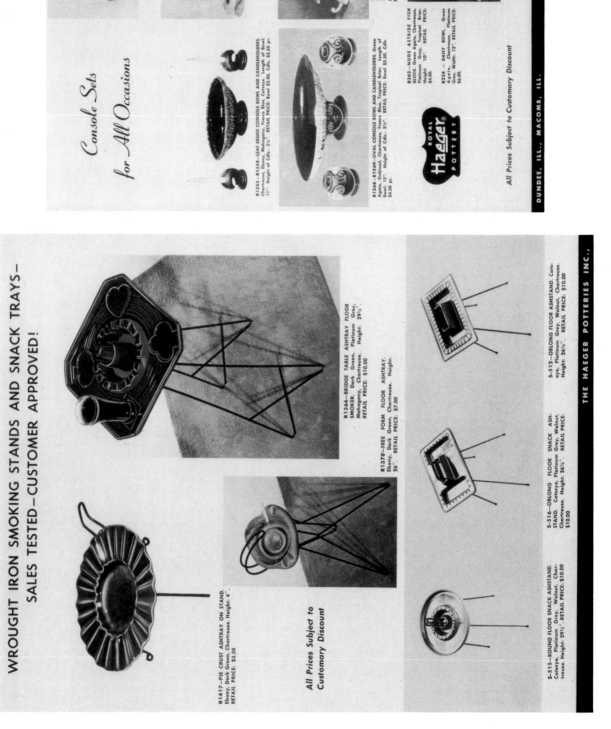

WROUGHT IRON SMOKING STANDS AND SNACK TRAYS— SALES TESTED—CUSTOMER APPROVED!

R1417—PIE CRUST ASHTRAY ON STAND. Ebony, Dark Green, Chartreuse. Height: 4". RETAIL PRICE: $3.30

R1366—BRIDGE TABLE ASHTRAY FLOOR SMOKER. Dark Green, Platinum Grey, Mahogany, Chartreuse. Height: 29½". RETAIL PRICE: $10.00

R1378—FREE FORM FLOOR ASHTRAY. Ebony, Dark Green, Chartreuse. Height: 26". RETAIL PRICE: $7.00

S-515—ROUND FLOOR SNACK ASHSTAND. Catseye, Platinum Grey, Walnut, Chartreuse. Height: 29½". RETAIL PRICE: $10.00

S-516—OBLONG FLOOR SNACK ASHSTAND. Catseye, Platinum Grey, Walnut, Chartreuse. Height: 26½". RETAIL PRICE: $10.00

S-512—OBLONG FLOOR ASHSTAND. Catseye, Platinum Grey, Walnut, Chartreuse. Height: 26½". RETAIL PRICE: $10.00

All Prices Subject to Customary Discount

THE HAEGER POTTERIES INC.,

Stock This New Cascade Group for Fresh Customer Interest

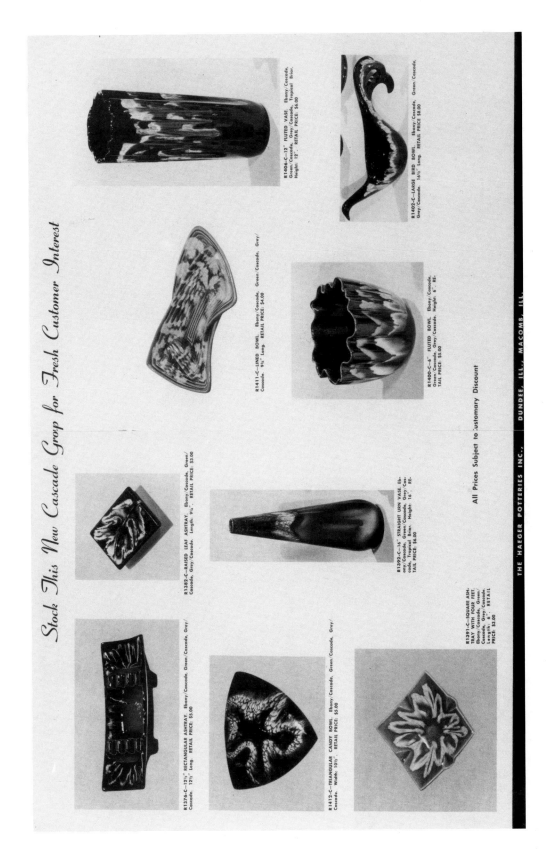

R1406-C—13" FLUTED VASE. Ebony/Cascade, Green/Cascade, Grey/Cascade, Tropical Briar. Height: 13". RETAIL PRICE: $6.00

R1402-C—LARGE BIRD BOWL. Ebony/Cascade, Green/Cascade. Grey/Cascade. 16½" Long. RETAIL PRICE: $8.00

R1411-C—LINED BOWL. Ebony/Cascade, Green/Cascade, Grey/Cascade. 9¼" Long. RETAIL PRICE: $4.00

R1400-C—6" FLUTED BOWL. Ebony/Cascade, Green/Cascade, Grey/Cascade. Height: 6". RETAIL PRICE: $5.00

R1382-C—RAISED LEAF ASHTRAY. Ebony/Cascade, Green/Cascade, Grey/Cascade, Tropical Briar. Length: 9¼". RETAIL PRICE: $3.00

R1392-C—16" STRAIGHT URN VASE. Ebony/Cascade, Green/Cascade, Grey/Cascade, Tropical Briar. Height: 16". RETAIL PRICE: $6.00

R1391-C—SQUARE ASH-TRAY WITH FOUR FEET. Ebony/Cascade, Green/Cascade, Grey/Cascade. Length: 6". RETAIL PRICE: $3.00

R1376-C—12½" RECTANGULAR ASHTRAY. Ebony/Cascade, Green/Cascade, Grey/Cascade. 12½" Long. RETAIL PRICE: $5.00

R1412-C—TRIANGULAR CANDY BOWL. Ebony/Cascade, Green/Cascade, Grey/Cascade. Width: 10½". RETAIL PRICE: $5.00

All Prices Subject to Customary Discount

THE HAEGER POTTERIES INC.,   DUNDEE, ILL.,   MACOMB, ILL.

REFRESH YOUR STOCK WITH THESE SPARKLING

New Planter Creations

Ever Popular Figurine Planters to Enchant Your Customers

HAEGER FIGURINES FOR *those Important Decorator Touches*

R-1375—WICKER BASKET, Green Agate, Tropical Briar, White Lattice, Turquoise Green Dec. Height 6". RETAIL PRICE $4.00.

R-1293—ACANTHUS PLANTER, Chartreuse, Ebony, Green Agate, Tropical Briar, Turquoise Green Dec. Height 9". RETAIL PRICE $3.00.

A-546—BASKET PLANTER, Dark Green Cascade, Ebony Cascade, Grey Cascade, White Lattice, Turquoise Green Dec. Height 6" RETAIL PRICE $3.00.

R-1462—WHEELBARROW PLANTER, Catseye, Chartreuse, Ebony, Tropical Briar, Turquoise Green Dec. Length 10" RETAIL PRICE $3.00.

R-1421—SINGLE HANDLED BOWL, Green Agate, Tropical Briar, White Lattice, Turquoise Green Dec. Length 15" RETAIL PRICE $4.50.

R-1838—BOWL ON 3 FEET, Dark Green, Cascade, Ebony Cascade, Grey Cascade, Pebble Coral, Length 10" RETAIL PRICE $3.00.

R-1262—HORSE PLANTER, Catseye, Ebony, Walnut, Turquoise Green Dec. Length: 16½" RETAIL PRICE $7.00.

R-1352—SEAGULL FISH BOWL, Catseye, Cotton White, Ebony, Height: 13½", RETAIL PRICE $4.50.

R-1229—GAZELLE BOWL, Chartreuse, Ebony, Green Agate, Walnut, Length: 11". RETAIL PRICE $4.00.

R-1341—GREYHOUND PLANTER, Catseye, Ebony, Walnut, Length: 12". RETAIL PRICE $4.00.

R-254—DONKEY PLANTER, Chartreuse, Ebony, Green Agate, Tropical Briar, Length: 11¼". RETAIL PRICE $3.00.

R-1336—COCKER SPANIEL, Walnut, Height: 8½". RETAIL PRICE $4.00.

R-1340—POODLE FIGURINE, Charcoal, Cotton White, Walnut, Height 8". RETAIL PRICE $3.00.

R-1342—STANDING COCKER FIGURINE, Charcoal, Cotton White, Walnut, Height: 7½". RETAIL PRICE $3.00.

R-462—PANTHER Ebony, Length: 18" RETAIL PRICE $3.00.

R-1381—GIRAFFE & YOUNG, Catseye, Cotton White, Walnut, Height: 13½". RETAIL PRICE $10.00.

R-1296—DOE & FAWN, Catseye, Cotton White, Walnut, Height: 11¾" RETAIL PRICE $9.00.

R-1407—THUNDER & LIGHTNING FIGURINE, Ebony, Green Stone, Tropical Briar, Height 17½" RETAIL PRICE $15.00.

R-1388—MARE & FOAL, Ebony, White, Walnut, Walnut, Height 9½". RETAIL PRICE $10.00.

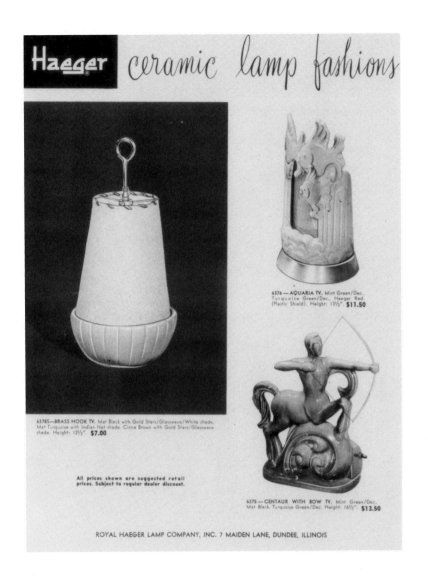

Haeger *ceramic lamp fashions*

6376 — AQUARIA TV. Mint Green/Dec., Turquoise Green/Dec., Haeger Red. (Plastic Shield). Height: 13½". **$11.50**

6378S—BRASS HOOK TV. Mat Black with Gold Stars/Glassweave/White shade. Mat Turquoise with Indian Nat shade. Cinna Brown with Gold Stars/Glassweave shade. Height: 12½". **$7.00**

All prices shown are suggested retail prices. Subject to regular dealer discount.

6375 — CENTAUR WITH BOW TV. Mint Green/Dec., Mat Black, Turquoise Green/Dec. Height: 16½". **$13.50**

ROYAL HAEGER LAMP COMPANY, INC. 7 MAIDEN LANE, DUNDEE, ILLINOIS

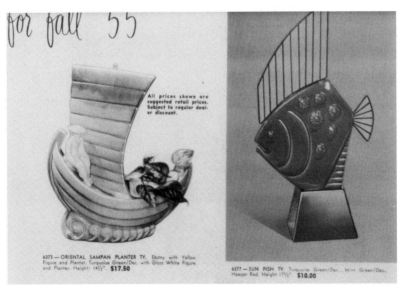

for fall 55

All prices shown are suggested retail prices. Subject to regular dealer discount.

6373 — ORIENTAL SAMPAN PLANTER TV. Ebony with Yellow Figure and Planter. Turquoise Green/Dec. with Gloss White Figure and Planter. Height: 14½". **$17.50**

6377 — SUN FISH TV. Turquoise Green/Dec., Mint Green/Dec., Haeger Red. Height: 17½". **$10.00**

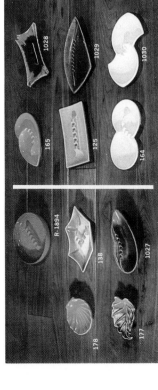

117 12" Free Form Ashtray. Cotton White, Reseda Yellow, Oxblood, Black Mistique: $2.30.

135 12" Free Form Ashtray. Cotton White, Mandarin Orange, Blue/Green, Misty Mint: $2.30.

1009 11½" Lined Ashtray. Misty Mint, Reseda Yellow, Mandarin Orange, Blue/Green, Cotton White, Blue Indigo: $2.30. Gold Tweed: $3.00.

1014 9" Free Form Ashtray. Black Mistique, Blue/Green, Oxblood, Blue Indigo: $2.30.

153 10½" Free Form Ashtray. Cotton White, Mandarin Orange, Blue/Green, Black Mistique, Blue Indigo: $2.30.

173 10" Free Form Textured Ashtray. Mandarin Orange, Reseda Yellow, Black Mistique: $2.30 ($24.00 dozen). Gold Tweed: $3.00.

1008 9½" Palette Ashtray. Black Mistique, Mandarin Orange, Blue/Green, Cotton White, Blue Indigo: $2.30. ($24.00 dozen).

1019 9" 18th Century Ashtray. Misty Curry, Mandarin Orange, Misty Mint, Porcelain White: $2.30. Gold Tweed: $3.00.

R-1836 10" Ashbowl. Black Mistique, Cotton White, Mandarin Orange: $2.30.

SP12 13½" Pallet Ashtray. Mandarin Orange, Cotton White, Curry, Blue/Green, Blue Indigo: $2.30.

1006 11" Free Form Ashtray. Mandarin Orange, Cotton White, Blue/Green, Blue Indigo: $2.70.

1001S 13" Oval Ashtray. Reseda Yellow, Mandarin Orange, Blue/Green, Cotton White: $3.50. Gold Tweed: $3.50.

1021 13" Traditional Ashtray. Oxblood, Cotton White, Blue/Green: $2.70.

1022 13" Free Form Ashtray. Oxblood, Curry, Blue/Green: $2.70.

128 13" Triangular Modern Ashtray. Blue/Green, Cotton White, Mandarin Orange, Reseda Yellow: $2.70. Gold Tweed: $3.50.

1003 Not Available

149 11" Rectangular Ashtray. Oxblood, Mandarin Orange, Blue/Green, Black Mistique: $3.50. Gold Tweed: $4.50.

1005 11" Fluted Ashtray. Misty Mint, Mandarin Orange: $3.00. Gold Tweed: $4.00.

192 12" Free Form Ashtray. Cotton White, Mandarin Orange, Blue/Green, Oxblood: $3.30.

1016-S 19" Convex Long John Ashtray. Black Mistique, Blue/Green, Mandarin Orange: $5.00.

1017-S 19" Concave Long John Ashtray. Black Mistique, Curry, Blue Indigo: $5.00.

162 16" Ashtray. Cotton White, Mandarin Orange, Blue/Green: $7.00.

1004 15" Large Modern Ashtray. Cotton White, Oxblood, Blue/Green: $7.00.

R-1735 11½" Shell Ashtray. Cotton White, Mandarin Orange, Blue/Green: $3.50.

ASHTRAYS
Suggested Retail: $2.00 - $2.50

1020 7" Plume Ashtray. Blue/Green, Misty Mint, Curry: $2.00. Gold Tweed: $3.00.

127 11" Flared Ashtray. Cotton White, Blue/Green, Black Mistique, Blue Indigo: $3.50. Gold Tweed: $3.50.

1015 11" Free Form Ashtray with Pipe Rest. Cotton White, Mandarin Orange, Curry: $2.50.

110-H 16" Leaf Ashtray. Misty Mint, Cotton White, Mandarin Orange: $3.50. Gold Tweed: $4.50.

170-S 12½" Rectangular Ashtray. Oxblood, Mandarin Orange, Blue/Green, Black Mistique: $3.50. Gold Tweed: $4.50.

R-1723 14" Executive Ashtray. Cotton White, Oxblood, Black Mistique: $10.00.

Suggested Retail: $2.75 and under

1028 1029 1030

165 125 164

177 178 R-1894 1027 138

SPECIAL ASSORTED 36-PACK
A 36-pack consisting of your choice of the six ashtrays in the Special Offer Group (165, 125, 164, 1028, 1029 and 1030) in the regular glazes, may be ordered at the $18.00 per dozen price ($54.00 for the 36-pack unit).

ASHTRAYS Priced in Dozen Lots
Suggested Retail: $1.00 - $2.00

178 4½" Shell Ashtray. Mandarin Orange, Cotton White, Reseda Yellow, Blue/Green, Blue Indigo: $12.00 Dozen (Minimum Two Dozen). Gold Tweed: $2.00 Each.

177 5½" Leaf Ashtray. Mandarin Orange, Cotton White, Reseda Yellow, Blue Indigo: $12.00 Dozen (Minimum Two Dozen). Gold Tweed: $2.00 Each.

R-1894 7" Round Ashtray. Mandarin Orange, Oxblood, Curry, Blue/Green: $2.00 Each (in One Dozen Lots, $1.50 Each).

138 8¼" Diamond Shape Ashtray. Mandarin Orange, Cotton White, Misty Mint, Mat Black, Reseda Yellow, Dark Green: $13.20 Dozen (Minimum Three Dozen, Six of each Color).

1027 8" Free Form Ash Bowl. Mandarin Orange, Cotton White, Blue/Green: $18.00 Dozen (Sold only in dozen lots).

SPECIAL OFFER GROUP
Suggested Retail: $1.50

165 9½" Free Form Ashtray. Cotton White, Reseda Yellow, Curry, Mandarin Orange: $1.70 Each ($18.00 a Dozen). Gold Tweed: $2.50 Each.

125 8" Rectangular Ashtray. Black Mistique, Haeger Red, Mandarin Orange, Cotton White, Reseda Yellow, Blue Indigo: $1.70 Each ($18.00 a Dozen). Gold Tweed: $2.50 Each.

164 8½" Figure Eight Ashtray. Misty Mint, Haeger Red, Cotton White, Blue Indigo: $1.70 Each ($18.00 a Dozen).

1028 8" Rectangular Ashtray. Black Mistique, Blue/Green, Mandarin Orange: $1.70 Each ($18.00 a Dozen).

1029 8" Ashtray. Mandarin Orange, Mat Black, Blue/Green: $1.70 Each ($18.00 a Dozen).

1030 8" Ashtray. Blue/Green, Cotton White, Haeger Red: $1.70 Each ($18.00 a Dozen).

Suggested Retail: $3.50 and under

18SS 13" Leaf Ashtray. Mandarin Orange, Curry: $3.30. Gold Tweed: $4.00.

155 13½" Shell Ashtray. Cotton White, Mandarin Orange, Blue Indigo: $3.50. Gold Tweed: $4.50.

1002 13" Modern Ashtray. Cotton White, Oxblood, Curry, Blue Indigo: $3.50.

144 8½" Shell Ashtray. Reseda Yellow, Blue Indigo: $4.00. Gold Tweed: $5.00.

R-1311 11" Square Divided Ashtray. Cotton White, Mandarin Orange, Black Mistique: $5.00. Gold Tweed: $6.50.

R-1755 14" Executive Ashtray. Cotton White, Mandarin Orange, Oxblood: $6.50.

Suggested Retail: $4.00, $5.00 and up

NEW! Blue Indigo

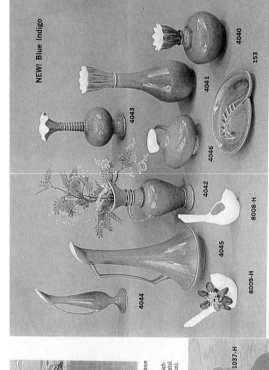

For those who like the emphatic accent, Haeger Artware provides bright, bold Blue Indigo. For those who prefer subtle nuances in color, there's soft, subdued Bristol Blue. As is true of all Haeger glazes, these are Color-Cued to today's home fashions. Also, Haeger Artware is Color-Coordinated in a wide selection of vases, candleholders, ashtrays, planters and decorative figurines to make it easy to choose harmonizing designs and unified accessories for the contemporary, traditional or provincial home.

153 10½" Ashtray. Cotton White, Mandarin Orange, Blue/Green, Black Mistique, Blue Indigo: $2.30.

4040 9" Vase. Mandarin Orange, Blue Indigo, Blue/Green: $4.50. Gold Tweed: $5.50.

4041 16" Vase. Mandarin Orange, Blue Indigo, Blue/Green: $6.50.

4042 12½" Etruscan Vase. Blue Indigo, Cotton White, Blue/Green: $6.00.

4043 12" Etruscan Vase. Blue Indigo, Cotton White, Blue/Green: $5.00. Gold Tweed: $6.00.

4044 14" Etruscan Vase. Blue Indigo, Cotton White, Bristol Blue. Gold Tweed: $6.00.

4045 18½" Pitcher. Blue Indigo, Cotton White, Mandarin Orange: (Lots of 6, Each: $5.50).

4046 6½" Etruscan Pitcher. Blue Indigo, Cotton White, Bristol Gold Tweed: $6.00.

8008-H 8" Bird. Porcelain White, Reseda Yellow, Blue Indigo, Bristol Blue: $2.50.

8009-H 6½" Bird. Porcelain White, Reseda Yellow, Blue Indigo, Bristol Blue: $2.50.

1-H 23" Vase. Mandarin Orange, Black Mistique, Blue Indigo: $11.00.

9-H 7½" Candle Bowl. Mandarin Orange, Black Mistique, Blue Indigo: $5.50.

13-H 6" Vase. Mandarin Orange, Black Mistique, Blue Indigo: $3.00.

25-H 14" Vase. Mandarin Orange, Black Mistique, Blue Indigo: $5.00.

26-H 12" Vase. Mandarin Orange, Black Mistique, Blue Indigo: $6.00.

144 8½" Shell Ashtray. Reseda Yellow, Blue Indigo. Gold Tweed: $4.00.

627 12½" Cat on Wood. Mat Black, Blue Indigo: $5.00.

1762 20" Rooster. Haeger Red Decorated, Gold Tweed, Blue Indigo: $16.50.

1810 12" Pheasant. Reseda Yellow, Blue Indigo, Blue/Green: $5.50. Gold Tweed: $6.50.

1811 14" Cock. Reseda Yellow, Blue Indigo, Blue/Green: $6.50.

3017 14" Bowl. Reseda Yellow, Blue Indigo, Blue/Green: $6.00. Gold Tweed: $9.00.

4012 13" Pitcher Vase. Cotton White/Turquoise, Blue/Green, Curry, Blue Indigo: $7.00. Gold Tweed: $9.00.

Suggested Retail Prices.

New Accessories For the Home!

1033-H 11" Ashtray. Mandarin Orange, Blue/Green, Bristol Blue, Reseda Yellow: $2.50. Gold Tweed: $3.50.

1034-H 9" Round Ashtray. Mandarin Orange, Blue/Green, Blue, Reseda Yellow: $2.50. Gold Tweed: $3.50.

1035-H 9" Round Ashtray. Mandarin Orange, Blue/Green, Bristol Blue, Reseda Yellow: $2.50.

1036-H 9" Round Ashtray. Mandarin Orange, Blue/Green, Bristol Blue, Reseda Yellow: $2.50.

1037-H 10½" Ashtray. Mandarin Orange, Blue/Green, Bristol Blue, Reseda Yellow: $2.50.

1038-H 9" Round Ashtray. Mandarin Orange, Blue/Green, Blue, Reseda Yellow: $2.50.

3018 5" Candleholder. Mandarin Orange, Blue/Green, Reseda Yellow: $2.50 Each.

8008-H 8" Bird. Porcelain White, Reseda Yellow, Blue Indigo, Bristol Blue: $2.50.

8009-H 6½" Bird. Porcelain White, Reseda Yellow, Blue Indigo, Bristol Blue: $2.50.

NEW! Ashtrays decorated with COINS!

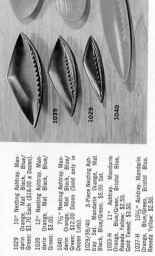

Actual coins embedded in the bottom surface make these immediate conversation pieces, unusual gifts.

1031 6½" Coin/Decorated Ashtray: Oxblood, Mat Black, Bristol Blue: $2.30 Each ($24.00 a Dozen).

1032 7" Coin/Decorated Ashtray: Oxblood, Mat Black, Bristol Blue: $2.30 Each ($24.00 a Dozen).

New Concepts in Ashtray Design!

1029 10" Nesting Ashtray. Mandarin Orange, Mat Black, Blue/Green: $1.70 Each ($18.00 a Dozen).

1039 12" Nesting Ashtray. Mandarin Orange, Mat Black, Blue/Green: $3.00.

1040 7½" Nesting Ashtray. Mandarin Orange, Mat Black, Blue/Green: $12.00 Dozen (Sold only in Dozen Lots).

1029/39/40 3-Piece Nesting Ashtray Set. Mandarin Orange, Mat Black, Blue/Green: $5.00 Set.

1041 11" Ashtray. Mandarin Orange, Mat Black, Blue Indigo: $3.00.

1042-S 10½" Ashtray. Mandarin Orange, Mat Black, Blue/Green: $4.00.

1043-S 10" Ashtray. Mandarin Orange, Mat Black, Blue/Green: $2.00.

1042/43 3-Piece Ashtray Set. Mandarin Orange, Mat Black, Blue/Green: $7.00 Set.

NEW! Low Table Accessories

8022-B 16¼" Bull Ash Bowl. Blue Indigo, Amber, Oyster White: $10.00.

8024-B 10" Horse Ash Bowl. Blue Indigo, Amber, Oyster White: $7.00.

8021-B 10" Elephant Ash Bowl. Blue Indigo, Amber, Oyster White: $7.00.

8023-B 12¾" Brahma Bull Ash Bowl. Blue Indigo, Amber, Oyster White: $7.00.

Suggested Retail Prices.

13

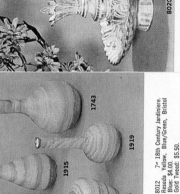

New Designs in GOLD TWEED

1035-H 9" Round Ashtray. Gold Tweed: $3.50. Mandarin Orange, Blue/Green, Bristol Blue, Reseda Yellow: $2.50.

1038-H 9" Round Ashtray. Gold Tweed: $3.50. Mandarin Orange, Blue/Green, Bristol Blue, Reseda Yellow: $2.50.

3023 18" Low Oval Bowl. Gold Tweed: $6.50. Blue/Green, Blue Indigo: $5.00.

4040 9" Vase. Gold Tweed: $5.50. Mandarin Orange, Blue Indigo, Blue/Green: $4.50.

4041 16" Vase. Gold Tweed: $6.50. Mandarin Orange, Blue Indigo, Blue/Green: $5.00.

4047-H 12" Vase. Gold Tweed: $8.00. Blue Indigo, Cotton White, Black Mistique: $6.00.

8010/11 Two-Tiered Chip 'n Dip. Gold Tweed: $8.00 Set. Misty Mint, Reseda Yellow, Bristol Blue, Porcelain White: $5.00 Set.

8012 7" 18th Century Jardiniere. Gold Tweed: $5.50. Reseda Yellow, Blue/Green, Bristol Blue: $4.00.

8013 6" 18th Century Jardiniere. Gold Tweed: $4.50. Reseda Yellow, Blue/Green, Bristol Blue: $3.00.

8014 5" 18th Century Jardiniere. Gold Tweed: $3.50. Reseda Yellow, Blue/Green, Bristol Blue: $2.50.

8015/16 Mediterranean Lavabo Set. Gold Tweed: $15.00 Set. Porcelain White, Peasant Olive: $11.00 Set.

8025-S 11" Double Server. Gold Tweed: $5.50. Porcelain White, Black Mistique: $6.00.

8026-S Triple Server, not illustrated. Same design as 8025-S Double Server. Gold Tweed: $7.00. Porcelain White, Black Mistique: $5.00.

UNUSUAL CONVERSATIONAL PIECES

That add a personal decorative touch to those blank corners or become the focal point of a room. These whimsical youngsters are sure to draw attention of young and old alike at any time of the year. They can be planted, used for unusual seasonal arrangements or left empty. Good with or without candles. Candles and flowers not included.

Suggested Retail Prices.

NEW! Fountain styled in the Mediterranean mode

Gracefully designed for an elegant effect.

8020 17" Mediterranean Styled Fountain. Gold Tweed, Oyster White: $70.00. U.S. Pat. No. 2,973,904

Fanciful creations to hold candles/flowers/plants! Gay, amusing decorations!

3020-Z 13" Chicken Planter. Bristol Blue, Amber, Porcelain White: $7.50.

3021-Z 6" Chicken Candleholder. Bristol Blue, Amber, Porcelain White: $6.00.

3022-Z 9" Chicken Candleholder-Planter. Bristol Blue, Amber, Porcelain White: $7.00.

16

NEW! Bristol Blue

RG-68-X 7" Bud Vase. Curry, Black Mistique, Cotton White, Mandarin Orange, Bristol Blue, Blue Indigo: Each $2.00 (Sold only in Lots of 12, three colors to a dozen). Gold Tweed: $2.50.

335 9" Compote. Cotton White/Turquoise, Curry, Blue Indigo, Bristol Blue: $6.00. Gold Tweed: $7.00.

336 4" Candleholder. Cotton White/Turquoise, Curry, Blue Indigo, Bristol Blue: $3.00 Pair. Gold Tweed: $6.00 Pair.

707-S 7½" Candy Box. Mandarin Orange, Cotton White, Curry, Blue/Green, Blue Indigo, Blue: $5.50. Gold Tweed: $6.50.

889 5" Lighter, Oxblood, Black Mistique, Mandarin Orange, Curry, Bristol Blue: $4.50.

1035-H 9" Round Ashtray. Mandarin Orange, Blue/Green, Blue, Reseda Yellow: $2.50. Bristol Blue: $3.50.

1037-H 10½" Ashtray. Mandarin Orange, Blue/Green, Bristol Blue, Reseda Yellow: $2.50.

1743 21½" Onion Jug Vase. Oxblood, Cotton White/Turquoise, Mandarin Orange, Bristol Blue: $9.00.

1915 15" One Stem Vase. Cotton White/Turquoise, Mandarin Orange, Oxblood, Black Mistique, Blue Indigo, Bristol Blue: $4.00. Gold Tweed: $5.00.

1919 10" One Stem Vase. Cotton White/Turquoise, Mandarin Orange, Oxblood, Black Mistique, Blue Indigo, Bristol Blue, Curry: $3.00. Gold Tweed: $4.00.

3020-Z 13" Chicken Planter. Bristol Blue, Amber, Porcelain White: $7.50.

3021-Z 6" Chicken Candleholder-Planter. Bristol Blue, Amber, Porcelain White: $6.00.

4034 7" Boutique Vase. Etruscan Blue, Etruscan Orange, Etruscan Yellow: $7.50. Cerulean Gold: $9.00. Black Mistique, Bristol Blue: $4.00.

4035 12" Boutique Vase. Etruscan Blue, Etruscan Orange, Etruscan Yellow: $6.50. Cerulean Gold: $8.00. Black Mistique, Bristol Blue: $3.50.

4043 12" Etruscan Vase. Blue Indigo, Cotton White, Bristol Blue: $6.00.

8012 7" 18th Century Jardiniere. Reseda Yellow, Blue/Green, Bristol Blue: $4.00. Gold Tweed: $5.50.

8013 6" 18th Century Jardiniere. Reseda Yellow, Blue/Green, Bristol Blue: $3.00. Gold Tweed: $4.50.

8014 5" 18th Century Jardiniere. Reseda Yellow, Blue/Green, Bristol Blue: $2.50. Gold Tweed: $3.50.

NEW! Whimsical Patio Planters

8017 19" Mermaid Patio Planter. Sagebrush, Brushed Grey: $40.00.

8018 19" Female Patio Planter. Sagebrush, Brushed Grey: $30.00.

8019 21" Male Patio Planter. Sagebrush, Brushed Grey: $30.00.

15

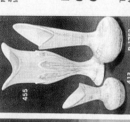

ETRUSCAN GLAZES

NOTE: Ashtrays shown above also available in new Cerulean Gold.

New CERULEAN GOLD

The treasured look of these designs is attained by splashing 22 carat gold on a heavenly blue to achieve a combination of delicate gold tracery and bold gold accents. The effect is different on each piece (fired three times) to give additional interest to the unusual shapes.

23

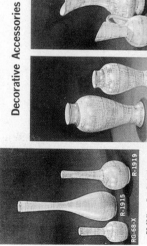

Decorative Accessories

150A/05 Lavabo, 15" Top, 16" Bottom. Gold Tweed: $20.00 Set.

842/843 Traditional Lavabo, 14" Top, 12" Bottom. Gold Tweed: $15.00 Set. In Porcelain White: $11.00 Set.

885 20" Large Electric Fountain. U.L. Approved. Gold Tweed: $95.00. U.S. Pat. No. 2,973,904

709 12½" Horn O' Plenty. Gold Tweed: $6.50. In Cotton White/Turquoise, Blue/Green: $5.00.

436 18" Classic Urn. Gold Tweed: $10.00. In Cotton White/Turquoise: $9.00.

306 12½" Bowl. Gold Tweed: $8.00. In Blue/Green, Misty Mint, Cotton White/Turquoise: $7.00.

R-1285 5" Calla Lily Candleholder. Gold Tweed: $5.00 Pair. In Mandarin Orange, Cotton White, Reseda Yellow, Curry, Misty Mint, Blue/Green, Blue Indigo: $4.00 Pair.

RG-68-X 7" Bud Vase. Gold Tweed: $2.50. In Black Mistique, Blue/Green, Cotton White, Mandarin Orange, Blue Indigo, Bristol Blue: $2.00 (Sold only in Lots of 12, three colors to a dozen).

R-1915 15" One Stem Vase. Gold Tweed: $5.00. In Cotton White/Turquoise, Mandarin Orange, Oxblood, Black Mistique, Bristol Blue, Blue Indigo: $4.00.

R-1919 10" One Stem Oriental Vase. Gold Tweed: $4.00. In Cotton White/Turquoise, Mandarin Orange, Oxblood, Black Mistique, Bristol Blue, Blue Indigo: $3.00.

4030 12" Traditional Vase. Gold Tweed: $6.50. In Black Mistique, Mandarin Orange, Cotton White, Blue/Green: $5.00.

4031 9" Traditional Vase. Gold Tweed: $5.00. In Black Mistique, Mandarin Orange, Cotton White, Bristol Blue, Blue/Green: $4.00.

4012 13" Colonial Pitcher Vase. Gold Tweed: $9.00. In Cotton White/Turquoise, Blue/Green, Curry, Blue Indigo: $7.00.

RG-82-X 9" Jug Vase. Gold Tweed: $4.50.

4000-S 12" Leaf Vase. Gold Tweed: $6.00. In Cotton White/Turquoise, Curry: $5.00.

499-S 7" Leaf Vase. In Reseda Yellow, Blue/Green: $5.50.

413 9" Vase. Gold Tweed: $4.50. In Cotton White/Turquoise, Curry, Blue/Green: $3.50.

455 16" Classic Vase. Gold Tweed: $7.50. In Cotton White/Turquoise, Blue/Green: $6.00.

R-1752 16" Eccentric Vase. Gold Tweed: $7.00. In Cotton White/Turquoise, Blue/Green, Black Mistique: $6.00.

All Prices Suggested Retail.

Big, handsome
Floor Planters
from Haeger

407

900

899

857-W

8001

8002

896-W

8005-Z

857W   16" Jardiniere (12"
Opening) with Walnut Tripod.
Cotton White/Turquoise, Black
Mistique: $18.00.
Gold Tweed: $20.00.

900   18" Floor Planter,
Black Mistique, Blue/Green:
$15.00.

407 20" Urn Vase. Por-
celain White: $30.00.

8001   14" Spanish   Floor
Planter with   Stand. Black/
Green, Cotton White, Mat
Black: $20.00.

899   13"   Floor   Planter,
Black Mistique, Blue/Green:
$15.00.

896-W   16" Floor Planter
with Walnut Stand. Black
Mistique, Blue/Green, Cotton
White/Turquoise: $20.00.

896   16" Floor   Planter
without Stand. Black Mis-
tique, Blue/Green, Cotton
White/Turquoise: $15.00.

8005-Z   13½" Mediter-
ranean Planter with Iron
Stand. Black/Green, Mat
Black, Brushed Gray: $25.00.

8002   14" Spanish Floor
Planter   with   Stand. Black/
Green, Mat Black, Cotton
White: $20.00.

411-H   23" Urn. Mandarin
Orange, Black Mistique:
$17.50.

All Prices Suggested Retail.

828-W

RG-90-W

RG-91

RG-91-W

411-H

828-W   13"   Pot with
Stand. Cotton   White/Tur-
quoise,   Blue/Green: $17.00.
828   13" Pot   without
Stand: $14.00.

RG-90-W   8" Jardiniere
with Wire Stand. Mat White,
Mat Black: $5.70.
RG-90   8" Jardiniere without Stand: $3.50.

RG-91-W   12"   Jardiniere
with Wire Stand. Mat White,
Mat Black: $8.00.
RG-91   12" Jardiniere without Stand: $5.50.

26

382

518

R-31

3008-H

R-1224

633

634

R-1913

4023

1018

4022

4024

3000

489

879-H/880-H

4018

4017

4019

613

3014-Z

612

1024

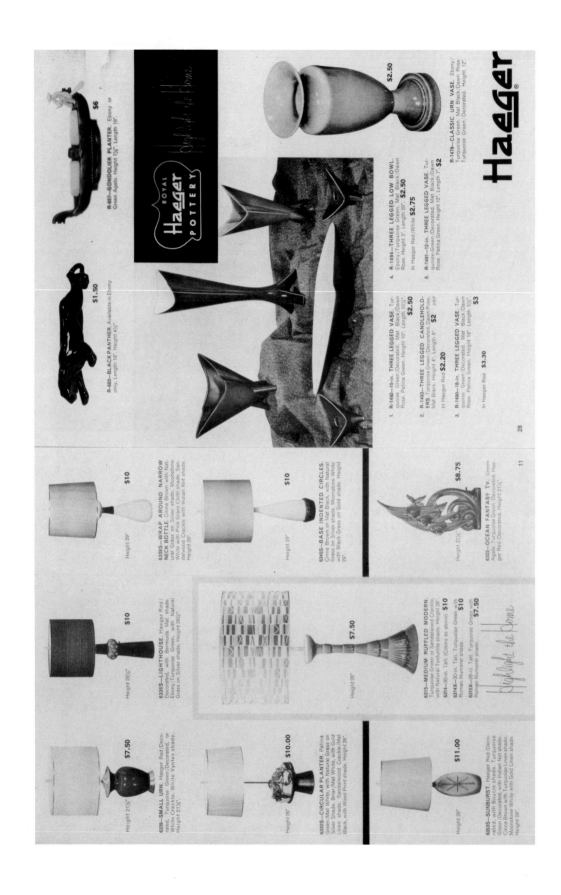

R-683—GONDOLIER PLANTER. Ebony or Green Agate. Height 7½", Length 18". **$6**

R-683—BLACK PANTHER. Available in Ebony only. Length 18", Height 4½". **$1.50**

Haeger®

ROYAL Haeger POTTERY

$2.50

1. R-1492—10-in. THREE LEGGED VASE. Turquoise Green./Decorated, Mat Black/Dawn Rose, Patina Green. Height 10", Length 10½". **$2.50**

2. R-1493—THREE LEGGED CANDLEHOLDERS. Turquoise Green./Decorated, Dawn Rose, Mat Black. Height 4", Length 6". **$2** pair
   In Haeger Red **$2.20**

3. R-1490—18-in. THREE LEGGED VASE. Turquoise Green./Decorated, Mat Black/Dawn Rose, Patina Green. Height 18", Length 5½". **$3**
   In Haeger Red **$3.30**

4. R-1494—THREE LEGGED LOW BOWL. Ebony/Turquoise Green, Mat Black/Dawn Rose. Height 3", Length 20". **$2.50**
   In Haeger Red/White **$2.75**

5. R-1491—12-in. THREE LEGGED VASE. Turquoise-Green./Decorated, Mat Black/Dawn Rose, Patina Green. Height 12", Length 7". **$2**

R-1479—CLASSIC URN VASE. Ebony/Turquoise Green, Mat Black/Dawn Rose, Turquoise Green./Decorated. Height 12".

28

6339S—SMALL URN. Haeger Red/Decorated, Turquoise Green./Decorated, or White Crackle. White Vyntex shade. Height 21½". **$7.50**

6338S—LIGHTHOUSE. Haeger Red/Decorated, with Bermuda Mat shade. Ebony/Turquoise Green, with Natural Grass on Silver shade. Height 20½". **$10**

6338S—WRAP AROUND NARROW NECK BOTTLE. Cinna Brown with Natural Grass on Silver shade. Moonstone White with Pink Grass Cloth shade. Sandalwood Crackle with Indian Mat shade. Height 29". **$10**

634SS—BASE INDENTED CIRCLES. Cinna Brown or Mat Black, with Natural Grass on Silver shade. Moonstone White with Black Grass on Gold shade. Height 29". **$10**

6322—OCEAN FANTASY TV. Green Agate. Turquoise Green./Decorated, Haeger Red /Decorated. Height 21½". **$8.75**

11

6335—CIRCULAR PLANTER. Patina Green Mat White, with Natural Grass on Silver Shade. Briar Mat White, with Gold Linen shade. Sandalwood Crackle/Mat Black, with Wood Print shade. Height 26". **$10.00**

6315—MEDIUM RUFFLED MODERN. Turquoise Green or Sandalwood Crackle, with Natural Texturtile shade. Height 28". **$10**

6314X—30-in. Tall. (Colors as above) **$10**

6314X—30-in. Tall. Turquoise Green with Roman Numeral shade. **$10**

6315X—26-in. Tall. Turquoise Green with Roman Numeral shade. **$7.50**

6353S—SUNBURST. Haeger Red/Decorated, with Boucle shade. Turquoise Green /Decorated, with Indian Mat shade. Cinna Brown with Turquoise Linen shade. Moonstone White with Gold Linen shade. Height 29". **$11.00**

The Haeger *Potteries* INC.

7 MAIDEN LANE, DUNDEE, ILLINOIS

Return Postage Guaranteed

Litho in U.S.A.

A. R1737S Oblong Cigarette Box & Ashtray
4¼" x 10½" - Haeger Red
B. R1311 Square Divided Ashtray 11" Square -
White Stone Lace
C. R1618 Rectangular Cigarette Box & Ashtray
6½" x 3" x 10½" - Turquoise Green/Decorated
D. R1735 Shell Ashtray 9½" x 11½" - Sable
E. R1714S Rectangular Ashtray 9" x 12" - Turquoise
Green/Decorated
F. R1673/74/75 Free Form Nesting Ashtray Set
8" x 12", 6" x 9", 4" x 6" - Saffron
G. R1738S Oval Ashtray 9¼" x 10½" - Mat Black
H. R1663 9" Free Form Ashtray - Turquoise Green/
Decorated
I. R1731 Leaf Ashtray 8½" x 16½" - Catseye

J. R1665 S Shaped Ashtray/Cigarette Box
Combination 5" x 14" - Saffron
K. R1723 14" Executive Ashtray - Turquoise
Green/Decorated
L. R1718/19/20 Freeform Ashtray Set 6¼" x 10½",
7¼" x 12", 8½" x 13½" - Turquoise
Green/Decorated
M. R1601 Fluted Ashtray 8½" x 1¾" x 8½" - Saffron
N. R1608 Tear Drop Ashtray 3½" x 1¾" x 14½" -
Dark Green/Stipple
O. R1634S Leaf Ashtray 7¼" x 2" x 12½" -
Ebony/Stipple
P. R1688S Small Rectangular 6" Cigarette Box -
Haeger Red
Q. R1602 Horseshoe Ashtray 8" x 1" x 8½" - Antique

Haeger

ARTWARE AND LAMPS

the Great Name in American Ceramics

1957

The Haeger *Potteries* INC. 7 MAIDEN LANE, DUNDEE, ILLINOIS

Haeger® Flower-ware

Rings Like Rare Old Porcelain

A. RG73 14″ S Shaped Bowl
B. RG74 9″ S Shaped Bowl
C. RG60 Oval Footed Bowl 3¼″ x 5¾″ x 11¾″
*D. RG65 Small Leaf Bowl 9½″ x 6″
E. RG64 Large Leaf Bowl 14″ x 8½″
F. RG72 8″ Goblet Vase
G. RG56 9″ Compote Bowl
H. RG42 Medium Flower Pitcher 4″ x 10″
I. RG61 Tall Oval Compote Bowl 12¼″ x 6½″ x 6″
*J. RG53 Posy Stand & Candleholder 6″ x 3¼″
K. RG63 6″ Square Compote Bowl
L. RG75 18″ Vase
*M. RG68 Bud Vase 7″
*N. RG37 6″ Triangular Bowl
O. RG77 6″ Bean Pot Planter
P. RG76 8″ Bean Pot Planter

** Prepacked Items. See Wholesale Price List.*

Haeger's new Artware to beautify the home

			COLORS SHOWN
A.	R1740S	Candlesticks for R1739 6¼″ x 6¼″	Turquoise Green Decorated
B.	R1739S	Oval Bowl 17″ x 11″	Turquoise Green Decorated
C.	R1731	Leaf Ashtray 8½″ x 16½″	Turquoise Green Decorated
D.	R1738S	Oval Ashtray 10¼″ x 9¼″	Oyster White
E.	R1726	Candlesticks for R1725 7¼″ x 5¼″	Gold Lustre
F.	R1725	Tall Console Bowl 12½″ x 7¼″	Gold Lustre

			COLORS SHOWN
E.	R1726	Candlesticks for R1725 7¼″ x 5¼″	Gold Lustre
G.	R1718	13½″ Freeform Ashtray	Oyster White
H.	R1724	15″ Contemporary Vase	Turquoise Green Decorated
I.	R1714S	9″ x 12″ Rectangular Ashtray	Gold Lustre
J.	R1661B	Box 6¾″ x 6¾″	Gold Lustre
K.	R1715S	10″ Round Ashtray	Sable
L.	R1724	15″ Contemporary Vase	Gold Lustre

Haeger

Designed for Today's Living

			COLORS SHOWN
A.	R1730	Candy Jar 7¼" x 10"	Haeger Red
B.	R1712S	11" Cat Vase	Antique
C.	R1726	Candlestick for R1725 7¼" x 5¼"	White Stone Lace
D.	R1725	Tall Console Bowl 12¾" x 7¼"	White Stone Lace
C.	R1726	Candlestick for R1725 7¼" x 5¼"	White Stone Lace
E.	R1711S	18" Cat Vase	Saffron
F.	R1702	12" Contemporary Vase	White Stone Lace
G.	R1742	Egyptian Cat 20"	Sable
H.	R1701	9" Traditional Vase	Saffron
I.	R1728	Candlestick for R1727 5¼" x 7½" x 4"	Turquoise Green Decorated
J.	R1727	Low Roman Bowl 5" x 20¼"	Turquoise Green Decorated

			COLORS SHOWN
I.	R1728	Candlestick for R1727 5¼" x 7½" x 4"	Turquoise Green Decorated
K.	R1708	Small Horse Planter 11" x 5½" x 11"	Ebony/Decorated
L.	R1722	14" Oriental Square Bowl	Turquoise Green Decorated
M.	R1705	Small Horn of Plenty 4¾" x 12"	Antique
	R1704	Medium Horn of Plenty 7" x 14¾"	
	R1696	Large Horn of Plenty 8½" x 18½"	
N.	R1733	Candy Box with Tassel Handle 8½" x 8½"	Sable
O.	R1732	12" Tall Footed Bowl	White Stone Lace
P.	R1717S	6½" Candy Box	Turquoise Green Decorated
Q.	R1716S	8" Flatsided Vase	Antique

R1657 Cookie Barrel 12½" high
Colorful roomy old fashioned Cookie Barrel
Packed 4 in carton. Wt. 24 lbs.
Saffron color only

R1699 Cookie Jar 11" high
Available in Antique, Mint Green Decorated or Saffron Decorated
Packed 6 in carton. Wt. 26 lbs.
2 each color

R1582S Cream Pitcher 4" x 4½"
R1583S Sugar Bowl 4½" x 4½"
R1584S Tea Pot 7½" x 6¼"
R1585S Coffee Pot 7" x 10¼"

R1588S Divided Relish Dish 5½" x 2" x 17¼"

R1683S Divided Leaf Server 14"

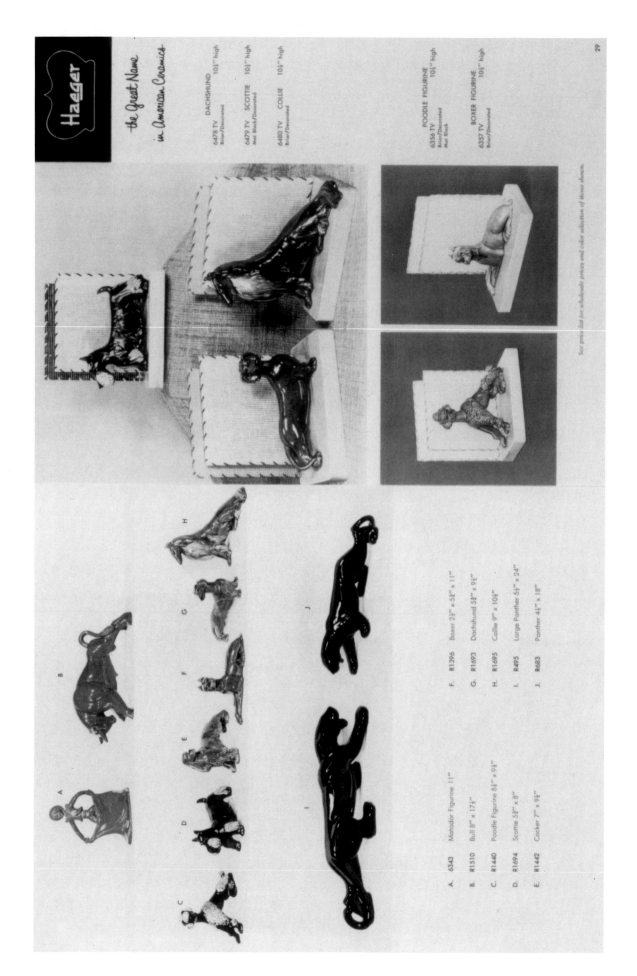

Haeger

the Great Name in American Ceramics

6478 TV DACHSHUND 10½" high
Briar/Decorated

6479 TV SCOTTIE 10½" high
Mat Black/Decorated

6480 TV COLLIE 10½" high
Briar/Decorated

POODLE FIGURINE 10½" high
6356 TV
Briar/Decorated
Mat Black

BOXER FIGURINE 10½" high
6357 TV
Briar/Decorated

29

See price list for wholesale prices and color selection of items shown.

A. 6343 Matador Figurine 11"

B. R1510 Bull 8" x 17½"

C. R1440 Poodle Figurine 8½" x 9½"

D. R1694 Scottie 5½" x 8"

E. R1442 Cocker 7" x 9½"

F. R1396 Boxer 2½" x 5½" x 11"

G. R1693 Dachshund 5½" x 9½"

H. R1695 Collie 9" x 10½"

I. R495 Large Panther 5½" x 24"

J. R683 Panther 4½" x 18"

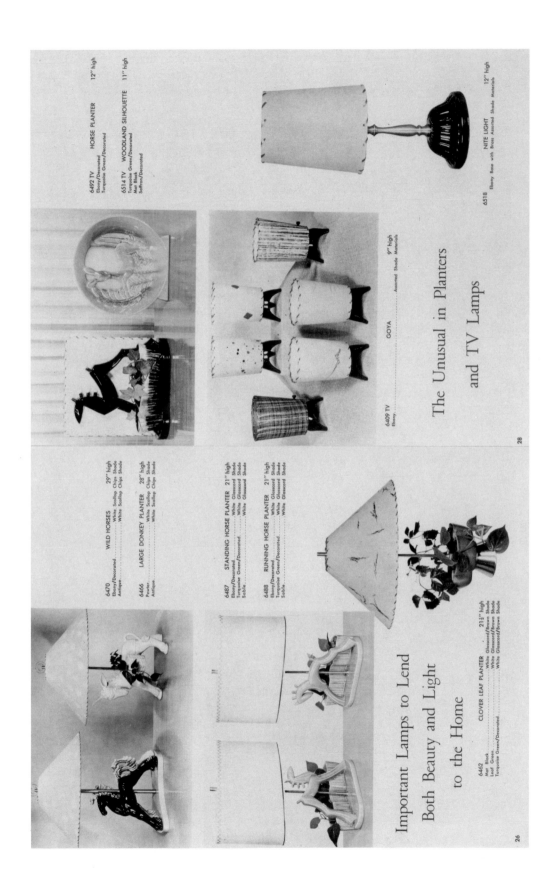

6492 TV   HORSE PLANTER   12" high
Ebony/Decorated
Turquoise Green/Decorated

6514 TV   WOODLAND SILHOUETTE   11" high
Turquoise Green/Decorated
Mat Black
Saffron/Decorated

6518   NITE LIGHT   12" high
Ebony Base with Brass and Assorted Shade Materials

6409 TV   GOYA   9" high
Ebony .... Assorted Shade Materials

The Unusual in Planters
and TV Lamps

28

6470   WILD HORSES   29" high
Ebony/Decorated .... White Scallop Chips Shade
Antique .... White Scallop Chips Shade

6466   LARGE DONKEY PLANTER   28" high
Pewter .... White Scallop Chips Shade
Antique .... White Scallop Chips Shade

6487   STANDING HORSE PLANTER   21" high
Ebony/Decorated .... White Glasscord Shade
Turquoise Green/Decorated .... White Glasscord Shade
Sable .... White Glasscord Shade

6488   RUNNING HORSE PLANTER   21" high
Ebony/Decorated .... White Glasscord Shade
Turquoise Green/Decorated .... White Glasscord Shade
Sable .... White Glasscord Shade

6462   CLOVER LEAF PLANTER   21½" high
Mat Black .... White Glasscord/Brown Shade
Leaf Green .... White Glasscord/Brown Shade
Turquoise Green/Decorated .... White Glasscord/Brown Shade

Important Lamps to Lend
Both Beauty and Light
to the Home

26

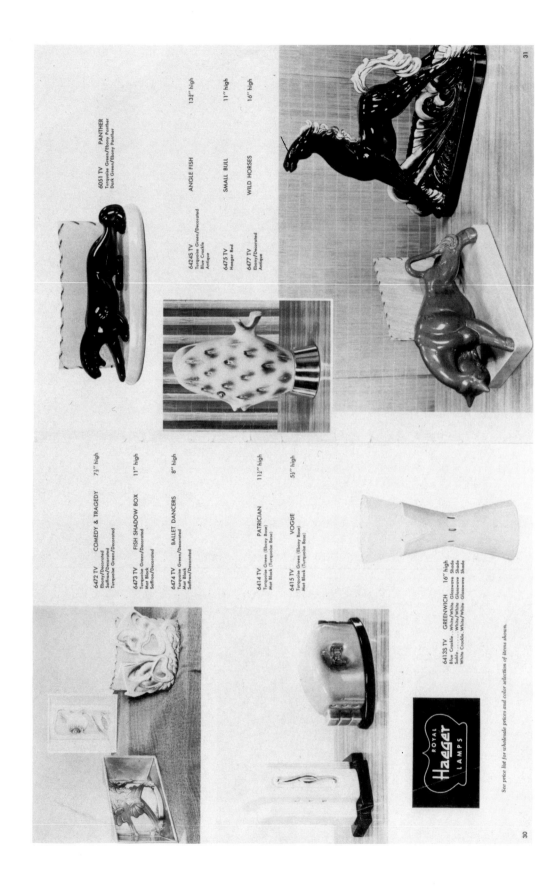

6051 TV　PANTHER
Turquoise Green/Ebony Panther
Dark Green/Ebony Panther　13½″ high

6424S TV　ANGLE FISH
Turquoise Green/Decorated
Blue Crackle
Antique

6475 TV　SMALL BULL　11″ high
Haeger Red

6477 TV　WILD HORSES　16″ high
Ebony/Decorated
Antique

6472 TV　COMEDY & TRAGEDY　7½″ high
Ebony/Decorated
Saffron/Decorated
Turquoise Green/Decorated

6473 TV　FISH SHADOW BOX　11″ high
Turquoise Green/Decorated
Mat Black
Saffron/Decorated

6474 TV　BALLET DANCERS　8″ high
Turquoise Green/Decorated
Mat Black
Saffron/Decorated

6414 TV　PATRICIAN　11½″ high
Turquoise Green (Ebony Base)
Mat Black (Turquoise Base)

6415 TV　VOGUE　5½″ high
Turquoise Green (Ebony Base)
Mat Black (Turquoise Base)

6413S TV　GREENWICH　16″ high
Blue Crackle．White/White Glassware Shade
Sable．．．．White/White Glassware Shade
White Crackle．White/White Glassware Shade

ROYAL
Haeger
LAMPS

See price list for wholesale prices and color selection of items shown.

30　　　31

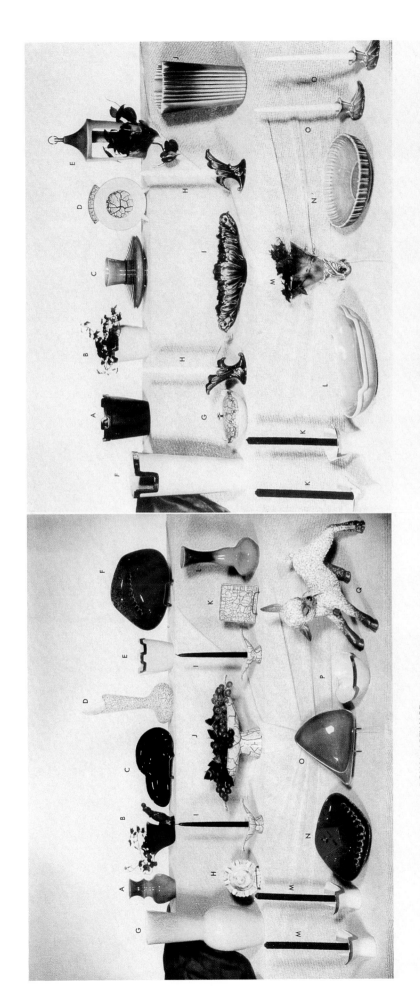

A. R1773S 7" Slip Pot
B. R1772S 6" Slip Pot
C. R1763 Low Disc Vase 7" x 12" x 5"
D. R1751 Circular Flatsided Vase 9½" x 8"
E. R1768S Round Hanging Planter 16" x 7"
F. R1769S 16" Round Vase
G. R1770S Round Candy Box 7½"
H. R1765 Chandleholder 5½" x 5½"

I. R1764 14" Leaf Bowl
J. R1753 12" Fluted Vase
K. R1775S Candleholder 4" x 4"
L. R1771S 14" Oval Bowl
M. R1783 Wall Pocket 8" x 8" x 3½"
N. R1778 12" Round Bowl
O. R437 Leaf Candleholders 3" x 5"

See price list for wholesale prices and color selection of items shown.

ROYAL ARTWARE

			COLORS SHOWN
A.	R1779	8" Vase	Turquoise Green Decorated
B.	R1777	Calabash Planter 5½" x 10" x 6"	Briar
C.	R1754	Modern Ashtray 14"	Ebony
D.	R1752W	16" Eccentric Vase	White Stone Lace
E.	R1772S	6" Slip Pot	Oyster/Gold Edge
F.	R1755H	14" Executive Ashtray	Carnival
G.	R1706	18" Contemporary Vase	Pearl Shell
H.	R1784	Round Ashtray 6½"	Tweed
I.	R1760F	Candleholders 2½" x 8"	Antique Marble

			COLORS SHOWN
J.	R1759F	21" Console Bowl	Antique Marble
K.	R1785	6" Square Ashtray	Antique Marble
L.	R1776	12" Vase	Turquoise Green Decorated
M.	R1775S	Candleholder 4" x 4"	Oyster/Gold Edge
N.	R1766S-H	Diamond Shaped Ashtray & Cigarette Box Combination 12½" x 9"	Carnival
O.	R1780	Pearl Shell Ashtray 7" x 11"	Turquoise Green Decorated
P.	R1774S	7" Round Ashtray	Oyster/Gold Edge
*Q.	R1782	Large Lamb Figurine 15" x 18"	White Stone Lace

* Prepacked Items. See Wholesale Price List.

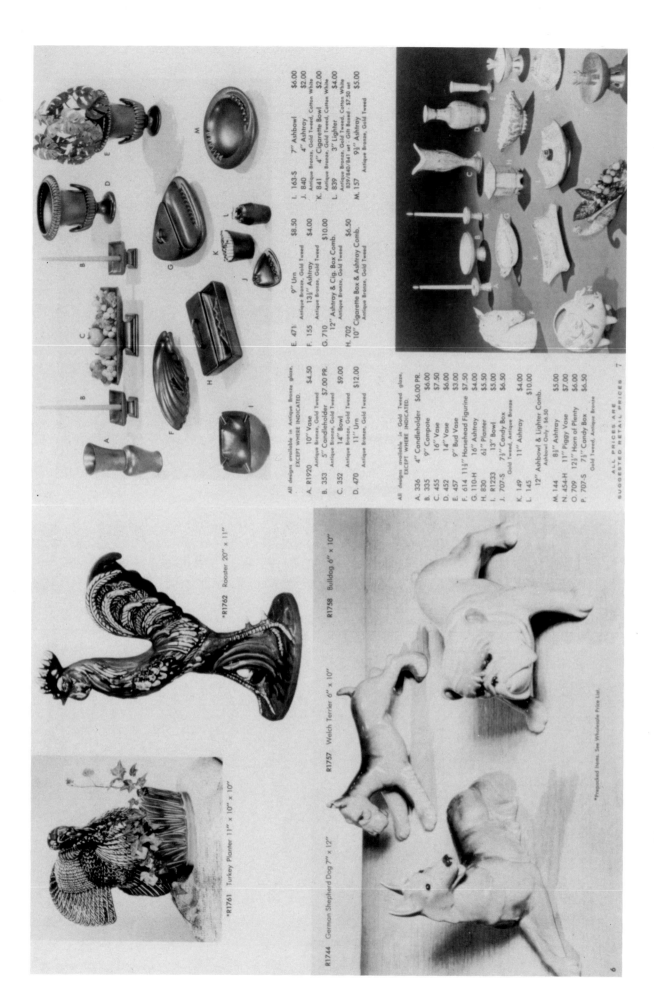

All designs available in Antique Bronze glaze.
EXCEPT WHERE INDICATED.

A.	R1920	10" Vase	$4.50
		Antique Bronze, Gold Tweed	
B.	353	5" Candleholder	$7.00 PR.
		Antique Bronze, Gold Tweed	
C.	352	14" Bowl	$9.00
		Antique Bronze, Gold Tweed	
D.	470	11" Urn	$12.00
		Antique Bronze, Gold Tweed	
E.	471	9" Urn	$8.50
		Antique Bronze, Gold Tweed	
F.	155	13½" Ashtray	$4.00
		Antique Bronze, Gold Tweed	
G.	710	12" Ashtray & Cig. Box Comb.	$10.00
		Antique Bronze, Gold Tweed	
H.	702	10" Cigarette Box & Ashtray Comb.	$6.50
		Antique Bronze, Gold Tweed	
I.	163-S	7" Ashbowl	$6.00
J.	840	4" Ashtray	$2.00
		Antique Bronze, Gold Tweed, Cotton White	
K.	841	4" Cigarette Bowl	$2.00
		Antique Bronze, Gold Tweed, Cotton White	
L.	839	3" Lighter	$4.00
		Antique Bronze, Gold Tweed, Cotton White	
		839/840/841 set: Gift Boxed	$7.50 set
M.	157	9½" Ashtray	$5.00
		Antique Bronze, Gold Tweed	

All designs available in Gold Tweed glaze.
EXCEPT WHERE INDICATED.

A.	336	4" Candleholder	$6.00 PR.
B.	335	9" Compote	$6.00
C.	455	16" Vase	$7.50
D.	452	14" Vase	$6.00
E.	457	9" Bud Vase	$3.00
F.	614	11½" Horsehead Figurine	$7.50
G.	110-H	16" Ashtray	$4.00
H.	830	6½" Planter	$5.50
I.	R1233	13" Bowl	$5.00
J.	707-S	7½" Candy Box	$6.50
		Gold Tweed, Antique Bronze	
K.	149	11" Ashtray	$4.00
L.	145	12" Ashbowl & Lighter Comb.	$10.00
		Ashbowl Only: $6.50	
M.	144	8½" Ashtray	$5.00
N.	454-H	11" Piggy Vase	$7.00
O.	709	12½" Horn of Plenty	$6.00
P.	707-S	7½" Candy Box	$6.50
		Gold Tweed, Antique Bronze	

ALL PRICES ARE
SUGGESTED RETAIL PRICES   7

*R1761 Turkey Planter 11" x 10" x 10"

*R1762 Rooster 20" x 11"

R1744 German Shepherd Dog 7" x 10"

R1757 Welch Terrier 6" x 10"

R1758 Bulldog 6" x 10"

*Prepacked items. See Wholesale Price List.

6

102

Bulk Rate
U. S. Postage
PAID
Permit No. 17

The Haeger Potteries INC.
7 MAIDEN LANE, DUNDEE, ILLINOIS
Return Postage Guaranteed

FLOWERWARE

A. RG81   12" Vase
B. RG82   9" Jug Vase
C. RG83   Square Fluted Vase 7" x 5"
D. RG26   Small Glad Vase 10"
E. RG79   4½" Square Planter

F. RG78   Rectangular Planter 4½" x 8" x 3"
G. RG84   10" Round Fluted Vase
H. RG80   16" Low Bowl
I. RG85   Round Candleholder 2" x 4½"

PRINTED IN U.S.A.

11

6526 WELSH TERRIER TV   Height 10½"
Sable/Decorated

6538 BULLDOG   Height 8½"
Sable/Decorated

6524 SHEPHERD DOG TV   Height 11"
Sable/Decorated

Haeger

6522 DONKEY PLANTER TV   Height 10"
Sable
Oyster

6525 LEOPARD SHADOW BOX TV   Height 11"
Turquoise/Decorated
Mat Black

6523 HORSE TV   Height 12"
Mat Black/Gold
Sable

Haeger
ARTWARE AND LAMPS
the Great Name in American Ceramics
1958

The Haeger Potteries INC. 7 MAIDEN LANE, DUNDEE, ILLINOIS

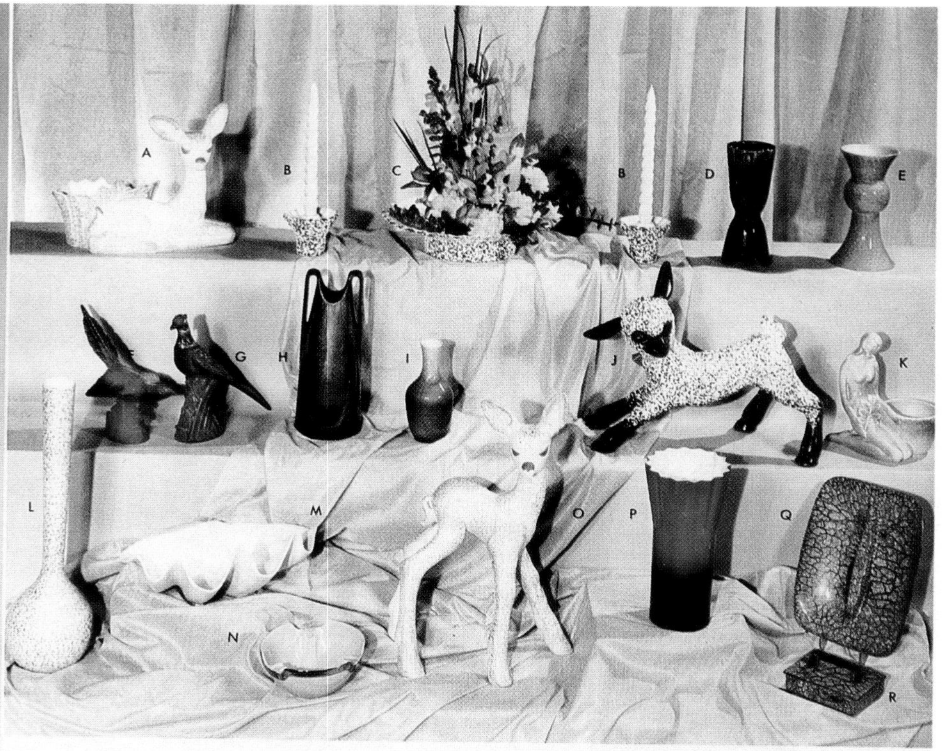
A
B
C
B
D
E
G
H
I
J
K
L
M
O
P
Q
N
R

Haeger's new Artware to beautify the home

A. R1829 Fawn Figurine Planter $12\frac{3}{4}$" x $6\frac{3}{4}$" x 14" Peach Stone with Gold
B. R1817S Pleated Candleholders $3\frac{1}{2}$" x $4\frac{1}{2}$" x $4\frac{1}{2}$" White Stone Lace
C. R1818S 15" Pleated Bowl $3\frac{1}{4}$" x 15" x 15" White Stone Lace
D. R1798 10" Modern Vase - Sherwood Green
E. R1799 Traditional Vase $10\frac{1}{4}$" x $5\frac{1}{4}$" - Pearl Shell
F. R1810 Pheasant Figurine $9\frac{1}{4}$" x $6\frac{1}{2}$" x $12\frac{1}{4}$" Carnival
G. R1811 Cock Pheasant Figurine $10\frac{1}{2}$" x $3\frac{3}{4}$" x 14" Carnival
H. R1812S 13" Two Handled Vase $13\frac{1}{2}$" x 5" Sherwood Green
I. R1796 Classic Bud Vase 8" x $3\frac{3}{4}$" - Royal Blue
J. R1782 Large Lamb Figurine 15" x 18" White Stone Lace
K. R1808 Girl Figurine Planter $9\frac{1}{2}$" x $5\frac{3}{4}$" x $8\frac{1}{4}$" Pearl Shell
L. R1743 Onion Jug Vase $21\frac{1}{2}$" x 6" - Peach Stone
M. R1822 Large Shell Bowl $6\frac{3}{4}$" x $9\frac{1}{2}$" x $14\frac{1}{4}$" Mat White
N. R1774S 7" Round Ashtray - Oyster/Gold Edge
O. R1806 Large Fawn Figurine $21\frac{1}{4}$" x $7\frac{1}{4}$" x $14\frac{1}{2}$" Peach Stone with Gold
P. R1815 12" Pleated Vase - Bittersweet
Q. R1714S-G Rectangular Ashtray 9" x 12" Gold Lustre
R. R1618B-G Rectangular Cigarette Box - Gold Lustre 6" x $4\frac{1}{2}$"

4

R1224   Large Gypsy Girl 6¼" x 16½" x 13"

A.   R1761   Turkey Planter 11" x 10" x 10"
B.   R1698   Horse Planter 6" x 17¼" x 17"
C.   R1709   Elephant Planter 11½" x 18" x 14"
D.   R1742   Egyptian Cat 20"
E.   R1741   Rooster Planter 6¼" x 10" x 19½"
F.   R1692   Large Poodle 20" x 18"
G.   R1697   Donkey Planter 10½" x 17" x 14"
H.   R1762   Rooster 20" x 11"

11

![Haeger]

Designed for Today's Living

A.   R1796   Classic Bud Vase 8" x 3½"
              Bittersweet
B.   R1813S 12" Two Handled Vase - Mat White
C.   R1814S Pleated Vase 15" - White Stone Lace
D.   R1805   18" Draped Vase - Ebony Cascade
E.   R1828   Large Grab Neck Pitcher 21" x 6"
              White Stone Lace
F.   R1804   18" Contemporary Vase - Pearl Shell
G.   R1776W 12" Vase - Green Stone Lace
H.   R1800   One Stem Vase 12" x 4" - Bittersweet
I.   R1781   Diane 10" x 8" - Antique Bronze
J.   R1285   Calla Lily Candleholder 5" x 5"
              Green Stone Lace
K.   R1809   Round Draped Bowl 4½" x 11"
              Green Stone Lace

L.   R1824   Palm Leaf Centerpiece 4" x 5" x 26"
              Pearl Shell
M.   R1817S Pleated Candleholder 4" x 4½"
              Royal Blue
N.   R1816S 9½" Pleated Bowl - Royal Blue
O.   R795   Folded Candleholder 3½" x 3" x 6"
              Peach Stone/Gold
P.   R1794   Folded Console Bowl 5½" x 17½"
              Peach Stone/Gold
Q.   R1826   Large Leaf Dish 3" x 14¼" x 21½"
              Sherwood Green
R.   R1827   Small Leaf Dish 1¼" x 6½" x 11½"
              Sherwood Green
S.   R1807   Rearing Horse Planter
              16" x 6" x 12½" - Ebony Cascade

See price list for wholesale prices and color selection of items shown.

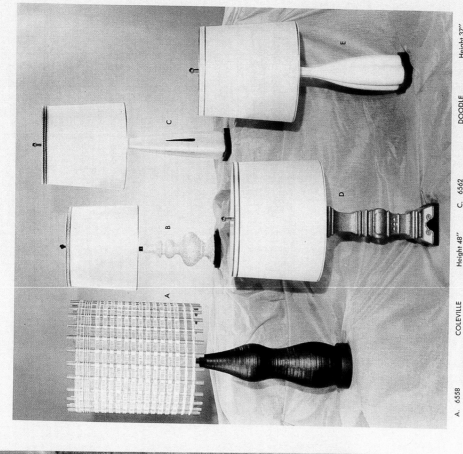

A. 6558   COLEVILLE   Height 48"

White		Winston Star Shade
Peach Stone/Gold		Winston Star Shade
Antique Bronze (Shown)	Gold	Winston Star Shade
Gold Lustre	White	Winston Star Shade
Bittersweet	White	Winston Star Shade

*6558X (See Wholesale Price List)

B. 6563   WILMINGTON   Height 30"

Green Stone Lace (Shown)	White Plastic Shade
Sherwood Green	White Plastic Shade
Tweed	White Plastic Shade
White Stone Lace	White Plastic Shade

C. 6562   DOODLE   Height 37"

Mat White/Gold	White Fabric Shade
Peach Stone/Gold (Shown)	White Fabric Shade
Ebony/Cascade	White Fabric Shade

D. 6555   SHINTO SHRINE CANDLE   Height 34"

Antique Bronze	White Irish Linen Shade
Antique Silver (Shown)	White Irish Linen Shade
White Crackle	White Irish Linen Shade

E. 6554   PANDORA   Height 36"

Peach Stone/Gold (Shown)	White Plastic Shade
Green Stone Lace	White Plastic Shade
Sherwood Green	White Plastic Shade

24

Haeger Flower-ware®

Rings Like Rare Old Porcelain

A.	RG63	6" Square Compote Bowl
B.	RG1	16" Window Box
C.	RG89	6" Jardiniere
D.	RG28	6" Rose Bowl
E.	RG87	12" Round Vase
F.	RG79	4½" Square Planter
G.	RG41	Large Pitcher 5½" x 14½"
H.	RG90	8" Jardiniere
I.	RG56	9" Compote Bowl
J.	RG72	8" Goblet Vase

K.	RG26	Small Glad Vase 10"
L.	RG78	Rectangular Planter 4½" x 8" x 3"
M.	RG42	Medium Flower Planter 4" x 10"
N.	RG65	Small Leaf Bowl 9½" x 6"
O.	RG60	Oval Footed Bowl 3½" x 5½" x 11½"
P.	RG86	16" Pitcher
Q.	RG25	13" Glad Vase
R.	RG68	7" Bud Vase
S.	RG85	Round Candleholder 2" x 4½"
T.	RG80	16" Low Bowl

See price list for wholesale prices and color selection of items shown.

13

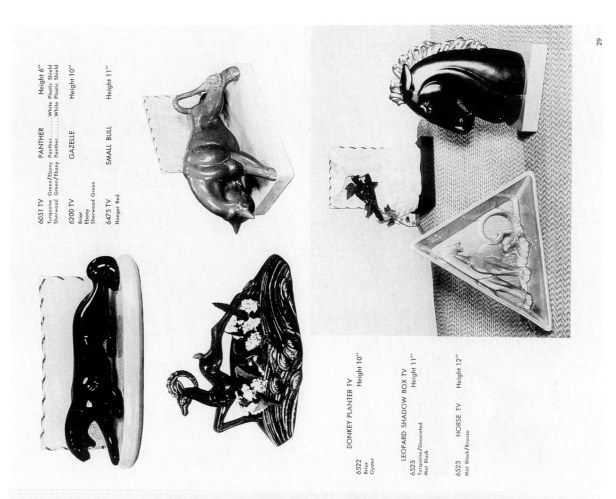

29

PANTHER Height 6"
6051 TV
Turquoise Green/Ebony Panther...White Plastic Shield
Sherwood Green/Ebony Panther...White Plastic Shield

GAZELLE Height 10"
6200 TV
Briar
Ebony
Sherwood Green

SMALL BULL Height 11"
6475 TV
Haeger Red

DONKEY PLANTER TV Height 10"
6522
Briar
Oyster

LEOPARD SHADOW BOX TV Height 11"
6525
Turquoise/Decorated
Mat Black

HORSE TV Height 12"
6523
Mat Black/Bronze

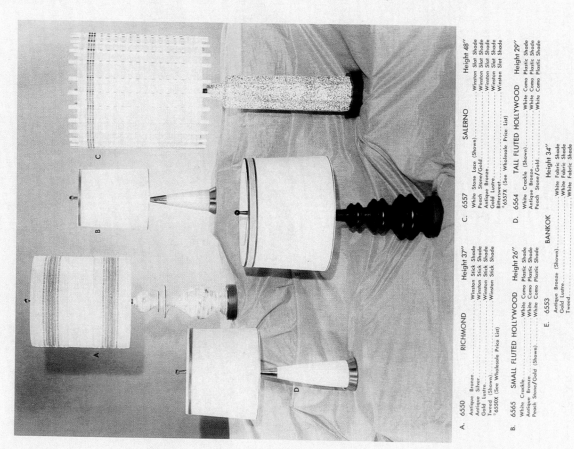

25

RICHMOND Height 37"
A. 6550
Antique Bronze
Antique Silver
Gold Lustre
Tweed (Shown)
*6550X (See Wholesale Price List)

SMALL FLUTED HOLLYWOOD Height 26"
B. 6565
White Crackle
Antique Bronze
Peach Stone/Gold (Shown)

BANKOK Height 34"
E. 6553
Antique Bronze (Shown)
Gold Lustre
Tweed

SALERNO Height 48"
C. 6557
White Stone Lace (Shown)......Winston Slot Shade
Peach Stone/Gold..............Winston Slot Shade
Antique Bronze................Winston Slot Shade
Gold Lustre...................Winston Slot Shade
Bittersweet...................Winston Slot Shade
*6557X (See Wholesale Price List)

TALL FLUTED HOLLYWOOD Height 29"
D. 6564
White Crackle (Shown)........White Como Plastic Shade
Antique Bronze...............White Como Plastic Shade
Peach Stone/Gold.............White Como Plastic Shade

RICHMOND
Winston Stick Shade
Winston Stick Shade
Winston Stick Shade
Winston Stick Shade

SMALL FLUTED HOLLYWOOD
White Como Plastic Shade
White Como Plastic Shade
White Como Plastic Shade

BANKOK
White Fabric Shade
White Fabric Shade
White Fabric Shade

107

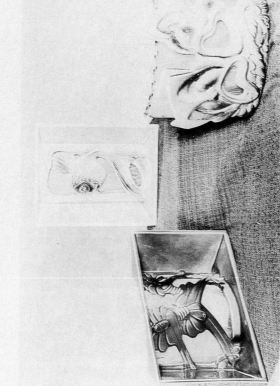

6492 TV   HORSE PLANTER   Height 12"
Ebony/Decorated
Turquoise Green/Decorated
Briar

6514 TV   WOODLAND SILHOUETTE   Height 11"
Turquoise Green/Decorated
Mat Black

6473 TV   FISH SHADOW BOX   Height 11"
Turquoise Green/Decorated
Mat Black
Sherwood Green

6472 TV   COMEDY & TRAGEDY   Height 7½"
Ebony/Decorated
Sherwood Green
Turquoise Green/Decorated

6474 TV   BALLET DANCERS   Height 8"
Turquoise Green/Decorated
Mat Black

31

The Haeger Potteries INC.
7 MAIDEN LANE, DUNDEE, ILLINOIS
Return Postage Guaranteed

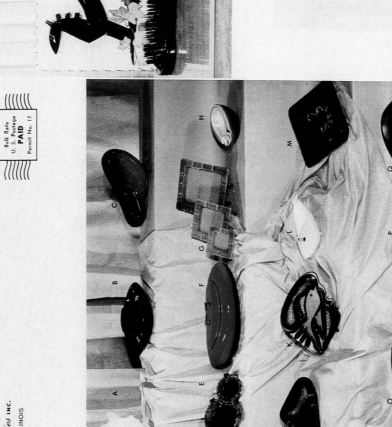

A. R1823   Large Shell Ashtray 2" x 11¼" x 13¼"
Mat White
B. R1766S   Diamond Shaped Ashtray & Cigarette Box
Combination 12½" x 9" - Ebony Cascade
C. R1754H   Modern Ashtray 14" - Carnival
D. R1827   Small Leaf Dish 6½" x 11½" - Pearl Shell
E. R1819 20 21   Nesting Ashtray Set 8¾", 6¾", 4¾"
Sherwood Green
F. R1607   Free Form Executive Cigarette Box & Ashtray
Combination 9¼" x 17" - Bittersweet
G. R1429 30 31   Square Nesting Ashtray Set
8¾", 6¾", 4¾" - Pearl Shell
H. R1787   Egg Shaped Ashbowl 4" x 5¾" x 7"
Royal Blue
I. R1311   Square Divided Ashtray 11"
White Stone Lace

J. R1788A   Triangular Ashtray 2¼" x 6¾" x 10"   Litho in U.S.A.
Antique Bronze
K. R1790   Modern Fish Motif Ashtray 9½" x 13"
Mat Black/Bronze
L. R1791   11" Free Form Ashtray & Cigarette Box
Combination 5" x 11" - Mat White
M. R1786   10" Square Roman Key Ashtray 10" x 10"
Ebony Cascade
N. R1618H   Rectangular Cigarette Box & Ashtray
Combination 6½" x 3" x 10½" - Haeger Red
O. R1735   Shell Ashtray 9½" x 11½" - Turquoise
P. R1665   S Shaped Ashtray/Cigarette Box
Combination 5" x 14" - Pearl Shell
Q. R1789A   Free Form Ashtray and Cigarette Box
Combination 2½" x 10½" x 12"
Antique Bronze

32

The Haeger Potteries Inc.

7 MAIDEN LANE, DUNDEE, ILLINOIS

Return Postage Guaranteed

A. R1843   Candleholder for Console Bowl 4'' - Pumpkin
B. R1842   Console Bowl 18'' x 5¼'' x 2¼'' Pumpkin
C. R1847   Convex Centerpiece Bowl & Candleholders Comb. 13'' x 13'' White Stone Lace
D. R1867S   Candleholders for Bowl 3½'' - Bamboo
E. R1866S   Console Bowl 13''x6''x2¾'' - Bamboo
F. R1828   Large Grab Neck Pitcher 21'' x 6'' Smoke Rings

A. R1845   Duck Figurine 9'' x 6'' Golden Sand
B. R1844   Duck Figurine 9'' x 6'' Golden Sand
C. R1841   Hen Cardinal 7½'' x 6½'' Carnival
D. R1840   Cock Cardinal 10'' x 5½'' Haeger Red & Black
E. R1846   Horse Figurine 13'' x 11'' - Ebony
F. R1855   Girl Night Stand 10'' x 7''
G. R1839   Lamb Figurine 6'' x 6'' Turquoise Green
H. R1838   Lamb Figurine 6'' x 5'' Gloss White
I. R1848   Donkey Planter 13''x 15'' - Pewter

A. R1879S   Ashtray 7¾'' x 11'' - Turquoise Green
B. R1766   Diamond Shaped Ashtray & Cigarette Box 12¼'' x 9'' - Jewel Tone
C. R1850   Oval Ashtray 8½'' - Ebony Cascade
D. R1849   Oval Ashtray 8'' - Ebony Cascade
E. R1870S   Rectangular Cigarette Box 6¼'' x 5'' Turquoise Green
F. R1872S   Five Rest Ashtray 6'' - Bittersweet
G. R873H   Free Form Ash Bowl 8½'' x 8'' Jewel Tone
H. R1873S   Three Rest Ashtray 8½'' Turquoise Green

SEE PRICE LIST FOR WHOLESALE PRICES
AND COLOR SELECTION OF ITEMS SHOWN.

A. RG102   One Stem Vase 10'' - Lilac
B. RG98   Dutch Boy Planter 9'' - Mat White
C. RG99   Dutch Girl Planter 9¼'' - Mat White
D. RG94   Sitting Duck Figurine 6¼'' - Lilac
E. RG95   Flying Duck Figurine 8'' - Lilac
F. RG101   Oval Basket 8½'' - Leaf Green
G. RG103   Rectangular Flower Block 8'' x 5½'' Leaf Green
H. RG97   Oval Bowl 14'' - Earth Brown
I. RG100   Covered Jar 5½'' - Slate
*J. RG92   Handled Bud Vase 7''
K. RG93   Bud Vase 7'' - Slate

* ALL DESIGNS ARE AVAILABLE IN MAT WHITE, MAT BLACK, LEAF GREEN, SLATE, LILAC, AND EARTH BROWN.

A. R1857   Tennessee State Ashtray
           13" x 5"

B. R1856   Michigan State Ashtray
           10" x 9"

C. R1830   Kentucky State Ashtray
           11" x 5"

D. R1858   Texas State Ashtray
           11" x 11"

E. R1893   Maine State Ashtray
           12½" x 8"

F. R1892   Illinois State Ashtray
           11½" x 7½"

WROUGHT IRON
Snack and Ashtray Stand   14" x 17"

A. R1859-60

NOTE . . . Prices subject to change without notice.

SEE PRICE LIST FOR WHOLESALE PRICES
AND COLOR SELECTION OF ITEMS SHOWN.

A. R1882S   Vase 12¼" x 5½"

B. R1877S   Vase 12" x 5½"

C. R1884S   Clock Dial Wall Planter
            8½" x 3"

D. R1876S   Wall Planter 9"

E. R1881S   Hanging Planter 13" x 6"

F. R1878S   Hanging Planter 7½"

G. R1868S   Vase 14"

A. R1504   Lavabo
           Urn 9½" x 15"
           Bowl 16" x 6½"

B. R1506   Lavabo
           Urn 7" x 13"
           Bowl 6" x 6¼"

SEE PRICE LIST FOR WHOLESALE PRICES AND COLOR SELECTION OF ITEMS SHOWN.

7

8

110

Haeger

Designed for Today's Living

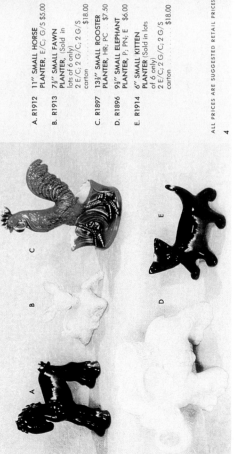

A. R1902 9" FLATSIDED VASE, W/CH; BG $6.00
B. R1901 10" LINED VASE, W/CH; BG $5.00
C. R1937S 12" FRILLED TOPPED VASE, E/C; SR; PC $7.50
D. R1919 10" ONE STEM ORIENTAL VASE, SR; W/CH; WSL .. $3.50
E. R1920 10" OPEN ORIENTAL VASE, SR; W/CH; G/C .. $3.50
F. R1900 6" LINED VASE, W/CH; BG $4.00

A. R1915 15" ONE STEM VASE, SR; W/CH; WSL .. $5.00
B. R1932S 14" ROPE VASE, BG; G/G; P/Gold $6.00
C. R1898 18" VASE, PN; W/CH; P/G $10.00
D. R1916 18" GOURD VASE, SR; G/C; W/CH .. $7.00

A. R1233 13" ACANTHUS BOWL, PC; E/C; T $4.00
B. R1904 20" LOW BOWL & CANDLEHOLDER, PN; BG $8.00
C. R1934S 21" ROPE CANDLEHOLDER, BG; G/G ...... pr. $5.00
D. R1933S 14" ROPE CONSOLE BOWL, BG; G/G .. $5.00
E. R1938S 11" SCALLOPED CENTERPIECE BOWL, PC; P; WSL $4.00

ALL PRICES ARE SUGGESTED RETAIL PRICES.

5

A. R1946 9" FLUTED VASE, E/C; G/C $4.00
B. R1945 7½" FLUTED VASE, E/C; G/C $3.00
C. RG87-X 12" ROUND VASE, E/C; T; PC $4.00
D. R1944 6" FLUTED VASE, E/C; G/C $2.50
E. RG84-X 10" FLUTED VASE, E/C; T; PC $4.00

A. R1912 11" SMALL HORSE PLANTER, E/C; G/S $5.00
B. R1913 7½" SMALL FAWN PLANTER, (Sold in lots of 6 only) 2 E/C; 2 G/C; 2 G/S carton $18.00
C. R1897 13½" SMALL ROOSTER PLANTER, HR; PC $7.50
D. R1896 9½" SMALL ELEPHANT PLANTER, P; PN; E $6.00
E. R1914 6" SMALL KITTEN PLANTER (Sold in lots of 6 only) 2 E/C; 2 G/C; 2 G/S carton $18.00

ALL PRICES ARE SUGGESTED RETAIL PRICES.

4

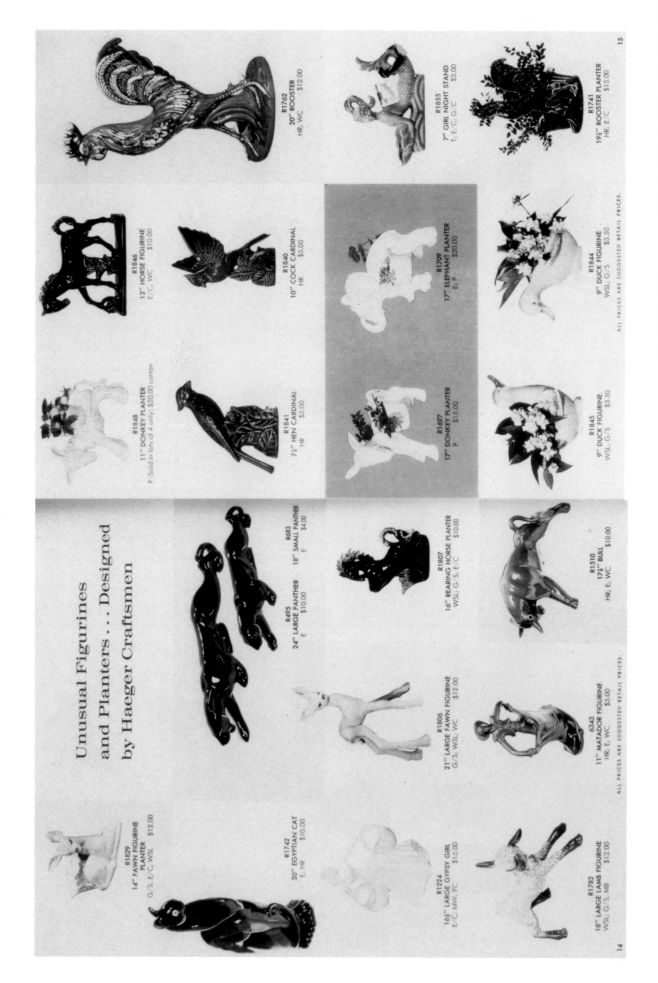

R1762
20" ROOSTER
HR; WC $12.00

R1855
7" GIRL NIGHT STAND
T; E/C; G; C $3.00

R1741
19¾" ROOSTER PLANTER
HR; E/C $15.00

R1846
13" HORSE FIGURINE
E/C; WC $10.00

R1840
10" COCK CARDINAL
HR $5.00

R1709
17" ELEPHANT PLANTER
E; P $20.00

R1844
9" DUCK FIGURINE
WSL; G/S $3.50

R1848
11" DONKEY PLANTER
P; Sold in lots of 4 only; $20.00/carton

R1841
7½" HEN CARDINAL
HR $5.00

R1697
17" DONKEY PLANTER
P $15.00

R1845
9" DUCK FIGURINE
WSL; G/S $3.50

ALL PRICES ARE SUGGESTED RETAIL PRICES.

15

Unusual Figurines and Planters . . . Designed by Haeger Craftsmen

R683
18" SMALL PANTHER
E $4.00

R495
24" LARGE PANTHER
E $10.00

R1807
16" REARING HORSE PLANTER
WSL; G/S; E/C $10.00

R1510
17½" BULL
HR; E; WC $10.00

R1806
21" LARGE FAWN FIGURINE
G/S; WSL; WC $12.00

6343
11" MATADOR FIGURINE
HR; E; WC $5.00

R1829
14" FAWN FIGURINE PLANTER
G/S; E/C; WSL $12.00

R1742
20" EGYPTIAN CAT
E; HR $10.00

R1224
16½" LARGE GYPSY GIRL
E/C; MW; PC $15.00

R1782
18" LARGE LAMB FIGURINE
WSL; G/S; MB $12.00

ALL PRICES ARE SUGGESTED RETAIL PRICES.

14

Royal Haeger
Jardinieres
and Planters

A. R1886S 13" JARDINIERE $13.00
E/C, W/CH, G/C

B. R1887S 8" JARDINIERE $5.00
E/C, W/CH, G/C, PN

C. R1888S 6" JARDINIERE $4.00
E/C, W/CH, G/C, PN

A. R1905 18" BIRD WALL PLAQUE $5.00
PN; E/C, G/F

B. R1906 18½" BIRD WALL PLAQUE $5.00
PN; E/C, G/F

C. R1504 LAVABO - 15" URN - 16" BOWL set $16.00
WSL

D. R1506 LAVABO - 13" URN - 6" BOWL set $12.00
WSL

ALL PRICES ARE SUGGESTED RETAIL PRICES.

18

R1826
21½" LEAF DISH $10.00
PC; E/C, T

R1822
14" SHELL BOWL $7.50
E/C, MW, T

LEFT
R1943
20" PINEAPPLE VASE $25.00
PN; W/CH

RIGHT
R1891S
17" HINDU SNAKE JAR $20.00
G/C, G/S, WSL, SR

R1851
20" RECTANGULAR PLANTER $6.00
WSL; G/S, PN

R1931S
20" UMBRELLA STAND $15.00
P; E/C, G/C

R1811
14" COCK PHEASANT FIGURINE $5.00
HR; MW

R1810
12" PHEASANT FIGURINE $5.00
HR; MW

ALL PRICES ARE SUGGESTED RETAIL PRICES.

17

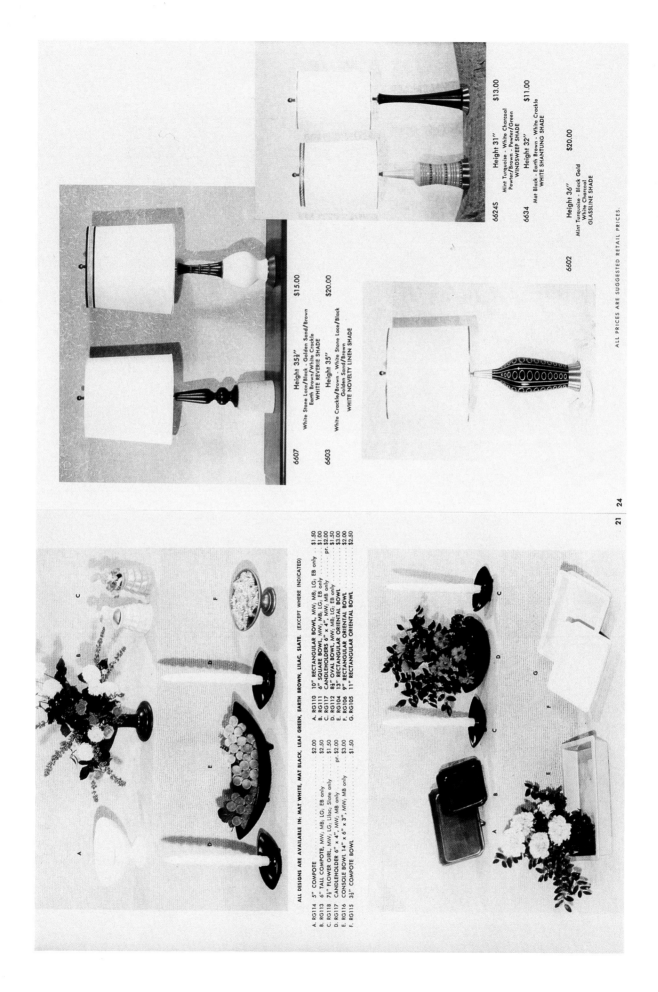

6607
Height 35½" $15.00
White Stone Lace/Black - Golden Sand/Brown
Earth Brown/White Crackle
WHITE REVERIE SHADE

6603
Height 35" $20.00
White Crackle/Brown - White Stone Lace/Black
Golden Sand/Brown
WHITE NOVELTY LINEN SHADE

6624S
Height 31" $13.00
Mint Turquoise - White Charcoal
Pewter/Brown - Pewter/Green
WINDSWEEP SHADE

6634
Height 32" $11.00
Mat Black - Earth Brown - White Crackle
WHITE SHANTUNG SHADE

6602
Height 36" $20.00
Mint Turquoise - Black Gold
White Charcoal
GLASSLINE SHADE

ALL PRICES ARE SUGGESTED RETAIL PRICES.

21   24

ALL DESIGNS ARE AVAILABLE IN: MAT WHITE, MAT BLACK, LEAF GREEN, EARTH BROWN, LILAC, SLATE. (EXCEPT WHERE INDICATED)

A. RG114 5" COMPOTE $2.00
B. RG113 6" TALL COMPOTE, MW; MB, LG; EB only $2.50
C. RG118 7½" FLOWER GIRL, MW; LG; Lilac; Slate only $1.50
D. RG117 CANDLEHOLDER 6" x 4", MW; MB only .... pr. $2.00
E. RG116 CONSOLE BOWL 14" x 6" x 3", MW; MB only $3.00
F. RG115 3½" COMPOTE BOWL $1.50

A. RG110 10" RECTANGULAR BOWL, MW; MB, LG; EB only $1.50
B. RG111 6" SQUARE BOWL, MW; MB, LG; EB only $1.00
C. RG117 CANDLEHOLDERS 6" x 4", MW; MB only ...... pr. $2.00
D. RG112 8½" OVAL BOWL, MW; MB, LG; EB only $1.50
E. RG104 13" RECTANGULAR ORIENTAL BOWL $3.00
F. RG106 9" RECTANGULAR ORIENTAL BOWL $2.00
G. RG105 11" RECTANGULAR ORIENTAL BOWL $2.50

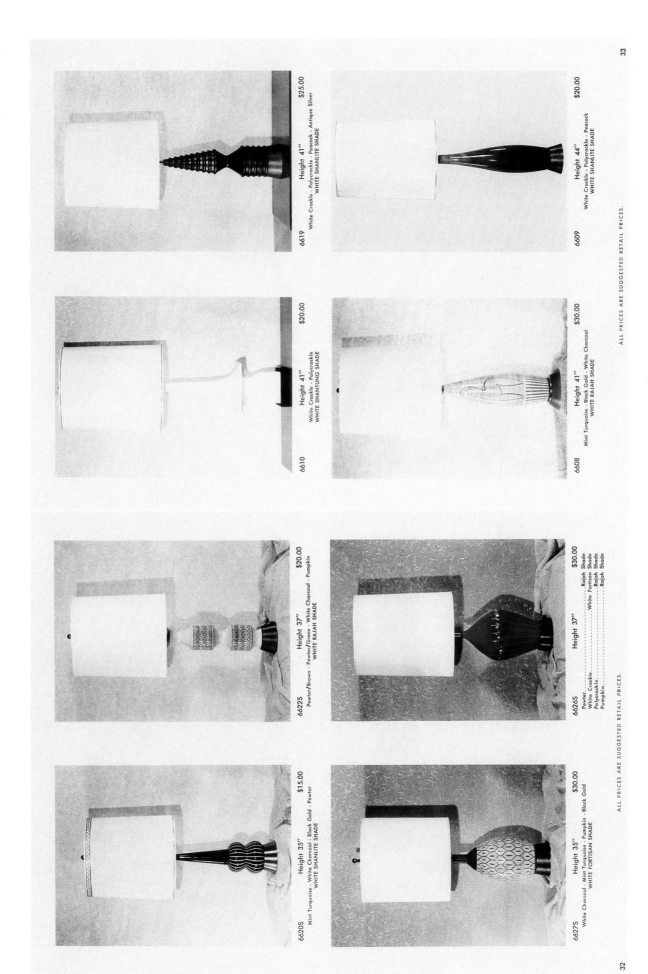

6619
Height 41"
White Crackle - Polycrackle - Peacock - Antique Silver
WHITE SHANLITE SHADE
$25.00

6609
Height 44"
White Crackle - Polycrackle - Peacock
WHITE SHANLITE SHADE
$20.00

6610
Height 41"
White Crackle - Polycrackle
WHITE SHANTUNG SHADE
$20.00

6608
Height 41"
Mint Turquoise - Black Gold - White Charcoal
WHITE RAJAH SHADE
$30.00

ALL PRICES ARE SUGGESTED RETAIL PRICES.

6622S
Height 37"
Pewter/Brown - Pewter/Green - White Charcoal - Pumpkin
WHITE RAJAH SHADE
$20.00

6626S
Height 37"
Pewter................Rajah Shade
White Crackle........White Fortisan Shade
Polycrackle..........Rajah Shade
Pumpkin..............Rajah Shade
$30.00

6620S
Height 35"
Mint Turquoise - White Charcoal - Black Gold - Pewter
WHITE SHANLITE SHADE
$15.00

6627S
Height 35"
White Charcoal - Mint Turquoise - Pumpkin - Black Gold
WHITE FORTISAN SHADE
$30.00

ALL PRICES ARE SUGGESTED RETAIL PRICES.

32

115

The **Haeger** *Potteries* INC.
7 MAIDEN LANE, DUNDEE, ILLINOIS
Return Postage Guaranteed

A. R1926 16½″ EXECUTIVE ASHTRAY COMB.,
PN; BG $10.00
B. R1665 14″ S SHAPED ASHTRAY COMB.,
E/C; RT; G/C $5.50
C. R1929 13″ RECTANGULAR ASHTRAY COMB.,
PN; BG $7.00
D. R1899 21″ SCULPTURED ASHTRAY,
RT; JT; EM $5.00

A. R1756 14″ LEADER ASHTRAY,
E; T; WC, DG $2.00
B. R1894 7″ ASHTRAY,
WSL; T; PN; WC; DG $1.50
C. R1942S 7″ ROUND ASHTRAY,
E/C; PN; PC $2.00
D. R1836S 10″ ASH BOWL, T; E/C; G/C; JT $2.00
E. R1941S 6″ ROUND ASHTRAY,
G/C; E/C; PN $2.00

ALL PRICES ARE SUGGESTED RETAIL PRICES.

A. R1940S 7½″ ROUND ASHTRAY, E; T; DG $1.50
B. R1911 7″ Ashtray, MW; EB; LG $3.00
C. R1910 12″ WHALE ASHTRAY, T; E; PC $3.00
D. R1907 11½″ FREE FORM ASHTRAY,
G/C; E/C; WC $2.50
E. R1909 10″ ROUND ASHTRAY,
WC; E; DG $2.00
F. R1939S 10″ RECTANGULAR ASHTRAY,
WC; EM; PN $2.50

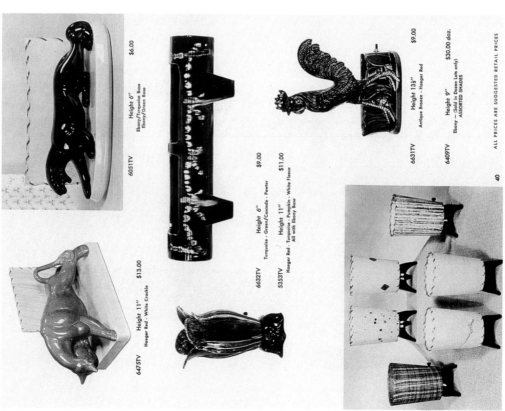

6051TV Height 6″ $6.00
Ebony/Turquoise Base
Ebony/Green Base

6475TV Height 11″ $13.00
Haeger Red - White Crackle

6653ZTV Height 6″ $9.00
Turquoise - Green/Cascade - Pewter

5353TV Height 11″ $11.00
Haeger Red - Turquoise - Pumpkin - White Fleece
All with Ebony Base

6631TV Height 13½″ $9.00
Antique Bronze - Haeger Red

6409TV Height 9″ $30.00 doz.
Ebony — (Sold in Dozen Lots only)
ASSORTED SHADES

ALL PRICES ARE SUGGESTED RETAIL PRICES

40

116

307 8" BOWL $4.00
Beige Agate, Jade Crackle,
Persimmon Texture

310-H 18½" DOUBLE
SHELL BOWL $7.00
Jade Crackle, Turquoise
Blue, Ebony/Cascade

311 7" DOUBLE SHELL
CANDLEHOLDER $5.00 pr.
Jade Crackle, Turquoise
Blue, Ebony/Cascade

306 12" BOWL $6.00
Beige Agate, Jade Crackle,
Persimmon Texture

R1923 5½" CANDLEHOLDER $6.00 pr.
Black Gold, White Charcoal,
Turquoise Blue

R1922 12½" CONSOLE BOWL $6.00
Black Gold, White Charcoal,
Turquoise Blue

A. 808-H 16½" LEAF DISH $5.00
Dark Green, Ebony/Cascade, Beige Agate

B. 301-H 15" SPIRAL BOWL $7.00
White Charcoal, Jade Crackle,
Ebony/Jeweltone, Haeger Red

C. 305 14" FOLDED BOWL $6.00
Persimmon Texture, Turquoise Blue/Black,
Beige Agate

D. 302-H 16" BOWL WITH HANDLE $7.00
Green/Cascade, Ebony/Cascade,
Haeger Red, Turquoise Blue

E. 807-H 20½" LOBSTER DISH $7.50
Haeger Red

RG101-X 8½" OVAL BASKET $3.00
White Charcoal

ALL PRICES ARE SUGGESTED RETAIL PRICES.

A. 107 12½" FREE FORM ASHTRAY $2.50
Beige Agate, Ebony/Cascade, White Crackle

B. 101-H 12" FISH ASHTRAY $5.00
Emeraldtone, Ebony/Jeweltone, Azure Crackle

C. 102-H 13" BUTTERFLY ASHTRAY $5.00
Ebony/Cascade, Green/Cascade

D. 104 12½" SNUFFER SAFETY
ASHTRAY $3.00
Turquoise Blue/Black, Dark Green/Turquoise
Blue, White Crackle/Mat Black

E. SP-12 13½" PALLET ASHTRAY $2.00
Green/Cascade, Ebony/Cascade,
White Crackle

A. R1945 7" FLUTED VASE $3.00
Ebony/Cascade, Green/Cascade
Beige Agate

B. R1746 6" CANDLEHOLDERS .... $3.00 pr.
Green/Cascade, Ebony/Cascade

C. R1745 14" CONSOLE BOWL $3.00
Green/Cascade, Ebony/Cascade

D. 305 14" FOLDED BOWL $6.00
Persimmon Texture, Turquoise Blue/Black,
Beige Agate

E. 309 6" BOAT SHAPED
CANDLEHOLDER .... $5.00 pr.
Turquoise Blue/Black, White Stone Lace,
Persimmon Texture

F. 308 18½" BOAT SHAPED BOWL $7.00
Turquoise Blue/Black, White Stone Lace,
Persimmon Texture

G. 301-H 15" SPIRAL BOWL $7.00
White Charcoal, Jade Crackle,
Ebony/Jeweltone, Haeger Red

A. 312-H 18" SWAN BOWL $10.00
Jade Crackle, Ebony/Cascade, Beige Agate

B. 406 13" FOLDED VASE $6.00
Turquoise Blue, Beige Agate, Ebony/Cascade

C. 410-H 23" VASE WITH SPIRAL $10.00
Haeger Red, White Crackle, Azure Crackle

D. 405 17" GLADIOLA VASE $10.00
White Stone Lace, Persimmon Texture,
Gloss White

E. 408 18½" VASE WITH HANDLE $6.00
(In Lots of 6 - $5.00)
Turquoise Blue, Ebony/Cascade,
Green/Cascade

ALL PRICES ARE SUGGESTED RETAIL PRICES.

117

Handsome Wall Decorations by Haeger

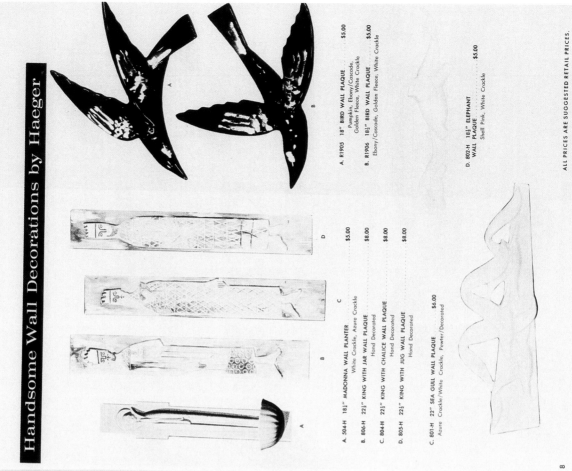

A. R1905 18" BIRD WALL PLAQUE $5.00
        Pumpkin, Ebony/Cascade,
        Golden Fleece, White Crackle

B. R1906 18½" BIRD WALL PLAQUE $5.00
        Ebony/Cascade, Golden Fleece, White Crackle

D. 802-H 18½" ELEPHANT
        WALL PLAQUE $5.00
        Shell Pink, White Crackle

A. 504-H 18½" MADONNA WALL PLANTER $5.00
        White Crackle, Azure Crackle

B. 806-H 22½" KING WITH JAR WALL PLAQUE ... $8.00
        Hand Decorated

C. 804-H 22½" KING WITH CHALICE WALL PLAQUE .. $8.00
        Hand Decorated

D. 805-H 22½" KING WITH JUG WALL PLAQUE ... $8.00
        Hand Decorated

C. 801-H 22" SEA GULL WALL PLAQUE $6.00
        Azure Crackle/White, Pewter/Decorated

7   8

601-H 18¼" POODLE $10.00
        Pink/White, Mat Black/White

505 12" x 23" MERMAID PLANTER $15.00
        Jade Crackle, Beige Agate

404-H 10½" DUCK VASE $5.00
        Haeger Red, Persimmon Texture,
        Jade Crackle

401-H-X 4" QUAIL $2.00
        Persimmon Texture, White
        Charcoal, Haeger Red

503-H 19" x 17" DOLPHIN PLANTER $25.00
        Ebony/Cascade, Jade Crackle

A. 403-H 12½" ROOSTER
        VASE $6.00
        Persimmon Texture, Jade
        Crackle, Haeger Red

B. 401-H 8½" QUAIL VASE $5.00
        Persimmon Texture, White
        Charcoal, Haeger Red

C. 402-H 8½" x 15"
        QUAIL VASE $5.00
        Ebony/Cascade, Green/Cascade,
        Haeger Red

D. 502-H 13" BULL
        FIGHTER PLANTER $7.00
        Haeger Red, Ebony/Cascade

E. 501-H 21½" BULL
        PLANTER $15.00
        Haeger Red, Ebony

118

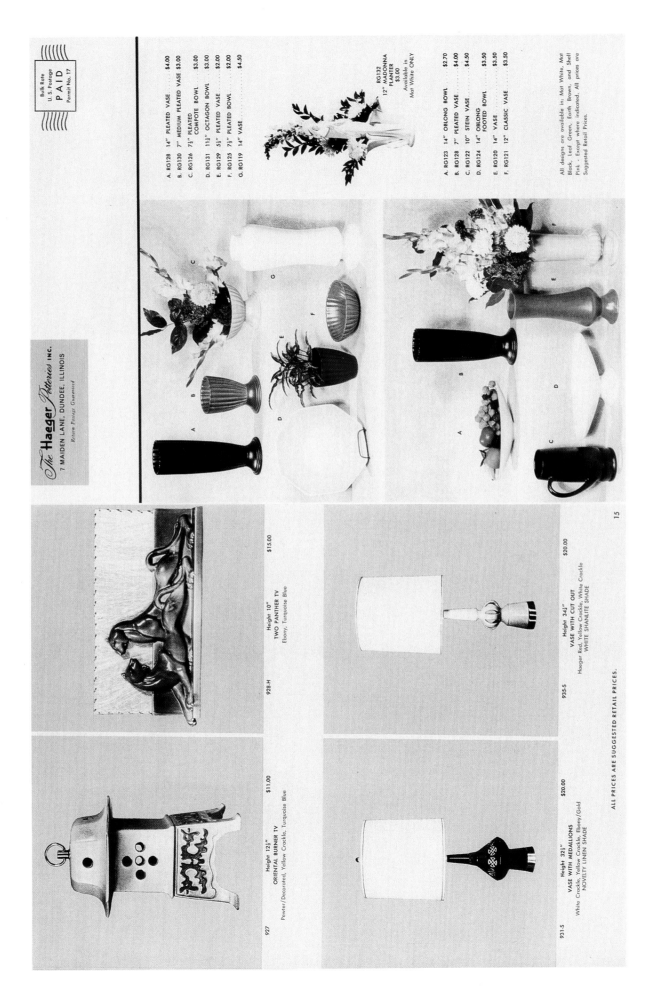

Bulk Rate
U. S. Postage
PAID
Permit No. 17

The Haeger Potteries Inc.
7 MAIDEN LANE, DUNDEE, ILLINOIS
Return Postage Guaranteed

A. RG128 14" PLEATED VASE $4.00
B. RG130 7" MEDIUM PLEATED VASE $3.00
C. RG126 7½" PLEATED COMPOTE BOWL $3.00
D. RG131 11½" OCTAGON BOWL $3.00
E. RG129 5½" PLEATED VASE $2.00
F. RG125 7½" PLEATED BOWL $2.00
G. RG119 14" VASE $4.50

RG132
12" MADONNA
PLANTER
$3.00
Available in
Mat White ONLY

A. RG123 14" OBLONG BOWL $2.70
B. RG128 7" PLEATED VASE $4.00
C. RG122 10" STEIN VASE $4.50
D. RG124 14" OBLONG FOOTED BOWL $3.50
E. RG120 14" VASE $3.50
F. RG121 12" CLASSIC VASE $3.50

All designs are available in: Mat White, Mat Black, Leaf Green, Earth Brown, and Shell Pink. - Except where indicated. All prices are Suggested Retail Prices.

927
Height 12½"
ORIENTAL BURNER TV
$11.00
Pewter/Decorated, Yellow Crackle, Turquoise Blue

928-H
Height 10"
TWO PANTHER TV
$15.00
Ebony, Turquoise Blue

931-S
Height 32½"
VASE WITH MEDALLIONS
$20.00
White Crackle, Yellow Crackle, Ebony/Gold
NOVELTY LINEN SHADE

935-S
Height 34½"
VASE WITH CUT OUT
$20.00
Haeger Red, Yellow Crackle, White Crackle
WHITE SHANLITE SHADE

ALL PRICES ARE SUGGESTED RETAIL PRICES.

15

814-H-X   Horsehead mounted on
            1" plywood 11" x 30" $21.00
814-H   17" Horsehead $15.00
            Mat Black/Gold, Silver/Copper
            Antique Bronze/Gold
R1941-S   6" Round Ashtray $2.00
            Ebony/Cascade, White Crackle,
            Turquoise Blue, Orange
R1941-S   Gold Tweed 22K Gold $3.00

306   12" Bowl $6.00
            Persian Blue, Jade Crackle, Green Texture
306   Gold Tweed 22K Gold $7.50

818-817-H-X $50.00 per set
            Fighting Cock Plaques mounted on
            1" plywood 32" x 16"
818-H   20" Fighting Cock $20.00
817-H   22" Fighting Cock Plaque $20.00
            Majolica

815-H   15½" Candleholder Compote $10.00
            Mother of Pearl, Haeger Red, Antique Silver
815-H   Gold Tweed 22K Gold $12.00
118   7½" Square Ashtray $3.50
            Ebony/Jeweltone, Jade Crackle, Emeraldstone
118   Gold Tweed 22K Gold $4.50

816-H   22" Bull Fighter Plaque $25.00
            Majolica

301-H   15" Spiral Bowl $7.50
            Ebony/Jeweltone, Purple/Jeweltone
            Emeraldstone
301-H   Gold Tweed, 22K Gold $9.00

3

Haeger
ARTWARE AND LAMPS
the Great Name in American Ceramics
1960

The **Haeger** *Potteries* INC.   7 MAIDEN LANE, DUNDEE, ILLINOIS

120

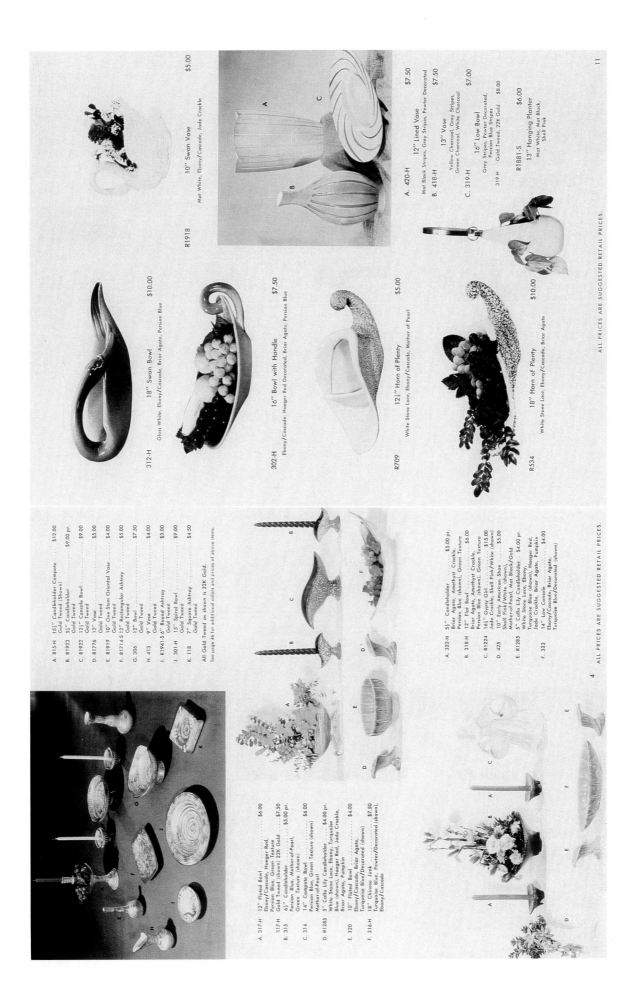

R1918
10" Swan Vase $5.00
Mat White, Ebony/Cascade, Jade Crackle

A. 420-H 12" Lined Vase $7.50
Mat Black Stripes, Grey Stripes, Pewter Decorated

B. 418-H 13" Vase $7.50
Yellow Charcoal, Grey Stripes, Green Charcoal, White Charcoal

C. 319-H 16" Low Bowl $7.00
Grey Stripes, Pewter Decorated, Persian Blue Stripes
319-H Gold Tweed, 22K Gold $8.00

R1881-S 13" Hanging Planter $6.00
Mat White, Mat Black, Shell Pink

ALL PRICES ARE SUGGESTED RETAIL PRICES.

312-H 18" Swan Bowl $10.00
Gloss White, Ebony/Cascade, Briar Agate, Persian Blue

302-H 16" Bowl with Handle $7.50
Ebony/Cascade, Haeger Red Decorated, Briar Agate, Persian Blue

R709 12½" Horn of Plenty $5.00
White Stone Lace, Ebony/Cascade, Mother of Pearl

R534 18" Horn of Plenty $10.00
White Stone Lace, Ebony/Cascade, Briar Agate

A. 815-H 15½" Candleholder Compote $12.00
Gold Tweed (Shown)
B. R1923 5½" Candleholder .... $9.00 pr.
Gold Tweed
C. R1922 12½" Console Bowl $9.00
Gold Tweed
D. R1776 12" Vase $5.00
Gold Tweed
E. R1919 10" One Stem Oriental Vase $4.00
Gold Tweed
F. R1714-S 12" Rectangular Ashtray $5.00
Gold Tweed
G. 306 12" Bowl $7.50
Gold Tweed
H. 413 9" Vase $4.00
Gold Tweed
I. R1941-S 6" Round Ashtray $3.00
Gold Tweed
J. 301-H 15" Spiral Bowl $9.00
Gold Tweed
K. 118 7" Square Ashtray $4.50
Gold Tweed

All Gold Tweed as shown is 22K Gold.
See page 46 for additional colors and prices of above items.

A. 322-H 5½" Candleholder .... $5.00 pr.
Briar Agate, Amethyst Crackle, Persian Blue (shown), Green Texture
B. 318-H 12" Flat Bowl $6.00
Briar Agate, Amethyst Crackle, Persian Blue (shown), Green Texture
C. R1224 16½" Gypsy Girl $15.00
Jade Crackle, Shell Pink/White (shown)
D. 425 10" Early American Shoe $5.00
Shell Pink/White (shown), Mother-of-Pearl, Mat Black/Gold
E. R1285 5" Calla Lily Candleholder .... $4.00 pr.
White Stone Lace, Ebony, Turquoise Blue (shown), Haeger Red, Jade Crackle, Briar Agate, Pumpkin
F. 323 14" Low Console $4.00
Ebony/Cascade, Briar Agate, Turquoise Blue/Decorated (shown)

ALL PRICES ARE SUGGESTED RETAIL PRICES.

A. 317-H 12" Fluted Bowl $6.00
Ebony/Cascade, Haeger Red, Persian Blue, Green Texture
317-H Gold Tweed (shown) 22K Gold $7.50
B. 315 6½" Candleholder .... $5.00 pr.
Persian Blue, Mother-of-Pearl, Green Texture (shown)
C. 314 14" Compote Bowl $6.00
Persian Blue, Green Texture (shown), Mother-of-Pearl
D. R1285 5" Calla Lily Candleholder .... $4.00 pr.
White Stone Lace, Ebony, Turquoise Blue (shown), Haeger Red, Jade Crackle, Briar Agate, Pumpkin
E. 320 10" Fluted Bowl $4.00
Ebony/Cascade, Briar Agate, Turquoise Blue/Decorated (shown)
F. 316-H 18" Chinese Junk $7.50
Turquoise Blue, Pewter/Decorated (shown), Ebony/Cascade

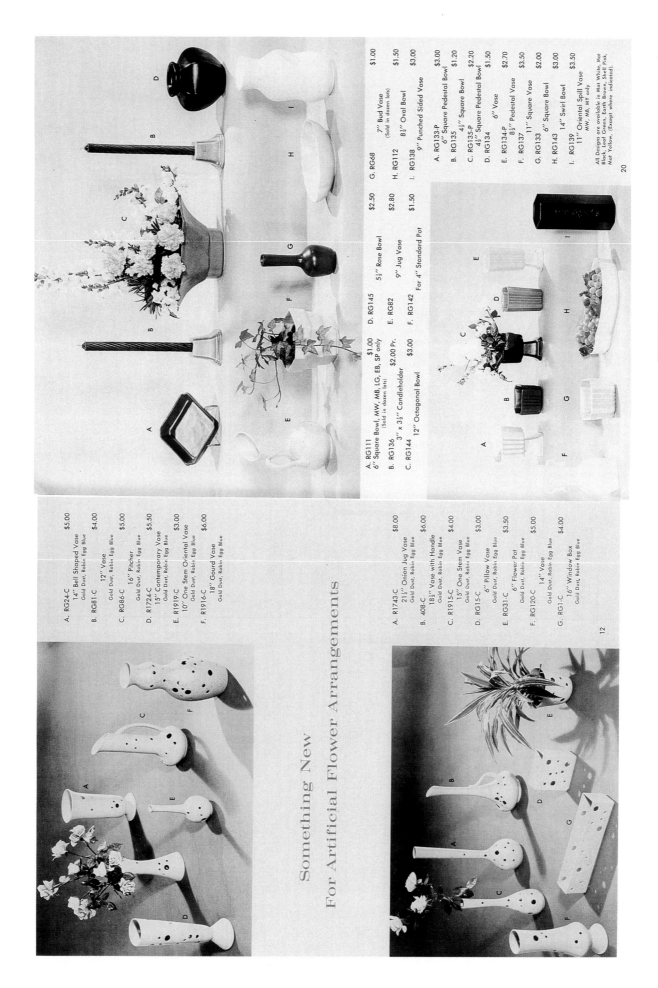

A. RG111   6" Square Bowl, MW, MB, LG, EB, SP only $1.00
(Sold in dozen lots)
B. RG136   3" x 3½" Candleholder $2.00 Pr.
C. RG144   12" Octagonal Bowl $3.00
D. RG145   5½" Rose Bowl $2.50
E. RG82   9" Jug Vase $2.80
F. RG142   For 4" Standard Pot $1.50
G. RG68   7" Bud Vase $1.00
(Sold in dozen lots)
H. RG112   8½" Oval Bowl $1.50
I. RG138   9" Punched Sided Vase $3.00

A. RG133-P   6" Square Pedestal Bowl $3.00
B. RG135   4½" Square Bowl $1.20
C. RG135-P   4½" Square Pedestal Bowl $2.20
D. RG134   6" Vase $1.50
E. RG134-P   8½" Pedestal Vase $2.70
F. RG137   11" Square Vase $3.50
G. RG133   6" Square Bowl $2.00
H. RG143   14" Swirl Bowl $3.00
I. RG139   11" Oriental Spill Vase $3.50
MW, MB, MY only

All Designs are available in Mat White, Mat Black, Leaf Green, Earth Brown, Shell Pink, Mat Yellow. (Except where indicated).

20

A. RG24-C   14" Bell Shaped Vase $5.00
Gold Dust, Robin Egg Blue
B. RG81-C   12" Vase $4.00
Gold Dust, Robin Egg Blue
C. RG86-C   16" Pitcher $5.00
Gold Dust, Robin Egg Blue
D. R1724-C   15" Contemporary Vase $5.50
Gold Dust, Robin Egg Blue
E. R1919-C   10" One Stem Oriental Vase $3.00
Gold Dust, Robin Egg Blue
F. R1916-C   18" Gourd Vase $6.00
Gold Dust, Robin Egg Blue

Something New
For Artificial Flower Arrangements

A. R1743-C   21½" Onion Jug Vase $8.00
Gold Dust, Robin Egg Blue
B. 408-C   18½" Vase with Handle $6.00
Gold Dust, Robin Egg Blue
C. R1915-C   15" One Stem Vase $4.00
Gold Dust, Robin Egg Blue
D. RG15-C   6" Pillow Vase $3.00
Gold Dust, Robin Egg Blue
E. RG31-C   6" Flower Pot $3.50
Gold Dust, Robin Egg Blue
F. RG120-C   14" Vase $5.00
Gold Dust, Robin Egg Blue
G. RG1-C   16" Window Box $4.00
Gold Dust, Robin Egg Blue

12

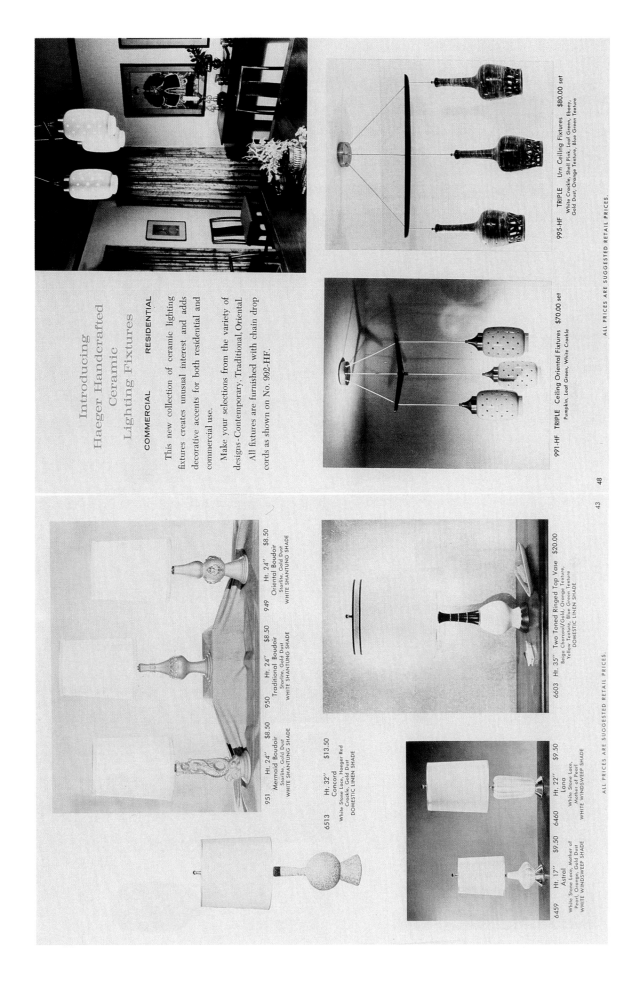

Introducing
Haeger Handcrafted
Ceramic
Lighting Fixtures

COMMERCIAL   RESIDENTIAL

This new collection of ceramic lighting fixtures creates unusual interest and adds decorative accents for both residential and commercial use.

Make your selections from the variety of designs-Contemporary, Traditional, Oriental. All fixtures are furnished with chain drop cords as shown on No. 992-HF.

995-HF   TRIPLE   Urn Ceiling Fixtures $80.00 set
White Crackle, Shell Pink, Leaf Green, Ebony,
Gold Dust, Orange Texture, Blue Green Texture

991-HF   TRIPLE   Ceiling Oriental Fixtures $70.00 set
Pumpkin, Leaf Green, White Crackle

ALL PRICES ARE SUGGESTED RETAIL PRICES.

48

43

951   Ht. 24″ $8.50
Mermaid Boudoir
Starlite, Gold Dust
WHITE SHANTUNG SHADE

950   Ht. 24″ $8.50
Traditional Boudoir
Starlite, Gold Dust
WHITE SHANTUNG SHADE

949   Ht. 24″ $8.50
Oriental Boudoir
Starlite, Gold Dust
WHITE SHANTUNG SHADE

6513   Ht. 32″ $13.50
Concord
White Stone Lace, Haeger Red
Crackle, Gold Dust
DOMESTIC LINEN SHADE

6603   Ht. 35″   Two Toned Ringed Top Vase $20.00
Beige Charcoal/Gold, Orange Texture,
Yellow Texture, Blue Green Texture
DOMESTIC LINEN SHADE

6459   Ht. 17″ $9.50
Astral
White Stone Lace, Mother of
Pearl, Orange, Gold Dust
WHITE WINDSWEEP SHADE

6460   Ht. 22″ $9.50
Lana
White Stone Lace,
Mother of Pearl
WHITE WINDSWEEP SHADE

ALL PRICES ARE SUGGESTED RETAIL PRICES.

123

Bulk Rate
U. S. Postage
P A I D
Permit No. 17

The Haeger Potteries Inc.
7 MAIDEN LANE, DUNDEE, ILLINOIS
Return Postage Guaranteed

A. 811-H 10½" Plume Lighter
(Gift Boxed - $6.30)
White Charcoal, Yellow Charcoal (shown),
Green Charcoal (shown), Jade Crackle,
Ebony/Cascade, Persian Blue $6.00
811-H Gold Tweed, 22K Gold
(Gift Boxed $7.30) $7.00
B. 812-H 10½" Fish Lighter
(Gift Boxed $6.30) $6.00
Persian Blue (shown), Jade Crackle,
Ebony/Jeweltone (shown), Amethyst Crackle
C. 108-H 8" Fish Ashtray
Haeger Red (shown), Purple Jeweltone $2.50
D. 813-H 10½" Classic Lighter
(Gift Boxed - $6.30)
Pumpkin, White Crackle (shown), Dark Green
Turquoise Blue Decorated, Haeger Red $6.00
E. 702 10" Rec. Cig. Box & Ashtray
Ebony/Cascade (shown), White Crackle
(shown), Orange Decorated $5.00

A. 119 14" Sculptured Ashtray
Ebony/Cascade, White Crackle,
Haeger Red (shown) $3.00
B. 118 7" Square Ashtray
Ebony/Jeweltone (shown), Jade Crackle,
Emeraldtone $3.50
118 Gold Tweed, 22K Gold $4.50
C. 107 12½" Free Form Ashtray
Ebony/Cascade, White Crackle,
Pumpkin (shown) $2.50
D. 117 12" Free Form Ashtray
Ebony/Cascade, Turquoise Blue,
White Crackle (shown) $2.00
E. 109-S 7" Square Porch Ashtray
Persian Blue, Haeger Red,
Jade Crackle (shown) $2.50
109-S Gold Tweed, 22K Gold $3.50
F. R1907 11" Free Form Ashtray, White Crackle,
Briar Agate (shown) $2.50

A. 114 12" Violin Ashtray
Ebony/Jeweltone, Haeger Red,
Emeraldtone (shown) $3.50
B. R1894 7" Round Ashtray,
White Stone Lace, Pumpkin,
Shell Pink (shown), White Crackle, Turquoise Blue $1.50
C. 112 5" Free Form Miniature
(Sold in lots of 12)
Ebony/Jeweltone (shown), Purple Jeweltone,
Emeraldtone $1.00
D. 115 8" Free Form Ashtray
Ebony/Jeweltone (shown), Purple Jeweltone,
Emeraldtone $2.00
E. 116 11" Free Form Ashtray
Ebony/Jeweltone (shown), Purple Jeweltone,
Emeraldtone $3.00
112/115/116 Set .... $5.00 set
F. 113 4½" Sculptured Miniature
(Sold in lots of 12)
Haeger Red (shown), Orange (shown),
White Crackle, Turquoise Blue $1.00
113 Gold Tweed, 22K Gold $2.00
G. 111-H 9" Glove Ashtray
Mat White, Ebony/Jeweltone, Purple
Jeweltone (shown), Emeraldtone $2.00
H. 110-H 16" Leaf Ashtray
White Crackle, Persian Blue,
Jade Crackle (shown) $3.00

52

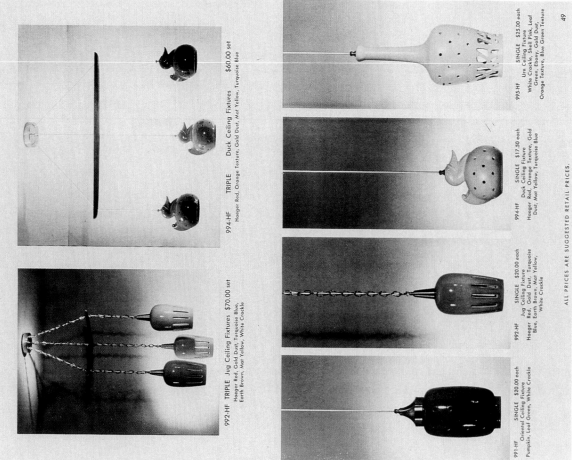

992-HF TRIPLE Jug Ceiling Fixtures $70.00 set
Haeger Red, Gold Dust, Turquoise Blue,
Earth Brown, Mat Yellow, White Crackle

994-HF TRIPLE Duck Ceiling Fixtures $60.00 set
Haeger Red, Orange Texture, Gold Dust, Mat Yellow, Turquoise Blue

991-HF SINGLE $20.00 each
Oriental Ceiling Fixture
Pumpkin, Leaf Green, White Crackle

992-HF SINGLE $20.00 each
Jug Ceiling Fixture
Haeger Red, Gold Dust, Turquoise
Blue, Earth Brown, Mat Yellow,
White Crackle

994-HF SINGLE $17.50 each
Duck Ceiling Fixture
Haeger Red, Orange Texture, Gold
Dust, Mat Yellow, Turquoise Blue

995-HF SINGLE $25.00 each
Urn Ceiling Fixture
White Crackle, Shell Pink, Leaf
Green, Ebony, Gold Dust,
Orange Texture, Blue Green Texture

ALL PRICES ARE SUGGESTED RETAIL PRICES.

49

124

1960 FALL SUPPLEMENT

A. 109-S   7" Square Ashtray
Gold Tweed (Shown), Green Gold Tweed . . $3.50
B. 426-S   6" Oriental Vase
Beige Gold Tweed . . . $4.00
C. R1285   5" Calla Lily Candleholder
Persian Blue (Shown), Amethyst Crackle
(Shown), Moss Green, Turquoise Blue . $4.00 pr.
D. 330   12" Round Fluted Bowl
(Shown), Haeger Red, Briar Agate,
Amethyst Crackle, Pumpkin . . . $5.00
E. 324-S   16" Rectangular Bowl
Ebony/Cascade, Briar Agate,
Turquoise Blue (Shown) . . . $6.50
F. 329-H   20" Pheasant Bowl
Persian Blue, Amethyst Crackle (Shown),
Ebony/Cascade, Haeger Red . . . $8.00
G. RG136-X 3" Candleholder
Decorated (Shown) . . . $3.00 pr.
H. RG131-X 11" Octagon Bowl
Ebony/Cascade (Shown), Briar Agate . $4.00
I. 325-H   17" Shell Bowl
Ebony/Cascade (Shown), Briar Agate . $8.00
Ebony/Cascade, Briar Agate (Shown)

A. RG137-X 11" Square Vase . . . $4.00
Ebony/Cascade, Persian Blue, Moss Green,
Green Texture (Shown)
B. R1919   10" One Stem Vase . . . $3.00
Haeger Red, Amethyst Crackle, White
Lava (Shown)
C. RG68-X   7" Bud Vase . . . $2.00
Persian Blue, Green Texture (Shown),
Orange Texture (Shown), Amethyst
Crackle (Shown), Blue Green Texture
(Shown), White Lava
(Maximum 3 colors to dozen)
D. RG138-X 9" Punch Sided Vase . . . $3.50
Ebony/Cascade, Amethyst Crackle,
Pumpkin (Shown)
E. 430-H   11" Vase . . . $5.00
Amethyst Crackle, Ebony/Cascade
F. RG82-X   9" Jug Vase . . . $3.50
Ebony/Cascade, Persian Blue (Shown),
Green Texture
G. RG145-X 5¼" Rose Bowl . . . $3.00
Ebony/Cascade (Shown), Briar Agate
H. RG114-X 5" Compote . . . $3.00
Ebony/Cascade, Briar Agate (Shown)

A. R1743   21½" Onion Jug Vase . . . $8.00
Haeger Red, Amethyst Crackle, Green
Texture (Shown), Pumpkin, Persian
Blue, White Lava
B. R1752   16" Eccentric Vase . . . $6.00
White Lava, Ebony/Cascade (Shown) . $4.00
C. RG87-X   12" Round Vase . . . $4.00
Ebony/Cascade, Moss Green (Shown),
Briar Agate
D. 410-H   23" Vase with Spiral . . . $10.00
Persian Blue, Green Charcoal, Beige
Charcoal/Gold (Shown)
E. R1916   18" Gourd Vase . . . $5.00
White Lava, Ebony/Cascade (Shown) . $4.00
F. R1776   12" Vase
Green Texture
G. R1724   15" Contemporary Vase . . . $5.50
Green Texture (Shown), White Lava
H. R1915   15" One Stem Vase . . . $4.00
White Lava, Pumpkin (Shown), Green
Texture, Amethyst Crackle
I. R1920   10" Open Oriental Vase . . . $3.50
Ebony/Cascade (Shown), Briar Agate,
Green Texture
J. R1406   12" Fluted Vase . . . $5.00
Green Charcoal (Shown), Moss Green,
Ebony/Cascade
K. R1702   12" Contemporary Vase . . . $4.50
Ebony/Cascade, Green Texture, Moss
Green (Shown), White Lava

2

Haeger ®
the Great Name in American Ceramics

ARTWARE AND LAMPS

The Haeger Potteries INC.   7 MAIDEN LANE, DUNDEE, ILLINOIS

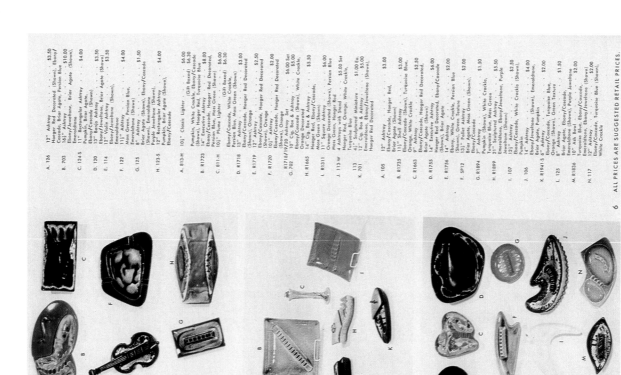

A. 126 12" Ashtray
Haeger Red Decorated (Shown), Ebony/ Cascade, Brier Agate, Persian Blue ... $3.50
B. 703 16½" Ashtray ... $10.00
Emeraldtone, Brier Agate (Shown)
C. 124-S 11" Rectangular Ashtray ... $4.00
Ebony/Jeweltone, Brier Agate, Pumpkin, Brier Agate (Shown)
D. 120 13" Banjo Ashtray ... $3.50
Beige Gold Tweed, Ebony/Cascade (Shown)
E. 114 12" Violin Ashtray ... $3.50
Ebony/Jeweltone, Brier Agate (Shown)
F. 122 9" Oriental Vase ... $4.00
Emeraldtone (Shown)
G. 125 11½" Ashtray ... $1.50
Moss Green, Persian Blue, Emeraldtone (Shown), Emeraldtone
H. 123-S 8" Ashtray ... $4.00
Brier Agate (Shown), Ebony/Cascade
Purple Jeweltone Ashtray
12" Rectangular Ashtray
Pumpkin, Brier Agate (Shown)

A. B13-H 10½" Classic Lighter (Gift Boxed) ... $6.00
Pumpkin, White Crackle ... $6.30
B. R1723 14" Executive Ashtray ... $8.00
Ebony/Cascade, Haeger Red Decorated, Persian Blue, Moss Green (Shown)
C. B11-H 10½" Plume Lighter ... $6.00
Ebony/Cascade, Haeger Red Decorated ... $6.30
Orange Decorated
D. R1718 13" Ashtray ... $3.00
Ebony/Cascade, White Crackle, Persian Blue, Moss Green (Shown)
E. R1719 13" Ashtray ... $6.00
Ebony/Cascade, Hanger Red Decorated (Shown), Orange
F. R1720 10" Ashtray ... $2.00
Ebony/Cascade, Hanger Red Decorated (Shown), Orange
R1718/19/20 Ashtray Set ... $6.00 Set
K. 702 10" Cig. Box & Ashtray ... $5.00
Ebony/Cascade, Hanger Red Decorated
H. R1665 13" Ashtray ... $6.00
Hanger Red, Ebony/Cascade (Shown), Brier Agate
I. R1311 11" Square Ashtray ... $3.00
Ebony/Cascade, Persian Blue (Shown), Orange
J. 113-W 11" Ashtray ... $5.00 Set
Orange Decorated (Shown), Persian Blue
Moss Green, Hanger Red
Hanger Red, Orange, White Crackle
113 Turquoise Blue ... $1.00 Ea.
K. 701 4½" Sculptured Miniature ... $5.00
Ebony/Cascade, Hanger Red Decorated
Emeraldtone, Ebony/Jeweltone (Shown), Hanger Red Decorated

A. 105 12" Ashtray ... $3.00
Ebony/Cascade, Haeger Red, Brier Agate (Shown)
B. R1735 11½" Shell Ashtray ... $3.00
Ebony/Cascade (Shown), Turquoise Blue,
C. R1663 9" Ashtray ... $2.50
Ebony/Cascade, Haeger Red Decorated
D. R1755 11" Ashtray ... $6.00
Haeger Red Decorated, Ebony/Cascade (Shown), Brier Agate
E. R1756 14" Ashtray ... $2.00
Ebony/Cascade, White Crackle, Purple Jeweltone (Shown)
F. SP12 12½" Pallet Ashtray ... $2.00
Ebony/Cascade, Green Texture
G. R1894 13½" Ashtray ... $1.50
Brier Agate, Moss Green (Shown)
H. R1899 21" Sculptured Ashtray ... $5.50
Turquoise Blue, Moss Green
I. 107 10" Ashtray ... $6.00
Haeger Red Decorated, Ebony/Jeweltone, Emeraldtone, Ebony/Cascade, Purple
J. 106 12½" Ashtray ... $2.50
Ebony/Cascade, White Crackle, Purple
K. R1941-S 14" Ashtray ... $4.00
Ebony/Jeweltone (Shown), Emeraldtone, Pumpkin
L. 125 6" Ashtray ... $2.00
Brier Agate, Ebony/Cascade
Brier Agate, Ebony/Cascade
Turquoise Blue, Green Texture
M. R1836 10" Ash Bowl ... $1.50
Emeraldtone (Shown), Purple Jeweltone ... $2.00
N. 117 12" Ashtray ... $2.00
Ebony/Cascade, Turquoise Blue (Shown), White Crackle

ALL DESIGNS ARE AVAILABLE IN GOLD TWEED, GREEN GOLD TWEED, AND BEIGE GOLD TWEED EXCEPT WHERE INDICATED. GOLD TWEEDS ARE 22 K GOLD.

A. R1504/05 Lavabo - 15" Urn 16" Bowl ... $20.00 set
Gold Tweed Only
B. 510-H 19" St. Francis Figurine ... $12.00
Beige Gold Tweed, Gold Tweed Only
C. 421-S 12" Vase ... $6.50
D. RG63-X 6" Oriental Vase ... $3.50
E. 426-S 6" Oriental Vase ... $5.00
F. 429-S 12½" Vase ... $6.50
G. 121 9" Square Vase ... $6.00
Gold Tweed ONLY
121-WF 9" Square Ashtray with Floor Stand ... $11.00
(Not Shown), Gold Tweed ONLY
H. RG114-X 15" Compote ... $4.00
I. 324-S 16" Rectangular Bowl ... $8.00
J. 109-S 7" Square Ashtray ... $3.50
K. 125 8" Rectangular Ashtray ... $2.50
Gold Tweed ONLY
L. 114 12" Violin Ashtray ... $4.50
M. 120 13" Banjo Ashtray ... $4.50
Beige Gold Tweed ONLY
N. R1899 21" Sculptured Ashtray ... $6.50
Ebony/Cascade

A. 424 14" Oriental Vase ... $6.50
Beige Gold Tweed, Gold Tweed ONLY
B. R1916 18" Gourd Vase ... $7.00
C. R1285 7" Calla Lily Candleholder ... $5.00 pr.
Gold Tweed ONLY
D. 319-H 16" Low Bowl ... $7.00
E. B11-H 10½" Plume Lighter ... $7.00
(Gift Boxed)
Green Gold Tweed, Gold Tweed ONLY
F. 317-H 12" Fluted Bowl ... $7.30
G. RG115-X 3½" Compote ... $3.00
H. RG145-X 5½" Rose Bowl ... $4.00
I. 430-H 11" Vase ... $6.00
Green Gold Tweed, Beige Gold Tweed ONLY
J. 113 4½" Sculptured Miniature ... $2.00
K. 325-H 17" Shell Bowl ... $10.00
Green Gold Tweed, Gold Tweed ONLY
L. 125 8" Rectangular Ashtray ... $2.50
Gold Tweed ONLY

A. R1920 10" Open Oriental Vase ... $4.50
Green Gold Tweed, Beige Gold Tweed ONLY
B. R1752 16" Eccentric Vase ... $7.00
C. 322-H 5½" Candleholder ... $6.00 pr.
D. 31B-H 21" Flat Bowl ... $7.00
E. R1724 15" Contemporary Vase ... $6.50
F. 414 12" Vase ... $8.00
G. 813-H 10½" Classic Lighter ... $7.00
Beige Gold Tweed, Gold Tweed ONLY (Gift Boxed)
H. 329-H 20" Pheasant Bowl ... $7.30
Gold Tweed ONLY
J. 702 10" Cig. Box & Ashtray ... $10.00
J. RG68-X 7" Bud Vase ... $6.50
K. 113-W 4 Ashtrays with Stand ... $2.50
113 4½" Sculptured Miniature ... $9.00 set
L. R1730 10" Candy Jar ... $6.50

948-JC   22" BALLISTER $75.00
Double - Gold, Gold Cord
948-JC   22" BALLISTER (Available) $40.00
Single - Gold, Gold Cord

967-JC   13½" POTBELLIED STOVE $85.00
Double - Mat Black/Gold
Black/Red Rope Cord

6594-SC/973-JC   SCULPTURED GLOBE 11½" - Triple - White & Gold $85.00
SMALL VASE 8" - White & Gold Cord
6594-SC/JC (Available)
SCULPTURED GLOBE 11½"
Single - Turquoise & White - White Lava
Fancy Cord with Tassel - $45.00
Plain Cord no Tassel - $35.00

6594-SC/6459-JC   Harlequin $130.00 Set
1 SCULPTURED GLOBE 11½"
Green Cord
5 ASTRAL 7"
1 Lavender, 1 Yellow, 1 Orange Ice,
1 Turquoise, 1 Sweet Pea Pink
Multi Cord

ROYAL HAEGER'S
NEW CEILING FIXTURES
JUANITA CAROL LINE

No electrical installation needed.

The Juanita Carol Line is a completely new idea in ceiling fixtures in a variety of styles and colors.

The fixtures are unique and so practical. They are attached to the ceiling by hooks and are suspended by handsome heavy twisted cords, the extension of one of the cords can be attached to a wall or base plug in any room in the house. This makes the fixtures portable and no special installation is ever needed.

Each one of the fixtures is individual and original because of the uses of cords and tassels. Completely fresh in approach and ideas, these fixtures add a new dimension to lighting and decorating.

1943-JC   20" PINEAPPLE $75.00
Single - Briar Shaded, Leaf Green Top
Green Cord
409-JC   12" PINEAPPLE (Available) $85.00
Double - Briar Shaded, Leaf Green Top
Green Cord

ALL PRICES ARE SUGGESTED RETAIL PRICES.

8

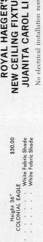

6001   Height 36"   COLONIAL EAGLE $30.00
Gold Tweed . . . . . White Fabric Shade
Gold (Shown) . . . . White Fabric Shade

6015-H   Height 42"   CLASSIC $31.50
Gold Tweed (Shown) . . Embroidered Tree Shade
Green Gold Tweed . . . Embroidered Tree Shade

6015-H   Height 42"   CLASSIC $25.00
Amethyst Crackle . . . Lavender Fabric Shade

6594-SC   Height 33"   CUT OUT GLOBE $31.50
Gold Tweed (Shown) . . Rough Textured Fabric Shade
Harlequin . . . . . . Rough Textured Fabric Shade
Chalk White . . . . . Rough Textured Fabric Shade
Turquoise/White Lava . Rough Textured Fabric Shade

6596-SC   Height 39"   CUT OUT VASE $31.50
Gold Tweed (Shown) . . White Fabric Shade
Harlequin . . . . . . White Fabric Shade
Chalk White . . . . . White Fabric Shade
Turquoise/White Lava . White Fabric Shade

ALL GOLD TWEED LAMPS 22 K GOLD

ALL PRICES ARE SUGGESTED RETAIL PRICES.   7

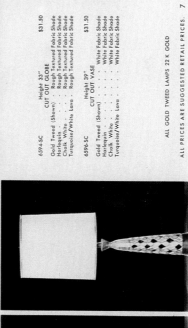
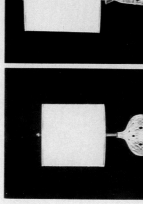
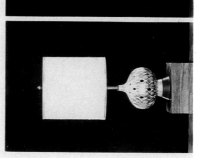

976-H   Height 36"   EPERGNE URN $30.00
Gold Tweed (Shown) . . White Fabric Shade

6002   Height 41"   CONTEMPORARY COLUMN $25.00
Gold Tweed (Shown) . . Seeded Satin Shade
Harlequin . . . . . . Seeded Satin Shade

6002   Height 41"   CONTEMPORARY COLUMN $21.50
White Crackle . . . . Seeded Satin Shade

127

All designs below are available in Gold Tweed, Green Gold Tweed, and Tan Gold Tweed, EXCEPT WHERE INDICATED.

A. 436	18" Urn	$10.00		
	Gold Tweed only			
B. 419	14" Urn	$18.00		
	Gold Tweed only			
C. 405	17" Vase	$10.00		
	Gold Tweed only			
D. 438	18" Vase	$10.00		
	Gold Tweed only			
E. RG 82-X	9" Vase	$4.50		
	Gold Tweed only			
F. RG 150-X	8" Urn	$5.00		
	Gold Tweed only			
G. 328-S	5½" Candleholder	$6.00		
	Gold Tweed only			
H. RG 145-X	5½" Bowl	$4.00		
	Gold Tweed, Green Gold Tweed			
I. 450	6" Bowl	$4.50		
	Gold Tweed only			
J. 340	16" Bowl	$10.00		

"GOLD TWEED" by Haeger

A delightful accent to the home is Haeger's Gold Tweed - Ashtrays - Bowls - Vases - Figurines. Adaptable to all decors.

Each design is beautifully handcrafted and decorated in Gold Tweed, Green Gold Tweed, and Tan Gold Tweed, 22 Karat Gold Tweed glaze.

These designs are best sellers for quick turnover.

ALL PRICES ARE SUGGESTED RETAIL PRICES

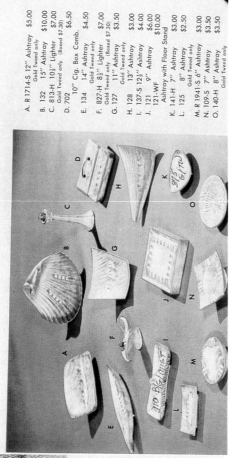

A. R 1714-S	12" Ashtray	$5.00	
	Gold Tweed only		
B. 132	15" Ashtray	$10.00	
C. 813-H	10½" Lighter	$7.00	
	Gold Tweed only	(Boxed $7.30)	
D. 702	10" Cig. Box Comb.	$6.50	
E. 134	14" Ashtray	$4.50	
	Gold Tweed only		
F. 827-H	8½" Lighter	$7.00	
	Gold Tweed only	(Boxed $7.30)	
G. 127	11" Ashtray	$3.50	
	Gold Tweed only		
H. 128	13" Ashtray	$3.00	
I. 137-S	12½" Ashtray	$4.00	
J. 121	9" Ashtray	$6.00	
121-WF	Ashtray with Floor Stand	$10.00	
K. 141-H	7" Ashtray	$3.00	
L. 125	8" Ashtray	$2.50	
	Gold Tweed only		
M. R 1941-S	6" Ashtray	$3.00	
N. 109-S	7" Ashtray	$3.50	
O. 140-H	8" Ashtray	$3.50	
	Gold Tweed only		

Haeger *Artware*
the Great Name in American Ceramics

A. 436 - 18" Urn - Mat White, Surf Green, Green, Green Agate, Lilac Tweed - $10.00.
B. 452 - 14" Vase - Surf Green, Mediterranean Blue, Nutmeg Texture - $5.00.
453 - 16" Vase - Green Agate, Ebony/Cascade, Briar Agate, Mat White - $6.00. (Lots of 6 - $5.00).
D. 408 - 18½" Vase - Turquoise Blue, Ebony/Cascade, Lilac, Moss Green - $6.00 (lots of 6 - $5.00).
E. 451 - 11" Vase - Surf Green, Green Agate, Lilac - $4.00.
F. 449 - 16" Vase - White Lava/Turquoise, Lilac, Surf Green - $5.00. Mediterranean Blue, Nutmeg Texture - $7.00.
G. 438 - 18" Vase - Cotton White/Decorated, Surf Green - $8.00. Gold Tweed - $10.00.
H. 445-H - 10" Vase - Persian Blue, Green Agate - $5.50.
I. 413 - 9" Vase - Ebony/Cascade, Briar Agate, Green Agate, Gold Tweed - $3.00. Gold Tweed, Tan Gold Tweed - $4.00.
J. 439 - 12" Vase - Green Agate, Lilac - $4.00. Gold Tweed - $5.00.

A. R1285 - 5" Candleholder - Ebony/Cascade, Moss Green, Lilac, Turquoise Blue, Haeger Red, Green Agate, Briar Agate, Amethyst Crackle, Pumpkin - $4.00 pr. Gold Tweed - $5.00 pr.
B. 332 - 14" Bowl - Briar Agate, Green Agate, Lilac - $4.00.
C. 336 - 4" Candleholder - Green Agate, Lilac - $4.00 pr. Mediterranean Blue - $6.00 pr.
D. 335 - 9" Compote - Green Agate, Lilac, Mediterranean Blue, Nutmeg Texture - $6.00.
E. R1233 - 13" Bowl - Ebony/Cascade, Briar Agate, Moss Green - $4.00.
F. 316-H - 18" Bowl Moss Green, Ebony/Cascade - $7.50.
G. 337 - 9" Vase - Lilac, Surf Green - $5.50. Nutmeg Texture, Mediterranean Blue - $6.50.
H. 441-S - 71" Vase - Lilac, Surf Green - $5.50. Nutmeg Texture, Mediterranean Blue - $6.50.

A. 334 - 7" Candleholder - Pumpkin, Lilac, Green Agate - $5.00 pr.
B. 333 - 16" Bowl - Pumpkin, Lilac, Green Agate - $5.00.
C. R1746 - 6" Candleholder - Ebony/Cascade, Briar Agate, Lilac - $3.00 pr.
D. R1745 - 14" Bowl - Ebony/Cascade, Briar Agate, Lilac - $3.00.
E. 331-S - 16" Bowl - Lilac, Surf Green - $6.00 Mediterranean Blue, Nutmeg Texture - $7.00.
F. 339 - 9" Bowl - Briar Agate, Green Agate, Lilac - $3.00.
G. 337 - 9" Bowl - White Lava, Haeger Red, Briar Agate - $2.50.

8

ALL PRICES ARE
SUGGESTED RETAIL PRICES

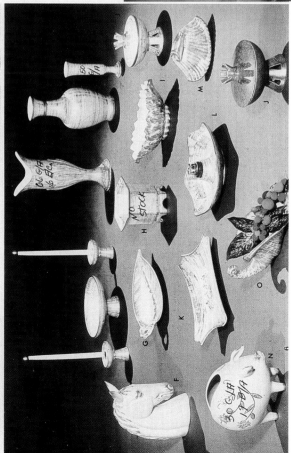

6

A. 3660 - 13" Vase - Mat White, Ebony/Cascade, Green Agate - (lots of 4) - $7.00.
B. 421 - 18" Urn - Moss Green, White Lava, Surf Green - $10.00.
C. R1285 - 5" Candleholder - Pumpkin, Ebony/Cascade, Moss Green, Lilac, Turquoise Blue, Hoeger Red, Green Agate, Briar Agate, Amethyst Crackle - $4.00 pr. Gold Tweed $5.00 pr.
D. 323 - 14" Bowl - Ebony/Cascade, Briar Agate, Lilac, Moss Green - $4.00.
E. R1702 - 12" Vase - Ebony/Cascade, Lilac, Moss Green, White Lava $4.50
F. 415 - 5" Vase - Ebony/Cascade, Briar Agate, Moss Green - (lots of 12) - $1.50.
G. R1946 - 9" Vase - Briar Agate, Green Agate, Lilac, White Lava - $4.00.
H. 130 - 12" Bowl, Turquoise Blue, Briar Agate, Green Agate, Lilac, Ebony/Cascade - $5.00.
I. R1944 - 6" Vase - Amethyst Crackle, Briar Agate, Green Agate - $2.50.

A. R466 14½" Bowl $4.00 Ebony/Cascade, Briar Agate, Pumpkin, Amethyst Crackle

B. R1285 5" Candleholder $4.00 pr. Ebony/Cascade, Moss Green, Lilac, Turquoise Blue, Pumpkin, Hoeger Red, Green Agate, Briar Agate, Amethyst Crackle, Gold Tweed $5.00 pr.

A. 306 12" Bowl Gold Tweed $7.50
B. 807-H 20½" Dish Hoeger Red $7.50
C. R1824 26" Leaf Bowl $8.50 Ebony/Cascade, Pumpkin, Moss Green

A. R1730 - 10" Candy Jar - Ebony/Cascade, Hoeger Red, Amethyst Crackle, Surf Green $5.00, Gold Tweed, Tan Gold Tweed $6.50
B. 444-H .11½" Vase - Cotton White/Decorated, Ebony/Cascade, Green Agate - $5.00
C. 612 - 12" Rooster - Hoeger Red Decorated $6.50, Gold Tweed $8.00
D. 613 - 10½" Hen - Hoeger Red Decorated $5.50, Gold Tweed $7.00
E. 445-H - 10" Vase - Persian Blue, Ebony/Cascade, Green Agate - $5.50.
F. 450 - 6" Bowl - Ebony/Cascade, Hoeger Red, Surf Green - $3.50 Gold Tweed, Mediterranean Blue, Nutmeg Texture - $4.50
G. 706 - 9" Candy Box - Hoeger Red, Ebony/Cascade, Lilac - $4.50.
H. 426-S - 6" Vase - White Lava, Amethyst Crackle, Lilac - $4.00, Gold Tweed, Tan Gold Tweed $5.00
I. 443-H - 10" Vase - Green Agate, Ebony/Cascade, Briar Agate - $4.00, Gold Tweed $5.00.

A. R1752 16" Vase - White Lava, Ebony/Cascade, Green Agate - $6.00, Gold Tweed, Green Gold Tweed, Tan Gold Tweed $7.00.
B. 447 8" Vase - White Lava/Turquoise, Mediterranean Blue, Nutmeg Texture - $3.50
C. R1891 13" Jar - Green Agate, White Lava - $15.00, Mediterranean Blue, Nutmeg Texture - $20.00.
D. 449 16" Vase - White Lava, Turquoise, Lilac, Surf Green - $6.00, Mediterranean Blue, Nutmeg Texture $7.00.
E. 825-H 8" Pot - White Lava, Moss Green, Green Agate - $4.50
F. R1760 21" Candleholder - Ebony, White Lava $4.00 pr.
G. R1759 21" Bowl - Ebony/Cascade, Briar Agate, $6.00
H. R1753 14" Ashtray - Hoeger Red Decorated, Ebony/Cascade, Briar Agate, White Lava - $6.00.
I. 322-H 5½" Candleholder - White Lava, Amethyst Crackle, Green Agate - $5.00 pr. Gold Tweed $6.00 pr.
J. 318-H 12" Bowl - White Lava, Amethyst Crackle, Green Agate $6.00 Gold Tweed $7.00.
K. R1311 11" Ashtray - Hoeger Red Decorated, Persian Blue, Moss Green, White Lava - $6.00
L. 337 9" Bowl - White Lava, Hoeger Red, Briar Agate $2.50
M. 128
N. 129 12" Ashtray - Pumpkin, White Lava, Green Agate - $2.00 Gold Tweed, Green Gold Tweed, Tan Gold Tweed $3.00.

A. 3315 - 16" Bowl - Lilac, Surf Green $6.00, Mediterranean Blue, Nutmeg Texture $7.00.
B. 439 12" Vase - Green Agate, Lilac - $4.00 Gold Tweed $5.00
C. 451 11" Vase - Surf Green, Green Agate - Lilac - $4.00, Mediterranean Blue, Nutmeg Texture - $5.00.
D. 809-H 8" Planter - Lilac, Persian Blue, Moss Green - $3.50.
E. 813-H 10½" Lighter - Ebony/Cascade, Turquoise Blue/Dec. Pumpkin, White Crackle, Hoeger Red, Lilac $6.50, Boxed Gold Tweed $7.00, $7.30
F. 138 8½" Ashtray - Lilac, Green Agate, Briar Agate, Ebony/Cascade, Turquoise Blue, Purple Jewelltone (lots of 12) - $3.00
G. 139 5" Candy Box - Hoeger Red, Ebony/Cascade, White Crackle, Lilac $3.50
H. 706 9" Candy Box - Hoeger Red, Ebony/Cascade, Lilac - $4.50
I. 339 19" Bowl - Briar Agate, Green Agate, Lilac $3.00, White Crackle, Lilac $2.00.
N. SP12 13½" Ashtray - Ebony/Cascade, Briar Agate, Moss Green $2.00
O. 113 4½" Bowl - Turquoise Blue, Lilac, Briar Agate - (lots of 12) $1.00

A. 446 10" Vase - White Lava/Turquoise, Mediterranean Blue, Nutmeg Texture - $4.50
B. R1920 10" Vase - Surf Green, Ebony/Cascade, Nutmeg Texture $4.00
C. 349 15" Vase - White Lava, Orange Texture $4.00, Gold Tweed, Mediterranean Blue, Nutmeg Texture $5.00
D. 452 14" Vase - Surf Green, Green Agate, Lilac $5.00, Mediterranean, Nutmeg Texture $6.00
E. 451 11" Vase - Surf Green, Green Agate, Lilac $4.00, Mediterranean Blue, Nutmeg Texture $5.00
F. 829 9" Pot - White Lava, Surf Green $4.00
G. 330 4" Candleholder - Green Agate, Lilac, Mediterranean Blue, Nutmeg Texture $6.00 pr.
H. 335 9" Compote - Green Agate, Lilac $5.00
J. 129 13" Ashtray - Moss Green, Hoeger Red Decorated $3.00, Mediterranean Blue, Nutmeg Texture $3.00
K. R1714-S 12" Bowl - Ebony/Cascade, Briar Agate, Gold Tweed, Mediterranean Blue, Nutmeg Texture $4.50
L. 459 4" Bowl - Green, Lilac $3.00

HAEGER'S VOLUME SELLING ASHTRAYS FOR QUICK TURNOVER $1.00 - $3.00

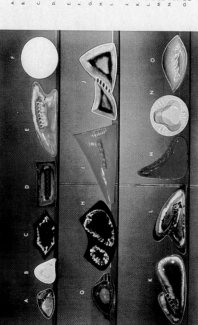

A. 112 - 5" Ashtray - Ebony/Cascade, Purple Jewelltone, Emeraldtone - (Lots of 12) - $1.00
B. 113 - 4 1/2" Ashtray - Haeger Red, Pumpkin, White Crackle, Turquoise Blue, Lilac, Brior Agate - (Lots of 12) - $1.00
C. 138 - 8 1/2" Ashtray - Lilac, Green Agate, Brior Agate, Ebony/Cascade, Turquoise Blue - (Lots of 12) - $1.50
D. 125 - 8" Ashtray - Emeraldtone, Haeger Red, Brior Agate, Moss Green, Lilac - (Lots of 12) - $1.50
E. SP-12 (3)" Ashtray - Ebony/Cascade, Brior Agate, Turquoise Blue, Moss Green - $1.50
F. R1894 - 7" Ashtray - Pumpkin, White Crackle, Turquoise Blue, Ebony/Cascade - $2.00
G. 115 - 8" Ashtray - Ebony/Cascade, Emeraldtone, Purple Jewelltone - $2.00
H. 117 - 12" Ashtray - Ebony/Cascade, Turquoise Blue, White Crackle, Lilac - $2.50
I. 128 - 12" Ashtray - White Lava, Ebony/Cascade - $2.50
J. 129 - 13" Ashtray - Moss Green, Haeger Red Decorated, Ten Gold Tweed - $3.00
K. 130 - 12" Ashtray - Haeger Red, Lilac, Green Agate - $2.00
L. 135 - 12" Ashtray - Brior Agate, Ebony/Cascade, Purple Jewelltone - $2.00
M. R1720 - 10 1/2" Ashtray - Ebony/Cascade, Turquoise Blue, Mediterranean Blue, Nutmeg - $3.00
N. R1941-S - 6" Ashtray - Ebony/Cascade, Turquoise Blue, Moss Green, Lilac - $2.00 Gold Tweed, Tan Gold Tweed, Green Gold Tweed - $3.00
O. R1836 - 10" Ashtray - Turquoise Blue, Ebony/Cascade, Lilac, Emeraldtone - $2.00

LARGE ASHTRAYS FOR THE EXECUTIVE AND FOR LARGE COFFEE TABLES $3.50 - $8.00

R1663 9" Ashtray $2.50
Ebony/Cascade, Haeger Red Decorated, Green Agate, Brior Agate

A. 119 - 14" Ashtray - Ebony/Cascade, Turquoise Blue, Green Agate, Brior Agate - $3.00
B. 140 H 8" Ashtray - Orange Texture, Surf Green - $2.50 Gold Tweed - $3.50
C. 127 11" Ashtray - White Crackle, Brior Agate, Ebony/Cascade $2.50 Gold Tweed - $3.50
D. 105 13" Ashtray - Ebony/Cascade, Haeger Red, Brior Agate, Lilac - $3.00
E. 116 11" Ashtray - Ebony/Cascade, Emeraldtone, Purple Jewelltone - $3.00
F. R1719 12" Ashtray - Ebony/Cascade, Haeger Red Decorated, Pumpkin - $3.50
G. 131 9" Ashtray - Ebony/Cascade, Emeraldtone, Purple Jewelltone - $3.00
H. 129 13" Ashtray - Moss Green, Nutmeg Texture - $3.00
I. 110 H 16" Ashtray - Moss Green, Amethyst Crackle, Persian Blue - $3.00
J. 139 9" Ashtray - Briar Agate, Lilac, Green Agate - $3.00
K. 138-S 11 1/2" Ashtray - Brior Agate, Lilac, Green Agate - $3.00
L. R1735 11 1/2" Ashtray - Ebony/Cascade, Turquoise Blue, Pumpkin, White Crackle - $3.50

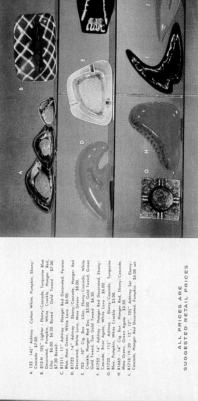

A. 115-112 11", 8", 5" Ashtray Set - Ebony/Cascade, Emeraldtone, Purple Jewelltone - $5.00 set
B. R1714-S 12" Ashtray - Gold Tweed, Mediterranean Blue, Nutmeg Texture - $5.00
C. 113 W 41" Ashtray With Stand - Haeger Red, Pumpkin, White Crackle, Turquoise Blue, Lilac, Brior Agate - $5.00 set
D. 106 14" Ashtray - Ebony/Cascade, Brior Agate, Moss Green, Pumpkin, Emeraldtone - $4.00
E. 122 11 1/2" Ashtray - Moss Green, Pumpkin, Emeraldtone - $4.00
F. 123-S 12" Ashtray - Turquoise Blue, Brior Agate, Ebony/Cascade - $4.00
G. 109-S 7" Ashtray - Moss Green, Amethyst Crackle $2.50 Gold Tweed, Green Gold Tweed, Tan Gold Tweed - $3.50
H. R1718 13" Ashtray - Ebony/Cascade, White Crackle, Haeger Red Decorated, Pumpkin - $3.00
I. 107 (21)" Ashtray - Ebony/Cascade, White Crackle, Amethyst Crackle, Pumpkin - $3.50
J. 134 14" Ashtray - Pumpkin, Ebony/Cascade, Green Agate - $3.50 Gold Tweed - $4.50

ALL PRICES ARE
SUGGESTED RETAIL PRICES

Glazes are burn proof • Excellent safety features • Wide color selection
Each ashtray complete with felt protection

126 12" Ashtray $2.50
Haeger Red Decorated, Ebony/Cascade, Brior Agate, Green Agate, Persian Blue

A. 133 - 14 1/2" Ashtray - Cotton White, Pumpkin, Ebony/Cascade - $7.00
B. B134 - 10 1/2" Lighter - Ebony/Cascade, Turquoise Blue Decorated, Pumpkin, White Crackle, Haeger Red, Lilac - $6.00 $6.30 Boxed - Gold Tweed - $7.00 $7.30 Boxed
C. R1311 - 11" Ashtray - Haeger Red Decorated, Persian Blue, Moss Green, White Lava - $5.00
D. R1723 - 14" Ashtray - Ebony/Cascade, Haeger Red Decorated, White Lava, Moss Green - $8.00
E. 702 - 10" Cig. Box - Ebony/Cascade, White Crackle, Haeger Red Dec. - $5.00, Gold Tweed, Green Gold Tweed, Tan Gold Tweed - $6.50
F. R1755 - 14" Ashtray - Haeger Red Decorated, Ebony/Cascade - $6.00
G. R1725 - 11 1/2" Ashtray - Ebony/Cascade, Turquoise Blue, Pumpkin, White Crackle - $3.00
H. R1665 - 14" Cig. Box - Haeger Red, Ebony/Cascade, Moss Green, Amethyst Crackle - $3.50
I. R1718/19/20 13", 12", 10 1/2" Ashtray Set - Ebony/Cascade, Haeger Red Decorated, Pumpkin - $8.00 set

ALL PRICES ARE
SUGGESTED RETAIL PRICES

*Haeger ashtrays are styled and sized for every use in homes, offices,
and restaurants - Buy by the dozen*

All designs below are available in Gold Tweed, EXCEPT WHERE INDICATED.

A. 439	12″ Vase	$5.00
B. 815-H	15½″ Candleholder Compote	$12.00
C. 424	14″ Vase	$6.50
	Gold Tweed, Antique Bronze	
D. 430-H	11″ Vase	$6.00
	Gold Tweed, Antique Bronze	
E. 325-H	17″ Bowl	$10.00
F. R1224	16½″ Gypsy Girl	$17.50
G. R1730	10″ Candy Jar	$6.50
	Gold Tweed, Antique Bronze	
H. 329-H	20″ Bowl	$10.00

"GOLD TWEED" by Haeger

A. R31	15″ Vase	$13.50
B. 359	14″ Bowl	$13.00
	Gold Tweed, Faience	
C. 346	15″ Bowl	$15.00
D. 465	14″ Vase	$7.50
E. 350-H	11″ Cat Candleholder	$6.00
F. 354-S	6″ Vase	$7.50
G. 461	6″ Vase	$3.50
H. 459	6″ Vase	$3.50
I. 458	6″ Vase	$3.50
J. 467-S	6″ Cut Out Vase	$5.00

A. R1776	12″ Vase	$5.00
B. 322-H	5½″ Candleholder	$6.00 PR.
C. 318	12″ Bowl	$7.00
D. R1752	16″ Vase	$7.00
E. 413	9″ Vase	$4.00
F. R1920	10″ Vase	$4.50
	Gold Tweed, Antique Bronze	
G. 306	12½″ Bowl	$7.50
H. RG115-X	3½″ Compote	$3.00
I. RG114-X	5″ Compote	$4.00
J. R1919	10″ Vase	$4.00
K. RG68-X	7″ Bud Vase	$2.50

ALL PRICES ARE
SUGGESTED RETAIL PRICES

5

VASES

PLANTERS

ASHTRAYS

CANDY DISHES

BOWLS

URNS

Haeger *Artware*

the Great Name in American Ceramics

FIGURINES

JARDINIERES

CENTERPIECES

PITCHERS

CANDLE-HOLDERS

THE HAEGER POTTERIES, INC., 7 MAIDEN LANE, DUNDEE, ILLINOIS

A. 465 - 14" Vase - Green Agate, Lilac, Ebony Cascade - $6.00. Gold Tweed - $7.50.
B. 464 - 9" Vase - Lilac, Avocado - $3.50.
C. 468-S - 15" Vase - Cotton White/Turquoise, Avocado - $7.00. Gold Tweed - $8.50.
D. 469 - 15" Vase - Ebony Cascade, Lilac, Avocado - $4.50.
E. RG63.X - 6" Compote - Cotton White/Mat Turquoise, Cotton White/Mat Yellow, Cotton White/Mat Black - $4.00.

F. 463-H - 10" Vase - Lilac, Avocado - $5.00.
G. 350-H - 11" Cat Candleholder - Avocado, Bitter Orange - $5.00. Gold Tweed - $6.00.
H. 354-S - 11" Bowl - Cotton White/Turquoise, Avocado - $6.00. Gold Tweed - $7.50.
I. 461 - 6" Vase - Briar Agate, Lilac, Green Agate. Lots of 12 - $2.50. Gold Tweed - $3.50.
J. 459 - 6" Vase - Briar Agate, Ebony Cascade, Green Agate. Lots of 12 - $2.50. Gold Tweed - $3.50.
K. 458 - 6" Vase - Avocado, Cotton White/Turquoise, Lilac. Lots of 12 - $2.50. Gold Tweed - $3.50.
L. 351 - 8" Bowl - Cotton White/Mat Turquoise, Cotton White/Mat Yellow, Cotton White/Mat Black - $3.00. Gold Tweed - $4.00.

A. 472 - 14" Vase - Green Agate, Lilac, Cotton White/Turquoise - $6.00. (Lots of 6 - $5.00 ea.). Green Agate, Lots of 12 - $8.00. Gold Tweed - $10.00.
B. 436 - 18" Urn - Cotton White/Turquoise - $8.00. Gold Tweed - $10.00.
C. 353 - 5" Candleholder - Cotton White/Turquoise, Avocado - $5.00 PR. Gold Tweed, Antique Bronze - $7.00 PR.
D. 352 - 14" Bowl - Cotton White/Turquoise, Avocado - $7.00. Gold Tweed, Antique Bronze - $9.00.
E. 358 - 11" Candleholder - Cotton White/Turquoise, Bitter Orange - $3.50. Gold Tweed, Antique Bronze - $4.50.
F. 706 - 9" Candy Box - Lilac, Haeger Red, Cotton White/Turquoise - $4.50.
G. R1730 - 10" Candy Jar - Ebony Cascade, Cotton White/Turquoise, Haeger Red - $5.00. Gold Tweed, Antique Bronze - $6.50.
H. R709 - 121" Horn of Plenty - Cotton White/Turquoise, Bitter Orange - $5.00. Gold Tweed - $6.00.
I. 339 - 9" Bowl - Cotton White/Mat Black, Cotton White/Mat Yellow, Cotton White/Mat Turquoise - $3.00.
J. 711-S - 71" Candy Box - Lilac, Cotton White/Turquoise, Bitter Orange - $5.00.
K. RG178.X - 6" Bowl - Cotton White/Mat Turquoise, Cotton White/Mat Yellow, Cotton White/Mat Black - $2.00.
L. RG179.X - 9" Bowl - Cotton White/Mat Turquoise, Cotton White/Mat Yellow, Cotton White/Mat Black - $2.00.

ALL PRICES ARE
SUGGESTED RETAIL PRICES

9

A. 334 - 7" Candleholder - Lilac, Bitter Orange, Cotton White/Turquoise - $5.00 PR.
B. 333 - 16" Bowl - Lilac, Cotton White/Turquoise, Bitter Orange - $5.50.
C. 473 - 141" Vase - Avocado, Bitter Orange - $7.00. Gold Tweed - $8.00.
D. R1285 - 5" Candleholder - Ebony Cascade, Moss Green, Lilac, Green Agate, Cotton White, Bitter Orange, Avocado - $4.00 PR. Gold Tweed - $5.00 PR.
E. 332 - 14" Bowl - Briar Agate, Green Agate, Lilac - $4.50.
F. 336 - 4" Candleholder - Green Agate, Lilac, Bitter Orange - $4.00 PR. Gold Tweed - $6.00 PR.
G. 335 - 9" Compote - Green Agate, Lilac, Bitter Orange - $5.00. Gold Tweed - $6.00.
H. R1746 - 6" Candleholder - Ebony Cascade, Briar Agate, Lilac - $3.00 PR.
I. R1745 - 14" Bowl - Ebony Cascade, Briar Agate, Lilac - $3.00.
J. R1233 - 13" Bowl - Ebony Cascade, Briar Agate, Moss Green, Bitter Orange - $4.00. Gold Tweed - $5.00.

A. 439 - 12" Vase - Lilac, Bitter Orange - $4.00. Gold Tweed - $5.00.
B. 472 - 14" Vase - Green Agate, Lilac, Cotton White/Turquoise - $6.00. (Lots of 6 - $5.00).
C. R1743 - 211" Vase - Haeger Red, Cotton White - $8.00. Gold Tweed - $10.00.
D. 438 - 18" Vase - Avocado, Cotton White/Turquoise - $8.00. Gold Tweed - $10.00.
E. 473 - 141" Vase - Avocado, Bitter Orange - $7.00. Gold Tweed - $8.00.
F. 359 - 14" Bowl - Avocado, Lilac - $10.00. Gold Tweed, Faience - $13.00.
G. R1730 - 10" Candy Jar - Ebony Cascade, Haeger Red, Cotton White/Turquoise - $5.00. Gold Tweed, Antique Bronze - $6.50.
H. 349-H - 12" Bowl - Lilac, Avocado - $5.00.
I. R1919 - 10" Vase - Haeger Red, Bitter Orange, Avocado, Cotton White/Turquoise - $3.00. Gold Tweed - $4.00.
J. 711-S - 71" Candy Box - Lilac, Cotton White/Turquoise, Bitter Orange - $5.00.
K. 467-S - 6" Vase - Avocado - $4.00. Gold Tweed - $5.00.

A. 452 - 14" Vase - Green Agate, Lilac, Bitter Orange - $5.00. Gold Tweed - $6.00.
B. R31 - 15" Vase - Lilac, Avocado - $11.00. Gold Tweed - $13.50.
C. RG86-X - 16" Pitcher - Ebony Cascade, Moss Green - $5.00.
D. R1702 - 12" Vase - Ebony Cascade, Lilac, Avocado - $4.50.
E. RG81-X - 12" Vase - Cotton White/Turquoise - $4.00.
F. 449 - 16" Vase - Lilac, Cotton White/Turquoise - $6.50. Gold Tweed - $7.00.
G. 408 - 181" Vase - Ebony Cascade, Bitter Orange, Lilac, Moss Green - $6.00. (Lots of 6 - $5.00).
H. 450 - 6" Bowl - Haeger Red, Bitter Orange, Lilac, Cotton White/Turquoise - $3.50. Gold Tweed - $4.50.
I. 337 - 9" Bowl - Haeger Red, Lilac, Cotton White/Turquoise - $2.50.
J. RG114-X - 5" Compote - Ebony Cascade, Briar Agate, Green Agate, Cotton White/Turquoise, Bitter Orange - $3.00. Gold Tweed - $4.00.
K. RG82-X - 9" Vase - Ebony Cascade, Green Agate - $3.50. Gold Tweed - $4.50.

ALL PRICES ARE
SUGGESTED RETAIL PRICES

8

HAEGER'S VOLUME SELLING ASHTRAYS FOR QUICK TURNOVER ... BUY BY THE DOZEN

Glazes are burn proof • Excellent safety features • Wide color selection • Each ashtray complete with felt protection

A. 113   4½" Ashtray $1.00
Haeger Red, Cotton White, Bitter Orange
(Lots of 12)

B. 138   8½" Ashtray $1.00
Lilac, Green Agate, Briar Agate,
Ebony Cascade, Bitter Orange
(Lots of 12)

C. 160   7" Ashtray $2.00
Ebony Cascade, Bitter Orange, Green Agate

D. 156   8" Ashtray $2.00
Briar Agate, Bitter Orange, Green Agate
Gold Tweed - $3.00

E. 125   8" Ashtray $1.50
Ebony Cascade, Briar Agate,
Green Agate, Haeger Red
(Lots of 12)

F. R1894   7" Ashtray $1.50
Gold Tweed, Antique Bronze - $2.50

G. 5P-12   13½" Ashtray $2.00
Ebony Cascade, Briar Agate, Moss Green, Lilac

H. 135   12" Ashtray $2.00
Briar Agate, Ebony Cascade, Cotton White

I. 130   12" Ashtray $2.00
Haeger Red, Lilac, Cotton White, Green Agate

J. 117   12" Ashtray $2.00
Ebony Cascade, Bitter Orange, Avocado,
Briar Agate, Lilac

K. 153   10½" Ashtray $2.00
Cotton White, Ebony Cascade, Lilac

L. 154   12½" Ashtray $2.50
Moss Green, Lilac, Briar Agate

M. 129   13" Ashtray $2.50
Moss Green, Haeger Red, Cotton White,
Ebony Cascade

N. 128   13" Ashtray $2.50
Bitter Orange, Cotton White, Avocado
Gold Tweed - $3.00

A. R1836   10" Ashbowl $2.00
Lilac, Avocado, Ebony Cascade

B. 146-S   11" Ashtray $2.50
Ebony Cascade, Briar Agate, Green Agate

C. 107   12½" Ashtray $2.50
Ebony Cascade, Lilac,
Briar Agate, Bitter Orange

D. 127   11" Ashtray $2.50
Briar Agate, Bitter Orange, Avocado
Gold Tweed - $3.50

E. 119   14" Ashtray $3.00
Ebony Cascade

F. 159   9" Ashtray $2.50
Bitter Orange, Avocado

G. 148-S   9" Ashtray $3.00
Briar Agate, Haeger Red, Cotton White

H. 155   13½" Ashtray $3.00
Avocado, Cotton White, Bitter Orange
Gold Tweed, Antique Bronze - $4.00

I. 105   12" Ashtray $3.00
Ebony Cascade, Haeger Red, Briar Agate
Gold Tweed - $4.00

J. R1735   11" Ashtray $3.00
Ebony Cascade, Cotton White,
Briar Agate, Bitter Orange

K. 149   11" Ashtray $3.00
Green Agate, Haeger Red,
Briar Agate, Bitter Orange

L. 110-H   16" Ashtray $3.00
Cotton White, Moss Green, Bitter Orange
Gold Tweed - $4.00

Styled and Sized for Every Use in Homes, Offices and Restaurants

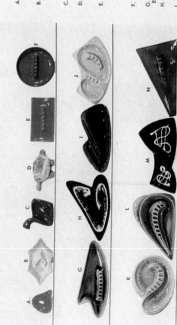

A. 162   16" Ashtray $6.00
Cotton White, Bitter Orange, Avocado

B. R1723   14" Ashtray $8.00
Ebony Cascade, Haeger Red,
Cotton White, Moss Green

C. 133   14½" Ashtray $7.50
Cotton White, Moss Green

D. 158   14" Ashtray $7.00
Bitter Orange, Avocado

E. R1311   11" Ashtray $6.00
Haeger Red, Moss Green, Cotton White
Gold Tweed - $7.00

F. R1755   14" Ashtray $6.00
Haeger Red, Ebony Cascade, Cotton White

A. 150   8" Ashbowl $2.50
Bitter Orange, Avocado, Lilac

B. 151   7" Ashbowl $2.00
Bitter Orange, Avocado, Lilac

C. 152   6" Ashbowl $1.50
Bitter Orange, Avocado, Lilac
150/151/152   Ashbowl Set $5.00 SET

D. 134   14" Ashtray $3.50
Bitter Orange, Ebony Cascade, Avocado
Gold Tweed - $4.50

E. R1718   13" Ashtray $3.00
Ebony Cascade, Haeger Red, Bitter Orange

F. R1719   12" Ashtray $2.50
Ebony Cascade, Haeger Red, Bitter Orange

G. R1720   10½" Ashtray $2.00
Ebony Cascade, Haeger Red, Bitter Orange
R1718/19/20   Ashtray Set $6.00 SET

H. 157   9½" Ashtray $4.00
Avocado, Bitter Orange, Cotton White
Gold Tweed, Antique Bronze - $5.00

I. 144   8½" Ashtray $4.00
Moss Green, Lilac, Cotton White, Bitter Orange
Gold Tweed - $5.00

J. 113-W   4½" Ashtray with Stand $5.00 SET
Haeger Red, Cotton White, Bitter Orange

K. 163-S   7" Ashbowl $5.00
Cotton White, Ebony Cascade, Bitter Orange
Antique Bronze - $6.00

ALL PRICES ARE SUGGESTED RETAIL PRICES

The Haeger Potteries Inc.

7 MAIDEN LANE, DUNDEE, ILLINOIS

Return Postage Guaranteed

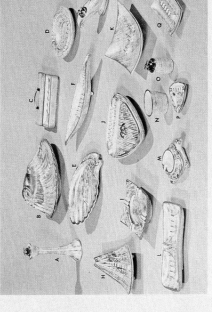

A. 702 - 10" Cigarette Box - Ebony Cascade, Lilac, Haeger Red, Cotton White - $5.00, Gold Tweed, Antique Bronze - $6.50.

B. 813-H - 10½" Lighter - Ebony Cascade, Haeger Red, Lilac, Avocado, Bitter Orange, Briar Agate, Cotton White - $6.00; Boxed - $6.30. Gold Tweed - $7.00; Boxed $7.30.

C. 708 - 16½" Cigarette Box - Cotton White, Moss Green, Haeger Red - $10.00.

D. 827-H - 8½" Lighter - Moss Green, Lilac - $6.00; Boxed - $6.30. Gold Tweed - $7.00; Boxed - $7.30.

E. 145 - 12" Ashbowl & Lighter Comb. - Cotton White, Bitter Orange, Moss Green - $9.00; (Ashbowl Only) - $6.50. Gold Tweed - $10.00; (Ashbowl Only) - $7.50.

F. 710 - 12½" Ashtray Comb. - Antique Bronze, Gold Tweed, Cotton White - $8.00. Gold Tweed, Antique Bronze $10.00.

G. 841 - 4" Cigarette Bowl - Antique Bronze, Gold Tweed, Cotton White - $2.00.

H. 839 - 3" Lighter - Antique Bronze, Gold Tweed, Cotton White - $4.00.

I. 840 - 4" Ashtray - Antique Bronze, Gold Tweed, Cotton White - $2.00. 839/840/841 Gift Boxed - $7.50 SET.

All designs below available in Gold Tweed.

A. 813-H	10½" Lighter Boxed - $7.30	$7.00
B. 132	15" Ashtray	$10.00
C. 702	10" Cigarette Box	$6.50
D. 157	9½" Ashtray	$5.00
E. 155	13½" Ashtray	$4.00
F. 134	14" Ashtray	$4.50
G. 827-H	8½" Lighter Boxed - $7.30	$7.00
H. 128	13" Ashtray	$3.00
I. 109-S	7" Ashtray	$3.50
J. 710	12½" Cigarette Box	$10.00
K. 127	11" Ashtray	$3.50
L. 137-S	12½" Ashtray	$4.00
M. 156	8" Ashtray	$3.00
N. 841	4" Cigarette Bowl	$2.00
O. 839	3" Lighter	$4.00
P. 840	4" Ashtray	$2.00
	839/840/841 Set	$7.50 Boxed
Q. 125	8" Ashtray	$2.50

24

ALL PRICES ARE SUGGESTED RETAIL PRICES

All designs are available in Mat White, Mat Black, Leaf Green, Stone Gray, Shadow Rose, Mat Yellow, EXCEPT WHERE INDICATED.

A. RG173	7" Vase	$2.50
B. RG183	10" Vase	$4.50
C. RG170	8" Bowl	$3.00
D. RG172	10" Bowl	$4.00
E. RG181	4" Bowl	$2.00

F. RG175/176	9" Bowl with Flower Block	$4.00 SET
G. RG171	7" Vase	$2.50
H. RG187	8" Bowl	$1.30
I. RG186	9" Bowl	$1.50
J. RG185	8" Bowl	$1.10

K. RG179	8" Bowl (Lots of 12)	$1.50
L. RG178	6" Bowl (Lots of 12)	$1.50
M. RG180	6" Bowl (Lots of 12)	$1.50
N. RG184	8" Bowl (Lots of 12)	$1.30

All designs are available in Sunrise Crackle, Amber Gold, Green Rings, UNLESS INDICATED OTHERWISE.

A. 22-H	10½" Vase	$5.00
B. 20-H	7½" Pitcher	$3.50
	Buff, Oyster, Light Green	
C. 833	4½" - 12 ounce Mug	$2.00
	Buff, Oyster, Light Green	
D. 3-H	12" Pitcher Vase	$5.50
	Sunrise Crackle, Amber Gold, Buff	
E. 13-H	6" Vase	$3.00
F. 21-H	16½" Vase	$7.50
G. 7-H	7" Ashtray	$1.70
H. 23-H	13" Bowl	$5.00
I. 5-H	5½" Vase	$3.00
J. 10-H	7½" Vase	$4.00

16

ALL PRICES ARE SUGGESTED RETAIL PRICES

135

A. 835	13" Bacchus Lavabo Urn	$15.00
	Leaf Green, Gold Tweed Faience - $18.00	
B. 836	17" Bacchus Lavabo Bowl	$10.00
	Leaf Green, Gold Tweed Faience - $12.00	
C. 361	Candleholder for 359	$7.00 PR.
	Avocado, Lilac Gold Tweed, Faience - $9.00 PR.	
D. 359	14" Bowl	$10.00
	Avocado, Lilac Gold Tweed, Faience -$13.00	
E. 837	8½" Girl Head	$10.00
	Faience, Gold Tweed	
F. 838	8½" Boy Head	$10.00
	Faience, Gold Tweed	

411-H	23" Urn	$15.00
	Orange/Texture, Cotton White, Avocado	
408	18½" Vase	$6.00
	Ebony Cascade, Bitter Orange, Lilac, Moss Green (Lots of 6 - $5.00)	
R1619-S	16" Pitcher	$6.00
	Ebony Cascade, Lilac, Avocado (Lots of 6 - $5.50)	
RG137-X	11" Vase	$4.00
	Cotton White/Turquoise, Moss Green Ebony Cascade	
RG68-X	7" Bud Vase	
	Cotton White, Green Agate, Lilac, Bitter Orange (Lots of 12 - $2.00) Gold Tweed - $2.50	

325-H	17" Bowl	$8.00
	Lilac Gold Tweed - $10.00	
331-S	16" Bowl	$6.00
	Cotton White/Turquoise, Lilac Gold Tweed - $8.00	
323	14" Bowl	$4.50
	Ebony Cascade, Briar Agate, Moss Green, Cotton White/Turquoise	

331-S

323

325-H

RG137-X

RG68-X

R1619-S

411-H

408

11

136

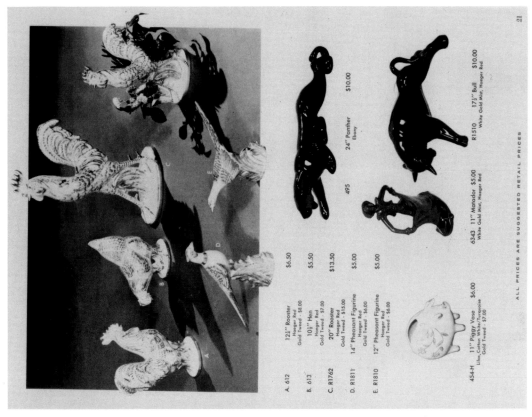

21

A. 612   12½" Rooster
          Haeger Red
          Gold Tweed - $8.00 $6.50

B. 613   10½" Hen
          Haeger Red
          Gold Tweed - $7.00 $5.50

C. R1762 20" Rooster
          Haeger Red
          Gold Tweed - $15.00 $13.50

D. R181T 14" Pheasant Figurine
          Haeger Red
          Gold Tweed - $6.00 $5.00

E. R1810 12" Pheasant Figurine
          Haeger Red
          Gold Tweed - $6.00 $5.00

495   24" Panther $10.00
          Ebony

R1510   17½" Bull $10.00
          White Gold Mist, Haeger Red

6343   11" Matador $5.00
          White Gold Mist, Haeger Red

454-H   11" Piggy Vase $6.00
          Lilac, Cotton White/Turquoise
          Gold Tweed - $7.00

ALL PRICES ARE SUGGESTED RETAIL PRICES

515/16/17   3-Piece Set/Chain & Bracket $6.00 Set
             Green Stoneware
             Cotton White/Turquoise Liner
             Gold Tweed - $7.50 Set

516/517 Set - Chain & Bracket - $5.00
             Florentine Gold, Gold Tweed - $6.00

513   12" Hexagonal Hanging Planter $5.50
       Green Stoneware, Tan Stoneware
       Gloss White, Gold Tweed

512   14" Hanging Planter $5.50
       Green Stoneware, Tan Stoneware
       Gloss White, Gold Tweed

New Wall Decorations

DESIGN DETAIL
FUNCTION - COLOR

842   14" Traditional Lavabo Top $3.00
       Cotton White/Turquoise, Gloss White
       Florentine Gold, Gold Tweed - $4.50

843   12" Traditional Lavabo Bottom $2.00
       Cotton White/Turquoise Liner, Gloss White
       Florentine Gold, Gold Tweed - $3.00

842/843 set - $5.00
842/843 set - Florentine Gold, Gold Tweed - $7.50

865-S   12½" Shell Wall Pocket $2.00
         Avocado, Mandarin Orange
         Green Stoneware
         Gold Tweed - $2.50

858   19½" Covered Jardiniere $10.00
         Gold Tweed

864-S   9½" Strawberry Jar $4.00
         Green Stoneware, Tan Stoneware
         Cotton White/Turquoise Liner
         Gold Tweed - $5.00

859   19" Large Jardiniere $10.00
         Green Stoneware, Tan Stoneware

YOUR WHOLESALE PRICES SHOWN

4

A. 626   12" Penguin on Wood Block $2.75
    Black/White
B. 624   12½" Pelican on Wood Block $2.75
    Gloss White, Green Stoneware, Tan Stoneware
C. 625   11½" Giraffe on Wood Block $2.75
    Gloss White, Green Stoneware, Tan Stoneware
D. & E. 627   12½" Cat on Wood Block $2.75
    Gloss White, Tan Stoneware, Mat Black

Be sure to include 621 Gazelle Head, 622 Horse Head and 623 Flying Fish in your order for a complete display and fast turnover. See page 2 Spring catalog.

868   12" Cherub Wall Planter (R & L) $2.50
    Green Stoneware
    Tan Stoneware, Gloss White
    Gold Tweed, Florentine Gold $3.50

518   13½" Cherub Compote $6.00
    Green Stoneware
    Mandarin Orange/White
    Florentine Gold - $7.50

519-H   11½" Mermaid on Dolphin $7.50
    Compote
    Green Stoneware
    Gold Tweed, Florentine Gold $8.75

505   23" Mermaid Planter $8.75
    Cotton White/Turquoise, Gold Tweed
514   14" Small Mermaid $5.00
    Cotton White/Turquoise, Mandarin Orange
    Gold Tweed, Florentine Gold

YOUR WHOLESALE PRICES SHOWN

5

AZTEC GOLD On All Designs

A. 5600   42" Large Oriental Urn $50.00
    Black Tortoise Shell Shade
B. 4001   8½" Small Bud Vase $2.50
C. R1915   15" One Stem Vase $4.00
D. R1919   10" One Stem Oriental Vase $3.00
E. 13-H   6" Vase $3.00
F. 1-H   23" Vase $10.00
G. 2-H   13" Vase $5.00
H. 191   16" Tear Drop $3.50
I. 1311   11" Square Divided Ashtray $3.50
J. 125   8" Rectangular Ashtray $2.00

FLORENTINE GOLD On All Designs

A. 868 R & L   12" Cherub Wall Planter $3.50 Ea.
B. 519-H   11½" Mermaid on Dolphin Compote $8.75
C. R1919   10" One Stem Oriental Vase $2.00
D. R1915   15" One Stem Vase $2.50
E. 449   16" Narrow Necked Vase $3.50
F. 411-H   23" Urn $8.75
G. 518   13½" Cherub Compote $7.50
H. R1224   16½" Gypsy Girl $8.75
I. 4003   16" Hexagonal Vase $3.25
J. 4002   13" Hexagonal Vase $3.00
K. 382   19" Candleholder $8.75
L. 711-S   7½" Square Candy Box $3.25
M. 385   10" Hexagonal Low Bowl $2.50
N. R1510   17½" Bull $7.50

A. 1-H   23" Vase $5.50
    Black/White Lava
B. 411-H   23" Urn $8.75
    Black/White Lava
C. 864-S   9½" Strawberry Jar $5.00
    Gold Tweed
D. 4003   16" Hexagonal Vase $3.25
    Black/White Lava
E. R1919   10" One Stem Oriental Vase $2.00
    Black/White Lava, Gold Tweed
F. R1730   10" Candy Jar $3.25
    Black/White Lava, Gold Tweed
G. 386   7" Planter and Candleholder $1.75
    Gold Tweed
H. 27-H   12" Footed Bowl $6.75
    Gold Tweed
I. 157   9½" Ashtray $2.50
    Black/White Lava, Gold Tweed
J. 514   14" Small Mermaid $5.00
    Gold Tweed
K. 413   9" Vase $2.00
    Black/White Lava, Gold Tweed
L. 165   8½" Free Form Ashtray $1.00
    Black/White Lava, Gold Tweed
M. 190   11" Rectangular Ashtray $3.00
    Gold Tweed
N. 185-S   13" Leaf Ashtray $2.00
    Gold Tweed

YOUR WHOLESALE PRICES SHOWN

3

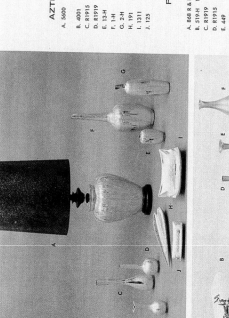

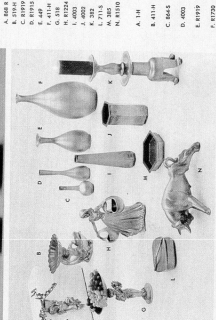

Haeger creates exciting contrasts with BLACK MISTIQUE

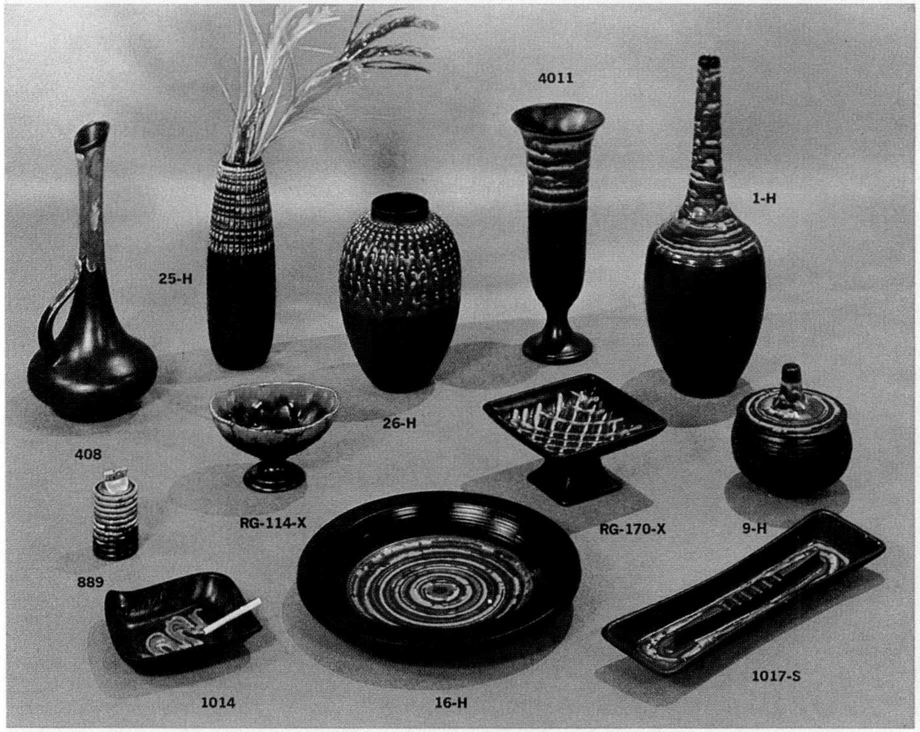

BLACK MISTIQUE Shown

1-H 23″ Vase $11.00
9-H 7½″ Candy Bowl 5.50
16-H 15″ Low Bowl 6.00
25-H 14″ Vase 5.00
26-H 12″ Vase 6.00
RG-114-X 5″ Compote 3.00
RG-170-X 8″ Pedestal Bowl 4.00
408 18″ Tall Necked Vase 6.00
889 5″ Cigarette Lighter 4.50
1014 9″ Free Form Ashtray 2.20
1017-S 19″ Concave Long John Ashtray 5.00
4011 16″ Chalice Vase 5.00

Shown on Cover

R-1915 15″ One Stem Vase $4.00
R-1919 10″ One Stem Oriental Vase 3.00
RG-68-X 7″ Bud Vase (1 doz. min.) 2.00

Prices: Suggested Retail

All prices subject to change.

© 1964, The Haeger Potteries, Inc.

Other Designs Available in BLACK MISTIQUE

2-H 13″ Vase $4.50
8-H 11½″ Bowl 5.50
13-H 6″ Vase 3.00
RG-56-X 9″ Compote Bowl 4.00
117 12″ Free Form Ashtray 2.20
125 8″ Rectangular Ashtray Doz. 18.00
127 11″ Flared Ashtray 2.50
149 11″ Rectangular Ashtray 3.00
153 10½″ Free Form Ashtray 2.20
170-S 12½″ Rectangular Ashtray 3.50
173 10″ Free Form Textured Ashtray 2.00
183-F 9″ Round Nesting Ashtray 3.50
184-F 7″ Round Nesting Ashtray 2.50
183-F/184-F Round Nesting Ashtray Set 6.00
352 14″ Rectangular Bowl 7.00
353 5″ Candleholder Pr. $5.00
358 11″ Tall Candleholder 3.50
388 16″ Oriental Kobuni Bowl 6.00
390 22″ Free Form Long Low Bowl 7.50
493 16″ Traditional Vase 6.00
715 7″ Nordic Cigarette Box 5.00
813 10½″ Classic Lighter 6.00
857 16″ Jardiniere on Tripod 17.00
1000 7″ Nordic Ashtray 2.50
1008 9½″ Palette Ashtray Doz. 24.00
1016-S 19″ Convex Long John Ashtray 5.00
R-1311 11″ Square Divided Ashtray 5.00
R-1730 10″ Candy Jar 5.50
R-1836 10″ Ashbowl 2.20
4004 12″ Nordic Vase 5.00
4005 18″ Nordic Vase 6.00
4006 6″ Nordic Vase 7.00

The Moorish influence on Mediterranean styles and color is stronger than ever today. Realizing a growing trend, Haeger evolves a velvety midnight-blue-black to form a bewitching background for vivid volcanoes of color in one of its new color glazes: BLACK MISTIQUE. Exhilarating oranges, reds, yellows and electric blues flow, swirl and erupt in bright profusion on each of 45 pieces to provide accents that are unusual and distinctive for room settings.

More NEW colors on the inside . . .

30

New Big and Bold designs—Bold NEW color: OXBLOOD

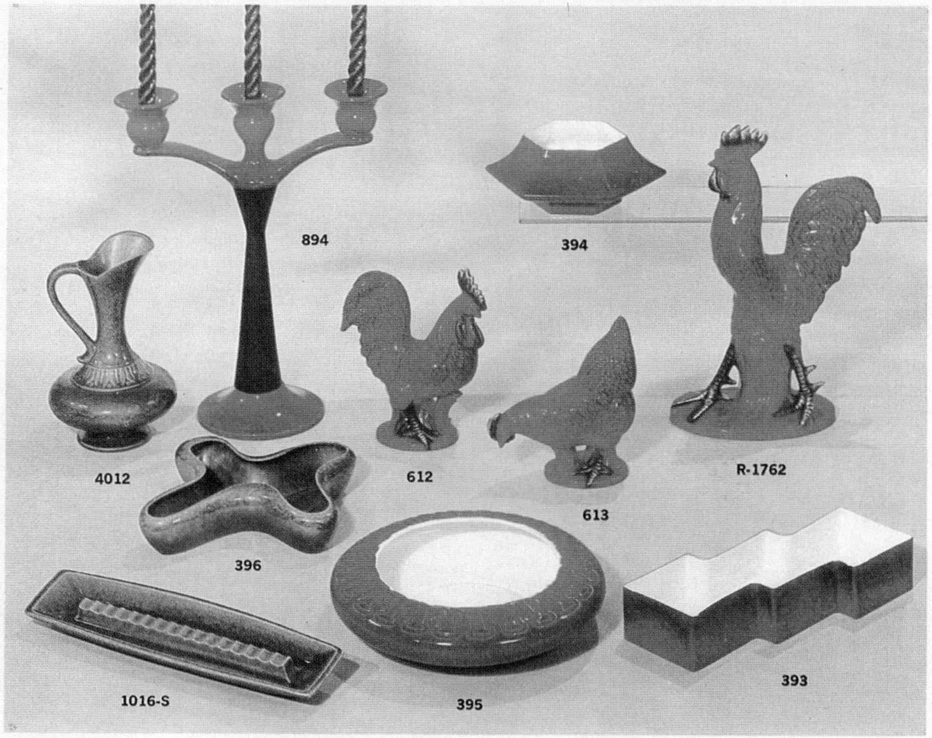

The warmest of reds, OXBLOOD, covers designs of impressive size to command attention in any setting. In contrast, popular BLUE/GREEN DRIP accents in a strong yet restrained manner.

Haeger Designs Shown Above

393 16″ Triple Bowl. Oxblood, Cotton White, Green Texture. $5.00
394 12″ Six-Sided Bowl. Oxblood, Cotton White, Mandarin Orange. $6.00
395 15″ Round Bowl. Oxblood, Cotton White, $7.50. Gold Tweed $10.00
396 15″ Free Form Bowl. Blue/Green Drip, Cotton White, Misty Mint. $5.00
612 12¼″ Rooster. Oxblood, Curry, Misty Mint. $6.50
613 10½″ Hen. Oxblood, Curry, Misty Mint. $5.50
894 22½″ Candelabrum. Oxblood/Black Wood, Cotton White/Walnut. $25.00
1016-S 19″ Ashtray. Blue/Green Drip, Black Mistique, Mandarin Orange. $5.00
R-1762 20″ Rooster. Oxblood, Gold Tweed. $15.00
4012 13″ Colonial Pitcher Vase. Blue/Green Drip, Cotton White, Curry, Green Texture. $7.00. Gold Tweed. $9.00

31

Other Designs Available in OXBLOOD

117 12″ Free Form Ashtray $2.20
125 8″ Rectangular Ashtray Doz. 18.00
129 13″ Free Form Ashtray 2.50
130 12″ Free Form Ashtray 2.20
148-S 9″ Rd. Contemporary Ashtray 3.00
149 11″ Rectangular Ashtray 3.00
164 8½″ Figure Eight Ashtray Doz. 18.00
170-S 12½″ Rectangular Ashtray 3.50
183-F 9″ Round Nesting Ashtray 3.50
184-F 7″ Round Nesting Ashtray 2.50
183-F/184-F Round Nesting Ashtray Set 6.00
188-S 7½″ Apple Ashtray 2.00
191 16″ Teardrop Ashtray 3.00
192 13″ Free Form Ashtray 3.00
382 19″ Candleholder $17.50
386 7″ Planter and Candleholder 2.50
631 9½″ Bull on Wood Base 13.50
702 10″ Cigarette Box and Ashtray Set 5.50
718 5″ x 9″ Cigarette Box 5.00
813 10½″ Classic Lighter 6.00
889 5″ Cigarette Lighter 4.50
1002 13″ Modern Ashtray 3.00
1004 15″ Large Modern Ashtray 7.00
1011 8″ Egg-Shaped Nesting Ashtray 2.20
1012 5¼″ Egg-Shaped Nesting Ashtray 1.50
1011/1012 Egg-Shaped Nesting Ashtray Set 3.50
1013 5½″ x 2½″ Deep, Two-piece Ashtray with Pipe Knocker 5.00
1014 9″ Free Form Ashtray $ 2.20
R-1510 17½″ Bull 12.00
6343 11″ Matador Figurine 5.00
R-1723 14″ Executive Ashtray 10.00
R-1730 10″ Candy Jar 5.50
R-1743 21½″ Onion Jug Vase 8.00
R-1755 14″ Executive Ashtray 6.50
R-1915 15″ One Stem Vase 4.00
R-1919 10″ One Stem Oriental Vase 3.00
4003 16″ Hexagonal Vase 5.00
4013 12″ Lotus Leaf Vase 3.50
4015 12″ Oriental Vase w/handles 10.00
4020 5½″ Peg-foot Vase w/handles 2.50
4021 5½″ Peg-foot Vase 2.00

Prices: Suggested Retail

Haeger captures the mood of the Near East with CURRY

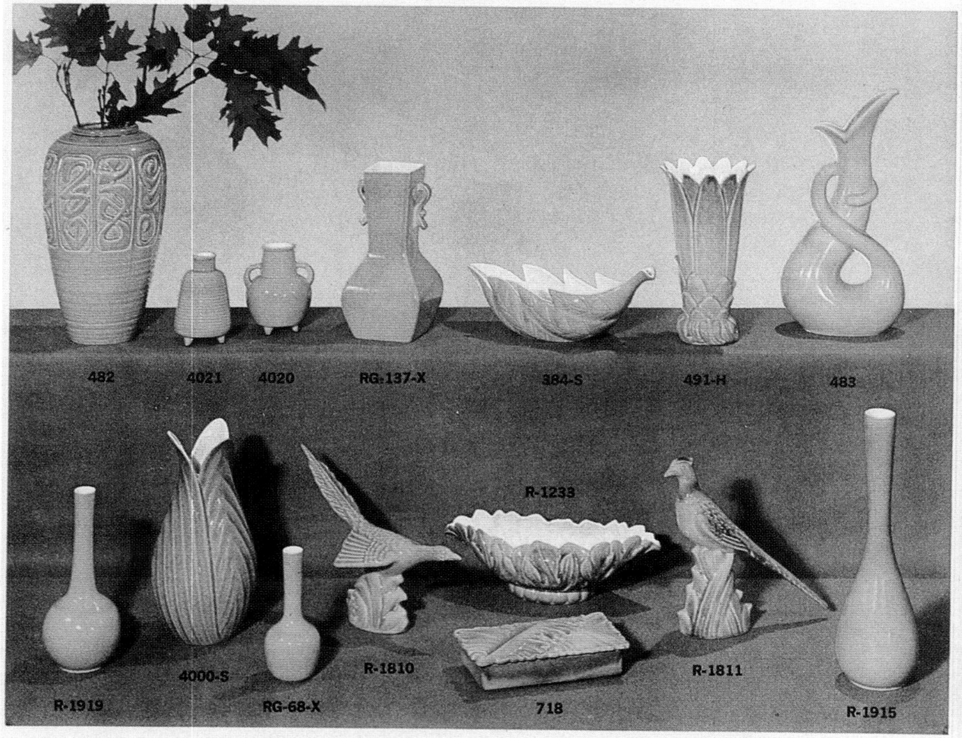

Giving new life to furnishings can be as simple as changing accessories with each new season. Haeger Artware, with such fashion-right colors as new CURRY, provides the quick and easy way to update rooms with fresh, fashionable accents.

CURRY Shown Above

RG-68-X 7" Bud Vase. Curry, Black Mistique, Blue/Green Drip, Cotton White, Green Texture, Mandarin Orange. (Lots of 12 only). $2.00 each. Gold Tweed. $2.50 each
RG-137-X 11" Square Vase. Curry, Mandarin Orange. $4.50. Florentine Gold. $5.50
384-S 14" Leaf Bowl. Curry, Misty Mint, Reseda Green. $5.00. Gold Tweed. $6.00
482 14" Traditional Vase. Curry, Cotton White, Mandarin Orange, Reseda Green. $8.00. Gold Tweed. $9.00
483 15" Exotic Vase. Curry, Blue/Green Drip, Cotton White, Mandarin Orange. $6.00. (Lots of 6 $5.00 each)
491-H 11½" Lily Vase. Curry, Cotton White, Misty Mint, Reseda Green. $5.00. Gold Tweed. $6.00
718 5" x 9" Cigarette Box. Curry, Blue/Green Drip, Misty Mint, Oxblood. $5.00
R-1233 13" Acanthus Bowl. Curry, Misty Mint, Reseda Green. $4.00. Gold Tweed. $5.00
R-1810 12" Pheasant Figurine. Curry, Misty Mint, Reseda Green. $5.50. Gold Tweed. $6.00
R-1811 14" Cock Figurine. Curry, Misty Mint, Reseda Green. $5.50. Gold Tweed. $6.00
R-1915 15" One Stem Vase. Curry, Black Mistique, Cotton White, Mandarin Orange, Oxblood. $4.00. Gold Tweed, Florentine Gold. $5.00
R-1919 10" One Stem Oriental Vase. Curry, Black Mistique, Cotton White, Mandarin Orange, Oxblood. $3.00. Gold Tweed, Florentine Gold. $4.00
4000-S 12" Leaf Vase. Curry, Cotton White, Misty Mint, Reseda Green. $5.00. Gold Tweed. $6.00
4020 5½" Peg-foot Vase w/handles. Curry, Mandarin Orange, Oxblood. $2.50
4021 5½" Peg-foot Vase. Curry, Mandarin Orange, Oxblood. $2.00

Other Designs Available in CURRY

SP-12 13½" Pallet Ashtray $2.20
RG-25-X 13" Glad Vase 7.00
RG-124-X 14" Oblong Footed Bowl 5.00
125 8" Rectangular Ashtray Dz. 18.00
128 13" Triangular Modern Ashtray 2.50
144 8½" Shell Ashtray 4.00
165 8½" Free Form Ashtray Dz. 18.00
185-S 13" Leaf Ashtray 3.00
335 9" Compote 5.00
336 4" Candleholder Pr. 4.00
379 8" Bowl 4.50
397 12" 18th Century Rd. Bowl 5.00
413 9" Vase 3.00
430-H 11" Vase 5.00
612 12¼" Rooster 6.50
613 10½" Hen 5.50
707-S 7½" Modern Candy Box 5.50
709 12½" Horn Plenty 5.00
711-S 7½" Square Candy Box 5.00
716 5" x 9" 18th Century Cigarette Box 5.00
717 9" 18th Century Candy Dish 6.00
878-H 14" Leaf Double Server $4.00
889 5" Cigarette Lighter 4.50
895 18" 18th Century Divided Server 5.00
1003 13" Leaf Ashtray 3.00
1011 8" Egg-Shaped Nesting Ashtray 2.20
1012 5¼" Egg-Shaped Nesting Ashtray 1.50
1011/1012 Egg-Shaped Nesting Ashtray Set 3.50
1013 5½" x 2½" Deep, Two-piece Ashtray with Pipe Knocker 5.00
1014 9" Free Form Ashtray 2.20
1017-S 19" Long John Ashtray 5.00
1019 9" 18th Century Ashtray 2.20
R-1285 5" Calla Lily Candleholder Pr. 4.00
R-1894 7" Round Ashtray 1.50
4007 14½" Modern Bud Vase 4.00
4008 10" Modern Bud Vase 3.00
4012 13" Colonial Pitcher Vase 7.00
4019 5½" Lined Vase 2.00

Prices: Suggested Retail

32

New cool MISTY MINT color—new Nodular Designs

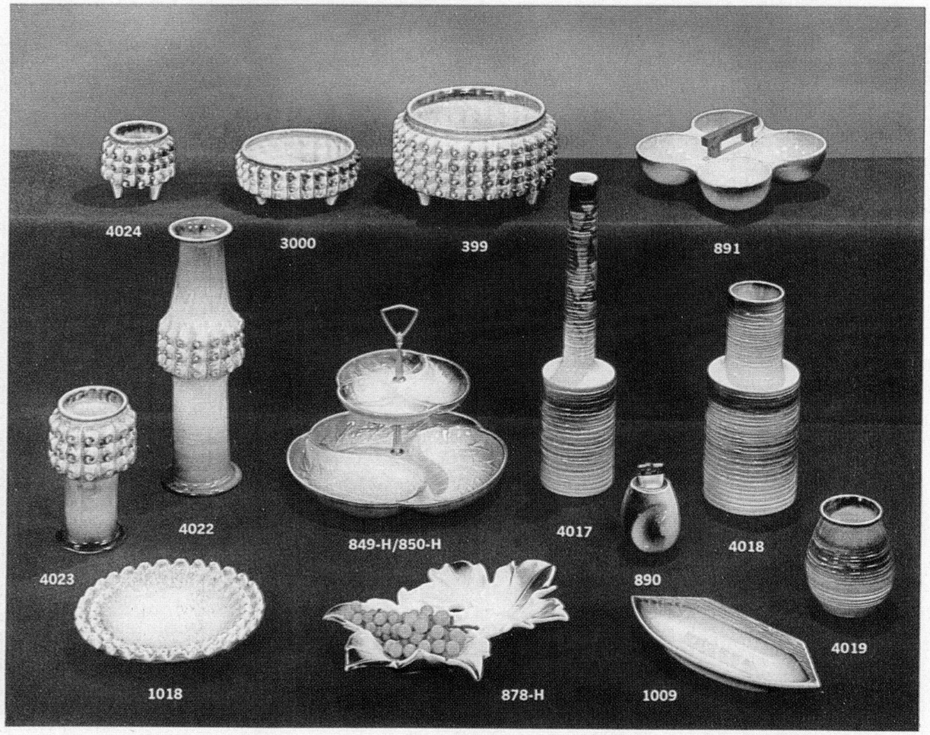

MISTY MINT Shown Above

399 10½" Large Planter Bowl. Misty Mint, Reseda Green. $10.00
849-H 8" Serving Tray. Misty Mint, Mandarin Orange, Porcelain White, Reseda Green. $2.50
850-H 12" Serving Tray. Misty Mint, Mandarin Orange, Porcelain White, Reseda Green. $3.50
849H/850H Two Tier Serving Tray. Misty Mint, Mandarin Orange, Porcelain White, Reseda Green. $5.00
878-H 14", Leaf Double Server. Misty Mint, Curry, Mandarin Orange, Reseda Green. $4.00. Gold Tweed. $6.00
890 5" Table Cigarette Lighter. Misty Mint, Blue/Green Drip, Cotton White. $4.00
891 9½" Four-Compartment Server w/wooden handle. Misty Mint, Blue/Green Drip, Porcelain White. $5.00
1009 11½" Lined Ashtray. Misty Mint, Green Texture, Reseda Green. $2.20. Gold Tweed. $3.00
1018 9½" Round Ashtray. Misty Mint, Reseda Green. $4.00
3000 7" Three-Legged Bowl. Misty Mint, Reseda Green. $5.00
4017 18" Lined Bud Vase. Misty Mint, Green Texture, Reseda Green. $5.50. Gold Tweed. $7.50
4018 12" Lined Bud Vase. Misty Mint, Green Texture, Reseda Green. $5.00. Gold Tweed. $7.00
4019 5½" Lined Bud Vase. Misty Mint, Green Texture, Curry, Reseda Green. $2.00. Gold Tweed. $4.00
4022 17" Vase. Misty Mint, Reseda Green. $7.50
4023 8" Vase. Misty Mint, Reseda Green. $5.00
4024 4½" Peg-foot Vase. Misty Mint, Reseda Green. $4.00

Other Designs Available in MISTY MINT

110-H 16" Leaf Ashtray $3.50
127 11" Flared Ashtray 2.50
128 13" Rectangular Modern Ashtray 2.50
135 12" Free Form Ashtray 2.20
138 8¼" Diamond Shape Ashtray Doz. 12.00
144 8½" Shell Ashtray 4.00
164 8½" Figure Eight Ashtray Doz. 18.00
188-S 7½" Apple Ashtray 2.00
306 12¼" Bowl 7.00
343 8" Lily Bowl 2.50
345-S 5" Loop Edge Bowl 3.50
384-S 14" Leaf Bowl 5.00
392 5" Lotus Leaf Candleholder Pr. 5.00
396 15" Free Form Bowl 5.00
397 12" 18th Century Round Bowl 5.00
455 16" Classic Vase 6.00
472 14" Oriental Vase 6.00
477 20" Bud Vase 5.00
491-H 11½" Lily Vase 5.00
499-S 7" Leaf Vase $ 5.50
514 14" Small Mermaid 10.00
612 12¼" Rooster 6.50
613 10½" Hen 5.50
716 5" x 9" 18th Century Cig. Box 5.00
717 9" 18th Century Candy Dish 6.00
718 5" x 9" Cigarette Box 5.00
848-H 18" Triple Server 3.50
854-H 18" Fish Tray 4.00
856-H 15" Chip and Dip 5.00
862-H 14" Rooster Chip and Dip 4.00
873-H 15" Egg Serving Plate 5.00
879-H 6½" Bud Serving Tray (Single) 2.50
880-H 12" Lily Leaf Serving Tray (Single) 3.50
879/880 Two-Tier Serving Tray 5.00
895 18" 18th Century Divider Server 5.00
1005 11" Fluted Ashtray $3.00
1019 9" 18th Century Ashtray 2.20
R-1233 13" Acanthus Bowl 4.00
R-1285 5" Calla Lily Candleholder Pr. 4.00
R-1619-S 16" Flower Pitcher 6.00
R-1735 11½" Shell Ashtray 3.00
R-1755 14" Executive Ashtray 6.50
R-1759 21" Console Bowl 7.00
R-1760 2½" Candleholder Pr. 4.00
R-1810 12" Pheasant Figurine 5.50
R-1811 14" Cock Figurine 5.50
R-1844 9" Duck Planter 3.50
R-1845 9" Duck Planter 3.50
3660 13" Glad Vase 7.50
4000-S 12" Leaf Vase 5.00
4011 16" Chalice Vase 5.00

Prices: Suggested Retail

34

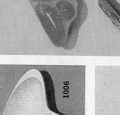

HAEGER

7 Maiden Lane
Dundee, Illinois 60118

Return Requested

Nesting Ashtray Set,
183-F/184-F. $6.00

Nesting Ashtray Set,
1011/1012. $3.50

2-pc. Ashtray w/pipe
knocker, 1013. $5.00

Prices: Suggested Retail

All prices subject to change.

The wonderful HAEGER world of ASHTRAYS

Fashionable NEW COLORS and exciting NEW DE-SIGNS join the already wide assortment of colors, sizes, and shapes in HAEGER ashtrays. New designs include a two-piece ashtray with pipe knocker, an ashtray with pipe rest, a new nesting ashtray. Each ashtray designed with safety rests. Each bottom finished with felt protectors where necessary. All with glazes that are burn-proof. Wide choice, too, of cigarette boxes and lighters.

813 10½" Classic Lighter. Black Mistique, Cotton White, Green Texture, Mandarin Orange, Oxblood, Reseda Green. $6.00. Gold Tweed. $7.00
1006 11" Free Form Ashtray, Blue/Green Drip, Cotton White, Green Texture, Mandarin Orange. $2.50
1008 9¼" Palette Ashtray. Black Mistique, Blue/Green Drip, Cotton White, Mandarin Orange. $2.00 (1 doz. min.)
1009 11½" Lined Ashtray. Green Texture, Misty Mint, Reseda Green. $2.20. Gold Tweed. $3.00
1011 8" Egg-Shaped Nesting Ashtray. Curry, Green Texture, Oxblood. $2.20
1012 5" Egg-Shaped Nesting Ashtray. Curry, Green Texture, Oxblood. $1.50
1011/1012 Egg-Shaped Nesting Ashtray Set $3.50
1013 5½" x 2½" deep. Two-Piece Ashtray with Pipe Knocker, Blue/Green Drip, Cotton White, Curry, Green Texture, Oxblood. (Alternate top: Mat Black) $5.00
1014 6½" Free Form Ashtray. Black Mistique, Blue/Green Drip, Curry, Oxblood. $2.20
1015 11" Free Form Ashtray with Pipe Rest. Cotton White, Green Texture, Mandarin Orange, Oxblood. $3.50
1017-S 19" Concave Long John Ashtray, Black Mistique, Blue/Green Drip, Curry. $5.00
1019 9" 18th Century Ashtray, Curry, Mandarin Orange, Misty Mint, Porcelain White. $2.20. Gold Tweed. $3.00

128 13" Triangular Modern Ashtray, Blue/Green Drip, Curry, Cotton White, Green Texture, Mandarin Orange, Misty Mint, Reseda Green. $2.50. Gold Tweed. $3.00
138 8½" Diamond Shape Ashtray, Cotton White, Dark Green Texture, Mat Black, Misty Mint, Orange. $1.00 (3 doz. min.)
183-F 6" Round Nesting Ashtray. Black Mistique, Blue/Green Drip, Mandarin Orange, Oxblood. $3.50
184-F 7" Round Nesting Ashtray. Black Mistique, Blue/Green Drip, Mandarin Orange, Oxblood. $2.50
183-F/184-F Round Nesting Ashtray Set $6.00
188-S 7½" Apple Ashtray. Mandarin Orange, Misty Mint, Oxblood. $2.00

36

Distinctive SIGNATURE Originals from Haeger

Individualized for discriminating tastes

SIGNATURE artware is especially designed for those individuals who prefer the hand-crafted look in accessories. Each of the designs, created by artists in residence at Haeger Potteries, is original. No two are exactly alike. Each piece is hand-thrown on the potter's wheel to attain the rugged textural quality beloved by individualists. Each piece is hand-glazed with specially compounded stone-like glazes in colors chosen to enhance its beauty. Each is signed by the ceramist-artists. The SIGNATURE on the bottom signifies an original creation.

SIGNATURE Designs Shown Above in GOLDEN MAPLE and TIGER LILY

HT-30 15" Big Bowl	$10.00
HT-31 10" Small Bowl	5.00
HT-32 8" Compote	10.00
HT-33 10" Large Ashtray	6.00
HT-34 5" Small Ashtray	2.00
HT-35 9" Large Vase	6.00
HT-36 9" Small Vase	
HT-37 2½" Cigarette Cup	3.00
HT-38 15" Large Hanging Planter with Bracket and Chain	20.00
HT-39 10" Small Hanging Planter with Bracket and Chain	10.00
HT-40 8" Table Planter	17.50

Prices: Suggested Retail

35

141

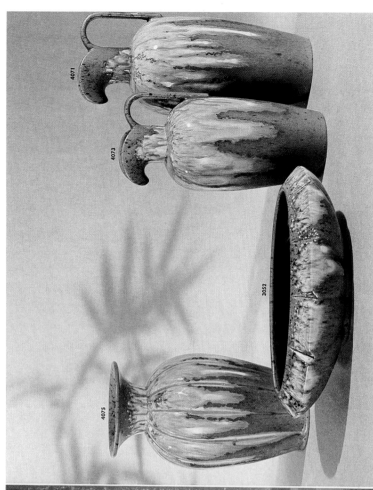

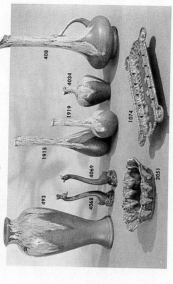

New Glaze – New Designs

Aqua Crystal

Reminiscent of sunshine thru the thin crest of a tall Hawaiian wave as it curls into iridescent foam.

408	18½" Vase		$7.00
493	16" Vase		8.00
1074	14" Traditional Ashtray		5.00
1915	15" One Stem Vase		5.00
1919	10" One Stem Vase		3.50
3051	9½" Oval Vase		4.50
3052	11" Contemporary Bowl		4.00
4034	7" Boutique Vase		4.00
4068	9" King Bud Vase	Ea.	2.50
4069	9" Queen Bud Vase	Ea.	2.50
4071	12" Pitcher Vase		6.00
4073	10" Pitcher Vase		6.00
4075	10" Vase		5.00

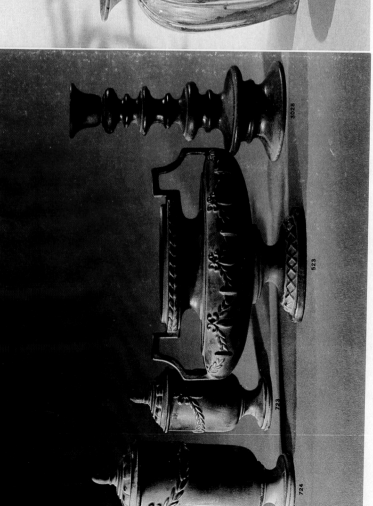

The Haeger Potteries, Inc.

HAEGER — the Great Name in American Ceramics—

The Haeger Potteries, Inc., Seven Maiden Lane, Dundee, Illinois 60118

6

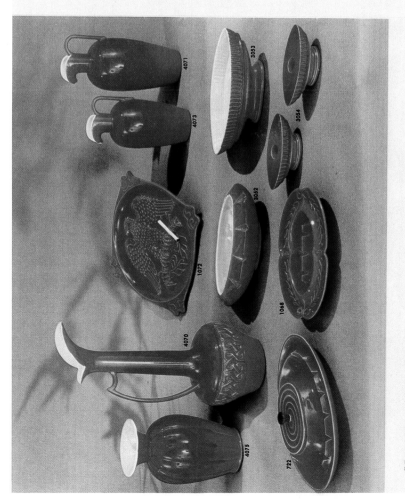

Mandarin Orange

722	12"	Cigarette Box/Ashtray	$6.50
1068	10"	Ashtray	2.80
1072	12"	Early American Eagle Ashtray or Wall Plaque	7.50
3052	11"	Contemporary Bowl	4.50
3053	11"	Empire Bowl	4.00
3054	5½"	Candleholders - - Pr.	4.00
3053/54		3-Pc. Empire Bowl Console Set - Set	8.50
4070	18"	Pitcher Vase	7.00
4071	12"	Pitcher Vase	6.00
4073	10"	Pitcher Vase	5.00
4075	10"	Vase	5.00

More Colors Available on All Designs—See Price List

890	5"	Lighter	$ 5.00
1056	6"	Free Form Ashtray (3 doz. min.) - Doz.	12.00
1068	10"	Ashtray	2.80
1075	10½"	Contemporary Ashtray	4.00
3051	9½"	Oval Bowl	4.50
3052	11"	Contemporary Bowl	4.50
3053	11"	Empire Bowl	4.50
*3054	5½"	Candleholders - - Pr.	4.00
*3053/54		3-Pc. Console Set	8.50
4068	8¾"	King Bud Vase	2.50
4071	12"	Pitcher Vase	6.00
4073	10"	Pitcher Vase	5.00
4075	10"	Vase	5.00

*Candles and Floral Arrangement not included.

ALL PRICES ARE SUGGESTED RETAIL

4

143

1045	15″	Ashtray	4.50
1054	9½″	Circular Ashtray	4.50
1056	6″	New Form Ashtray	2.50
1063	9½″	New Form Ashtray	3.50
1072	12″	Early American Eagle Wall Plaque or Ashtray	10.00
		Acanthus Bowl	7.00
1233	13″	Lavabo Top/16″ Bottom	
*1504/5	15″	(See Page 9) Set	25.00
1810	12″	Pheasant	7.50
1811	14″	Cock	7.50
1894	7″	Ashtray	3.50
3034	18″	Round Bowl	18.00
3040	12″	Oblong Bowl	6.50
3041	8″	Round Bowl	5.50
*3043	17½″	Candleholder Ea.	15.00
4043	12″	Etruscan Vase	7.00
4044	14″	Etruscan Pitcher Vase	11.00
4054	16″	Oriental Vase	15.00
4055	16″	Oriental Vase	15.00
*4056	10″	Oriental Vase	6.50

More Colors Available on All Designs—See Price List

*Fruit, Floral Arrangement, Planting and Candles not included.

11

Etruscan Blue, Orange, Ivory

All designs illustrated on pages 6 and 7 available in Etruscan Blue, Etruscan Orange and Etruscan Ivory.

RG68X	7″	Bud Vase		$ 3.50
155	13½″	Shell Ashtray		5.50
165	8½″	Ashtray		2.50
173	10″	Ashtray		3.50
183	9″	Nesting Ashtray		6.00
184	7″	Nesting Ashtray		4.00
183/184		2-Pc. Nesting Set	Set	10.00
325	17″	Shell Bowl		11.50
*335	9″	Compote		9.00
*336	4″	Candleholders	Pr.	6.50
*335/336		3-Pc. Console Set	Set	15.00
364	16″	Lily Bowl		8.00
*382	19″	Candleholder	Ea.	8.50
707	7½″	Candy Box		
721	9″	Early American Candy Bowl		8.50
813		Lighter		8.00
896W	16½″	Planter w/stand (ET/BL, ET/OR only)		23.00
896	16″	Floor Planter, without stand (ET/BL, ET/OR only)		17.00
1045	15″	Ashtray		4.50
1046	7″	Circular Ashtray		4.50
1058	10″	Free Form Ashtray		3.50

1059	13″	Free Form Ashtray		5.50
1063	9½″	New Form Ashtray		3.50
1066	9″	Early American Ashtray		4.00
1894	7″	Ashtray		3.50
1915	15″	One Stem Vase		5.50
1919	10″	One Stem Vase		4.50
3040	12″	Oblong Bowl		6.50
3041	8″	Round Bowl		5.50
*3045	10″	Early American Candleholder	Pr.	11.00
*3048	13″	Early American Bowl		7.50
*3045/48		3-Pc. Early American Set	Set	18.50
*4040	13″	Pitcher Vase		10.00
4042	9″	Vase		6.00
4043	12½″	Etruscan Pitcher Vase		9.00
4043	12″	Etruscan Vase		7.00
*4044	14″	Etruscan Pitcher Vase		6.50
*4050	12½″	Triple Etruscan Vase		11.00
4054	16″	Oriental Vase		15.00
4055	16″	Oriental Vase		15.00
4056	10″	Oriental Vase		6.50
4063	12½″	Early American Vase		9.00
4064	10″	Oriental Vase		7.00
4065	9″	Etruscan Vase		9.00

*Candles and Floral Arrangement not included.

More Colors Available on All Designs—See Price List

ALL PRICES ARE SUGGESTED RETAIL

7

Sebastiano Maglio

17

HANDTURNED CANDLEHOLDERS by HAEGER'S smiling Italian potter. These peasant figurine designs have special charm for homemakers. Their whimsical faces and stylized capes and coats in GREY/BLUE decorated, or GREY/GREEN decorated, add amusing decorative touches to dining tables, mantels, chests, or consoles. Each one has its own personality to make it a conversation piece.

Hand-Thrown

The following designs available only in GREY/BLUE decorated, GREY/GREEN decorated.

*HT-44	15″	Male Candleholder	$18.00
*HT-45	12½″	Female Candleholder	12.50
*HT-46	9″	Female Candleholder	9.00
HT-47	15″	Female Candleholder	18.00
HT-51	7″	Round Ashtray	5.50
HT-52	7″	Round Ashtray	5.50

The following designs available only in FAWN.

*HT-57	13½″	Mushroom Planter	15.00
HT-58	16½″	Mushroom Planter	17.50
HT-59	19½″	Mushroom Planter	20.00

°Candles and Planting not included.

ALL PRICES ARE SUGGESTED RETAIL

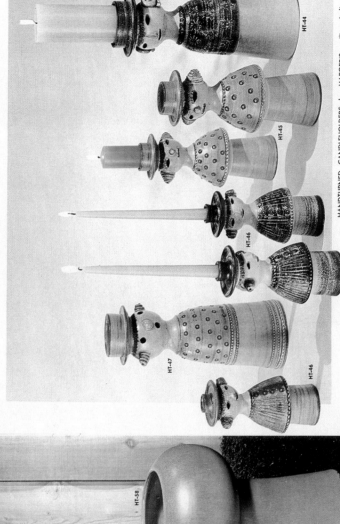

HANDTURNED PATIO PLANTERS of mushroom-shape, and in earth color, fresh and exciting as a Spring day! Perfect accents for a garden room, terrace, patio, porch, or entrance doorway. In smart contemporary design, these new patio planters will accommodate a variety of foliage, flowering plants, or herbs for the gourmet.

8031 Ht. 15″ Handcrafted Girl Planter Evergreen, Grey/Blue decorated, Grey/Green decorated $12.50 Ea.

8030 Ht. 17½″ Handcrafted Boy Planter Evergreen, Grey/Blue decorated, Grey/Green decorated $12.50 Ea.

16

Haeger's Exciting World of Ashtrays

Suggested Retail $1.10 Each

***138 $13.20 doz.
Three dozen minimum
order - Assorted colors

***Net, No Freight Allowance

Suggested Retail $1.10 Each

***1056 $13.20 doz.
Three dozen minimum
order - Assorted colors

*1894
*1030
*1028
*1029
*1057
**1061

*165

A SPECIAL PACK OF 36 - Assorted colors, Six designs your choice.
The package - $54.00 retail. SELL FOR $1.50.

No Freight Allowance On This Special Package.

**1079

*1044
*125

*1066

Suggested Retail $1.00 Each

***1078 $12.00 doz.
Three dozen minimum
order - Assorted colors

*1076
*1027

A SPECIAL PACK OF 36 - Assorted colors in six designs, $72.00 retail.
SELL FOR $2.00.

No Freight Allowance On This Special Package.

**1058
**1063

Special Promotional Packs

SP42 $4.50
M, Or, Orb
Ev, PC, CW

135
C/White,
M/Orange,
Peacock,
Evergreen

1046
Artichoke,
Peacock,
M/Orange,
Evergreen

1014
Oxblood,
M/Orange,
Peacock,
Evergreen

1834
Peacock,
M/Orange,
Evergreen, Aqua

1008
Peacock,
M/Orange,
C/White,
Evergreen

153
Artichoke,
Evergreen,
M/Orange,
Peacock,
C/White

117
Aqua, Oxblood,
Peacock,
Artichoke,
M/Orange

1062
Evergreen,
P/White,
M/Orange

SP42 - $4.50

1054
Peacock,
M/Orange,
Aqua, Evergreen,
Artichoke

SP12
M/Orange,
C/White,
Evergreen

1064
M/Orange,
Evergreen,
P/White

Suggested Retail Any Ashtray This Group $2.80.

1068
Evergreen,
M/Orange

20

HAEGER'S own Pompeian Bronze

724
725
3058
1066
1068
4063

"The Sculptured Look"

Covered jars and scalloped ashtray decorated in embossed
swags of original antique treasures, which inspired these designs.
Each is a handcrafted work-of-art reproduced by HAEGER to fill
today's need for Classic Accents.

Hexagonal vase, compote and ashtray in Pompeian Bronze
show their design debt to the classics of another era. The
fused ceramic glaze has the exact patina of ancient bronze.

More Colors Available on All Designs—See Price List

4063	12½"	$ 9.00
*3058	10½"	10.00
1066	9"	4.00
725	7½"	$ 7.50
724	10"	8.50
1068	10"	4.00

*Fruit not included.

Spice Gold

1073
1072
722

722	12"	Cigarette Box/ Ashtray	$6.50
1072	12"	Early American Eagle Ashtray or Wall Plaque	7.50
1073	16"	Oriental Ashtray	8.50

Smart Style in JARS 'N BOXES

Smart Style in JARS 'N BOXES have Today's
Design Appeal with old-fashioned use and con-
venience. Covered jars are useful for stick candies,
peppermints, gumdrops, sourballs.
Oblong box is just right for filter cigarettes.

The Total Look For Any Coffee Table.

8056
8057
727
721

721	9"	$6.50
8057	6½"	5.00
8056	5½"	4.00
727	5½"x3½"	4.00

ALL PRICES ARE SUGGESTED RETAIL

18

A Style and Color for Every Decor

LUXURY GLAZES . . . HAEGER'S Touch of Elegance for Special Occasions

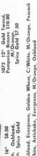

722 $8.00
Et/Bl, Et/Or

1006 $5.00
Et/Or, Et/Bl,
Et/Or

*813 $8.00

1311 $8.00
Et/Bl, Et/Iv,
Et/Or

184 $4.00
Et/Or, Et/Bl,
Et/Iv

1046 $4.50
Et/Or, Et/Bl,
Et/Iv

1063 $3.50
Et/Bl, Et/Or,
Et/Iv, Pom/Br

1056 $3.50
Et/Bl, Et/Or,
Et/Iv, Pom/Br

1058 $3.50
Et/Or, Et/Bl,
Et/Iv

1060 $10.00
Et/Bl, Et/Or,
Spice Gold

730 $4.00
1044 $3.00
173 $3.50
125 $3.00
128 $5.00
160 $2.50

Boot Set $15.00 — Gift Boxed.
Boot Set $15.00 — Gift Boxed.

B054
726
1076
1054 $4.50
144 $5.00
1056 $2.50

22

*Et/Bl, Et/Iv, Et/Or, Gold Tweed, Pom/Br.
Please refer to price list for more colors
available on these designs.

More Colors Available
on All Designs—See Price List

ALL PRICES ARE SUGGESTED RETAIL

HAEGER

1039 $3.50
Evergreen,
M/Orange,
Artichoke,
Oxblood, Peacock

1002 $4.00
Oxblood,
Evergreen,
C/White, Artichoke

1041 $3.50
M/Orange,
Evergreen,
Golden Wheat

1021 $3.50
M/Orange,
C/White,
Evergreen,
Artichoke

155 $4.00
M/Orange,
Evergreen

1059 $4.00
Peacock,
M/Orange,
Golden Wheat,
Evergreen

1733 $4.00
Evergreen,
M/Orange,
C/White

Retail this Group $3.50 — $4.00 each, as indicated.
Illustrated color is first listed under each design.

149 $4.00
Oxblood, Peacock,
Artichoke,
M/Orange, Aqua

1006 $3.50
M/Orange,
C/White,
Artichoke,
Evergreen,
Golden Wheat

1005 $3.50
Artichoke,
Evergreen,
Golden Wheat

128 $3.50
Evergreen, Peacock,
Aqua, C/White,
M/Orange

127 $3.50
Golden Wheat,
M/Orange,
Aqua, C/White,
Peacock

1075 $4.00
Peacock, Aqua,
M/Orange,
Evergreen

"King-size" Ashtrays to retail from $5.00 to $11.50 —
Color-matched Lighters.

1016 19" $4.00
Artichoke,
M/Orange,
Oxblood, C/White,
Evergreen, Aqua

*890 5" $5.00

1311 11" $5.50
M/Orange, Peacock,
Evergreen, C/White,
Golden Wheat

100 15" $8.50
Evergreen, Artichoke, Peacock,
M/Orange, Oxblood, Aqua

162 14" $8.50
Golden Wheat, C/White,
M/Orange, Oxblood

1723 14" 50
Evergreen,
Oxblood,
M/Orange,
Peacock,
Artichoke, Aqua

1072 12" Gold Tweed,
Pompeian Bronze $10.00
M/Orange,
Spice Gold $7.50

21

*813 10½" $7.00

1074 14" $5.00

1073 14" $8.50
Evergreen, Oxblood,
M/Orange, Spice Gold

1755 14" $7.50
Aqua, C/White, Peacock,
M/Orange, Artichoke, Evergreen

*813: Aqua, Artichoke, Oxblood, Golden Wheat, C/White, M/Orange, Evergreen, Peacock
**890: Golden Wheat, Oxblood, Artichoke, Evergreen, M/Orange, Oxblood

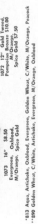

147

Mandarin Orange

1H	23"	Vase		$12.50
9H	7½"	Candy Bowl		6.50
26	12"	Vase		7.00
SP41/42/43		3-Pc. Smoking Set	Set	7.00
RG42X	10"	Pitcher		5.00
*RG56X	9"	Bowl		4.50
RG68X	7"	Bud Vase		2.50
RG92X	7"	Handled Bud Vase		2.50
RG124X	14"	Oblong Bowl		6.50
345	5"	Loop Edge Bowl		4.00
408	18½"	Vase		7.00
456	18"	Pitcher		7.00
477	20"	Bud Vase		6.00
483	15"	Vase		7.00
493	16"	Vase		8.00
616	15½"	Cat		6.50

More Colors Available on All Designs—See Price List.

ALL PRICES ARE SUGGESTED RETAIL.

24

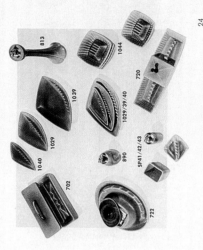

New Boot Set

A distinguished 3-piece gift set with masculine appeal. In SPICE GOLD color which suggests the patina of a briar pipe or a polished saddle, the Boot Lighter, Ashtray and Cigarette Box with horse's head motif combine smart design with practical purpose.

Additional colors illustrated on page 22.

Spice Gold Set — Gift Boxed - - - $10.00

Boot Set $10.00 — Gift Boxed.

R054 - $7.00

726 - $3.50

1076 - $1.70

Evergreen

890 $5.00

722 $6.50

182/84 Nesting $6.00 Set

Oxblood

720 $6.50

*1044 Stacking $1.70 ea.

890 $5.00

Color-Cued Smoking Accessories available individually or as sets.

Mandarin Orange

813 $7.00

702 $6.50

1029/39/40 Nesting - $5.50 Set

ALL PRICES ARE SUGGESTED RETAIL.

23

148

Peacock
The accent with a personality

1H	23"	Vase	$12.50
9H	7½"	Candy Bowl	6.50
26H	12"	Vase	7.00
SP41/42/43		3-Pc. Smoking Set	Set 7.00
RG56X	9"	Bowl	4.50
RG68X	7"	Bud Vase	2.50
RG92X	7"	Handled Bud Vase	2.50
*RG114X	5"	Compote	3.50
153	10½"	Ashtray	2.80
183	9"	Nesting Ashtray	3.50
183/84		2-Pc. Nesting Set	Set 6.00
408	18½"	Vase	7.00
493	16"	Vase	8.00
720	15"	Cigarette Box/Ashtray	6.50
813	10½"	Lighter	7.00
857W	16"	Jardiniere/Walnut Tripod	21.00
857	16"	Jardiniere (not shown)	15.00
1008	9½"	Ashtray	2.80
1014	9"	Ashtray	2.80
1054	9½"	Circular Ashtray	2.80
1066	9"	Early American Ashtray	2.20
1730	10"	Onion Jug Vase	6.50
1743	21½"	One Stem Vase	10.00
1915	15"	One Stem Vase	5.00
1919	10"	One Stem Vase	5.00
3034	18"	Round Bowl	13.50
*3038	12"	Bowl	7.50
3039	8"	Bowl	5.50
4001	8½"	Chalice Vase	3.00
4011	16"	Bud Vase	6.50
4030	12"	Vase	5.50
4031	9"	Vase	4.50
4034	7"	Boutique Vase	4.00
4038	14"	Vase	4.50
*4050	12"	Triple Etruscan Vase	8.50

*Floral Arrangement not included.

37

Haeger®

Peacock

36

149

Mr. Joseph F. Estes, President

As a customer you are a member of the Haeger Family. We thank you for the important part you have played in this success story. You will enjoy reading the enclosed history of our first 100 years.

Mr. L. J. Klein, Vice President for Sales

As we enter the second hundred years, the word "Craftsman" still characterizes Haeger. It has been a tradition with us to supply you with the finest possible products, your assurance of greater sales. This Centennial Edition of our catalog will assist you in preparing your next order.

COVER STORY—The cover story for our Centennial Issue was taken on the banks of the Fox River. Native clays from this shoreline and the nearby hills, were used in our original products.

4135
10"
$7.00

4134
11"
$7.00

4136
5½"
$6.00

8113
4"
$6.00

2022
9"
$6.00

centennial edition 1871/1971

Craftsmen for a century

THE HAEGER POTTERIES INC. / DUNDEE, ILLINOIS 60118

150

Alan Osterberg
from Germany
Haeger's New Contemporary Designer

Lime Decorated
Orange Decorated
Blue Decorated

Design	Size		Retail Price
2055	5"½		$ 3.00
2056	7½ "		4.00
2057	4½ "		3.50
3129	4¼ "		5.50
3130	10¾ "		10.00
4141	10½ "		9.00
4142	13"		7.00
4143	9½ "		6.00
8161	8"		6.00
8163	8"		12.00
8164	6½ "		9.00
8165/66	15"	Set	14.00
8167	3"		5.00

Flowers, plants and candles not included.
ALL PRICES ARE SUGGESTED RETAIL

Sascha Brastoff Los Angeles

Individual of rare talent. As a youngster, he displayed abilities which have led to famous exhibits in the permanent collections at the New York Metropolitan Museum of Art, Los Angeles County Museum, Sculpture Center of New York and many others, as well as commissions from famous personalities, many from Hollywood. Brastoff's intuitive design sense has carried him to world-wide prominence as a great talent in the ceramic arts, and we now bring you the touch of Brastoff in HAEGER ESPLANADE!

Roman Bronze

Lamp from
Royal Haeger
Lamp Collection

ALL PRICES ARE
SUGGESTED RETAIL

Eric Olsen is a distinguished Ceramist and Sculptor. His creative work began in his native Norway, continued for many years in the famous potteries of Staffordshire in England, before he joined Haeger in 1947. Ever since, his design talents have been dedicated to the development of Haeger's extensive lines in Lamps and Artwares.

Eric Olsen
from Norway
Director of Haeger Design Bureau

3088
8"
$6.00 Ea.

3078
7½" (Triple)
$5.00 Ea.

2006
8½"
$4.00 Ea.

721
9"
$7.50 Ea.

3074
4"
$3.00 Ea.

2025
6"
$4.00 Ea.

3102
9½" (Triple)
$6.00 Ea.

1048
10"
$5.00 Ea.

8097
16"
$10.00 Ea.

4103
16"
$10.00 Ea.

2043
6"
$2.50 Ea.

1086
13"
$5.00 Ea.

8086

2045
6"
$24.00 Doz.

728
11"
$12.00 Ea.

8085

8092

8084 $20.00 4-Pc. Set

8081

Peasant Olive

8088
11"
$11.00 Ea.

6

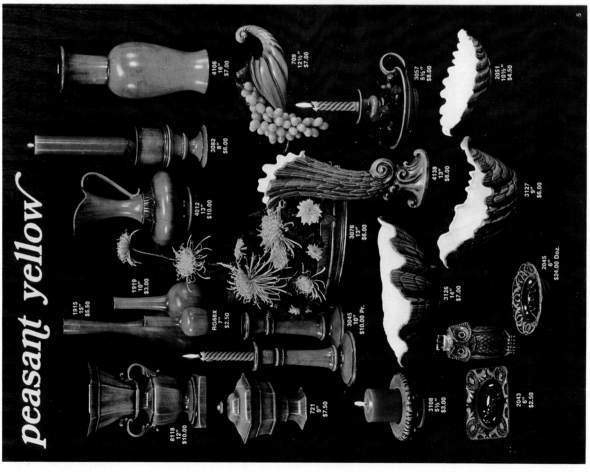

peasant yellow

5

4106
16"
$7.00

709
12½"
$7.00

3057
5½"
$8.00

2051
10½"
$4.50

3082
8"
$6.00

4012
13"
$10.00

4138
13"
$6.00

3127
9"
$6.00

3076
13"
$6.00

3126
14"
$7.00

1919
10"
$3.00

RG68X
$2.50

3045
10"
$10.00 Pr.

2045
6"
$24.00 Doz.

1915
15"
$5.50

8118
12"
$10.00

721
9"
$7.50

3108
5½"
$3.00

2043
6"
$2.50

152

peasant olive

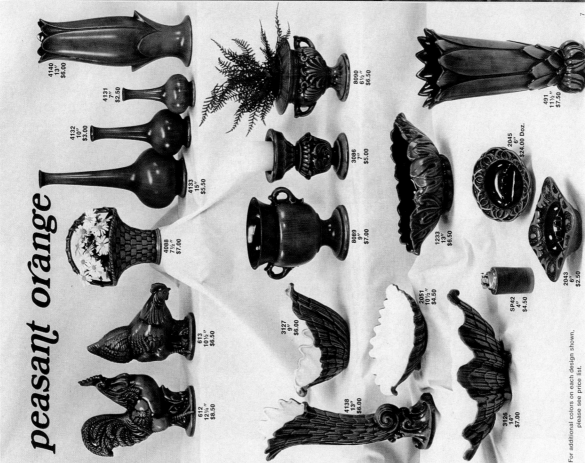

peasant orange

Antique
Dove White

Topaz Decorated

681
12"
$30.00

peasant flame

3045/3076 Set $16.00

13" Bowl

13" Bowl

13" Bowl

13" Bowl

3088
8"
$6.00

1233/3108 Set $12.50

1068
10"
$5.00

3102
9½"
$6.00

3093
6"
$7.00

3044/3077 Set $16.00

3057
5½"
$8.00

3086
7"
$5.00

3103
9½"
$6.00

709
12½"
$7.00

Peasant Olive
Wood Mount

628
10"
$13.50

Flowers, plants and candles not included.

Haeger Red only

1510
17½"
$17.50

10

520 Ht. 12½"
(Opening 10½")
$10.00

For additional colors
on each design shown,
please see price list.

peasant flame

3075
7½"
$5.00

3074
4"
$3.00

2006
8½"
$4.00

4140
13"
$6.00

3127
9"
$6.00

2051
10½"
$4.50

8097
12"
$10.00

8134
12"
$7.00

4138
13"
$6.00

3126
14"
$7.00

9

8142
6½"
$6.00

4122
12½"
$7.50

2034
9"
$5.00

735
$8.00

8141 Set
$20.00

Florawood Series
Topaz Decorated

8141
8"
$7.00

Peasant Green

4070
18"
$10.00

4128
18"
$10.00

4123
7"
$5.00

Peasant Flame

735
7"
$8.00

4127
18"
$10.00

154

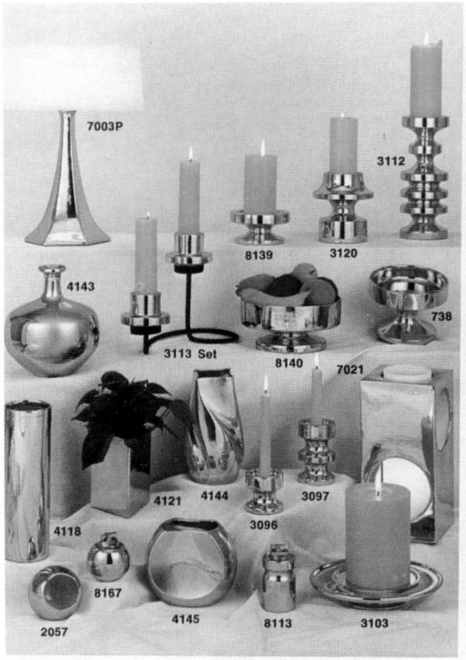

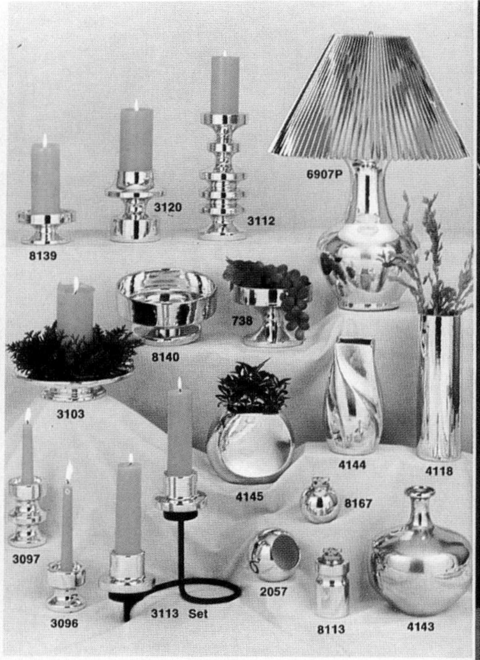

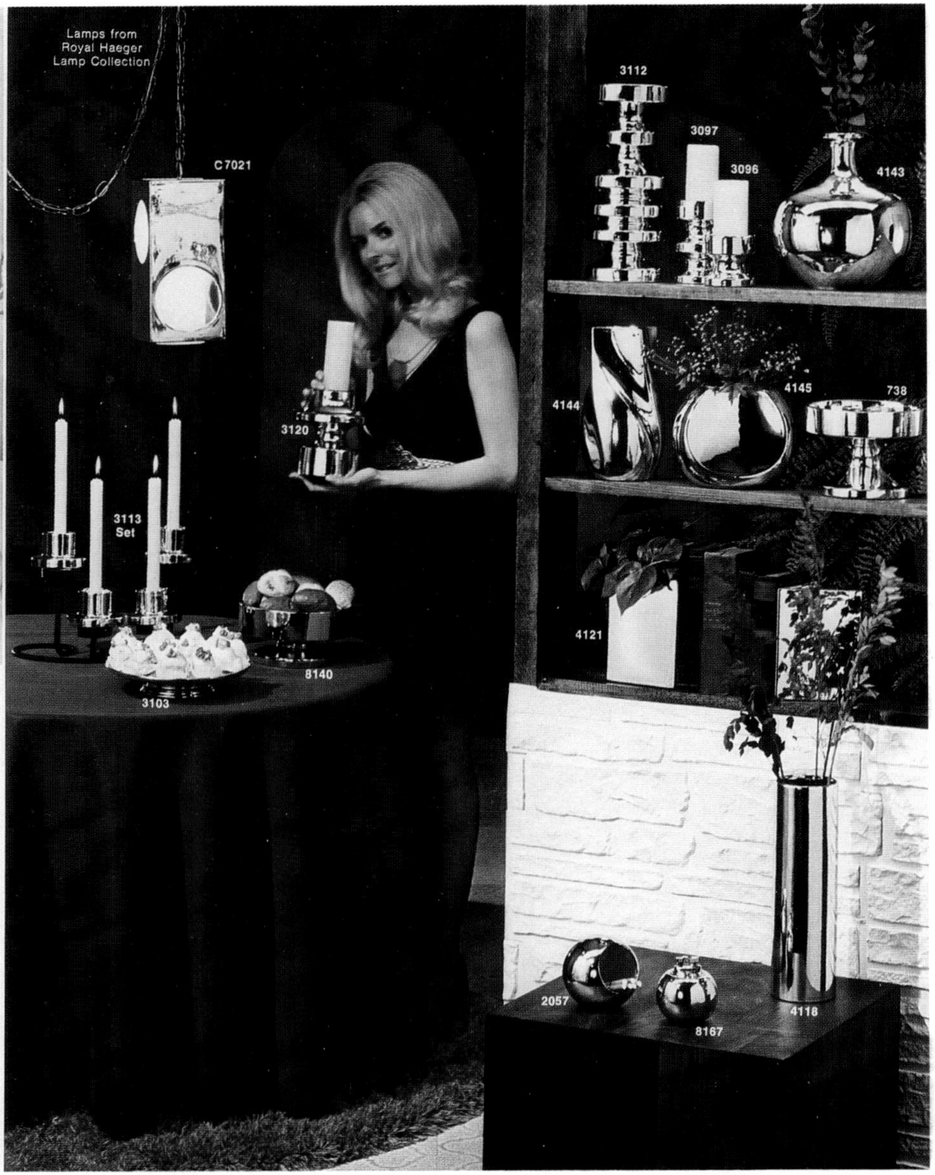

Mirror Chrome & Mirror Gold

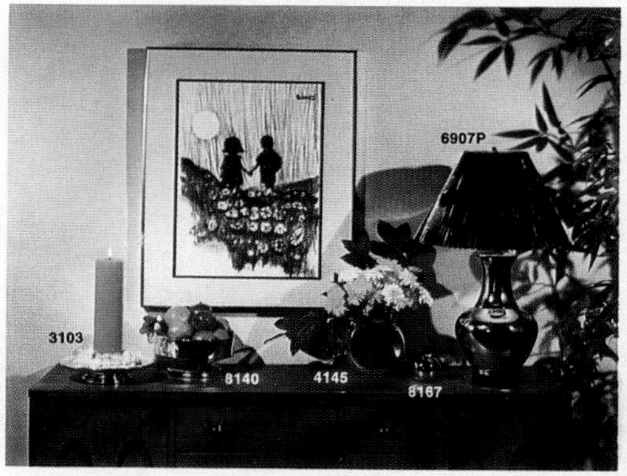

Design	Size	Retail Price Mirror Chrome	Retail Price Mirror Gold
738	6¾″	$ 8.00	$ 9.00
2057	4½″	5.00	5.50
3096	3″	4.00	4.50
3097	5″	4.50	5.00
3103	9½″	8.00	9.00
3112	11¾″	11.00	12.00
3113	3-pc. Set	14.00	15.00
3120	6⅝″	8.50	9.50
4118	12″	6.00	6.50
4121	6½″	5.50	6.50
4143	9½″	10.00	11.00
4144	9″	7.00	8.00
4145	6″	7.00	8.00
8113	4″	6.50	7.00
8139	5¼″	5.00	5.50
8140	8½″	10.00	11.00
8167	3″	6.50	7.00

Lamps from Royal Haeger Lamp Collection
SEE PRICE LIST

Flowers, plants and candles not included.
ALL PRICES ARE SUGGESTED RETAIL

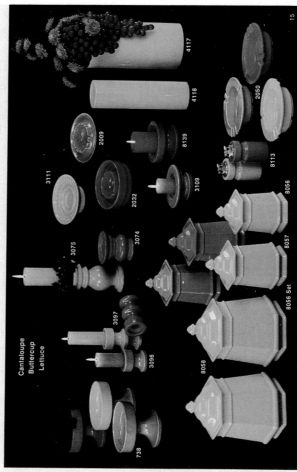

Porcelain White
Gloss Ebony
Pimento

Cantaloupe
Buttercup
Lettuce

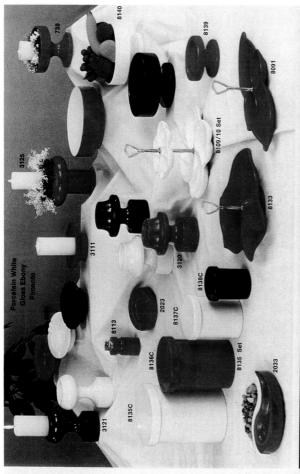

Lawrence Peabody
New Hampshire and Haiti

Lawrence Peabody's versatile "Mix and Match" collection, designed exclusively for HAEGER, boasts a color palette of six brilliant, high-gloss glazes.

Design	Height	Retail Price
738	7"	Ea. $ 6.00
1066	9"	2.50
1311	11"	7.00
2009	7"	2.50
2022	9"	5.00
2023	6"	2.00
2025	6"	2.00
2032	7"	4.00
2033	9"	3.50
2048	10"	3.00
2049	4½"	3.00
2050	7"	1.50
3074	4" (triple)	5.00
3075	7½" (triple)	5.00
3096	3"	2.50
3097	5" (triple)	3.00
3102	9½"	3.00
3109	5½"	6.00
3111	6"	3.00
3112	12"	Doz. 30.00
3113	12"	Ea. 8.00
3113 Set	3½"	Ea. 3.50
	(2 candleholders with iron stand)	
3118	9¾"	Set 11.00
3120	7"	Ea. 6.50
3121	8"	Ea. 6.00
3123	6½"	Ea. 6.00
3125	7"	Ea. 3.50
4117	12"	Ea. 6.00
4118	12"	Ea. 5.00
4121	6½"	Ea. 4.00
8056 Set	(4 pcs.)	Ea. 3.50
		Set 20.00
8091	15½"	Ea. 4.50
8109/10 Set	(See price list for individual pieces)	
8113	4"	Ea. 5.00
8133	7"	Set 7.00
8135 Set	14"	Ea. 5.00
	(4 pcs.)	Set 20.00
8139	5½"	Ea. 3.50
8140	8½"	Ea. 6.50

All designs available in Pimento, Cantaloupe, Porcelain White, Gloss Ebony, Buttercup, Lettuce.

Porcelain White

Gloss Ebony   Lettuce

Gloss Ebony

Porcelain White

Marigold Agate

741X 7" $8.00
8156X 4¾" $5.00
3116X 9" $7.00
2046X 5" $5.00
1066 9" $2.50
153 10½" $3.00
1092 11" $3.00
R668X 7" $2.50

Flowers, plants and candles not included.
ALL PRICES ARE SUGGESTED RETAIL

All Designs Illustrated are Available in Fern Agate or Marigold Agate

707 7½" $9.00
4144 9" $4.00
4145 6" $4.00
408 18½" $10.00
919 10" $3.00
4044 12" $5.50
1752 16" $8.00
4133 15" $5.50
4132 10" $3.00
4131 7" $2.50
1311 11" $7.00
890 5" $5.00
1054 9½" $3.00
1058 10" $2.50
4126 15" $6.00
4107 12" $6.00
3133 8" $8.00
2053 8" $2.50
2052 8" $2.50
2044 7½" $24.00 Doz.
4140 15" $6.00
4104 15" $10.00
4030 12" $6.00
3003/4 Set 12" $11.00 Set
4123 7" $5.00
2027 7½" $2.50
2028 7" $2.50

1091 11½" $3.00
1723 14" $15.00
1054 9½" $3.00
4131 7" $2.50
4132 10" $3.00
4030 12" $6.00
890 5" $5.00
1755 14" $8.00
728 11" $12.00
1735 11½" $4.50
1311 11" $7.00
4107 12" $6.00
1752 16" $8.00
1054 9½" $3.00
2011 8" $2.50
890 5" $5.00
1735 11½" $4.50
1091 11½" $3.00
1093 15" $3.00

18

Porcelain White

3075
4126
3109
3074
3125
3118
8146 Set
3111
8133
8109/10 Set
8110

17

4058/60 Set $12.00

1066
721
8087 Set
8063/3089 Set
3058
8081
8091
8063
8057
8056
8067 Set
3045 Pr.
8080
8079
8056 Set
8109
8058
3087
3057 5½" $8.00
8118
3055/4074 Set $10.00

Design	Size	Retail Price
721	9"	$ 7.50
1066	9"	2.50
2009	7"	3.50
2032	9¾"	2.50
3045	10"	Pr. 10.00
3058	10½"	7.00
3074	4"	3.00
3075	7½"	5.00
3087	7½"	5.00

8063/3089 Set $13.00 Set
8063 Pitcher — 9½"
3089 Bowl — 14"

Design	Size		Retail Price
3109	5½"		3.00
3111	6"	Doz.	30.00
3118	9½"		6.50
3125	9¼"		6.00
4126	15"		6.00
8056		Set	20.00
8056	5¾"		4.00
8057	6⅜"		4.50
8058	9"		7.50
8063	11"		6.50
8067	11½"	Set	25.00
8079	4½"		6.50
8080	3½"		3.00
8081	2 Pint		6.00
8087		Set	12.00
8091	15½"		4.50
8109/10	11¼"	Set	7.00
8110	4¼"		4.50
8113	4"		7.00
8118	12"		10.00
8133	14"		4.50
8146	9"	Set	25.00

Animal Figurines

649
9½"
$7.00

650
8½"
$7.50

656
6"
$11.50

655
11"
$13.50

307
10½"
$15.00

4841
Pulled Tulip Decanter
$35.00

642X
12"
$10.00

805
7"
$5.00

762
20"
$20.00

644
16"
$6.00

8100 L/R
8"
$13.00 Pr.

612X
12½"
$10.00

613
10½"
$6.50

613X
10½"
$8.00

612
12½"
$8.50

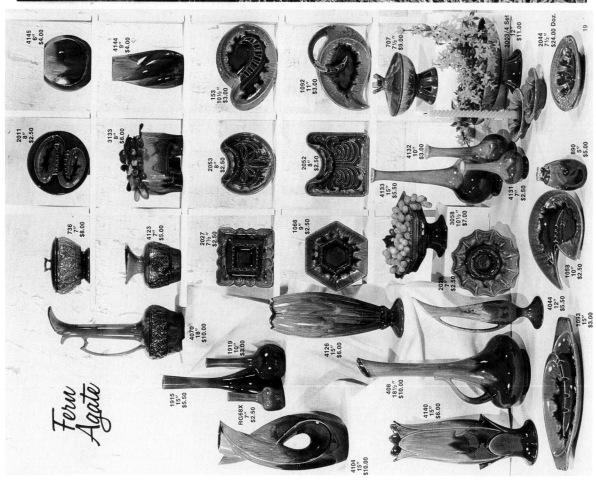

Fern Agate

4145
6"
$4.00

4144
9"
$4.00

153
10½"
$3.00

1092
11"
$3.00

707
7½"
$9.00

3003/4 Set
12"
$11.00

2044
7½"
$24.00 Doz.

2011
8"
$2.50

3133
8"
$8.00

2053
8"
$2.50

2052
8"
$2.50

4132
10"
$3.00

890
5"
$5.00

736
7"
$8.00

4123
7"
$5.00

2027
7½"
$2.50

1066
9"
$2.50

4133
15"
$5.50

4131
7"
$2.50

3058
10½"
$7.00

201
7½"
$2.50

1058
10"
$2.50

4070
18"
$10.00

1919
10"
$3.00

4044
12"
$5.50

1093
15"
$3.00

1915
15"
$5.50

RG68X
7"
$2.50

4126
15"
$6.00

408
18½"
$10.00

4140
15"
$6.00

4104
15"
$10.00

19

158

To Our Valued Haeger Dealers,

We present this edition as a ready reference to the NEW Royal Haeger Artware line. It is an extensive line encompassing all of today's style trends, produced by potters whose skills are attuned to the ever-changing consumer demands. We look forward to your use of Haeger as the single resource for your Ceramic Artware requirements.

Sincerely,

L. J. Klein
Vice-President Sales & Marketing

You are cordially invited to tour our factory facilities. Tours are conducted by experienced guides six times daily, Monday thru Friday. The knowledge gained from this memorable tour will enable you to sell our product with more profitable results.

Mr. Joseph F. Estes, President of The Haeger Potteries, Inc., personally escorting a group of children.

Chief of The HAEGER Design Staff
GLENN RICHARDSON
Glenn brings to us a totally new and refreshing approach to the designs of HAEGER lamps and artware.

MARTIE STRUBEL
. . . is the sculptress of "Magical Moment" figurines, where the charms and joys of children are captured in her designs.

Menagerie

693
17" x 11" x 11"

696
14" x 16" x 9"

697
15" x 18" x 12"

700
15" x 9" x 7"

698
14" x 14" x 10"

695
11" x 15" x 9"

2

CANDLE SHOPPE 1871-1971

3082 9" $6.00

3088 8" $6.00

3086 7" $5.00

709 12½" $7.00

3075 7½" $5.00

3057 5½" $8.00

3107 6" $3.00

3108 5½" $3.00

3074 4" $3.00

8134 12" $7.00

3093 6" $7.00

3102 9½" $6.00

3103 9½" $6.00

Haeger
Craftsmen for a century

PERMANENT SHOWROOMS

ATLANTA - Merchandise Mart • DALLAS - Trade Mart
NEW YORK - 225 Fifth Avenue • CHICAGO - Merchandise
Mart • MINNEAPOLIS - Midwest Merchandise Mart •
PORTLAND - 211 S.W. 9th St. • LOS ANGELES - Brack
Shops • DENVER - Denver Merchandise Mart • HIGH
POINT - Southern Furniture Exposition Bldg.

159

Brown Earth

4142
13"

4179
12"

3130
11"

4181
12"

4183
11½"

4185
5½"
(Opening 8")

4143
9½"

4182
12"

8202
8½"

8201
10½"

4161X
10½"

4160X
12"

4162X
7"

2094X
9"

2085X
6¾"

746
(w/o cover)

4132X
10"

4131X
7"

8167
3"

746
6½"

2057
4½"

Please refer to price list for additional colors.

Flowers, plants and candles not included.

White Earth

A collection that comes through with color to enhance any decor. The spirited feeling of our surrounding viewed in contemporary, yet traditional collection, reflecting our EARTH's own graphics.

Flowers and candles not included.

3130
11"

3142
4"

4152
7½"

3139
10¼"

8188
8"

746
6½"

4132X
10"

3144
21"

4131X
7"

8167
3"

4187
13"

208BX
6¾"

2057
4½"

Bennington Brown Foam

Haeger

818X
10"

1752X
16"

738X
7"

4178X
10"

1915X
15"

1919X
10"

RG68X
7"

116X

8140X
8½"

3139
10¼"

1066X
9"

131X
11"

2073X
6"

408X
18½"

8183X
12"

3142
4"

2094X
12"

1093X
15"

4106X
16"

8156X
5"

4044X
14"

4189
15½"

2046X
9"

1058X
10"

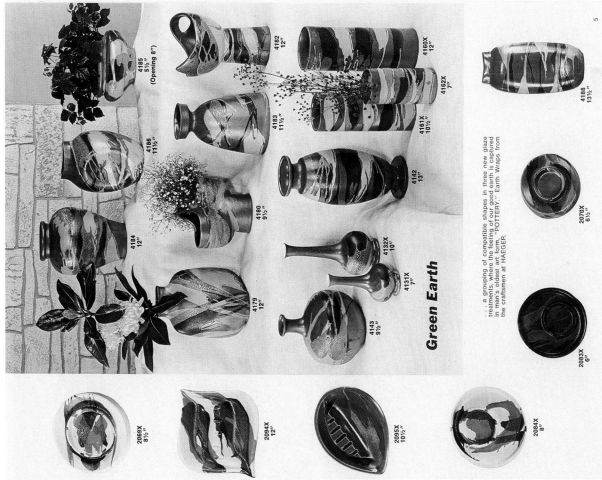

4185
5½"
(Opening 8")

4182
12"

4160X
12"

4186
11½"

4183
11½"

4162X
7"

4161X
10½"

4184
12"

4180
9½"

4142
13"

4132X
10"

4179
12"

4131X
7"

4143
9½"

Green Earth

. . . a grouping of compatible shapes in three new glaze treatments, where the feeling of our good earth is captured in man's oldest art form, "POTTERY." Earth Wraps from the craftsmen at HAEGER.

4188
13½"

2070X
6½"

2083X
6"

2069X
8½"

2094X
12"

2095X
10½"

2084X
8"

162

8193H
9"

4185H
10"
Opening

3139H
10½"
Opening

8207XH
9"
Opening

Please use the letter "H" to specify Hanging Planters.

Please refer to price list for additional colors.

8216
12"

8215
16"

The Haeger Potteries INC.

SEVEN MAIDEN LANE, DUNDEE, ILLINOIS 60118

Return Postage Guaranteed

Printed in U.S.A.

19

MULTI DIRECTIONAL MULTI DIRECTIONAL

4142
13"

4161X
10½"

4141
10½"

4152
7½"

4143
9½"

3130
11"

4162X
7"

746
6½"

8188
8"

3075X
7½"

307X
4"

3157
10½"

3144
21"

3142
4"

2057
4½"

8167
3"

2070X
6½"

2083X
6"

2084X
8"

2069X
8½"

MULTI-DIRECTIONAL — A collection that is both traditional and yet contemporary. A group that has elegance and sophistication, but blends into any surrounding. The white lines on the matte black ceramic are the key to HAEGER's MULTI-DIRECTIONAL.

U-L-T-I-D-I-R-E-C-T-I-O-N-A-L M-U-L-T-I-D-I-R-E-C-T-I-O-N-A-L

Brown Wrap - Green Wrap

4171
15"

4170
13"

3168
12"

4200
5½"

2109
6"

4106X
16"

3173
10"

3172
10"

2105
8"

4170
13"

4174
10"

3169
11"

3171
9"

4171
15"

4132X
10"

4133X
15"

3170
11"

4131X
7"

8207H
5"

4197
12"

4196
6"

3174
8"

24

For additional colors on each design shown, please see price list.

8216
12"

5005H
5½"

502
7"

8207H
5"

5001
8"

4185H
5½"

8215
16"

5000
8"

Flowers, plants and candles not included.

8219H
5½" Opening
7½" Depth

8228H
12½" Opening
6½" Depth

8226
Ht. 15½"

23

4199H

4199
7½" Opening
6½" Depth

4185H
8" Opening
5¼" Depth

8225-H: Ht. 15"

5000
8"

5001
8"

French White

8208
8½"

4168
13"

4190
10½"

4147
12"

2100
7"

8097
18"

4206
12"

4140
13"

3160
4½"

4149
10"

4070
18"

8182
8180
10"

4131
7"

4159
18"

4133
15"

8196/87 Set
14" Top
12½" Bottom

4203
12"

4132
10"

3075
7½"

8205H
7½"

748
6½"

3074
4"

5006H
8" Opening
9" Height

4205
12"

4158
18"

4148
15"

2067
7½"

4190
10½"

4193
6"

2043
6"

1068
10"

13" Bowl
3045/3076 Set

1762
20"
Peasant
Flame
only

3071
12"

612X
12¼"

613X
10½"

649
9½"

650
8½"

Antiqued Dove White only

30

White Wrap

4171
15"

3169
11"

4132X
10"

3172
10"

4195
4"
Avail. as H

4200
5½"

4133X
15"

4131X
7"

4185
5½"
Avail. as H

3173
10"

2105
8"

4202
10"

4172
10½"

2109
6"

4170
13"

3174
8"

4106X
16"

Flowers, plants and candles not included.

25

165

Ashtray Assortment I

2072
FA, MA, HR

2044
FA, MA, ET

2103
Now
ET, HR, TC

2070
PW, DK/BR, HR

2043
FA, MA, ET

2104
Now
FA, MA, HR

2071
FA, MA, ET

2106
Now
FA, ET, HR

2045
FA, MA, ET

Picture Vases
Assortment A

8097-18"

4159-18"

408-18½"

4070-18"

4103-18"

Special Offer— See Your
CERTIFICATE TO SAVINGS

Special Offer - See Your CERTIFICATE TO SAVINGS

Ashtray
Assortment II

2099
8¾"

1091
11½"

Colors listed on
enclosed wholesale
price list.

1054
9½"

153
10½"

New Vases
Assortment B

French White Antiqued
Peasant Olive
Peasant Flame

4206
12"

4205
12"

4203
12"

4204
12"

PERMANENT SHOWROOMS

ATLANTA - Merchandise Mart • BURLINGTON, MASS. - Gift & Decorative Center • CHICAGO - Merchandise Mart • COLUMBUS - Columbus Gift Mart • DALLAS - Dallas Trade Mart • DENVER - Denver Merchandise Mart • HIGH POINT - Southern Exposition Bldg. • LOS ANGELES - Los Angeles Furniture Mart • MINNEAPOLIS - Midwest Merchandise Mart • NEW YORK CITY - New York Merchandise Mart • SAN FRANCISCO - Western Furniture Mart

THE HAEGER POTTERIES, INC.

SEVEN MAIDEN LANE, DUNDEE, ILL. 60118 • PHONE 312 426-3441

Copyright 1974 The Haeger Potteries, Inc.   Printed in U.S.A.

Haeger
Craftsmen
for over a
century

4128
18"

4165
11¾"

8193
8'

8191
10½"

8200
12'

8190
8"

31

Hand Antiqued

8190H
8"

4012
13"

8193H
8"

709
12½"

1086
13"

642X
12"

628
13"

4122
12½"

8145
7½"

2092
9"

8134
12"
Zodiac

1233
13"

8141
8"

2045
6"

3162
5½"

8142
6½"

2034
9"

3166
10"

3161
11"

721
9"

SP42
4'

8191
10½"

8141
4 pc. Set

4150
15"

4176
12"

3160
4½"

3057
5½"

3153
4½"

4175
15½"

4088
7½"

All designs illustrated on pages 30
and 31 are available in French White/
Antiqued, Peasant Olive, Peasant
Flame, unless otherwise indicated.

Flowers, plants and candles not included.

166

"Playful Critters" Planters in hand-decorated STONEWARE.

5023
Height 6"
Width 7"

5024
Height 10"
Width 6"

5022
Height 5"
Length 10½"

5028
Height 12"
Width 8½"

5026
Height 6"
Length 9"

5027
Height 10"
Width 7"

5025
Height 9"
Width 6"

Plants not included.

Ceramic Figurines

649-9½"

650-8½"

628X-10½"

628-13"

612-12½"

613X

613

612

612X

642X-12"

820?H
6½" Opening
5" Ht.

5000
10" Opening
8" Ht.

4195X
8" Opening
5½" Height

8215
16" Ht.
11" Dia.

3174XH
8" Flare Top
3½" Ht.

4195X
6½" Opening
4" Height

8216
12" Ht.
10½" Dia.

Planters and Hangers in Earth Graphic wrap glazes available only from Haeger... leader in the field.

Plants and flowers not included.

8193H
8" Opening
8" Height

Peasant Olive

Buttercup

5005H
6" Opening
5½" Height

8190
8" Opening
8" Height

5006H
8" Opening
9" Height

5007
10" Opening
9" Height

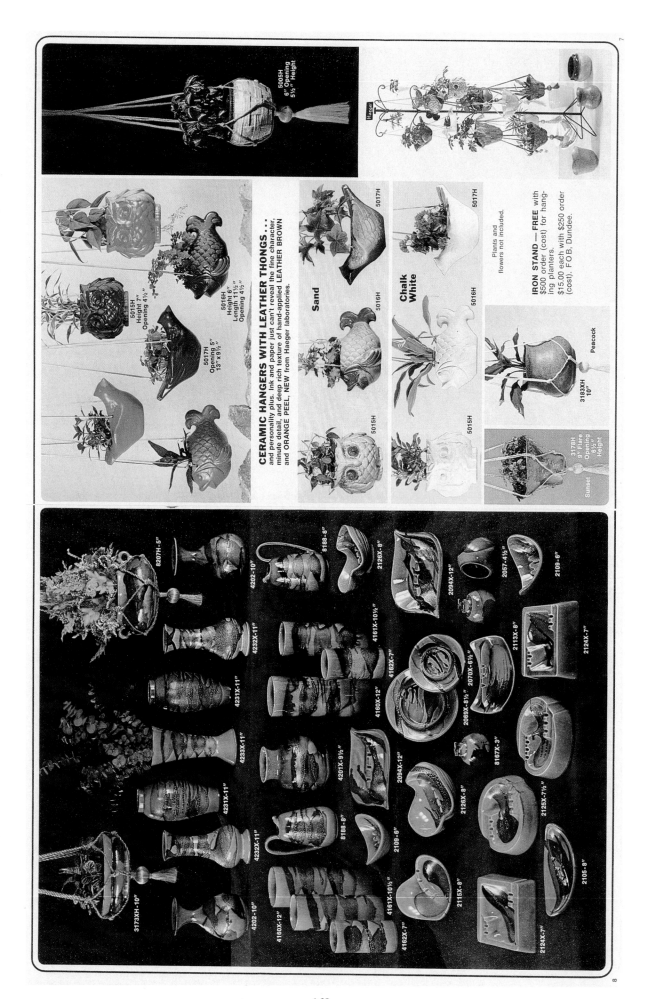

CERAMIC HANGERS WITH LEATHER THONGS...
and personality plus. Ink and paper just can't reveal the fine character, minute detail, and deep rich texture of hand-applied LEATHER BROWN and ORANGE PEEL, NEW from Haeger laboratories.

5005H
6" Opening
5½" Height

5015H
Height 7"
Opening 4½"

5016H
Height 6"
Length 11½"
Opening 4½"

5017H
Opening 5"
13"x9½"

5017H

5016H

5015H

Sand

5017H

5016H

5015H

Chalk White

3183XH
10"
Peacock

317BH
9" Flare
Opening
6½"
Height
Sunset

IRON STAND — FREE with $500 order (cost) for hanging planters.
$15.00 each with $250 order (cost). F.O.B, Dundee.

Plants and flowers not included.

820TH - 5"

4202 - 10"

8188 - 8"

2126X - 8"

2094X - 12"

2057 - 4½"

2109 - 6"

4232X - 11"

4161X - 10½"

2113X - 8"

4162X - 7"

4231X - 11"

4160X - 12"

2070X - 6½"

2124X - 7"

4233X - 11"

4201X - 9½"

2069X - 8½"

8167X - 3"

2094X - 12"

4231X - 11"

8188 - 8"

2126X - 8"

2125X - 7½"

2113X - 3"

4232X - 11"

2109 - 6"

2115X - 8"

2105 - 8"

3173XH - 10"

4202 - 10"

4160X - 12"

4161X - 10½"

4162X - 7"

2124X - 7"

168

Haeger

NEW Earth Graphics....
Fern Agate Wrap
Marigold Agate Wrap.
Designed to capture Earth's rich beauty and excitement for the home.

4184-12"

4195X

3175X-4"
Dia. 7"

4172X
10½"

3187X-5"

4131X

4132X

4131X

2069X

8167X

4200X

5000H-8"
Opening 10"
Dia. 12"

4185X

5000H

4172X-10½"

4200X-5½"

4195X-4"
Opening 6½"

3175X-4"
Dia. 7"

4131X-7"

4132X-10"

8167X-3"

2069X-8½"

4185XH
Height 5½"
Opening 8"

EXCLUSIVE HAEGER GLAZES-
All designs illustrated on these 2 pages are available also in Brown Wrap (page 10) and White Wrap (see bowl 4185X, page 6).

Flowers, plants and candles not included.

3187X-5"

4184-12"

4141-10½"

3187X-5"

8188-9"

4143X-9½"

4200X-5½"

3175X-4"
Dia. 7"

4152X-7½"

3173X-3½"
Opening 10"

2105
8"x4½"

746-5½"
Dia. 6½"

2109-3"
6"x5"

3172XH
Height 3"
Dia. 9½"

3172X

8207
Height 5"
Opening 6½"

8167X-3"

317X-2½"
9"x8½"

3174X
Height 3½"
Opening 7½"

2057-4"

4185X
Height 5½"
Opening 8"

4195X
Height 4"
Opening 6½"

3170
11"x10"
Height 4"

2085X-7"

4184-12"

Flowers, plants and candles not included.

"Brown Wrap Graphics"
Glaze treatment available only from HAEGER.

2113X-8"x6"

2111X
11"x5"

2094X
12"x10"

2070X-6½"

2069X-8½"

4160X-12"

4162X-7"

4161X-10½"

4171-15"

4170X-13"

4202-10"

4131X-7"

4172X-10½"

4132X-10"

Flowers, plants and candles not included.

169

STONEWARE
in beautiful
Sunset Colors

4208X-15"

3182-9"

3184-5"

3178-6½"

2111X-9"

2115X-8"

4170X-13"

1919X-10"

4207-13"

4160X-12"

4161X-10½"

4162X-7"

4202-10"

RG68XX-7"

3183H-6"

Flowers, plants and candles not included.

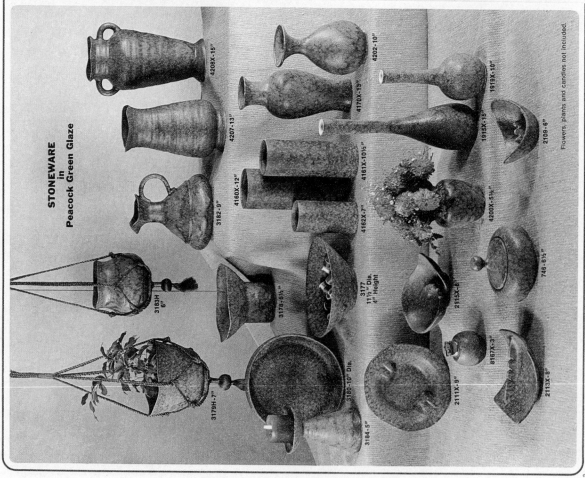

STONEWARE
in
Peacock Green Glaze

4208X-15"

4207-13"

4160X-12"

3182-9"

4170X-13"

4202-10"

1919X-10"

1915X-15"

4161X-10½"

4162X-7"

2109-6"

4200X-5½"

3177
11½" Dia.
4" Height

746-6½"

3183H
6"

3178-6½"

2115X-8"

8167X-3"

3179H-7"

3180-10" Dia.

2111X-9"

2113X-8"

3184-5"

Flowers, plants and candles not included.

170

RALEIGH BELAIR

More and more people are changing to RALEIGH for the taste, the real tobacco taste . . . and to BELAIR where you taste the light touch, just the right touch of menthol.

PREMIUM CATALOG

TASTEFUL LIVING

A. (#1145)—2800 COUPONS. BUFFET CART BY COSCO. Brass frame, 25" x 15½"; 31" high. Removable center tray snaps on top section for serving. 50" long.

B. (#1873)—2250 COUPONS. COFFEE TABLE BY FLOYD KNOBS. Hardwood with dark Oriental mahogany finish, 48" x 16"; 17" high. Matches table "N" (#1874).

C. (#1940)—650 COUPONS. PITCHER VASE BY HAEGER. Hand-fired ceramic; 18½" high. Specify orange or white. Matches ash tray "M" (#1070).

†D. (#1792)—9500 COUPONS. PORTABLE STEREO BY MAGNAVOX. Tilt down "Micromatic"; solid-state amplifier, two 8" oval speakers. Diamond/sapphire stylus, 45 RPM adapter, detachable wing-type speakers. 9½" deep, 16" high, 25" long.

E. (#1700)—825 COUPONS. FLOOR PILLOW BY EDSON. Striped upholstery fabric cover, soft Kapok filling; 24" sq. Specify Antique Gold, Marine Blue, Avocado Green, Burnished Orange or Char-Brown.

F. (#1714)—925 COUPONS. ARTIFICIAL BAMBOO PLANT. Washable, fadeproof polyethylene with natural bamboo stems. Break-resistant white container. 48" high overall.

G. (#1745)—800 COUPONS. PLANTER BY SCHWARTZ. Brass with tarnish-resistant finish; 15" x 4"; 4½" high. Plant not included.

H. (#1557)—2050 COUPONS. CHAIN LIGHT BY THOMAS. Shell chips on 11¼" white Fiberglass® sphere, antique brass trim and 15" chain; 20' cord with on/off switch. Complete with hanging hardware.

†K. (#1930)—11,675 COUPONS. PORTABLE TV BY G.E. Model M-152CVY series. All channel VHF-UHF. 12" diagonal tube, 74-sq. in. picture. 110-W., 120-V., 60 cycles, AC only.

L. (#1861)—950 COUPONS. HI-FI & TV STAND BY SPECO. Brass-plated steel, walnut-grain hardboard shelves, adj. record holders. 15½" wide, 17½" long, 25" high.

M. (#1070)—225 COUPONS. ASH TRAY BY HAEGER. Ceramic; 4½" x 8". Specify orange or white. Matches pitcher vase "C" (#1940).

N. (#1874)—1225 COUPONS. CHAIRSIDE TABLE BY FLOYD KNOBS. Clean sculptured lines; 17½" x 12"; 20" high. Matches coffee table "B" (#1873).

†Suggested for group savings.   ® Registered trademark

Page 2

Page 3

Notice on the top photo of the cover there is a Mandarin Orange Ashtray on the coffee table.
On the bottom photo Item C is a Mandarin Orange Vase and Item M is the same rectangular ashtray that is on the cover.
(See photo section to get model numbers)

171

Royal Haeger Pottery and Lamps

• See these new colorful Haeger Award winning designs, marked with the artist's name, now available at better stores everywhere.

THE HAEGER POTTERIES, INC. • DUNDEE, ILLINOIS

Royal Haeger

Lamps and Pottery

Complements to a gracious room—a handsome lamp created in the Haeger tradition of elegant simplicity—striking color accents reflected in the rich glazes of Royal Haeger Pottery. Available at better stores everywhere.

Haeger of Dundee

MAIDEN LANE   DUNDEE, ILLINOIS

"Conversation Pieces for the Home"

Royal **Haeger** Lamps and Pottery

Often a single piece of Royal Haeger Pottery, or a graceful Royal Haeger Lamp, exquisite in design, rich in the colors of the incomparable Haeger glazes, will lift a whole room from the commonplace to the charming. Ask for Royal Haeger Pottery and Lamps...at better dealers everywhere.

The
**HAEGER
POTTERIES**
Incorporated

DUNDEE, ILL.
MACOMB, ILL.

1950's Advertisement

Genuine **Haeger** Pottery

Beauty you'll always prize!

At dealers everywhere

The Haeger Potteries, Inc.
Macomb, Ill.   Dundee, Ill.
Also Makers of Royal Haeger Lamps

July 1946 Better Homes & Gardens Ad

1950's Advertisement

November 1948 Better Homes & Gardens

174

Left - #2069, Round Ashtray, reservoir in center, "White Earth Graphic Wrap" color, circa
1970's, molded on bottom: "Royal Haeger, 2069 ©, U.S.A.", 8 1/4" Dia. x 1 3/4" T.
Right - #2084, Round Ashtray, reservoir to the side, "White Earth Graphic Wrap" color,
circa 1970's, molded on bottom: "Royal Haeger ©, 2084 USA", 8 1/2" Dia. x 1 1/2" T.

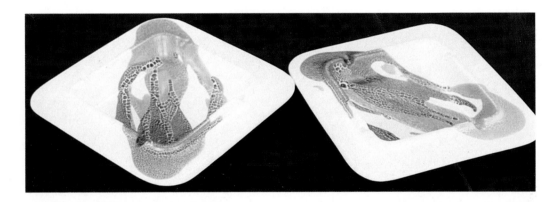

Left & Right - #2085, Pair of Square Ashtrays, "White Earth Graphic Wrap" color, circa 1970's,
molded on bottom: "Royal Haeger ©, 2085 U.S.A.", 6 3/4" Sq. x 1 1/4" T.

#2124, Square Ashtray, "Brown Earth Graphic
Wrap", circa 1970's, molded on bottom: "Haeger ©
USA 2124", 7" x 7" x 2" T.

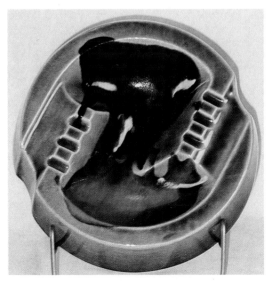

#2125X, Round Ashtray, "Fern Agate Earth
Graphic Wrap", circa 1970's, 7 3/4" Dia. x 1 3/4" T.

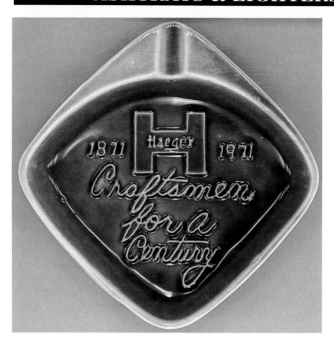

#R-1095, 1818-1968 Lincoln Ashtray, brown color, molded on bottom: "Illinois Sesquicentennial, Haeger 1095, © U.S.A.", 6 3/4" L x 4 3/8" W x 1" T.

Haeger Commemorative Ashtray, green color, molded inside: "Haeger 1871-1971, Craftsmen for a Century", molded on bottom: Haeger U.S.A.", 5 3/8" x 5 3/8" x 1" T.

Elephant Ashtray, blue color, marked with label on bottom: "1934, A Century of Progress", 4 1/2" L x 3 1/4" W x 1 7/8" T.

Advertising Ashtray, brown color, "1934, Century of Progress", molded on bottom: "Haeger", 4" W x 3 1/4" L x 1" T.

Advertising Ashtray, "A Century of Progress, 1934", green color, molded on bottom: "Haeger", 4 1/4" L x 3" T x 1" W.

Advertising Ashtray, "A Century of Progress, 1933-1934", brown color, no markings, 3 1/4" Dia.

Advertising Ashtray, "A Century of Progress, 1933-1934", green color, molded on bottom in diamond shape: "Haeger", 3" Dia.

#128, Ashtray, "Gold Tweed" color, molded on bottom: "Royal Haeger, 128 © USA", 13" L x 8" W x 2 1/2" T.

#127, Ashtray, "Gold Tweed" color, molded on bottom: "Royal Haeger USA ©", also stamped on bottom in gold: "Haeger Gold Tweed 22K Gold", 10 1/4" L x 9 1/2" W x 2" T.

#109-S, Square Ashtray, "Gold Tweed" color, molded on bottom: "Royal Haeger 109-S U.S.A.", 7" x 7" x 2 1/4" T.

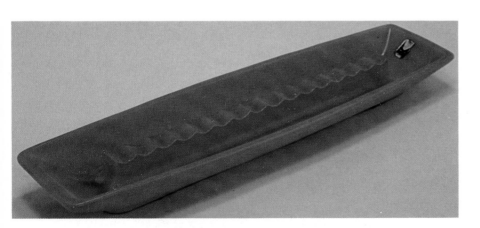

#1016-S, Convex Long John Ashtray, "Mandarin Orange" color, marked with foil label: "Haeger" in H design, also molded on bottom: "Royal Haeger © 1016-S USA", 18 1/4" L x 4 5/8" W x 1 5/8" T.

#889, Ribbed Table Lighter, "Mandarin Orange" color, circa 1950's-60's, marked with foil label: "Haeger" in H design, 3" Dia. x 5" T.

177

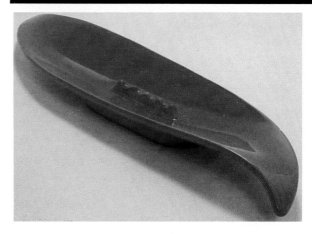

#128, Triangular Ashtray, "Mandarin Orange" color, molded on bottom: "Royal Haeger 128 © U.S.A.", 13 1/4" L x 2 1/2" T

#1045, Ashtray, "Mandarin Orange" color, molded on bottom: "Haeger, 1045, ©", 15" L x 1 1/4" T.

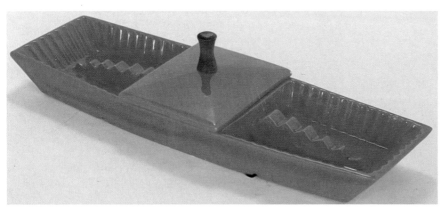

#720-S, Ashtray & Cigarette Holder with wooden handle on lid, "Mandarin Orange" color, molded on bottom: "Haeger, 720-S, ©, U.S.A.", 15 1/4" L x 3 1/2" T.

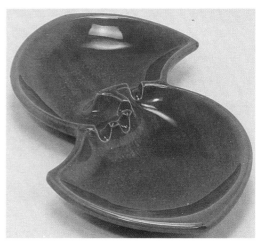

#1030, Ashtray, "Mandarin Orange" color, circa 1950's, molded on bottom: "Haeger, 1030, ©, USA", 9 1/8" L x 5 1/2" W x 1" T.

#153, Ashtray, "Mandarin Orange" color, molded on bottom: "Royal Haeger, ©, 153, USA", 10 3/4" L x 8" W x 1 1/2" T.

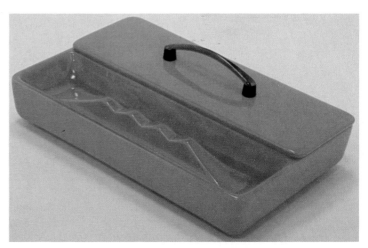

#702, Ashtray & Cigarette Holder, "Mandarin Orange" color, molded on bottom: "©, Royal Haeger, 702, USA", 10 1/4" L x 6 3/8" x 3 1/4" T.

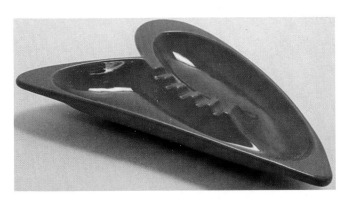

#135, Ashtray, "Mandarin Orange" color, molded on bottom: "Royal Haeger 135 © U.S.A.", 11 1/2" L x 1 3/8" T.

Stanley Snuffer Ashtray, green color, molded on bottom: "Stanley Snuffer, by Haeger, USA", 7" Dia. x 1 1/2" T.

#2009, Round Ashtray, green with white and brown, molded on bottom: "Haeger ©, 2009 USA", 7" Dia. x 1 3/4" T.

#2115, Ashtray, green color, molded on bottom: "Haeger", 7 3/4" W x 7 3/4" L x 2 1/2" T.

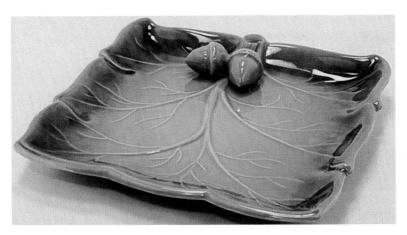

#2145, Square Leaf Ashtray with Acorns, green color, molded on bottom: "Haeger, © 1976, 2145", 9 3/4" x 9 3/4" x 1 1/2" T

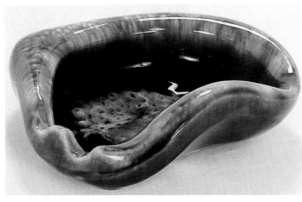

#R-873, Freeform Ashtray, "Green Agate" color, molded on bottom: "Royal Haeger R-873 U.S.A."

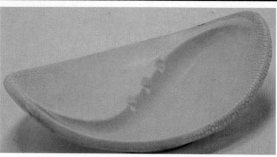

#2105, Ashtray, "Yellow Boco", molded on bottom: "Haeger, 2105 ©", 7 7/8" L x 4 3/4" W x 2 1/4" T.

#R-685, Horse Head Cigarette Box, "Green Agate" color, molded on bottom: "Royal Haeger R-685 USA", 6 3/4" L x 4" W x 5" T

#R-1894, Round Ashtray, transparent white glaze over red clay, molded on bottom: "Royal Haeger, R1894, U.S.A.", 7" Dia. x 1 1/2" T.

#134, Palm Leaf Ashtray, "Green Agate" color, molded on bottom: "Royal Haeger 134 USA", 19" L x 4 1/4" W x 2 1/4" T.

#175, Sands of Time Ashtray, green with olive green specks, molded on bottom: "Royal Haeger USA 175", 11 1/2" L x 6 1/4" W x 1 1/2" T.

Left - #R-125, Rectangular Ashtray, "Cotton White" color, molded on bottom: "Royal Haeger, ©, R125 USA", 8" L x 4 1/2" W x 1 1/4" T.
Right - #153, Ashtray, "Cotton White" color, molded on bottom: "Royal Haeger, ©, 153 USA", 11" L x 8" W x 1 1/2" T.

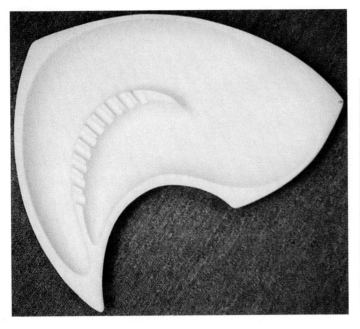

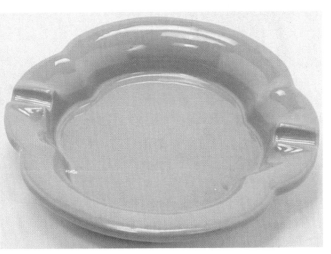

#162, Ashtray, "Cotton White", molded on bottom: "Royal Haeger © 162 U.S.A.", 15 1/4" L x 14" W x 1 1/2" T.

#2155, Ashtray, tan color, molded on bottom: "Haeger ©, 2155, USA", 7 1/2" Dia. x 1 1/2" T.

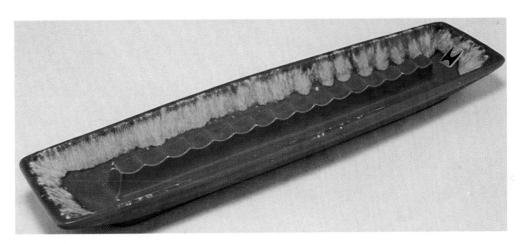

#1016-S, Convex Long John Ashtray, "Pumpkin" with cascade of cream, molded on bottom: "Royal Haeger, 1016-S, USA", also marked with foil label: "Haeger" in H design, 18" L x 4 1/2" W x 2" T.

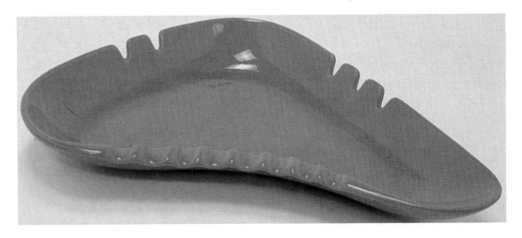

#R-1718, Boomerang Ashtray, orange color, molded on bottom: "Royal Haeger, R1718, U.S.A.", 13 1/2" L x 8" W x 1 3/4" T.

#R-1787, Egg Shaped Ashbowl, "Pearl Shell" color, molded on bottom: "Royal Haeger, R1787 U.S.A.",
6 1/4" x 5 3/4" W x 4" T.

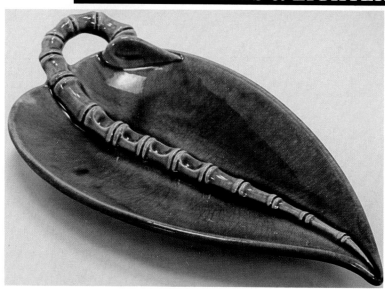

#110-H, Leaf Ashtray, "Jade Crackle" color, molded on bottom: "Royal Haeger, 110-H U.S.A.", 13 3/4" L x 7 1/2" W x 2 1/2" T.

#R-125, Rectangular Ashtray, "Briar Agate" color, molded on bottom: "Royal Haeger, © R-125 USA", 8" L x 4 1/2" W x 1 1/4" T.

#R-631, Leopard Cigarette Box, "Amber" color, 1940's, molded on bottom: "Royal Haeger, R631, U.S.A.", 6 1/2" L x 4" W x 5" T.

#R-811, Palette Ashtray, "Pearl Grey Drip" color, molded on bottom: "Royal Haeger R811 USA", 9 1/2" L x 6 1/4" W x 1 1/2" T.

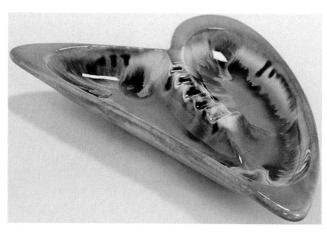

#135, Ashtray, "Briar Agate" color, molded on bottom: "Royal Haeger 135 © U.S.A.", 12" L x 7 1/2" W.

#R-1602, Horseshoe Ashtray with two horse heads inside, "Ebony" color, molded on bottom: "Royal Haeger R-1602 USA", also marked with crown foil label: "Royal Haeger", 8" W x 2 1/4" T.

#HJ-8, Rectangular Ashtray, green & blue with brown trim, *this was a piece made for another company*, molded on bottom: "Haeger", 11" L x 5" W x 2 1/4" T.

#138, Ashtray, "Turquoise & Blue", molded on bottom: "Royal Haeger 138 © U.S.A.", 8 1/2" L x 4 3/4" W x 1 1/2" T.

#130, Ashtray, "Turquoise", molded on bottom: "Royal Haeger 130 © USA", 12" L x 5 1/4" W x 1 1/2" T.

#135, Ashtray, "Purple Jewel Tone" *This color was achieved by dropping colored glass in the pottery and then firing it until melted*, molded on bottom: "Royal Haeger, 135 © USA", 12" L x 7 1/2" W x 1 1/2" T.

#153, Ashtray, purple color, circa 1960's-70's, molded on bottom: "Royal Haeger © 153 USA", 10 1/2" L x 7 3/4" W x 1 1/2" T.

Left - #2070, Round Ashtray, light tannish-brown with black streaks, molded on bottom: "Royal Haeger 2070 © U.S.A.", 6 1/2" Dia. x 1 1/2" T.
Right - #8167, Round Lighter, light tannish-brown with black streaks, not marked, lighter insert marked: "Japan", 3" Dia. x 3 1/2" T.

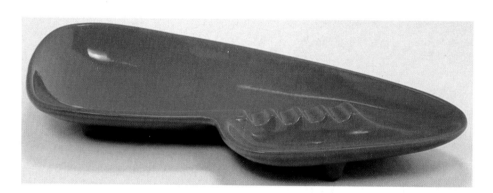

#130, Ashtray, "Haeger Red" color, molded on bottom: "Royal Haeger", 12" L x 1 1/4" T.

#113, Sculpted Miniature Ashtrays, "Haeger Red" color, molded on bottom: "Royal Haeger", 4 1/2" L x 1 1/4" T.

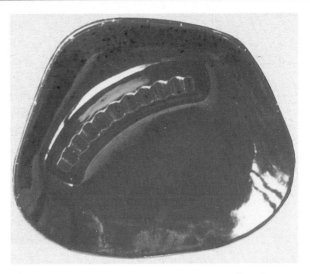

#R1755, Executive Ashtray, "Haeger Red" color,
marked on bottom *(unreadable)*, 14" W.

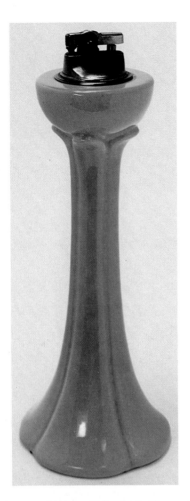

#813-H, Tall Cigarette Lighter, "Mandarin Orange" color, lighter
insert is marked: "Japan", molded on bottom: "Royal Haeger, 813-
H USA", 4 1/8" Dia. base x 2 7/8" Dia. top x 10 3/4" T.

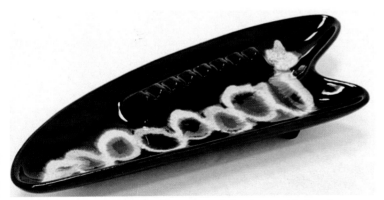

#SP-12, Palette Ashtray, "Ebony Cascade" color, molded on bottom:
"Royal Haeger SP-12 U.S.A.", 13 1/2" L x 5 1/2" W x 1 1/2" T.

#813-H, Tall Cigarette
Lighter, "Marigold Agate"
color, lighter insert is
marked: "Japan", molded
on bottom: "Royal
Haeger, 813-H U.S.A.",
4" Dia. base x 10 1/2" T.

#177, Leaf Ashtray, "Mandarin Orange" color, circa 1950's, molded on bottom: "Royal Haeger © 177 U.S.A.", *note: S in U.S.A. is backwards*, 5" L x 4" W x 1 1/8" T.

#8167, Round Lighter, blue with black streaks, not marked, 3" Dia. x 3 1/2" T.

#812-H, Fish Table Lighter, "Jade Crackle" color, circa 1960's, 4" Dia. base x 10" T.

#R-449, Leaf Ashtrays, "Mauve Agate" color, no markings, 3 1/2" W x 4 1/2" L x 1" T.

#3622, Ball Bookend Planters, "Chartreuse" color, marked
on bottom with foil label: "Genuine Haeger",
4 3/4" L x 5" W x 7" T.

#R-132, Ram Bookend Figure, mint green-blue
with brown and blue spots, no markings,
8 1/2" L x 4" W x 8" T

#R-641, Stallion Bookend Planter,
"Chartreuse" color, not marked,
5 1/2" L x 3 1/2" W x 8 3/4" T.

#R718, Ram Head Bookends, "Oxblood" color,
marked with crown foil label: "Royal-Haeger Dundee,
Illinois", 5" L x 4 1/4" W x 5 3/4" T.

#R-1144, Water Lily Bookends, green with white flowers, circa 1952, 5" L x 5" W x 7 1/2" T.

#R-638, Pair of Panther Planter Bookends, "Ebony" color, circa 1950's, molded on bottom: "Royal Haeger R638 USA", Left - 7 3/4" L x 5 1/4" W x 4" T., Right - 7 1/2" L x 5 1/4" W x 7 3/4" T.

#R-475, Calla Lily Bookends, "Amber" color, molded on bottom: "Royal Haeger R475 U.S.A.", 4 1/2" L x 4 1/2" W x 6 1/8" T.

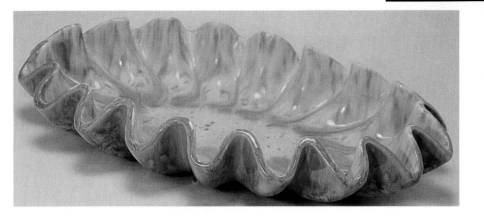

#R-309, Ruching Bowl, peach-blue-cream-white & green, molded on bottom: "Royal Haeger, by Royal Hickman, Made in USA 309", 15" L x 8" W x 3" T.

#R-1824, Palm Leaf Center-piece, "Pearl Shell" color, molded on bottom: "Royal Haeger R-1824 U.S.A.", 26" L x 4 3/4" W x 3 3/4" T.

#R-333, Bowl, "Lilac" color, molded on bottom: "Royal Haeger R-333 © USA", also marked with foil label: "Handcrafted, Haeger", 16 1/4" L x 7" W x 4 1/2" T.

#R-370, Dutch Cup Bowl, "Green Agate" color, molded on bottom: "Royal Haeger", 18 1/2" L x 3 1/2" T.

#R-759, Bowl, dark purple with light blue and white, molded on bottom: "#R-759", 6 1/2" Top Dia. x 3" T.

#RG-56, Compote Bowl, "Black Mistique" color, molded on bottom: "Royal Haeger © RG56 USA", 9" Dia. Top x 3" T.

#R-277, Spiral Plume Dish, "Peach Agate" color, circa 1942, molded on bottom: "Royal Haeger by Royal Hickman, Made in U.S.A., R-277", 7" L x 1" T.

#R-614, Scroll Bowl, "Green Agate" color, molded on bottom: "Haeger Award 1947, Prize Design, by S. Young, R 614 U.S.A.", 14 1/2" L x 12 1/2" W x 4 3/4" T.

#352, Rectangular Bowl, "Black Mistique" color, molded on bottom: "Royal Haeger © 352 USA", 14 1/2" L x 7 1/4" W x 4" T.

#364-H, Lily Bowl, yellow-orange with dark tips, molded on bottom: "Royal, Haeger, © 364H USA", also marked with foil label: "Handcrafted, Haeger", 16 1/4" L x 9 1/4" W x 2 1/4" T.

#R-466, Curving Bowl, "Briar Agate" color, molded on botttom: "Royal Haeger, R-466 U.S.A.", also marked with foil label: "Royal Haeger, Dundee, Illinois", 14 1/2" L

#R-309, Ruching Bowl, "Cloudy Blue" color, circa 1946, no markings, 15" L x 8" W x 2 1/2" T.

#3003, Compote, "Cotton White and Turquoise" color, molded on bottom: "Haeger © 3003 U.S.A.", also marked with foil label: "Haeger" in H design, 12" L x 4 1/2" T.

#H-740, Footed Bowl, "Green Agate" color, marked with rectangular blue & silver foil label: "The Great Name, Haeger ®, In American Ceramics", 15 3/4" L x 5 1/2" W x 3 1/2" T.

#R-1494, 50's Three Legged Low Bowl, pink & black, molded on bottom: "Royal Haeger R1494", 20 1/4" L x 6 1/2" W x 3 1/4" T.

#334 (also re-numbered #R-357), Scalloped & Waved Bowl, "White" color, molded on bottom: "Haeger USA 334", 15" L x 7 1/4" W x 2" T.

#R-358, Footed Bowl, "Mallow and Ebony", molded on bottom: "Royal Haeger R358 USA", 17 1/2" L x 8" W x 3 1/2" T.

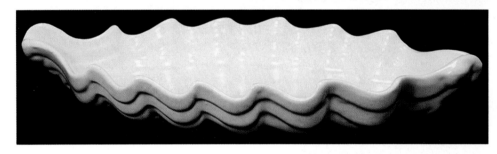

#R-1338, Modern Bowl, "Chartreuse and Ebony" color, marked with paper label: "Royal-Haeger, Dundee, Illinois", 13 1/4" L x 6 1/2" W x 3 1/2" T.

#329-H, Pheasant Bowl, "Gold Tweed" color, molded on bottom: "Royal Haeger © 329-H USA", 21 1/4" L x 7 1/4" W x 5 1/2" T.

#364-H, Lily Bowl, "Gold Tweed" color, molded on bottom: "Royal Haeger © 364H USA", also stamped in gold on bottom: "Haeger, Gold Tweed 22 K. Gold", 16 1/4" L x 9 1/4" W x 2 1/2" T.

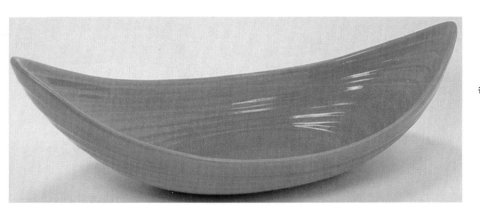

#373-H, Bowl, "Mandarin Orange" color, molded on bottom: "Royal Haeger", 15" L x 7" W x 4" T.

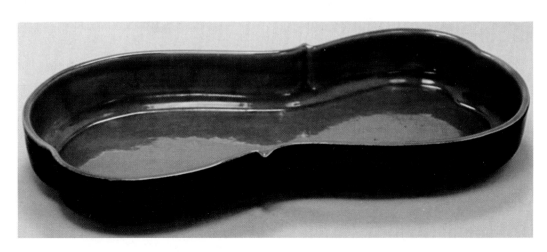

#R-484, Garden Bowl, "Chartreuse and Ebony" color, molded on bottom: "Royal Haeger U.S.A.", 13 1/2" L x 1 3/4" T.

#47, Bowl, "Chartreuse" color, circa 1938, molded on bottom: "Haeger U.S.A.", 13 1/4" Dia. x 2 1/2" T.

#362, Round Bowl, "Mandarin Orange" color, molded on bottom: "Royal Haeger 362 © USA", 12 1/4" Dia. x 2" T.

#W-2005, Garden Bowl, pink & white, molded on bottom: "Royal Haeger by Royal Hickman U.S.A. W2005", 14" L x 6" W x 2" T.

#878-H, Bud Serving Tray, "Mandarin Orange" color, circa 1950's, molded on bottom: "Haeger USA © 878H", 14" L x 9" W x 2" T.

#3177, Bowl, white-yellow-orange & reddish-brown, *note: pottery is rough like bisque*, marked on felt bottom: "Royal Haeger ®, U.S.A., The Haeger Potteries Inc. ©, Dundee, ILL.", 4 3/4" Dia. base x 11" Dia. Top x 4" T.

#3961, Square Dish, blue with black specs, circa 1967-68, made at Macomb, Illinois plant, molded on bottom: "Haeger 3961 U.S.A.", 8" x 8" x 2 1/2" T.

#3169, Two Handled Bowl, "White Earth Graphic Wrap", molded on bottom: "Royal, Haeger ©, 3169 USA", also marked with foil label: "Haeger (in H design), Craftsmen for a Century", 11 1/4" L x 8 3/4" W x 4 1/8" T.

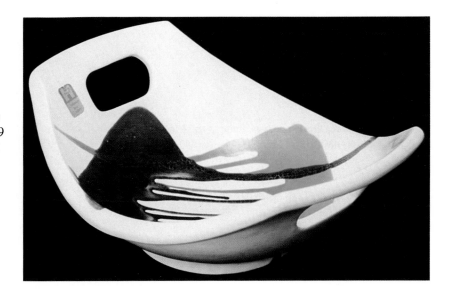

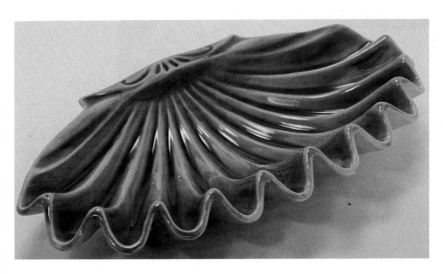

#R-297, Shell Bowl, "Chartreuse and Silver Spray" color, molded on bottom: "Royal Haeger, R297 U.S.A.", 14" L x 7 1/2" W x 2 3/4" T.

#S-552, "S" Bowl, *note: this is Studio Haeger*, marked on bottom: "Haeger U.S.A.", 14 1/4" L x 8" W x 2 1/4" T.

#101, Bowl, *note: this piece was made at the Macomb, Illinois plant, molded on bottom: "Haeger U.S.A.", 7 1/2" Top Dia. x 3 1/2" T.

#R-466, Curving Bowl, light blue & white, molded on bottom: "Royal Haeger, R466 U.S.A.", 14 3/4" L x 6" W x 3 1/2" T.

#R-442, Bowl with floral relief,
"Mauve Agate" color, no markings,
18 1/4" L x 6 1/4" W x 4 3/4" T.

#314, Compote Bowl, green & white
"Boco", molded on bottom: "Royal Haeger,
314 USA", 14" L x 5" W x 6 1/4" T.

#R-373, Bowl with applied flowers,
"Cloudy Blue and White" color, circa
1950's, no markings,
19" L x 6" W x 6 1/2" T

#R-476, Beaded Bowl, "Mauve Agate"
color, molded on bottom: "Royal
Haeger R476 U.S.A.",
14 3/4" L x 7 1/4" W x 4 3/4" T.

#R-1195, Abstract Fish Bowl, light pink with white spots, marked with crown foil label: "Royal Haeger ®", 14 1/2" L x 5 1/2" W x 4 1/8" T.

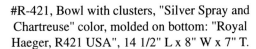

#R-421, Bowl with clusters, "Silver Spray and Chartreuse" color, molded on bottom: "Royal Haeger, R421 USA", 14 1/2" L x 8" W x 7" T.

#R-421, Bowl with clusters, "Green Agate and Chartreuse" color, molded on bottom: "Royal Haeger, R421 USA", 14 1/2" L x 8" W x 7" T.

#R-328, Oval Bowl with plume feet, "Mauve Agate" and cream color, molded on bottom: "R-328, Royal Haeger by Royal Hickman, U.S.A.", 16" L x 7 1/4" W x 5 5/8" T.

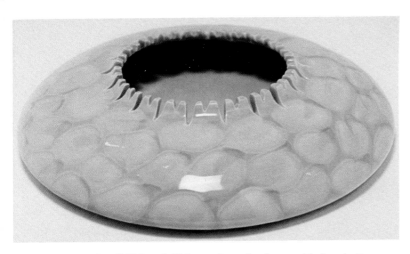

#R-290, Cut Out "V" Bowl, "Mauve Agate" color, molded on bottom: "Royal Haeger, R-290, U.S.A.", 10 1/4" Dia. x 2 1/2" T.

#R-481, Seashell on base, "Silver Spray and Chartreuse" color, molded on bottom: "Royal Haeger 481", 9 3/4" L x 9" W x 10 1/2" T.

#8172, Bowl Planter, "Roman Bronze" color, molded on bottom: "Haeger, Sascha B", *note: Sascha Brastoff was a well known California artist who designed this line.* 8 3/4" Dia. x 6 1/2" T.

#60, Bowl Planter, "Green Agate" color, circa 1936, no markings, 5 7/8" Top Dia. x 3 1/2" T.

#R-877, Open Leaf Bowl, "Ebony and Chartreuse" color, circa 1951, molded on bottom: "Royal Haeger, R877 USA", 13 3/4" L x 7 1/2" W x 2 1/4" T.

#342, Bowl, "Lilac" color, molded on bottom:
"Royal Haeger © 342 U.S.A.", 7" x 7" x 6" T.

#106, Bowl Planter, brown and dark purple, circa
1930, no markings, 8" Dia. x 3" T.

#3122-A, Ribbed Bowl, green, molded on bottom:
"Haeger USA", 7" Dia. x 2 1/2" T.

#R-1729, Tall Footed Bowl, beige and gold
(rough surface), molded on bottom:
"Royal Haeger, R1729 USA",
5" Base Dia. x 9 3/4" Top Dia. x 8 3/4" T.

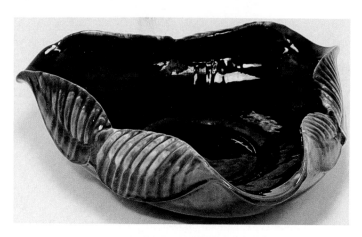

#R-112, Leaf Edged Bowl, "Green Agate" color, molded on
bottom: "Royal Haeger, Royal Hickman, Made In USA 112",
13 1/2" L x 2 1/2" T.

#746, Dish, "Brown Earth Graphic Wrap", *note:
could also have a lid*, stamped on felt bottom: "©
Royal Haeger U.S.A.", 7" Dia. x 2 1/2" T.

#R-224, Daisy Bowl, "Chartreuse" color, molded on bottom: "Royal Haeger USA", 11 3/4" Dia. x 2" T.

#450, 6" Bowl, "Gold Tweed" color, molded on bottom: "Royal Haeger 450 U.S.A.", 3 3/8" Base Dia. x 4 3/8" Top Dia. x 6" T.

#25, Three Footed Bowl, dark & light blue, circa 1914, molded on bottom: "Haeger" in diamond shape, 6" Dia. x 3 1/4" T.

#5, Three footed Compote, blue, circa 1914, no markings, 6 1/4" Dia. x 1 7/8" T.

#63, Bowl Planter, blue with light blue & green, circa 1918, no markings, 8 7/8" Dia. x 2 7/8" T.

#4195, Bowl, "White Earth Graphic Wrap" color, stamped on bottom: "Royal Haeger USA ©", 4 1/2" Base Dia. x 6 3/4" Top Dia. x 3 3/4" T.

#811, Bowl Planter, "Briar Agate" color, ink stamped on bottom: "Haeger", 6 1/2" Top Dia. x 3 3/4" T.

#RT-63, Square Compote, "Green Gold Tweed" color, circa 1960, marked on bottom: "Royal Haeger Green Gold Tweed USA RT63", 4" x 4" Base x 7" T.

#33, Bowl, "Briar Agate" color, marked on bottom: "Haeger U.S.A. 33", also marked with foil label: "Copyrighted Haeger ®, Macomb, ILL. Made in U.S.A.", 3 3/4" Base Dia. x 6" Top Dia. x 3" T.

#863, Round Diamond Pattern Bowl, tan with white interior, stamped on bottom: "Haeger, ©, USA, 863", 9 3/4" Dia. x 2 3/4" T.

#834, Octagon Bowl Planter with rope pattern relief, "Peasant Red and White" color, molded on bottom: "Haeger, No.834, U.S.A.", 4 1/4" Base x 8 1/2" Top x 4 1/4" T.

#34, Stemmed Candle Holder, mint green, circa 1910's-1920's, no markings, 5 1/4" Base Dia. x 10 1/2" T.

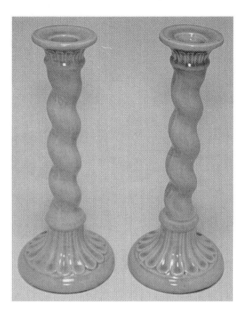

#120 (also #3044), Spiral Stemmed Candlesticks, yellow, circa 1917, no markings, 4" Base Dia. x 10" T.

#R-220, Candle Holder with two birds, "Mauve Agate" color, circa 1939, no markings, 3" x 3" Base x 7 1/2" T.

#R-203, Standing Double Fish Candle Holder, "Mauve Agate" color, no markings, 5" T.

#R-579, Double Tier Block Candle Holder, "Green Briar" color, *note: also came in a Three Tier Block #R-397*, no markings, 2" x 2" x 2 1/4" T.

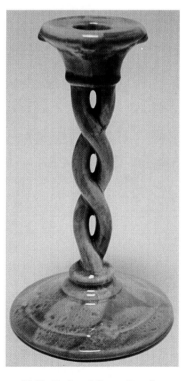

#243, Twisted Stem Candle Holder, "Peach Agate" color, circa 1927, no markings, 4 1/4" Base Dia. x 7 1/2" T.

#R-304, Fish Candle Holder, "Mauve Agate" color, no markings, 3 1/4" L x 2" W x 4 1/4" T.

#R-312, Cornucopia Candle Holders, left - "Chartreuse" color, right -"Silver Spray" color, marked with foil crown label: "Royal-Haeger, Dundee, Illinois", 5 3/4" L x 3" W x 5" T.

#R-1285, Lily Candle Holders, "Turquoise and Blue" color, marked with crown foil label: "Royal Haeger", 5 1/2" L x 3 1/4" W x 5" T.

#R-312, Cornucopia Candle Holder, "Green Briar" color, circa 1949, no markings, 5 1/2" L x 2 3/4" W x 5" T.

#R-1728, Roman Candle Holders, "Sable" color, molded on bottom: "Royal Haeger R1728 U.S.A.", 2 1/2" Base Dia. x 5 3/8" Top Dia. x 4 1/4" T.

#R-516, Swan Candle Holders, "Mauve Agate" color, no markings, 3 5/8" Base Dia. x 8" T.

#R-433, Triple Plume Candle Holder, "Mauve Agate" color, no markings, 11" L x 3 1/4" W x 5" T.

#R-418, Double Candle Holder, "Cloudy Blue" color, no markings, 8 1/2" L x 4" W x 6" T.

#R-220, Pair of Double Birds Candle Holders, "Cloudy Blue" color, no markings, 2 1/2" x 2 1/2" x 5 1/4" T.

#R-437, Leaf Candle Holders, "Ebony" color, no markings, 4 3/4" L x 2 3/4" T.

205

#815-H, Candle Holder Compote, "Gold Tweed" color, circa 1961, molded on bottom: "Royal Haeger 815H USA", 5 1/4" Base Dia. x 15 1/4" T.

#R-473, Twin Stalk Candle Holder, blue with white accents, no markings, 10 1/2" L x 4" W x 7 1/2" T.

#8487, Candle Holders, marked with paper label: "Studio Haeger", *note: made with red clay*, 3 1/2" Base Dia. x 7 1/4" T.

#HT-46, Pair of Female Candle Holders, blue with black & white, signed in the pottery on the inside of the molds: "Haeger Maglio", *note: these pieces were hand thrown by Sebastiano Maglio.* 3 1/4" Base Dia. x 3 3/4" Dia. of hat rim x 9 1/4" T.

#R-485, Double Candle Holder with Planter, Chartreuse, circa 1946, molded on bottom: "Royal Haeger USA R485", also marked with crown foil label, 7 1/2" L x 1 1/2" W x 3" T.

#R-185, Flower and Leaf Candle Holders, light blue with light green accents, marked with crown foil label: "Royal-Haeger By Royal Hickman", 5 3/4" x 5 1/2" x 2 1/2" T.

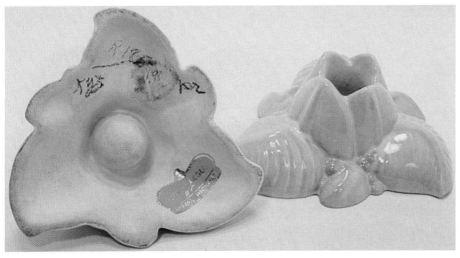

This is a photo of the label on the underside. The label is over 1 3/4" L. Also notice that there isn't any glaze on the underside of these pieces.

#3004, Candle Holders, "Blue Crackle" color, molded on bottom: "Haeger 3004 ©", 5 3/4" L x 3 1/4" W x 1 3/8" T.

#3004, Candle Holders, "Peacock" color, molded on bottom: "Haeger 3004 ©", 5 3/4" L x 3 1/4" W x 1 3/8" T.

#3068, Triple Candle Holder Dish, brown with white accents, molded on bottom: "Haeger U.S.A.", 12 1/4" Dia. x 3" T.

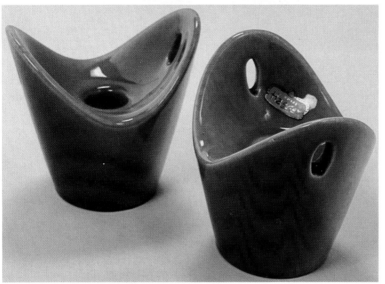

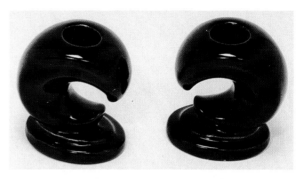

#R-1354, Edged Candle Holders, "Ebony" color, no markings, 3" L x 2" W x 3 1/2" T.

#1552-S, Candle Holders, "Turqoise and Blue" color, molded on bottom: "Royal Haeger", also marked with crown foil label: "Royal Haeger", 4" W x 4" T.

#3142, Candle Holder for large candles, "Brown Earth Graphic Wrap" color, 5 1/2" Dia. x 3 3/4" T.

Leaf Candle Holder & Planter, "Silver Spray" color, marked with oval foil label: "Haeger, Made in U.S.A.", 8" L x 4 3/4" W x 7 1/4" T.

#R-431, Lily Candy Bowl, "Mallow"
and aqua color, molded on bottom:
"Royal Haeger R431 USA", 7 1/2" Dia. x 6" T.

#R-1730, Candy Jar, "Mandarin Orange" color,
stamped on bottom: "Royal Haeger",
7" Top Dia. x 10" T.

#8170, Covered Dish with Rooster on lid, "Roman Bronze" color,
molded on bottom: "Haeger" and "Sascha B", 9" L x 5" W x 3" T.

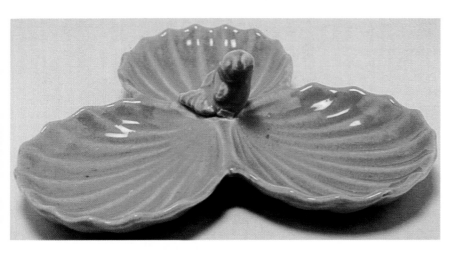

#R-459, Large Triple Candy Dish with Fish
Figure, blue, circa 1946, molded on bottom:
"USA", 8 1/2" L x 3" T.

Left - #R-459, Large Triple Candy Dish with Fish Figure, "Mauve Agate" color, molded on bottom: "USA", 8 1/2" x 3" T.
Right - #R-457, Triple Leaf Candy Dish with Bird Figure, "Mauve Agate" color, 8 1/2" x 3" T.

#707-S, Covered Dish, "Blue Crackle" color, molded on bottom: "© Royal Haeger U.S.A. 707-S", 7 1/2" Top Dia. x 4 3/8" Base Dia. x 6 3/4" T.

#R-431, Lily Candy Bowl, "Chartreuse and Yellow" color, molded on bottom: "Royal Haeger R431 USA", also marked with crown foil label: "Royal Haeger, Dundee, Illinois", 7 1/2" Dia. x 6" T.

#8044-H, Candy Dish with handle, "Mandarin Orange" color, molded on bottom: "Haeger © 8044-H", 8 3/4" x 8 3/4" x 6 1/2" T.

#8300, Toe Tapper with Flute, brown
textured, 4 1/4" x 8" T.

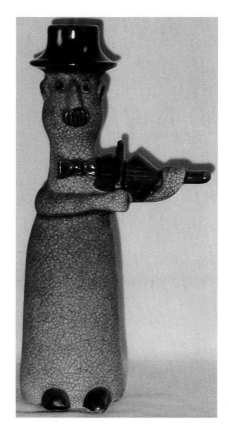

#8296, Toe Tapper with Violin,
brown textured, 3 3/4" x 9 1/4" T.

Toe Tappers, brown textured, from left to right:
#8297, Banjo Player, 2 1/2" Dia. x 12" T.
#8295, French Horn Player, 5 1/2" Dia. x 10" T.
#8299, Cymbals Player, 4 1/2" Dia. x 11 1/2" T.
#8294, Accordion Player, 5 1/2" Dia. x 10 1/2" T.
*note: there is one more figure to this series that is not
pictured on this page.*

Left - #RG-68, Bottle Vase, green with black specks (Flower-
Ware), molded on bottom: "Royal Haeger U.S.A. RG-68",
1 7/8" Base Dia. x 7 1/8" T.
Right - #RG-37, Triangular Bowl, green with black specks
(Flower-Ware), molded on bottom: "Royal Haeger RG-37",
3" Base Dia. x 6" W x 2 3/8" T.

Left - #8183-X, Pitcher Vase, orange and yellow with dark spots, stamped on bottom: "Haeger © USA", 3 7/8" Base Dia. x 12 1/4" T.
Middle - #R-1919, Onion Vase, orange and yellow with dark spots, stamped on bottom: "Royal Haeger © USA", 2 5/8" Base Dia. x 10 1/4" T.
Right - #8180, Pitcher Vase, orange and yellow with dark spots, stamped on bottom: "Haeger © USA", 3 3/8" Base Dia. x 10" T.

Left - #3045, Candle Holder, ebony and amber with yellow, circa 1967, *note: experimental glaze, very few produced.*, molded on bottom: "Haeger 3045 USA", 6" Base Dia. x 10" T.
Right - Jug, ebony and amber with yellow, circa 1967, *note: experimental glaze, very few produced*, no markings, 2 3/4" Dia. x 4" T.
*both pieces also had metal flakes in the glaze.

Left & Right - #R-312, Cornucopia Candle Holders, "Mauve Agate" color, no markings, 5 1/2" L x 3" W x 4 3/4" T.
Middle - #R-284, Trout Vase, "Mauve Agate" color, molded on bottom: "Royal Haeger USA 284", 9" L x 4 1/2" W x 7" T.

Left - #4232-X, Vase, "White Earth Graphic Wrap" color, marked
on felt: "Royal Haeger ®, U.S.A., The Haeger Potteries Inc. ©,
Dundee, ILL.", 4 3/8" Base Dia. x 3 7/8" Top Dia. x 11 1/8" T.

Right Front - #3187-X, Candle Holder, "White Earth Graphic
Wrap" color, marked on felt: "Royal Haeger ®, U.S.A.,
The Haeger Potteries Inc. ©, Dundee, ILL.",
5" Base Dia. x 5 3/8" Top Dia. x 5 1/8" T.

Right Back - #4161-X, Cylinder Vase, "White Earth Graphic
Wrap" color, marked on felt: "Royal Haeger ®, U.S.A.,
The Haeger Potteries Inc. ©, Dundee, ILL.", 4 1/8" Dia. x 10 7/8" T.

Left - #4233-X, Vase, "Brown Earth Graphic Wrap"
color, marked on bottom of felt:
"© Royal Haeger U.S.A.", 5" Base Dia. x 11" T.

Right - #2057, Ashbowl, "Brown Earth Graphic Wrap"
color, marked on bottom of felt:
"© Royal Haeger U.S.A.", 3 3/4" Dia. x 3 3/4" T.

Top - #R-453, Peacock Planter, "Mauve Agate" color,
molded on bottom: "Royal Haeger, R-453 USA",
9 3/4" W x 3 1/8" W x 10" T.

Bottom - #R-372, Fluted Bowl, "Mauve Agate" color,
molded on bottom: "Royal Haeger USA 372"
13 1/2" Dia. x 2" T.

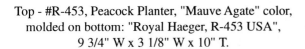

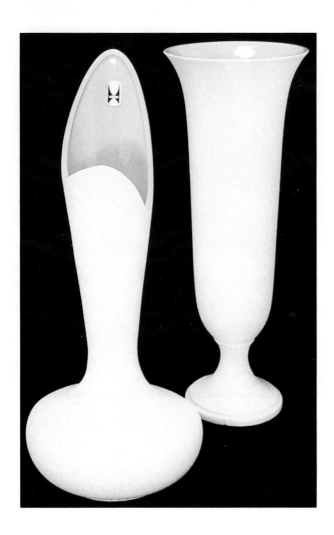

Left to Right:
#R-1752W Eccentric Vase,
"Cotton White and Turquoise",
marked with foil label "Haeger" in "H" logo,
4 3/4" Dia. base x 16 3/4" T.
(has an original JC Penney's Tag on it)

#4011 Chalice Vase, "Cotton White and Turquoise",
molded on bottom "Royal Haeger © 4011 U.S.A.",
4 5/8" Dia. base x 6 1/8" Dia. top x 16 1/8" T.

Left to Right:
#343 Bowl, "Cotton White and Turquoise",
molded on bottom "Royal Haeger 343 © U.S.A.", also
marked with a foil label "Haeger" in an "H" logo,
8" Dia. top x 3 1/4" T.

#489 Sculpted Vase, "Cotton White and Turquoise",
molded on bottom "Royal Haeger © 489 U.S.A.",
4" Dia. base x 4" Dia. top x 14 1/8" T.

Various "Cerulean Gold" color Vases, circa 1955.
#4034 Two Boutique Vases, 2 1/2" Dia. x 8" T.
#4035 Boutique Vase, 2 1/4" Dia. x 11 1/2" T
#4027 Boutique Vessel, 1 3/4" Dia. x 11 3/4" T

Left to Right:
#R-455 Bow Vase, white with blue bow,
molded on bottom "Royal Haeger USA R-455",
circa 1936, 5" Dia. x 14" T.

#3277 Bow Candle Holder, blue in color,
circa 1947, 3 1/4" Dia. base x 7 1/2" T.

#336 Candle Holders and #335 Compote,
"Blue Crackle" with hints of green
and rough textured, no markings.
Compote is
3 3/4" Dia. base x 10 1/8" Dia. top x 4 3/4" T.

Candle holder is
2 1/4" Dia. base x 4 1/4" Dia. top x 3 3/4" T.

Left to Right:
#257 Vase with relief design, "Briar Agate" color,
stamped on bottom "Haeger – USA – #257,
4 1/4" Dia. base x 4 3/4" Dia. top x 9 1/4" T.

#809 Pedestal Planter, brown, green, yellow and white, 1966-1972,
stamped on bottom, "Haeger – © – USA",
4 1/2" Dia. base x 8 1/4" Dia. top x 7 1/2" T.

#4131 small, #4132 medium and #4133 large
Set of Three Vases, "Peasant Orange" with black interior,
all stamped on bottom "Royal Haeger USA ©".
Small: 2 3/4" Dia. base x 7 1/4" T.
Medium: 3 1/8" Dia. base x 10 1/8" T.
Large: 4 1/8" Dia. base x 15 1/4" T.

Left to Right:
#4165 Vase, "Peasant Orange" with black interior,
stamped on bottom "Royal-Haeger – USA ©",
4 1/4" Dia. base x 4 3/8" Dia. top x 11 3/8" T.

#8142 Jar with floral in relief (lid is missing),
"Peasant Orange" with white interior,
stamped on bottom "Haeger – USA ©",
4 3/4" Dia. base x 4 1/4" Dia. top x 6 1/8" T.

Left to Right:
#R-321 Shell Vase, "Chartreuse" and white interior, molded on bottom "Royal Haeger – USA 321", 5" L x 3 1/2" W x 7 3/4" T.

#R-476 Beaded Bowl, "Chartreuse and Silver Spray" color, molded on bottom "Royal Haeger – R476 U.S.A.", 14 3/4" L x 7" W x 5" T.

Left to Right:
#R-557 Bowl, "Chartreuse and Silver Spray" color, molded on bottom "Royal Haeger – R557 USA", 15 3/4" L x 7" W x 5 3/4" T.

#R-527 Pillow Vase, "Chartreuse and Silver Spray" color, molded on bottom "Royal Haeger – R527 USA", 5 3/8" L x 3 1/4" W x 7 1/4" T.

Left to Right:
#3318 Colonial Flower Girl Planter, "Chartreuse", no markings, 6 1/2" L x 4 3/4" W x 9" T.

#3232 Double Branch Candleholder, "Chartreuse", foil label "Genuine - Haeger ®", 7"L x 2 7/8" W x 4 1/8" T.

#616 Teddy Bear Planter, circa 1938, "Chartreuse", no markings, 7" L x 3 1/4" W x 4 3/4" T.

#R-371 Whirling Bowl and
#R-438 Rosebud Candle Holders,
"Cloudy Blue" color,

Candle Holders are not marked, they are
4 1/4" L x 1 1/8" T.

#R-371 Bowl is marked on bottom
"Royal Haeger – R371 – U.S.A.",
12 3/4" L x 5 1/2" W x 2 1/2" T.

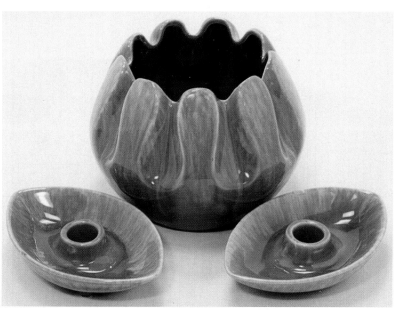

#345-S Scalloped and indented bowl, "Lilac",
molded on bottom "Royal Haeger © 345-S U.S.A.",
4 1/4" Dia. base x 5 1/8" T.

#R-1746 Candle Holders, "Lilac",
molded on bottom "Royal Haeger R1746 U.S.A.",
6" L x 3 3/4" W x 1 1/2" T.

#R-967 Starfish Bowl, "Pearl Grey Drip"
color,
molded on bottom "Royal Haeger – R 967
USA" and also a crown foil label
"Royal Haeger - Dundee, Illinois" ,
14 1/2" L x 14 1/4" W x 2 3/8" T.

#R-968 Starfish Candle Holders, "Pearl Grey
Drip" color,
molded on bottom "Royal Haeger-R 968-USA",
and also a crown foil label
"Royal Haeger - Dundee, Illinois" ,
4 7/8" L x 4 3/4" W x 1 1/4" T.

Far Left and Far Right:
#R-891 Pair of Tall Stem Vases,
"Green Briar" color,
molded on bottom "Royal-Haeger R891 USA",
also marked with crown foil label
"Royal Haeger, Dundee Illinois",
3 3/4" Dia. base x 12 1/4" T.

Middle Left:
#R-7285 & later #R-7465 Leaf Candle Holders,
"Green Briar" color,
no markings, 4" L x 2 7/8" W x 4" T.

Middle Right:
#R-103 Horse, "Green Briar" color,
no markings, 5 1/8" L x 3 3/4" W x 8 1/4" T.

Left to Right:
#318-H Bowl, "Amethyst Crackle" color, molded on bottom
"Royal Haeger – U.S.A. – 318-H",
4" Dia. base x 11 3/4" Dia. top x 5" T.

#R-1919 Onion Vase, "Amethyst" color, stamped on bottom,
"Haeger ® – U.S.A." and also a foil label that reads
"Haeger in H – Craftsmen – For A – Century",
2 3/4" Dia. base x 10 3/8" T.

219

Left to Right:
#4132-X Vase, lime green, "Boco" texture,
stamped on bottom "Royal Haeger USA ©",
and a paper label that reads
"Haeger-Style-USA-4132-X - Price",
3 1/4" Dia. base x 9 1/8" T.

#3170 Handled Dish, lime green, "Boco" texture,
molded on bottom "Royal Haeger - 3170 © USA",
a paper label that reads "Haeger-Style - 3170 - Price",
and a foil label (Rect. design, Haeger in "H")
that reads "Haeger-Craftsmen for a Century" ,
10 3/4" Dia. base x 3 3/4" T.

Left to Right:
#4001 Vase, "Green Marigold" in color, molded on
bottom "Haeger © – 4001 – USA",
2 1/8" Dia. base x 8 1/4" T.

#H-72 Two Owls on Planter, "Green Marigold" in color,
circa 1973-74, foil label "Copyrighted - The - Haeger ® -
Potteries, Inc. -Macomb, ILL. - Made In U.S.A.",
6" L x 5" W x 8 7/8" T.

#4149 Vase with leaves in relief, "Green Marigold" colored
stamped on bottom "Haeger © - USA",
5 1/8" Dia. base x 4 1/8" Dia. top x 12 1/8" T.

Left to Right:
#9-H Covered Dish, "Mandarin Orange", molded on
bottom "Early-American-By Haeger-© USA-9H",
a foil label reads "Haeger" in an 'H' logo, gold and black,
and a paper label that reads "9.H - Style",
3 1/4" Dia. base x 6 1/4" Dia. top x 7 1/2" T.

#R-1915 One Stem Vase, "Mandarin Orange",
foil label "Haeger" in an 'H' logo, gold and black,
3 1/8" Dia. base x 1 3/4" Dia. top x 15 1/4" T.

Three piece Horse & Boot Set, all are
"Rust Brown" in color, and all have the silver and
black "Haeger" (Big H) label.

#726-H Horse Cannister is molded on bottom,
"Haeger 726-H USA", circa 1967,
3" Dia. x 4 1/4" T.

#1076-H Horse Plate with stand is molded
on bottom "Haeger 1076-H USA", circa 1967,
5 1/4" Dia. x 1" T.

#8054 Boot Lighter molded on bottom
"Haeger #8054", circa 1967,
4 1/4" L x 2" W x 9 1/4" T.

Left to Right:
#3928 Gold Goblet, circa 1962-69,
stamped on bottom "Haeger - USA ©",
3 5/8" Dia. base x 4 1/2" Dia. top x 9 3/8" T.

#3968A Gold Vase, circa 1969-75,
foil label reads "Copyrighted - The- Haeger ® -
Potteries, Inc. - Macomb, ILL. - Made in U.S.A."
and a foil label that reads "22 - Carat - Gold",
4 1/8" Dia. base x 4 18/" Dia. top x 9 1/4" T.

All pictured here are of the same color and glaze, brown
glossy and matte with tan, all are marked with a printed foil
crown label "Royal-Haeger ® – Dundee, ILL." and are
stamped on bottom "Royal-Haeger - USA ©",
#8183-X Pitcher Vase, 3 3/4" Dia. base x 12" T.

#4131 Vase, 2 5/8" Dia. base x 7 1/4" T.

#4200 Planter, 2 1/2" Dia. base x 4 1/2" Dia. top x 51/2" T.

Left to Right:
#3819 Pedestal Planter, green and lighter green, stamped on bottom "Haeger © - U.S.A.",
4 7/8" Dia. base x 9 1/2" Dia. top x 7 1/2" T.

#725 Wall Pocket, green, circa 1952,
molded on back "Haeger - 725 USA", 6 1/2" L x 2 3/4" W x 5 1/4" T.

Left to Right:
#R-1121 Vase, "Green Agate" color, marked with foil crown label,
"Royal Haeger - Dundee, Illinois", 5 3/4" L x 3" W x 5 3/4" T.

#R-1170 Comedy & Tragedy Masks Planter, "Green Agate" color,
molded on bottom "Royal Haeger - R-1170 USA", 11" L x 4 1/4" W x 7 1/4" T.

#827 Vase, "Green Agate" color, marked with foil crown label
"Royal Haeger - Dundee, Illinois" also molded on bottom "Royal Haeger-827 USA",
5 1/4" L x 4" W x 10 1/2" T.

Fire Hydrant Cookie Jar, red with gold crackle trim. Gilded on outside "Fire Plug Cookies" also printed in ink on the bottom is "Royal Haeger", 8 1/2" Dia. x 12" T.

#8198 Gleep Cookie Jar, yellow-orange in color, molded in pottery, "© Haeger".

Keebler Treehouse Cookie Jar, in colors of green and brown, 7 1/4" Dia. x 11" T.

#R-188 Cookie Jar with shell designs at top and bottom, rose and blue in color, no markings, 7 1/4" dia x 10 1/2" T.

#612 Rooster and #613 Hen,
red with green and black accents .

The rooster mark is molded on bottom
"Royal Haeger 612 © USA",
8 1/2" L x 4" W x 11" T.

The hen mark is molded on bottom
"Royal Haeger 613 © USA",
8 1/2" L x 4" W x 10" T.

#612 Rooster and #613 Hen, circa 1973,
"Burnt Sienna" colored glaze.

The rooster is marked #612 and is
8 1/2" L x 4" W x 11" T.

The hen is marked #613 and is
8 1/2" L x 4" w x 10" T.

*Note: These pieces were made
from a 1967 design.*

#F-3 Pair of figural ducks, white, circa 1941,
no markings, 5" T x 3" L x 2" W.

#R-1762 Rooster, dark brown and white in color,
circa 1973, 14" L x 6" W x 20" T.

Note: These pieces were made from a 1967 design.

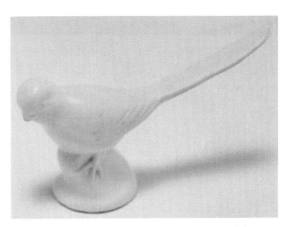

#6 Figural Bird, circa 1933, white, no markings,
4 1/2" L x 2 1/2" T x 1 1/4" W.

Left to Right:
#649 & 650 Figural Pigeons (Doves),
Left: 9 1/2" T   Right: 8 1/2"

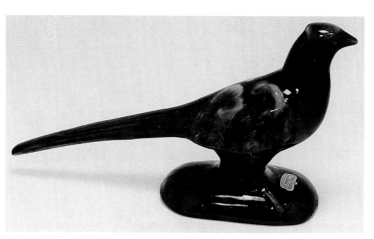

#R-130 Pheasant, "Green Agate" color,
crown foil label marked "Royal Haeger – Dundee, Illinois,
11 1/4" L x 3 1/2" W x 6" T.

#F-17 Wild Goose, white matte glaze, circa 1941,
no markings, 6 1/4" L x 2" W x 6 1/2" T.

#7 Cockatoo, pink,
1933, no markings,
4" L x 3" T.

Left to Right:

#650 Mourning Dove, rust brown color,
circa 1973, 10" L x 4" W x 7" T.

#649 Mourning Dove, white, circa 1973,
10" L x 5" W x 8" T.

#R-287 Wren House with two birds,
"Mauve Agate" in color. Molded on
bottom "Royal Haeger by Royal Hickman
USA #287", circa 1949,
7 1/4" L x 4 1/4" W x 9 1/2" T.

#R-287 Wren House with two birds,
"Mauve Agate" in color. Molded on
bottom "Royal Haeger #R287 USA",
7 1/4" L x 4 1/4" W x 9 1/4" T.

#R-434 Hen Pheasant, "Mauve Agate" color, no markings or numbers,
15" L x 4 1/2" W x 5 1/4" T.

#R-435 Rooster Pheasant, "Mauve Agate" in color,
no mark found, 13" L x 12" T.

#R-165 Pheasant, "Mauve Agate" in color,
molded on bottom "U.S.A.", 11" L x 6" W x 10 1/4" T.

Console Set, "Pearl Grey Drip" color, circa 1950's.
(Left to Right)
Tiger – #R-313   Oblong Bowl – #R-282   Tigress – #R-314

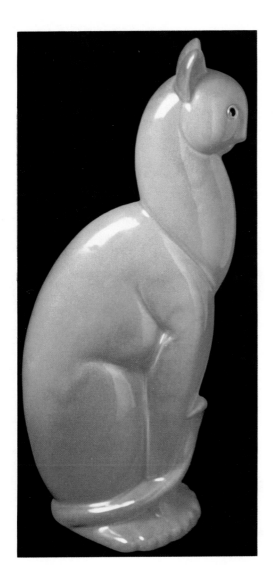
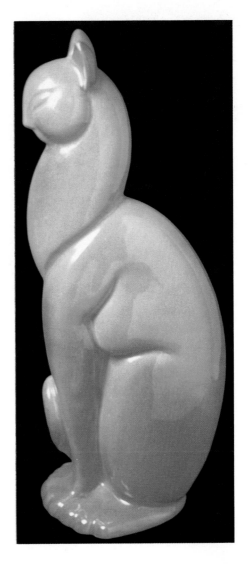

#616 Egyptian Cat, "Mandarin Orange" ,
marked on bottom "Royal Haeger ©616 U.S.A.",
circa 1950's, 15 1/2" T

*NOTE: One side of the cat has an open eye made of glass,
The other side of the cat has the eye closed.*

#R-313 Tiger, "Amber" colored, molded on bottom
"Royal Haeger R313 U.S.A.",
12 3/4" L x 4" W x 8 1/4" T.

#R-282 Planter, the centerpiece that goes with the two tigers
pictured above and below, "Amber" colored, no markings,
10" L x 4" W x 8" T.

#R-314 Tigress, "Amber" colored, molded on bottom
"Royal Haeger U.S.A.", 10 1/4" L x 41/4" W x 11" T.

#R-648 Panther sitting on a
Pedestal, "Ebony" color, circa
1950's, no markings,
2 7/8" Dia.base x 6" T.

#R-313 Tiger, "Amber" colored,
molded on bottom "Royal Haeger R313 U.S.A.",
12 3/4" L x 4" W x 8 1/4" T.

#R-649 Lying Panther, "Oxblood" color,
molded on bottom "Royal Haeger – R649 U.S.A.",
7 1/4" L x 2 1/2" W x 2 5/8" T.

#R-1131 Leopard, "Chartreuse" color, not marked,
7 1/2" L x 3 1/2" W x 7 3/4" T.

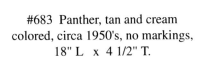

#683 Panther, tan and cream
colored, circa 1950's, no markings,
18" L   x 4 1/2" T.

#495 Panther, "Ebony" in color, with a foil crown label "Royal Haeger – Dundee, Illinois,
24 1/2" L x 4 3/4" W x 5 1/2" T.

Top:
#495 Panther, "Ebony" in color, with a crown label
24 1/2" L x 4 3/4" W x 5 1/2" T. *(as pictured above)*

Bottom:
#315 Panther, (Newer Edition) "Ebony", with silver and black foil label
"Royal-Haeger ® – Handcrafted in America", also marked with
a paper label "Haeger ® – American Made – 315 – Copyright 1994",
25 1/4" L x 4 3/4" W x 5" T.

**Notice: Difference between the older version and the newer is the size and
the tail comes up higher on the back paw of the new one.*

#R-412 Standing Fawn, pink color,
circa 1950's, no markings,
61/2" L x 3" W x 11 3/4" T.

#3108 Two Deer Abstract Vase, white,
circa 1942, no markings,
5" L x 2" W x 7 1/2" T.

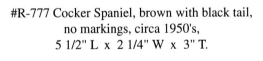

#R-777 Cocker Spaniel, brown with black tail,
no markings, circa 1950's,
5 1/2" L x 2 1/4" W x 3" T.

Leaping Gazelle TV Lamp, green and white, often mistaken for Haeger,
this lamp was made by Phil-Mar, 13 1/2" L x 5 1/8" W x 10 1/2" T.
Note: Frank Perry stayed on with Phil-Mar after Royal Hickman sold the pottery in Tennessee. This is why Phil-Mar lamps look similar to Royal Haeger lamps and figures.

#R-413 Sitting Fawn, dark brown
base with a muddish brown
overglaze, circa 1949, no markings,
6 1/2" L base x 3" W x 6 1/2" T

#R-318 Russian Wolfhound (head down),
"Green Briar" color, no markings, circa 1940's,
11 1/2" L x 3 1/4" W x 6 1/4" T.

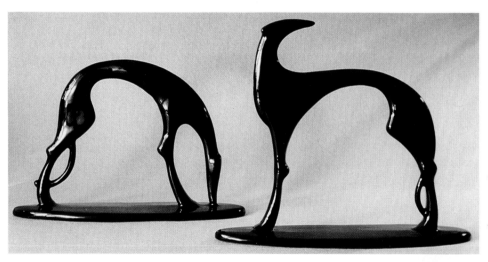

Left to Right:

#R-166 Greyhound (head down),
"Gun Metal" color, circa 1940's, 9" T.

#R-167 Greyhound (head up),
"Gun Metal" color, circa 1940's, 9" T.

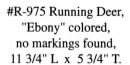

#R-975 Running Deer,
"Ebony" colored,
no markings found,
11 3/4" L x 5 3/4" T.

#R-424 Bucking Bronco,
"Amber" colored, circa 1940's, 13" T.

#R-451 Mare and Foal, "Amber" colored, circa 1943,
molded on bottom "Royal Haeger - R451-U.S.A.",
13" L x 4" W x 11" T.

#R-1265 Colt, brown color, with a crown foil label that
reads "Royal-Haeger – Dundee, Illinois,
7 1/2" L x 4 1/4" W x 6 1/2" T.

#R-479 The Prospector, "Amber" colored,
molded on bottom "Royal Haeger – R479 U.S.A.",
11 1/4" L x 7" T.

#3235 Deer (or Gazelle),
white, no markings,
1 1/2" Dia. x 5 1/4" T.

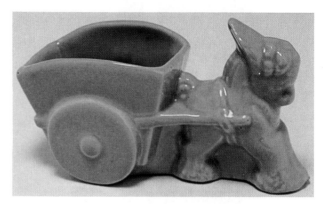

#3296 Donkey and Cart, blue in color,
circa 1943, no markings, 5" L x 3" W x 3" H.

#R-235 Colt Flower Holder, "Green Briar" color,
molded on bottom "Royal Haeger R235 U.S.A.",
7" L x 3 3/4" W x 12 1/2" T.

#R-402 Horse, circa 1942,
no markings, "Mallow" color,
51/2" L x 10 7/8" W x 5 1/2" T.

#502-H Bull Fighter Planter,
"Haeger Red" colored, molded on bottom
"Royal Haeger", 5 1/2" W x 13" T.

#R-379 Bull figure, "Mallow" colored,
circa 1941, 12" L x 3 1/2" W x 6 1/2" T.

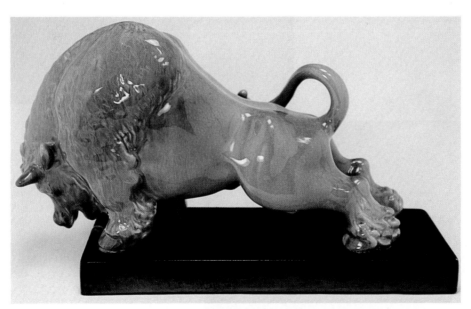

#R-379 Bull figure mounted on a rectangular "Ebony" base,
the bull is "Mallow" colored, molded on bottom
"Royal Haeger by Royal Hickman",
14" L x 4 3/4" W x 8 1/4" T.

237

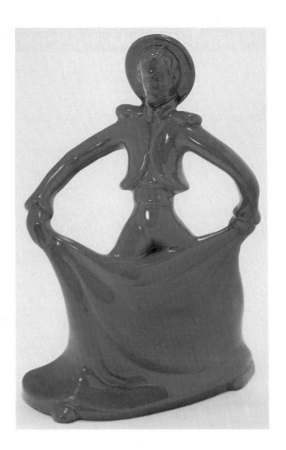

#6343 Matador, "Haeger Red" color, marked
with a gold foil crown label "Royal Haeger",
8 1/4" L x 4" W x 11 3/8" T.

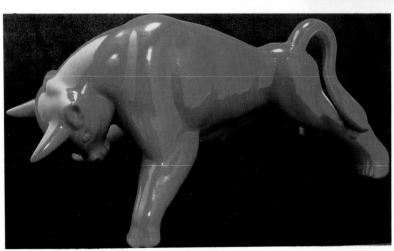

Top:
#R-1510 Bull, "Mandarin Orange",
no markings, 18" L x 8 1/4" T.

Bottom:
#R-1510 Bull, "Haeger Red",
no markings, 18" L x 8 1/4" T.

#R-138 Flying Fish, teal and yellow in color,
paper tag reads: "Haeger", 8" L x 4" W x 9" T.

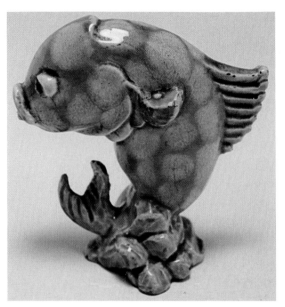

#R-284 Fish, "Amber" color,
(Royal Hickman design), no markings,
4" T x 3 1/2" L.

#3248 Rabbit, blue in color, no markings evident,
circa 1940's, 4" L x 4" W x 5" T.

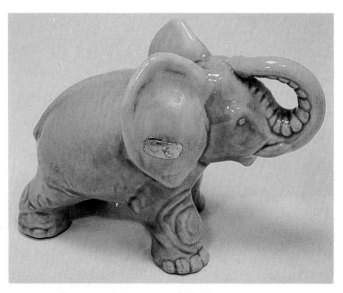

#R-784 Elephant, "Chartreuse & Honey" color,
crown foil label "Royal-Haeger – Dundee, Illinois",
8 1/4" L x 3 3/4" W x 6" T.

#648 Pair of Booties on square base, light blue,
marked with a foil label, "75th Anniversary",
4 5/8" L x 4" W x 3" T.
Note: from Junior "All American Series"

#R-1782 Lamb with silk ribbon and bell, "White Stone Lace",
marked with foil crown label "Royal-Haeger ®",
17" L x 8 1/2" W x 15" T.

Polar Bear Figures, musty gray-white in color, circa 1942, no markings.
#R-376A -Small standing Polar Bear
#R-375A - Small sitting Polar Bear
both are 5" L x 2" W x 2" T.

#R-375B - Large sitting Polar Bear
6 1/2" L x 5" W x 6 7/8" T.

#812 Lady Head, white,
circa 1936, no markings,
2 1/2" x 2 1/2" Base x 7" T.

#514 Mermaid with bowl, "Gold Tweed" color,
marked on bottom "Royal Haeger © 514 U.S.A.",
also marked with gold stamp "Haeger Gold Tweed 22K Gold".
(This has been seen in three different sizes.) 13 3/4" L x 10 3/8" T.

#837 Girl Head and #838 Boy Head, "Gold Tweed",
molded on bottom "Royal Haeger – © – (837 or 838) USA".
The girl is 6" L x 6" W x 8 1/2" T.
The boy is 5 1/2" L x 5 3/4" W x 8 3/4" T.

241

#R-1224 Gypsy Girl, brown and green
colored, no markings,
13 1/2" L x 6 1/2" W x 16 1/2" T.

#R-382 Peasant Man and #R-383 Peasant Woman,
both are "Green Agate" color.

The woman is molded on bottom "Royal Haeger R383 USA",
the base is 5" sq. and the height is 17".

The man is molded on bottom "Royal Haeger R382 USA",
the base is 5" sq. and the height is 17".

#R-363 Women riding fish flower block,
the left one is grey, green and white, the
right one is "Green Agate", neither one has markings.

#R-838 Frog figural flower block,
"Chartreuse", crown foil label,
"Royal-Haeger - Dundee, Illinois",
4 1/2" L x 3 1/4" W x 3 3/4" T.

#57 Swan Flower Frog,
green, white and beige,
circa 1918, no markings,
3" W x 3 1/4" L x 4" T.

#R-360 Pair of Fish figural flower block,
"Pearl Grey Drip" color, circa 1941,
no markings, 5" L x 3" W x 12" T.

#R-359 Two Birds figural flower frog,
"Cloudy Blue" color, no markings, circa 1940's,
5" Dia. base x 8 3/4" T.

#86 Mermaid with child,
green matte, no markings,
3 3/4" Dia. x 7" T.

#R-772 Stag flower block and #R-484 Garden Bowl, "Chartreuse" colored.

Stag is molded on bottom "Royal Haeger - R772 U.S.A.",
4" L x 2 1/2" W x 9" T.

Garden Bowl molded on bottom "Royal Haeger - R484 U.S.A.",
14" L x 6 1/4" W x 2" T.

#R-364 Nude with seal block,
"Green Briar" color
circa 1946, no markings,
5 1/2" Dia. base x 13 1/4" T.

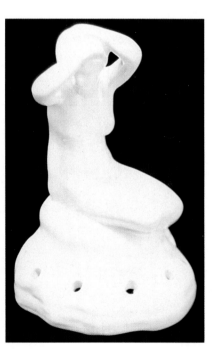

#77 Nude Bathing frog, white,
circa 1927, no markings,
5" Dia. base x 7" T.

#R-189 Sitting Nude flower frog,
"Mauve Agate" color no markings,
late 1930's to early 1940's,
4" Dia. base x 6" T.

244

#R-875 Colt Lamp Base Planter,
"Ebony Cascade" in color, no markings,
13" L x 5" W x 9" T.

#141 Lamp Base, purple, circa 1914,
first lamp base that Haeger produced,
no markings, 4 7/8" Dia. base x 9 3/4" T.

#5190 Bucking Bronco with
cactus finial, no markings, 26" T.

#R-455 Bow Lamp Base,
"Mauve Agate" color,
no markings,
5" Dia. base x 13 1/2' T.

#6204 Stallion Head Lamp, "Oxblood & White" color,
crown foil label "Royal-Haeger - Dundee, Illinois",
9" L x 4 1/4" W x 18" T base, 36" T (all over)

#1138 Cylinder Lamp with
Horse, "Oxblood" color,
manufacturing label on
bottom, 4 1/2" Dia. base x
11 1/2" T x 26" Tall with post.

#5240 Horse Head Wall Lamp,
"Ebony", circa 1947, crown foil label,
9 1/4" L x 5 1/4" Dia. base.

#5353 Petal Louvre Reflector Lamp,
"Walnut" colored, "Ebony" base,
no markings, circa 1954,
3 1/4" Dia. base x 11 1/4" T.

#R-1262 Prancing Horse TV Lamp, "Chartreuse and Honey"
color, (planter originally was #S-229), and has a
gold crown foil label "Royal Haeger Dundee, Illinois",
11 1/2" L x 5 1/2" W x 10 1/4" T.

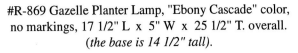

#R-869 Gazelle Planter Lamp, "Ebony Cascade" color,
no markings, 17 1/2" L x 5" W x 25 1/2" T. overall.
(*the base is 14 1/2" tall*).

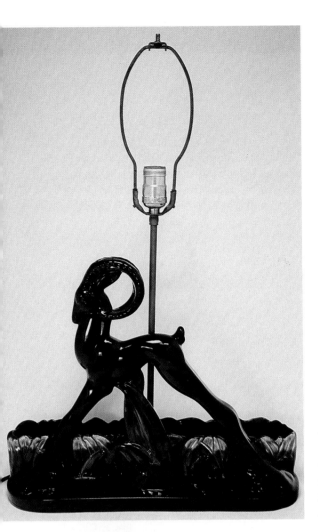

#5195 Fawn Table Lamp, "Ebony", marked with
foil label "Royal-Haeger, Dundee, Illinois" with red
metal tiered shade, 24 1/2" T.
Note: shade is not original.

#5473 Two Deer Abstract TV Lamp,
"Oxblood and White" color, no markings,
8" L x 5" W x 15 1/2" T.

#R-115 Gazelle Lamp, "Ebony",
labeled on outside (Gold Crown Label)
"Royal Haeger, Dundee, Illinois",
3" x 3 3/4" x 12 1/4" T,
with post it is 21 1/4" T.

#6051-TV Panther TV Lamp,
"Ebony and Turquoise" colored, molded on bottom
"Haeger USA", with a crown foil label on base that
reads "Royal Haeger ®",
13 1/4" L x 5 7/8" W x 5 7/8" T.

#6140 Sailfish TV Lamp, "Silver Spray" colored,
no markings, 9 1/4" L x 3 3/4" W x 9" T.

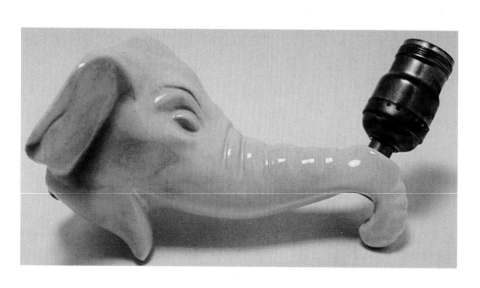

#5202 Parrot on Tree Lamp Base,
"Green Agate and Yellow Decorated",
circa 1947, no markings,
6 1/2" Dia. base x 17" T.

#5237 Elephant Head Wall Lamp,
white, no markings, circa 1947,
the base is 6" x 4 1/4" x 8" L.

#5401 Tree of Life Lamp, "Green Agate with
Chartreuse" color, marked with gold crown
foil label "Royal Haeger Dundee, ILL.",
7 1/2" L x 4 1/2" W x 7 1/2" T.
(including Finial 21 1/2" T.)

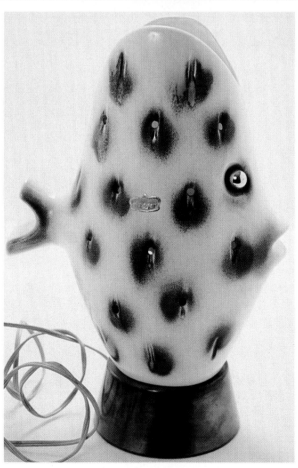

#6424S-TV: Angel Fish TV Lamp, "Antique" in color,
marked with foil label "Royal Haeger ®",
5 1/4" Dia. base x 13 3/4" T.

#5344 Lamp,
"Chartreuse and Honey",
gold crown label with silver letters,
"Royal Haeger, Dundee, ILL",
5 3/4" L x 4 1/2" W x 7 1/2" T.

Fish riding on a wave lamp,
yellow, no markings,
6" L x 4 1/4" W x 10 1/2" T base,
(20" overall.)

#3003 Lady Head Lamp Base,
green with brown accented color,
3 1/2" sq. x 14" T.

#4172 Cabbage Rose
Lamp with finial,
"Mauve Agate" color
circa 1941, no markings,
4 7/8" Dia. base x 25 1/4" T.

#5362 Fluted Ginger Jar Table Lamp with finial,
"Yellow Crackle" and "Ebony" base,
marked with foil label "Royal Haeger -
Dundee, Illinois", also has original paper
tag "A Royal Haeger Lamp",
5 3/4" Dia. base x 19" T.
(finial 4 3/8" T)

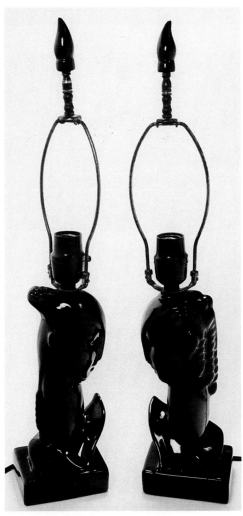

#5100 Modern Man & Lady Head Lamps,
"Ebony" color
3" x 4" rectangular base x 10" T.
(22" T. with post).

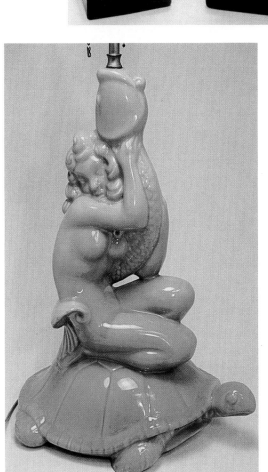

#5398 Mermaid Lamp Base,
grey mermaid and "Green Agate" base,
8 1/2" L x 7" W x 16" T.

#5205 Girl on Turtle Table Lamp,
turquoise, no markings,
13" L x 10" W x 19" T base.
(28 1/2" T. overall)

#5051 Toadstool Table Lamp (with original finial and shade),
"Amber" colored, crown foil label that reads
"Royal-Haeger - Dundee, Illinois,
6 1/4" Dia. base x 9 3/4" T base.
(21 1/2" T overall)

#5483 Modern Lamp Base,
"Mallow and Ebony" color, no markings,
11" Dia. base x 16" T base.
(29" T. overall)

#R-1504 & R-1505 Lion's Head Lavabo, "Turquoise-Blue".

The top piece #R-1504 is molded on back
"Royal Haeger - R-1504", 9 1/4" W x 14 1/2" T.

The bottom piece #R-1505 is not marked,
16" W x 6 1/4" T.

#R-1506 & R-1507 Lavabo, matte pink.

The top piece is molded on back "Royal
Haeger - R -1506", 8" W x 6 1/2" T.

The bottom piece is molded on back "Royal
Haeger - R-1507", 8" W x 6 1/2" T.

#8186 & #8187 Lavabo, cream and brown.

The top piece is molded on back "Royal-Haeger
© – 8186 USA", 6 1/2" W x 14 1/4" T.

The bottom piece is molded on back
"Royal-Haeger © - 8187 USA",
12 1/4" W x 5 1/4" T.

Shelf Clock, 9 1/4" L x 4" W x 17" T.
(The clock face was done by Kingswood)

Pagoda Clock with oriental man and woman,
"Silver Spray and Chartreuse" color, no markings,
7 7/8" L x 2 1/2" W x 9 1/4" T.

The clock is a Lanshire Self Starting model # SP-3,
patent date 1948, Lanshire Clock &
Instrument Corp., Chicago, U.S.A.

Harley Davidson Piggy Bank,
black with gold trim, molded on bottom
"© Harley Davidson 1982 Motor Co., Inc.",
11" L x 5 1/2" W x 7 1/4" T.
*Note: this piece had a very
low production number.*

Stein World's Fair 1933, yellow-brown, on the outside it reads "World's Fair - A Century of Progress, Chicago 1933", no markings on bottom, 3 1/2" Dia. base x 6 1/2" T.

Mermaid figure
gold tweed, 12 1/2" T.

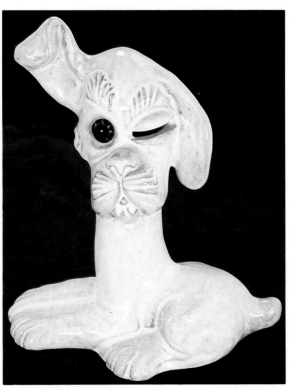

#8034 Dog Bank, white transparent color, marked on bottom "Haeger 8034 ©", 7 1/2" L x 8 1/2" T.

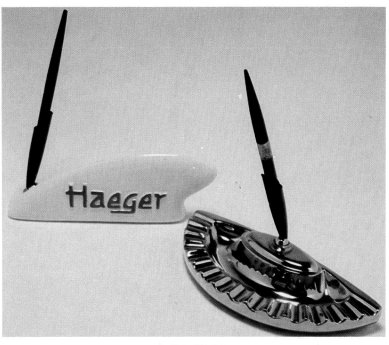

Left to Right:
Haeger advertising pen holder set, white with gilded letters, 8 1/2" L x 3 1/2" T.

"Midas Gold" Parker Pen and Ashtray set, molded on bottom "Parker USA", 8 1/4" L x 4" W.

Vase, marked on bottom
with stamp "Haeger U.S.A.",
4 1/2" Dia. base x 5 5/8" Dia. top x 12" T.

Vase, "Peach Agate" color,
no markings,
3 1/2" Dia. x 6" T.

Vase, "Peach Agate" color,
no markings, 5 3/4" Dia. base x 14" T.

Plate, Cup and Saucer,
"Peach Agate" color,
circa 1927, no markings.
Saucer – 5"
Plate – 7 1/4"
Cup – 3" x 3"

Horse Head, "Desert Red" with an "Ebony" base, circa mid 1930's, no markings, 4 3/4" base x 4 3/4" x 9" T.

Planter, light brown with darker specks throughout, stamped on bottom "Haeger © - USA", 4 1/2" x 4 1/2" base, 5" Dia. top x 9 1/4" T.

Flower Styled Vase, brown and rust colored, circa 1930's, 5 1/2" Sq. top x 7 1/4" T.

Horse, red in color, molded on bottom "Haeger U.S.A.", 4" L x 3" W x 6 1/4" T. *(by the designer Royal Hickman, this may have been an experimental piece)*

Floral Frog
(base for plastic flowers and plants),
brown base with green top,
stamped "Haeger" diamond marked
which is one of the earlier marks on
Haeger found in the 1930's,
3" Dia. x 1" T.

#845 Bowl Planter, green with lighter green cascade,
molded on bottom "Haeger" diamond shaped,
10" Dia. x 4" T.

Flower Frog, molded on bottom
"Haeger" in an early diamond logo,
*Note: this is a bottom view of the frog from above
showing the diamond mark.*

Pedestal Planter, green with lighter green cascade,
molded with early diamond logo with "Haeger" inside,
3 3/4" Dia. base x 7" Dia. top x 3 3/4" T.

Egg Paperweight, "Green Agate" colored,
circa 1950's, 5" L x 3" across sides.

#R-449 Set of four Leaf Trays, "Cloudy Blue" colored,
no markings, 4 1/2" L x 3 1/2" W x 1" T.

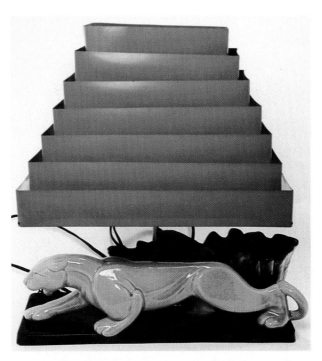

Panther Lamp/Planter, "Chartreuse & Ebony Cascade" color, with a gold crown label that reads "Royal Haeger, Dundee, Illinois", 17 1/2" L x 5 1/2" W x 5" T.

Sitting Panther Planter, brown with dark spots on a "Ebony" base.

Gondola Planter, pink and white accents, green and silver Haeger sticker, 16" L x 3 3/4" W x 3" T.

Panther on base, ink stamped "Haeger Designs of Dundee", 18 3/4" L x 5 1/8" W x 9 3/4" T.

Royal Haeger Lighter in Aladdin Lamp,
"Gold Tweed" color, marked on bottom with stamp,
"Haeger Gold Tweed 22K Gold",
12" L x 8 1/2" T.

Fish Planter, "Chartreuse" and grey,
no markings, 10" L x 4 1/4" W x 9" T.

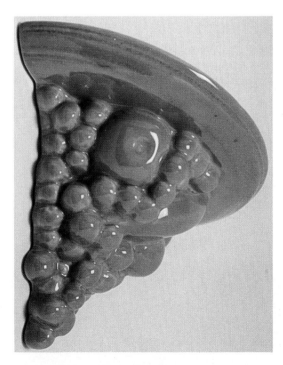

#R-531 Wall Shelf, "Mallow" color,
molded on back "Royal Haeger R-531 USA",
circa 1947, 7" L x 4 1/4" W x 4 3/4" T.

Fawn, green colored glaze, circa 1960,
gold crown label "Royal Haeger",
4 1/2" L x 2" W x 5 1/2" T.

Planter, "Briar Agate" color,
marked with a crown foil label
"Royal Haeger - Dundee, Illinois",
14" L x 4 3/8" W x 5 3/4" T.

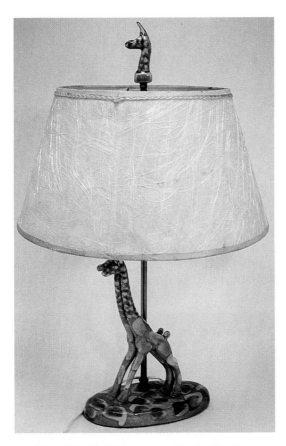

Two Giraffe Table Lamp, "Amber" color
with original finial and shade, no markings,
8 1/2" L x 3 1/2" W x 11" T base.
(22 1/2" overall)

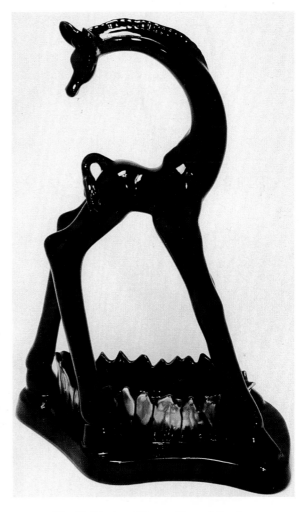

Giraffe Planter, "Ebony Cascade" color,
molded on bottom "Royal Haeger USA",
11" L x 6" W x 15 3/4".

Football Planter,
circa 1951, Macomb Line,
"Bennington Brown Foam"
color, 7 1/2" x 6".

Bell, yellow, made exclusively for Sears and has a
label on the outside that reads "Sears Best",
3 1/2" Dia. x 5" T.

Left to Right:
Figural Breast Pins, all are about 2 1/2" x 2 1/2".
1. Rooster, gilded   2. Giraffe, rose   3. Flower, "Chartreuse"
4. Hen and Drake Ducks, turquoise   5. Rooster, "Mauve Agate"
6. Hen and Drake Ducks, "Chartreuse"   7. Love Birds, pink & blue

Scottish Terrier Dogs Table Lamp,
"Cloudy Blue" color, no markings,
7 3/4" L x 5 1/4" W x 10" T base.

Greyhound Planter, white (Terra Madre),
marked with a paper label "Terra-Madre-by-Haeger".

Vase, yellow -green, circa 1930's,
diamond label "Haeger Pottery-Dundee, ILL",
3 1/2" Dia. base x 3 7/8" Dia. top x 6 3/4" T.

Planter, brownish color, marked with
an ink stamp "Haeger USA ©", circa 1950's,
5 1/2" Dia. x 6 1/4" T.

Earth Graphic Wrap Lamp Base,
"Green Earth Graphic Wrap",
21" x 10".
(36" x 10" overall)

Vase, marked on bottom with
stamp "Haeger U.S.A.",
2 5/8" Dia. base x 10 1/8" T.

#4058 & 4060 Pitcher and Wash Basin, brown matte and glossy.

#4058 Pitcher is stamped on bottom "Royal-Haeger-USA©",
also has a foil crown label "Royal-Haeger-Dundee, ILL.",
3 3/4" Dia. base x 10" T.

#4060 Basin is molded on bottom "Haeger-4060-U.S.A.",
15" L x 11 3/4" W x 3 3/4" T.

#8183 Pitcher Vase, "Bennington
Brown Foam", brown textured.

#8188 Pitcher, "Brown Earth Graphic Wrap",
marked on felt "Royal Haeger - U.S.A. -
The Haeger Potteries Inc. © - Dundee, ILL."
2 7/8" Dia. base x 8 7/8" T.

#3182 Pitcher "Sunset" color,
marked on bottom of felt "Royal Haeger U.S.A.,
Haeger Potteries Inc., Dundee, ILL.",
10" T x 9 1/2" Dia.

#R-698 Mexican Head Pitcher, "Green Briar" color,
molded on bottom "Royal Haeger - R-698 U.S.A.",
7 1/2" L x 4 1/4" W x 7 3/8" T.

#8229 Country Style Bean Pot,
blue and white and brownish-green,
stamped on bottom "Royal-Haeger - USA ©",
5" Dia. base x 5 1/2" Dia. top x 8" T.

#H-608 Pitcher with Rooster Handle,
"Persian Blue" color, molded on bottom
"Royal Haeger USA – H-608",
6 3/4" L x 4" W x 9" T.

#920 Soap Dish, Toothbrush Holder & Cup Holder,
blue, molded on bottom "Haeger © - 920 USA",
6 1/2" L x 5 1/2" W x 3" T.

#8011 Top Tier and #8010 Bottom Tier Chip 'n Dip Tray, "Misty Mint" colored, molded on bottom "Haeger 8010 © USA", 10" x 10" x 10 1/2".

1910 Green Cup, no markings, 2" Dia. base x 4 1/2" T. *(Experimental piece – Rare)*

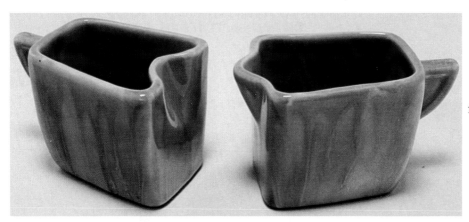

Sugar and Creamer Set, "Mauve Agate", factory molded on bottom "Evercraft USA", 2 1/2" L x 2" W x 2 1/2" T. *(possible contracting job for Haeger).*

#873-H Egg Serving Plate (Chicken shaped), "Reseda Yellow", molded on bottom "Royal Haeger 873 © U.S.A.", 14 3/4" L x 10 3/4" W x 1 3/4" T.

#575 Sugar and Creamer Set, white,
circa 1936, no markings,
3" Dia. base x 2 1/2" T.
(Reintroduced with new #3254 in 1946).

Four piece Serving Set,
circa 1971,

Cup, no markings, 3 1/4" Dia. x 4" T.

#3207-S Plate, molded "Haeger 3207-S USA",
also marked with 100th Anniversary label,
10 1/4" L x 8" W.

#3201 Salt and Pepper Shakers,
no markings, 2 1/4" Dia. x 4 3/4" T.

#8061 & #8062 Flour and Sugar Cannisters,
blue and white color, gold trim around
handle and lid edge.

Flour is molded on bottom
"Haeger USA 8062",
9" L x 7 1/2" Dia.

Sugar in molded on bottom
"Haeger USA 8061",
6 1/2" L x 5" Dia.

#R-1679-S Pitcher, "Turquoise-Blue",
marked on bottom
"Royal Haeger R-1679-S U.S.A." and marked
on a crown foil label "Royal Haeger",
3 3/4" Dia. base x 10 1/4" T.

Left to Right:
#4150 Urn, "Peasant Green", ink stamped on bottom
"Haeger © USA", 5 3/4" Dia. base x 15" T.

#8182 Water Pitcher, "Peasant Green",
ink stamped on bottom "Royal Haeger USA ©",
4 3/4" Dia. base x 11 3/4" T.

#R1582-S Cream Pitcher, "Turquoise" colored,
circa 1957, molded on bottom "Royal Haeger R1582-S",
2 1/4" Dia. base x 4 3/4" T.

#R1585-S Coffee Pot, "Turquoise" colored,
circa 1957, molded on bottom "Royal Haeger R1585-S",
3 1/2" Dia. base x 10 1/2" T.

*(also available with this set are
#R1584-S Tea Pot and, #R1583-S Sugar Bowl)*

#14 Fish Planter, yellow in color,
circa 1936, no markings,
3 1/2" L x 1 1/2" W x 3 1/2" T.

#3314 Horse Planter, white, no markings,
7 1/2" L x 3" W x 6" T.

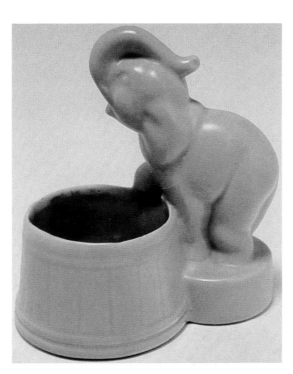

618 Elephant Planter, blue,
circa 1932, no markings,
5 1/4" L x 3 1/4" W x 6 1/2" T.

#617 Fawn Planter, yellow in color,
circa 1939, no markings, 4 1/4" Dia. x 6 1/2" T.

#R754 Donkey and Cart Planter, blue in color,
circa 1943, no markings, 11" L x 3 1/2" W x 5" T.

#B-3107 Lamb Planter, pink, no markings,
3" L x 3 1/2" W x 4 1/2" T.
(From the Junior "All American Series").

#3311 Cat Planter, blue in color, no markings,
circa 1946, 5 3/4" L x 3" W x 7" T.

#R-540 Turtle Planter, "Green Agate" colored,
molded on bottom "Royal Haeger - R540 U.S.A.",
13 1/2" L x 9 1/2" W x 4" T.

#R-766 Rudolph the Red Nosed Reindeer
Planter, "Desert Red Decorated", circa 1949,
molded on bottom "Royal Haeger - U.S.A.",
also marked with foil crown label,
6 1/2" L x 4 1/2" W x 9 1/4" T.

#R-1844 Duck Planter, "Jade Crackle" colored,
molded on bottom "Royal Haeger R1844 USA",
8" L x 7" W x 6 1/2" T.

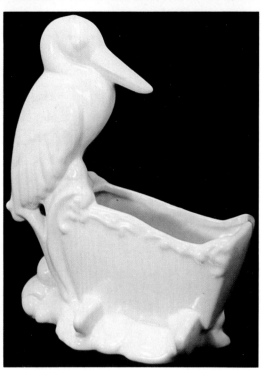

#B3322 Stork and Baby Bed Planter,
light pink, foil label reads "The Great Name -
Haeger ® - In American Ceramics",
7 3/4" L x 5" W x 10" T.

#8008-H Bird Planter,
"Blue Crackle", molded on
bottom "Haeger - © - 8008H -
USA", also with a H designed
foil label that reads "Haeger",
4 3/4" L x 2 3/4" W x 7 3/4" T.

#R-334 Fan Tail Pouter Pigeon Planter,
"Peach Agate" colored, molded on
bottom "Royal Haeger by Royal
Hickman Made in U.S.A.", circa 1934,
9" L x 8" W x 8" T.

#R-1747 Rabbit Planter, grey,
marked on bottom
"Royal Haeger - R1747 - U.S.A.",
5 3/4" L x 3" W x 8 3/4" T.

#R-182L Swan Planter,
"Peach Agate" color, no markings,
7 3/4" L x 3 1/8" W x 7 1/2" T.

#R-515 Swan Planter, "Mauve Agate"
colored, molded on bottom
"Royal Haeger R515 USA",
18" L x 4 1/2" W x 8 1/4" T.

#R-453 Peacock Planter, "Cloudy Blue" colored,
molded on bottom "Royal Haeger R-453 USA",
9" L x 3 1/2" W x 10" T.

#R-31 Peacock Planter, "Mauve Agate", molded on
bottom "Royal-Haeger - R31 - U.S.A.",
8" L x 5 1/4" W x 14 1/2"T.

#R-1402-C Large Bird Bowl, "Ebony Cascade" colored,
has a crown foil label "Royal-Haeger - Dundee, Illinois",
17 1/2" L x 4" W x 8" T.

#R-430 Swan Planter,
"Mauve Agate" colored, molded on bottom
"Royal Haeger - By - Royal Hickman - R 430 USA",
7" L x 3 1/4" W x 8 1/4" T.

#R-108 Pouter Pigeon Planter, "Mauve Agate" colored, circa 1938,
molded on bottom "Royal Haeger by Royal Hickman U.S.A.",
11 7/8" L x 4 1/2" W x 8 1/2" T.

273

#R-1226 Horse Planter, brown, with a
crown foil label "Royal-Haeger - Dundee, Illinois",
8" L x 3 1/2" W x 7 1/4" L.

#R-1761 Turkey Planter, molded on bottom
"Royal Haeger - R 1761 U.S.A.",
14" L x 10" W x 12" T.

#508 Donkey Planter, red transparent colored,
marked on bottom "© Royal Haeger, 508 U.S.A.",
7 1/2" x 9 1/4".

#6202 Greyhound TV Lamp and Planter, brown,
no markings, 11 1/2" L x 4 1/2" W x 6 1/4" T.

#R1146 Running Deer Planter, "Cotton White" colored, molded on bottom "Royal Haeger R-1146 USA", 11 1/4" L x 4" W x 6 1/2" T.

#R-869 Gazelle Planter, "Antique" colored, marked with foil crown label "Royal Haeger", 17" L x 13 3/4" T.

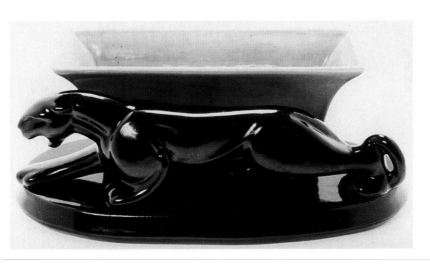

#3511 Panther Planter, "Ebony and Chartreuse", marked on bottom "Haeger-3511-U.S.A.", 13 1/2" L x 6" W x 5" T.

#R-1220 Gazelle Bowl, "Chartreuse & Honey" color,
with a foil crown label that reads
"Royal-Haeger - Dundee, Illinois",
11 1/4" L x 6 1/4" W x 7" T.

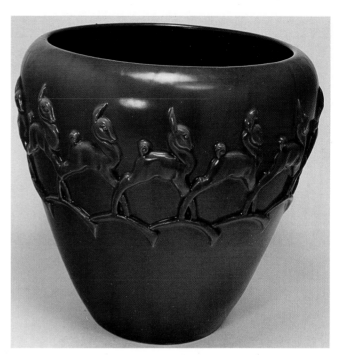

Prancing Deer Relief Border Planter,
"Oxblood" color, circa 1938, no markings,
10" Dia. top x 12 1/2" T.
(Also found in similar designs are #R-231 and #R-232)

#R-1734 Goat Planter, "Sable" colored,
marked with foil crown label "Royal Haeger ®",
13" L x 4 1/4" W x 9 1/2" T.

#R-1913 Bambi Deer Planter,
molded on bottom "Royal Haeger R-1913 U.S.A.",
also marked on foil label "handcrafted - Haeger",
8 3/4" L x 3 1/2" W x 7 1/2" T.

#R-1191 Sailfish Planter Bowl,
"Briar Agate" colored, no markings,
11" L x 5" W x 7 1/2" T.

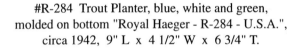

#R-284 Trout Planter, blue, white and green,
molded on bottom "Royal Haeger - R-284 - U.S.A.",
circa 1942, 9" L x 4 1/2" W x 6 3/4" T.

#R-284 Trout Planter, pearl carnival with
gold fins, molded on bottom
"Royal Haeger - R-284 - U.S.A.",
8" L x 4" W x 9 1/4" T.

#R-271 Sailfish Planter,
"Peach Agate" color,
marked on bottom "Royal Haeger 271",
13" L x 9" T.

#R-271 Sailfish Planter,
green with hints of light blue,
marked on bottom "Haeger R271 U.S.A.",
12 1/2" L x 9" T.

#5051 Koala Bear Planter,
"Bennington Brown Foam" colored.

#5084 Squirrel Planter, "Bennington Brown
Foam" colored, stamped on bottom
"Royal Haeger USA ©", 7" Dia. base x 7 1/4" T.

#5015 H Owl Hanging Basket, "Bennington Brown
Foam" colored, 8 1/2" x 7".

#5072 Planter with two cats,
"Bennington Brown Foam" colored, 6 1/2" x 10".

#5070 Planter with two hippos,
"Bennington Brown Foam", 10 1/2" x 5".

#5033 Lion Planter, "Bennington Brown Foam" colored, 6 3/4" x 8".

#5080 Hound Puppy in Shoe Planter, "Bennington Brown Foam" colored, 10 1/2" x 7", *(Possibly ad piece for Hound Dog Shoe Co.)*

#5073 Racoon with Bucket Planter, "Bennington Brown Foam" colored, 9" x 5 1/2".

#5025 "Playful Critters" Elephant Planter, "Bennington Brown Foam" colored, 6" W x 9" T.

#3054 Southern Belle with Nude Top
Planter, pink in color, molded on
bottom "Haeger U.S.A.",
designed by Royal Hickman,
4 7/8" Dia. base x 8" T.

Left to Right:
#R-1253 Little Sister holding basket,
white with black trim, circa 1952,
marked with label "Studio Haeger"
6" L x 4 1/2" W x 11 1/2" T.

#R-1254 Little Brother holding basket,
white with green trim, circa 1952,
marked with label"Studio Haeger"
6" L x 4 1/2" W x 11 1/2" T.

#RG-98 & #RG-99 Dutch Boy and Girl Planter,
matte white glaze, circa 1958, both statues
have 3 1/4" Dia. base x 9"T.

#RG98 Dutch Boy, molded on bottom
"Royal Haeger RG 98 USA".

#RG99 Dutch Girl, molded on bottom
"Royal Haeger RG 99 USA".

#3947 Boy and Girl on Tricycle Planter,
yellow, green and white, circa 1950-51,
marked with oval foil label
"Haeger - Made in U.S.A.",
6 3/4" L x 5" W x 7 1/2" T.

#3532 Flower Girl with Bowl,
brown and cream colored, molded on bottom
"Haeger - 3532 U.S.A.",
8 1/2" x 11 1/4" x 9 3/4" T.

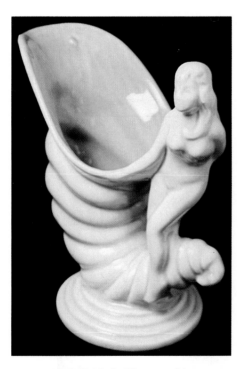

#R-859 Nude Woman with
Cornucopia Planter,
"Silver Spray and Chartreuse",
marked on bottom
"Royal Haeger R859 U.S.A.",
8" L x 4 3/4" Dia. base x 8 3/4" T.

#3910 Clown Jack-in-the-Box, pink,
stamped on bottom "Haeger - USA",
7" L x 6" W x 8 1/2" T.

#RG-132 Madonna Planter,
white, circa 1962, molded on bottom
"Royal Haeger RG132 USA",
5 1/2" L x 3 1/2" W x 11 1/2" T.

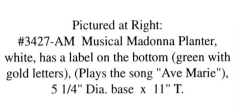

Pictured at Right:
#3427-AM Musical Madonna Planter,
white, has a label on the bottom (green with
gold letters), (Plays the song "Ave Marie"),
5 1/4" Dia. base x 11" T.

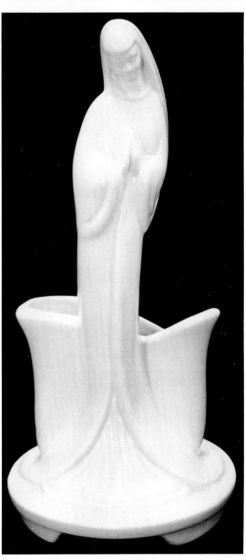

#990 Large Madonna Planter, white,
stamped on base "Haeger - U.S.A.",
10 1/4" L x 10 1/4" W x 13 1/4" T.

Pictured at Right:
#RG-118 Colonial Woman with
Basket Planter, pink, marked with
foil label "Haeger Flower-Ware"
and molded on bottom
"Royal Haeger - RG118 - U.S.A.",
3 1/4" L x 2 1/2" W x 7 1/2" T.

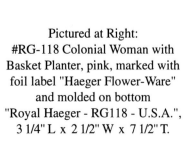

Madonna Planter, white, circa 1938, stamped on bottom "Haeger U.S.A. ©", 8 3/4" T.

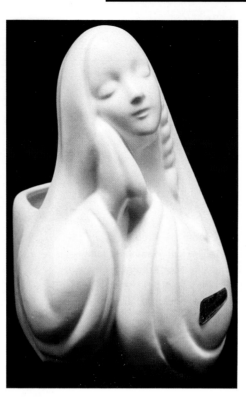

#RG-18 Madonna Planter, matte white finish, circa 1946, marked with "Royal Haeger Flower-Ware", 5" L x 7 1/4" W x 9 1/4" T.

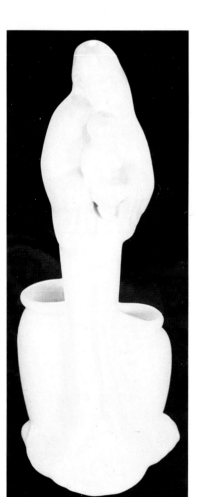

#3264 Madonna with Cherub Child Planter, white, marked on bottom with foil label "Genuine Haeger Pottery 75th Anniversary", 11" T.

#3932 L Boy holding up a Planter, white, by the Macomb Plant, 12" T.

#3855 Little Bo Peep Planter, light pink, circa 1959 by Macomb Plant, stamped on bottom "U.S.A." and a foil label (Rect. Green and silver) "The Great Name - Haeger ® - In American Ceramics", 3 1/2" Dia. base x 8 1/2" T.

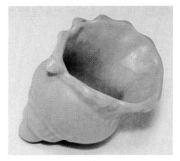

#368 Sea Shell Planter, green,
circa 1936, no markings,
3" W x 3 1/4" T.

#3280-B Buggy Planter, pink,
circa 1942, no markings,
6" L x 2 1/2" W x 5 1/2" T.

#3106 Oblong Vase Planter, "Chartreuse" colored,
marked on bottom with a foil label
"Haeger - Made in USA",
11 1/2" L x 4 1/2" W x 6 1/4" T.

#3244 Cornucopia Style Planter on a Seashell base,
blue in color, circa 1946, 4 3/4" L x 3 1/2" W x 5" T.

#3061 Cornucopia Planter,
white, molded on bottom
"Haeger - USA",
12" L x 4" W x 5 1/2" T.

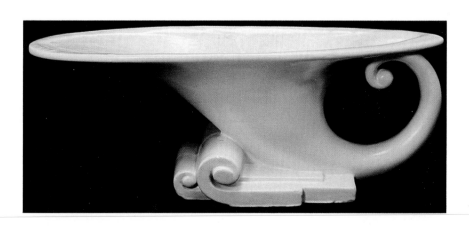

#R-460 Leaf Bowl, light green,
marked with a 75th Anniversary foil label
"Royal Haeger Pottery - 75th Anniversary",
12" L x 3 1/2" W x 5 1/4" T.

#R-483 Upright Shell Planter, "Mallow" color,
molded on bottom "Royal Haeger R-483 U.S.A.",
circa 1947, 10 1/2" L x 4 1/4" W x 10 1/2" T.

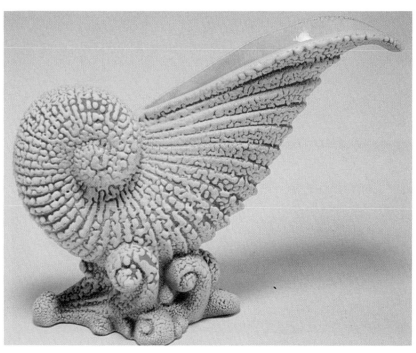

#R-298 Cornucopia Shell Vase,
"Boco" white and pink glaze, circa 1948,
factory molded on bottom "Royal Haeger by
Royal Hickman" "Made in USA R-298",
11" L x 4 1/4" W x 9" T.

#R-1460 Double Leaf Vase, "Antique" colored,
no markings, 8 3/4" L x 3 3/4" W x 10 3/4" T.

#R-575 Rose of Sharon Basket,
"Chartreuse" with red flowers on side, circa 1948,
molded on bottom "Royal Haeger R-575 USA",
7" Dia. x 8" T.

#R-321 Conch Shell, "Cloudy Blue"
colored, circa 1947,
no markings, 4 1/2" L x 3" W x 8" T.

#R-223 Triple Lily Planter,
white-lavender, 7 1/2" W.

#R-293 Violin Bowl Planter,
"Mallow" color, molded on bottom
"Royal Haeger R293 USA",
16" L x 5 3/4" W x 1 5/8" T.

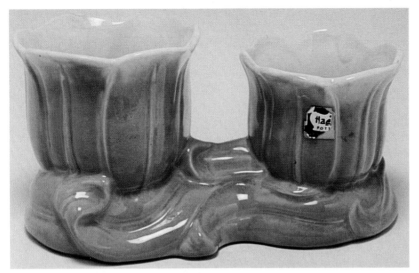

#R-525 Dual Tulip Planter, "Mallow" and white color,
circa 1947, factory molded on bottom
"Royal Haeger R-525 USA",
9 3/4" L x 4 1/2" W x 4 1/4" T.

#3212 Double Cornucopia
Planter, circa 1946,
"Green Briar" and white, no markings,
9 1/2" L x 3" W x 6 1/2" T.

#R-657 Gondolier Planter,
"Green Agate" with white color,
19" L x 6" W x 8 1/2" T.
(Oar is missing from man.)

#R-1293 Acanthus Planter, "Green Agate" colored,
marked with paper label
"Royal Haeger, Dundee, Illinois", 11" x 5 3/4".
(#6116 in TV Lamp form)

#R-709 Horn of Plenty, "Chartreuse" and brown
color, marked with foil crown label
"Royal-Haeger – Dundee, Illinois",
12 3/4" L x 5 1/8" W x 5 1/8" T.

Left to Right:
#394 Pilgrim Hat Planter, light brown,
stamped on bottom "Haeger - USA © - #394",
7 3/4" L x 7 1/2" W x 4 5/8" T.

#338 Cowboy Hat Planter, brown,
stamped on bottom "Haeger - USA © – #338",
8" L x 6 1/4" W x 3 7/8" T.

#R-1462 Wheelbarrow Planter,
"Briar Agate" colored, circa 1964,
9 1/2" L x 6" W x 5 1/2" T.

#R-1446 Basket Planter,
"Turquoise-Blue" color, no markings,
3 1/2" Dia. base x 6 1/2" Dia. top x 9" T.

#3292 Planter, aqua in color,
molded on bottom "Haeger USA",
11" L x 1 3/4" T.

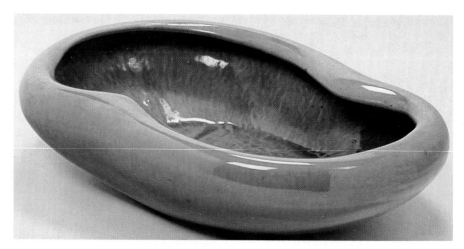

#3752 Planter, green in color, molded on bottom
"Haeger USA", 11" L x 2 3/4" T.

#R-1639-S Basket with metal
bracket, green in color,
molded on bottom "Royal Haeger -
U.S.A. - R1639-S" and a foil crown
label "Royal-Haeger ®",
4" Dia. base x 10" T to top of pot,
the handle is 14 1/2" T.

#3175 Planter, "Fern Agate Earth
Wrap Graphic" colored, no markings,
3 1/4" Dia. base x 4 1/2" Dia. top x 3 3/4" T.
(Possibly marked on missing felt)

Pictured at Right:
#R-1640-S Basket with metal bracket,
"Turquoise-Blue" color,
marked on bottom
"Royal Haeger, U.S.A., R-1640-S",
10 1/2" T with handle x 4" Dia. base.

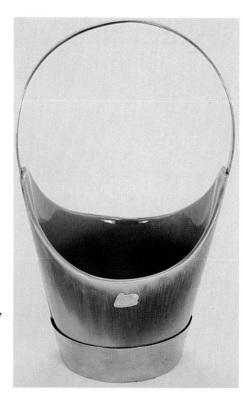

Pictured at Left:
#3174XH Planter/
Hanging Planter, "White
Earth Graphic Wrap",
8" Dia. flared top
x 3 3/4" T.

#3172 Planter, "Marigold Earth
Graphic Wrap" colored, stamped on bottom
"Royal-Haeger - USA ©",
4 7/8" Dia. base x 5 3/4" Dia. top x 3 1/2" T.

#5000 Planter, "Earth Graphic Wrap" colored,
10" Dia. opening x 12 1/2" Dia. x 8 1/4" T.

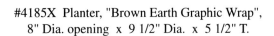

#4185X Planter, "Brown Earth Graphic Wrap",
8" Dia. opening x 9 1/2" Dia. x 5 1/2" T.

#8207H Planter/Hanging Planter,
"Brown Earth Graphic Wrap",
6 1/2" Dia. Opening x 10" Dia. x 5" T.

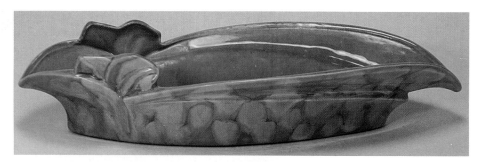

#R843 Planter, "Mauve Agate" colored,
molded on bottom "Royal Haeger - R843 USA",
15 3/8" L x 7 1/4" W x 3 1/2" T.

#R-281 Sphere with three feather
plumes, "Mauve Agate" colored,
no markings,
5 1/2" Dia. base x 9" T.

#776 Goblet shaped Planter, "Aqua
Tweed" colored, with a silver label that
reads "Copyright the Haeger ®" "Potteries
Inc. Macomb ILL", also gold ink stamped
on bottom "Haeger 22K Gold",
6 1/2" Dia. x 9" T.

#3085 Planter, pink and rose
in color, circa 1940's marked
with foil label "Haeger -
Made in U.S.A.",
7 1/2" L x 3 3/4" W
x 5 1/4" T.

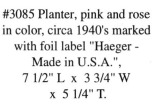

#R-510 Planter with Fish in Relief,
white with blue colors, marked on bottom
"Royal Haeger R510 U.S.A.",
15 1/4" L x 3 3/4" T.

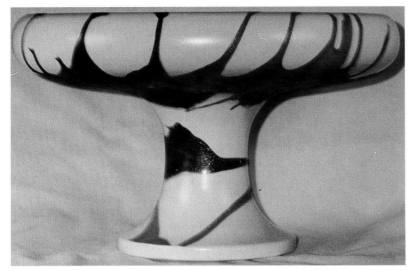

#3130 Pedestaled Planter, "White Earth Graphic Wrap",
11" Dia. x 7" T.

#R-936 Planter with leaves in relief,
"Pearl Grey Drip" color,
molded on bottom "Royal Haeger - R936
U.S.A.", and a crown foil label that reads
"Royal Haeger - Dundee, Illinois",
5" L x 3 1/4" W x 8" T.

#R-852 Triple Ball Planter, "Oxblood" color,
foil label reads "Genuine Haeger",
11 1/4" L x 4 3/4" W x 3 5/8" T.

#503 Planter, "Ebony" colored, circa 1927,
no markings, 4" Dia. base x 9 1/2" W x 6" T.

#5040 Planter, "Bennington Brown Sand" colored,
stamped on bottom "Royal Haeger USA ©",
8" Dia. x 6 3/4" T.

Bowl type Planter, green and aqua colored, molded on bottom
"Made for FTD® © F.T.D.A. 1979 By Haeger U.S.A.",
7 1/4" Dia. x 3" T.
(This type planter was sold exclusively for F.T.D.®)

#3880 Planter with metal bracket and
handle, green with black specks, marked
with foil label "Copyrighted - The -
Haeger ® - Potteries, Inc. - Macomb, ILL."
15 1/4" L x 5" W x 8 1/2" T.

Planter, green and black speckled, stamped on bottom
"Designed Exclusively for Florists Telegraph
Delivery Association Haeger USA", 6" Dia. x 5" T.

294

#167 Planter, yellow colored,
molded on bottom "Haeger U.S.A. 167",
3 1/2" Dia. base x 6 1/2" Dia. top x 5 1/4" T.

#667 Planter, yellow colored,
marked on bottom with stamp
"Haeger USA © #667", also marked
with a foil label "Copyrighted Haeger
® Macomb, ILL, Made in U.S.A.",
3 1/2" Dia. base x 5 1/4" Dia. top x 4 1/4" T.

Planter, marked on bottom
"Haeger U.S.A." and a paper label
that reads "Copyrighted The Haeger
Potteries, Inc., Macomb, ILL.",
5 5/8" x 5 5/8" x 4 3/4" T.

#4020 Planter, grey colored,
marked on bottom "Haeger 4020 U.S.A.",
7 1/2" x 5 1/4" x 3 1/2" T.

#8443 Round Planter, blue colored, marked with foil
label "Gardenhouse ™ - Haeger ® U.S.A.",
7" Dia. x 2 3/8" T. *(Pictured Gazebo)*

Display Sign "Haeger", tan brush stroked,
no markings, 7 3/4" L x 2 1/4" W x 2 1/4" T.

Crown Display Sign that reads
"Royal Haeger - Royal Hickman",
9" L x 2 3/4" W x 6" T.

Display Sign, green colored, that reads "Gardenhouse
by Haeger", 6 1/4" L x 2" W x 3" T.

Haeger Logo Sign,
brown in color, stamped on bottom
"Haeger U.S.A. ©", 8 3/4" L.

Royal Haeger Advertisement Sign,
brown in color, 7 1/2" L x 2" W x 3" T.

Top Photo is the front
that is molded "Royal Haeger".

Bottom photo is the back
that is molded "Craftsmen for a Century".

#3276 Swan Vase, matte white glaze,
circa 1946, no markings,
5 1/2" L x 3 1/2" W x 9 1/2" T.

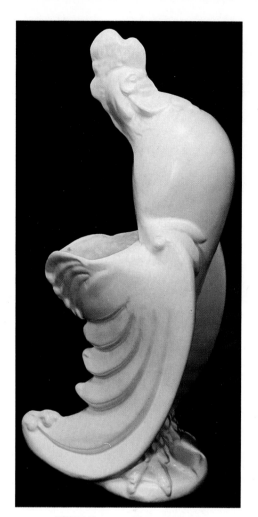

#3220 Rooster Vase, white,
no markings, 7" L x 4" W x 14" T.

#R36 Swan Vase, light blue in color,
marked on bottom "Royal Haeger
by Royal Hickman U.S.A. R36",
10" L x 15 1/2" T.

#R-182 Swan Vase, blue-green crackle
colored, circa 1950's, 8" T.

#R-285 Swan Vase, "Green Briar" colored,
circa 1947, molded on bottom
"Royal Haeger by
Royal Hickman – U.S.A. – 285",
5" L x 4" W x 8 1/2" T.

#R-186 Bird of Paradise, "Cloudy Blue" colored,
molded on bottom "Royal Haeger",
9" L x 4 1/4" W x 13 1/8" T.

#R-888 Vase with Bird on Branch, tan,
3 1/2" sq. base x 14 3/4" T.

#R-482 Three Feather Plume, "Mallow" color,
molded on bottom "Royal Haeger USA 482",
9 1/2" L x 4 1/2" W base x 14 1/2" T.

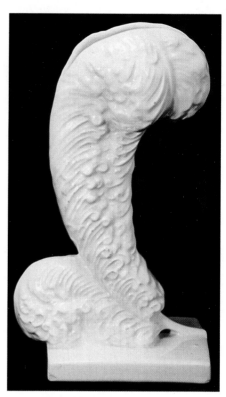

#R-248 Feather Plume Vase,
white, molded on bottom
"Royal Haeger - R 248 U.S.A.",
6" L x 3 3/8" W x 10" T.

#3225 Feather Plume Vase,
blue in color, marked with foil label
"Genuine - Haeger - Pottery",
5" L x 2 7/8" W x 6 1/4" T.

#3270 Leaf Vase, blue in color,
marked on bottom with a paper label that
reads "Genuine Haeger Pottery",
3 3/8" Dia. base x 8 1/8" T.

#R-301 Fan Vase *(Leaf)*, blue in color, marked with paper
label, "Royal Haeger Pottery - 75th Anniversary",
marked on bottom "Royal Haeger - R301 - U.S.A."
9 1/2" L x 9" T.

#R-355 Leaf Vase, "Mallow" color,
molded on bottom "Royal Haeger by Royal
Hickman - U.S.A.", 6 1/2" L x 3" W x 11" T.

#R-138 Leaf Vase "Green Briar" colored,
molded on bottom "Royal Haeger R138 U.S.A.",
12 1/2" L x 5 1/4" W x 12 1/2" T.

#R-826 Vase, brown and white in color,
molded on bottom "Royal Haeger R826 U.S.A.",
7 1/4" at top x 4 1/4" W x 9" T.

#R-320 Elm Leaf, "Green Briar"
colored, circa 1947, bottom marked
"R-320 Royal Haeger - Made in U.S.A."
6" x 12 1/2" T.

#33 Double Leaf Vase, "Peach Agate" color,
molded on bottom "Royal Haeger by Royal Hickman 33 USA",
16 3/4" L x 5 1/4" W x 13" T.

#3240 Two Leaf Vases,
both have the gold crown foil label
that reads "Royal Haeger",
2 3/4" L x 2" W x 3 1/2" T.

#36 Double Leaf Planter, white,
marked on bottom "Haeger U.S.A.",
17 1/2" L x 7" T.

#3053 Donkey Vase, white,
molded on bottom "Haeger USA",
5 3/4" L x 3" W x 9 1/4" T.

#R-427 Horse Vase, tan and white,
molded on bottom "Royal Haeger by
Royal Hickman USA R427",
5 3/4" L x 4" W x 10 3/4" T.

#R-857 Gazelle Head Vase,
molded on bottom
"Royal-Haeger - R857 USA",
3 7/8" Dia. base x 12 1/4" T.

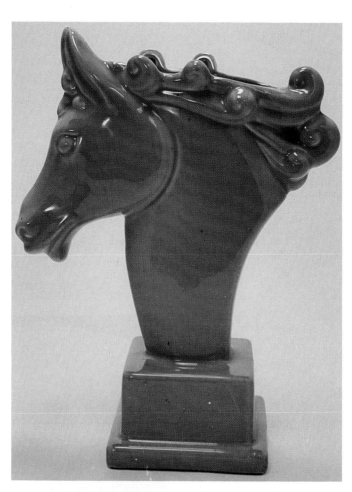

#R-393 Horse Head Vase (Pegasus), blue in color,
molded on bottom "Royal Haeger - 393 - USA",
8 1/2" L x 3 7/8" W x 11 1/4" T.

#3386 Gazelle Vase,
no markings,
4 3/8" L x 3 3/4" W x 12 1/8" T.

#R-647 Sunflower Vase, green,
molded on bottom
"Haeger U.S.A.",
3 3/4" Dia. base x 8 1/8" T.

#R-706 Running Deer Vase,
"Amber Crystal" colored, molded on bottom
"Royal Haeger R706 U.S.A.",
9 1/4" L x 4 7/8" W x 15 1/4" T.

#R-707 Standing Deer Vase,
"Ebony" colored, molded on
bottom "Royal Haeger - R707 U.S.A.",
7" L x 4 5/8" W x 15 1/4" T.

#186 Double Lily Vase, green,
circa 1936, no markings,
4 1/2" L x 3 3/4" W x 6" T.

#186 Double Lily Vase, "Peach Agate" color,
circa 1936, no markings,
6" L x 3 1/2" W x 6 1/2" T.

#R-455 Bow Vase, "Mauve Agate"
colored, molded on bottom
"Royal Haeger - USA - R455A",
5 1/4" Dia. base x 14 1/4" T.

#R-303 Laurel Wreath Bow Vase,
"Mauve Agate" colored,
(markings are too glazed over to read),
7 3/4" L x 4" W x 12" T.

#R-446 Lily Vase, blue in color,
circa 1943, no markings or labels,
4" x 7" base x 14 1/2" T.

#R-441 Deco Styled Circular Vase, "Mauve Agate"
colored, circa 1940's, no markings, 11 1/2" T.

#R-320 Elm Leaf, "Mauve Agate"
colored, circa 1947, molded on bottom
"Royal Haeger - Made in U.S.A. - R320"
4" x 4 1/2" Base x 12" T.

#R-441 Deco Styled Circular Vase,
"Peach Agate" color, no markings,
10" L x 4" W x 12 1/8" T.
(Extremely rare with silver overlay)

#R131 Basket Vase with Fruit, "Peach Agate" color,
no markings, 10 1/4" L x 3" W x 9" T.

#R-386 Basket Vase, "Mauve Agate" colored, circa 1943,
molded on bottom "Royal Haeger - R-386 - U.S.A.",
13 1/4" L x 4" W x 8 1/2" T.

#3528 Double Flower Vase, grey in color,
marked on bottom "Haeger U.S.A. 3528",
6 3/4" T.

#R-452 Morning Glory Vase,
"Mauve Agate" colored, marked on bottom
"Royal Haeger R-452 U.S.A.", 16 1/2" T.

#3531 Dancer with Lily Vase, white with "Chartreuse",
marked bottom "Haeger U.S.A.", 9 3/4" T.

#332A Cornucopia Vase,
"Cloudy Blue" colored,
molded on bottom
"Royal Haeger" (unreadable),
3 1/2" Dia. base x 6 3/4" T.

#R-426 Cornucopia Vase with Nude,
"Mauve Agate" colored, marked with foil crown label
"Royal Haeger Dundee, Illinois",
7 1/2" L x 8" T.

#R-426 Cornucopia Vase with Nude,
"Chartreuse" and white colored,
7 1/2" L x 8" T.

#332B Cornucopia Vase,
"Peach Agate" color,
molded on bottom
"Royal Haeger - by - Royal Hickman
- Made in USA",
4 1/2" L x 4 1/4" W x 10 3/4" T.

#R-701 Sea Shell, "Silver Spray" colored, circa 1949, molded on bottom "Royal Haeger - R701 - U.S.A.", 11" L x 3 1/2" W x 10 1/2" T.

#R-523 Fan Vase, "Green Briar" colored with white, molded on bottom "Royal Haeger - R523 USA", 16" L x 5 1/2" W x 10" T.

#3227 Double Shell Vase, "Green Agate" colored, no markings, 19" L x 7" W x 7" T.

#R-228 Cornucopia Vase, "Green Briar" colored,
molded on bottom "Royal Haeger - R 228 USA",
12 1/2" L x 4" W x 9" T.

#R-422 Butterfly Vase, "Mauve Agate" colored,
molded on bottom "Royal Haeger USA R-422"
circa 1940, 9" L x 3 3/4" W x 5 1/2" T.

#R-228 Cornucopia Vase, "Mauve Agate" colored,
circa 1939, molded on bottom "Royal Haeger U.S.A.",
12" L x 3 1/2" W x 9 1/2" T.

#R-246 Double Cornucopia Vase, "Mauve Agate" colored,
circa 1939, molded on bottom "Royal Haeger - Made in U.S.A.",
14" L x 4 1/2" W x 8 1/4" T.

Pictured at Left:
#R-332B Cornucopia Vases, "Mauve Agate" colored,
molded on bottom "Royal Haeger R332B USA",
4 1/4" Dia. base x 10 1/2" T.

#R-299 Snail, "Cloudy Blue" colored,
molded on bottom "Royal Haeger R299 U.S.A.",
11 1/4" L x 3 1/4" W x 7" T.

#R-299 Snail Vase, blue and white,
molded on bottom "Royal Haeger - R299 USA",
11 1/2" L x 3 1/4" W x 7" T.

#3105 Dancing Girl Vase,
green in color, no markings,
5 1/4" W x 8" T.

#3208 Fish Vase, white, with a green and silver
foil label that reads "Haeger - Made in USA",
4 1/2" L x 2" W x 5 1/2" T.

#R-322 Double Conch Shell Vase,
"Green Briar" colored, molded on bottom
"Royal Haeger", 10" L x 6 1/2" T.

Vase, "Ebony" colored, circa 1914
3 1/2" Dia. base x 8 1/4" T.
(1st art piece into production)

#141 Vase, dark blue-black, circa
1914, no markings,
4 1/2" Dia. base x 11 1/2" T.

#1037 Vase , blue in color,
circa 1940's, marked on bottom on a
paper label "Haeger Made in U.S.A.",
3 5/8" Dia. base x 9 1/2" T.

#19A Pair of Vases, blue with
light blue and green colors,
circa 1918, no markings,
3 1/4" Dia. base x 6" T.

#47 Vase, dark and light green,
circa 1938, no markings,
6" Dia. base x 15 1/2" T.

#39 Vase, dark rose in color,
circa 1918, no markings,
8 1/2" Dia. base x 6 7/8" T.

#628 A Pair of Vases, blue, circa 1938,
marked with a paper label
on bottom "Haeger",
3 1/2" Dia. base x 4" Dia. top x 9" T.

#39 Vase, blue and red in color,
circa 1918, no markings,
3 1/2" Dia. base x 3 3/4" T.

#43 Vase with three handles,
blue and red in color, circa 1927,
no markings, 4 3/4" Dia. x 6" T.

#182 Vase, blue and red in color,
circa 1936, no markings,
5 1/2" Dia. x 9" T.

#8237 Large Vase, green
with lighter green colors, marked on bottom
"Haeger" inside diamond logo, (very early logo),
6 1/2" Dia. base x 5" Dia. top x 7 3/4" T.

314

#186 Vase with leaf design molded into the vase, blue and white in color, circa 1939, no markings, 9" Dia. x 11 1/4" T.

#3015 Vase, green in color, circa 1946, molded on bottom "Haeger U.S.A.", 4" Dia. x 8" T.

#1018 Vase, pink in color, circa 1941, marked with Haeger label (green with gold letters on label), 2 1/2" Dia. base x 7 1/4" T.

#607 Vase, mint-blue colored, circa 1938, marked with label, 4" Dia. x 5 1/2" T.

#463 Round Vase with floral design in relief, green colored, circa 1930, no markings, 5 7/8" L x 4" W x 6 1/2" T.

#136 Vase, white,
circa 1935, no markings,
1 1/2" Dia. base x 5" T.

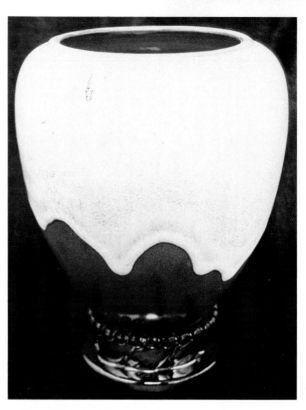

#R-337 Vase, charcoal grey and white, circa 1942,
no markings, 9" Dia. top x 11 1/2" T.

#R-454 Chinese Vase,
"Ebony" with textured white, circa 1936,
8" Dia. x 15 1/4" T.

#R-504 Bee Hive Vase, white and
pink in color, circa 1947, molded on bottom
"Royal Haeger USA R-504",
3 1/4" Dia. base x 7 3/4" T

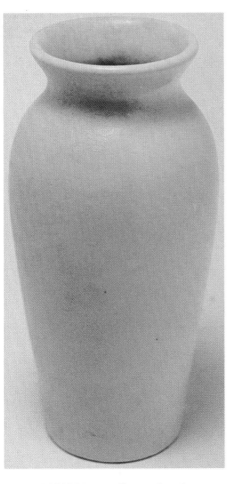

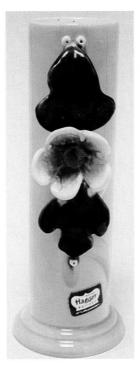

#R-580 Rose of Sharon Vase, yellow with decorated flowers, circa 1949, molded on bottom "Royal Haeger R-580 USA", and also has a crown foil label "75th Anniversary Haeger", 2 3/4" Dia. base x 10" T.

#2908 Vase, yellow colored,
circa 1930's,
3" Dia. base x 9 1/2" T.

#R-456 Wrap-around Spiral Vase,
"Yellow Drip" colored, molded on
bottom "Royal Haeger R456 USA",
5 1/4" Dia. base x 14" T.

#3059 Vase with sterling
overlay, blue in color,
molded on bottom
"Haeger U.S.A." and
also marked on overlay
"Sterling", 8" L x
3 3/4" W x 10 1/4" T.

#R-441 Circle Vase, blue with silver overlay, designed in 1940 for the National Silver Deposit Ware Co., molded on bottom "Haeger USA", also marked on overlay "Sterling", these vases were extremely expensive and very few were made, 10" L x 2" W x 11 3/4" T.

#R-1123 Pair of Vases with leaves in relief,
peach-tan and cream in color, crown foil label
"Royal-Haeger -Dundee, Illinois", 7" L x 2 1/2" W x 8" T.

#3617 Rectangle Vase, grey and pink
in color, circa 1952-1966,
marked with a green and silver foil
label "The Great Name - Haeger ® -
In American Ceramics" ,
4 1/2" L x 3 1/4" W x 6" T.

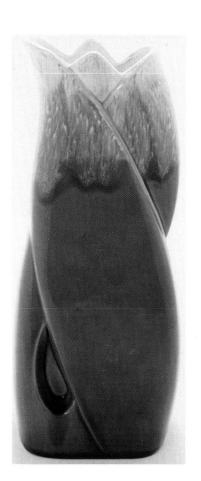

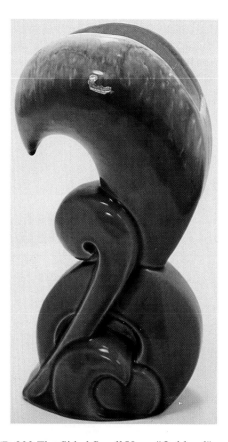

#R-893 Tulip Vase, "Oxblood" and
white in color, marked on bottom
"Royal Haeger - R893 - U.S.A.",
5" L x 3 3/4" W x 12 1/8" T.

#R-833 Flat Sided Scroll Vase, "Oxblood" and
white in color, molded on bottom "Royal Haeger -
R833 U.S.A.", and also marked with a crown foil
label "Royal-Haeger - Dundee, Illinois",
5 3/4" L x 4 1/8" W x 12" T.

#4044 Pitcher shaped Vase,"Green Agate" colored, molded
on bottom "Haeger 4044", and a foil label "Haeger" in 'H' design,
3 1/2" Dia. base x 13 3/4" T.

#R-651 Pillow Vase, "Green Agate" colored, molded on bottom "Royal Haeger – R651 USA", 5 1/4" L x 3" W x 7 3/4" T.

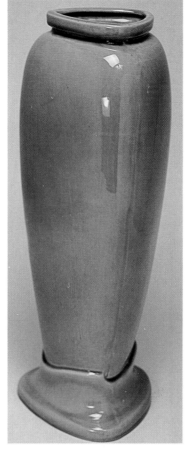

#W2002 also #R-490 Triangular Vase, "Chartreuse" colored, molded on bottom "Royal Haeger by Royal Hickman - Made in USA W2002", 5 1/2" x 5 5/8" base x 15 1/4" T.

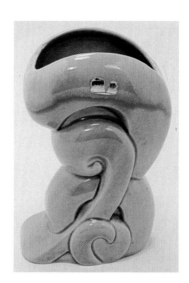

#R-900 Modern Scroll Vase, "Chartreuse & Honey" colored, marked with foil crown label "Royal Haeger - Dundee, Illinois" and molded on bottom "Royal Haeger - R900 U.S.A.", 4" L x 2 5/8" W x 6 1/4" T.

#R-830 Wave Styled Vase, "Green Agate & Chartreuse", molded on bottom "Royal Haeger R830 USA", 7" L x 6" W x 20 1/2" T.

#R-1235 Classic Bud Vase, "Chartreuse & Honey" colored, marked with paper label "Royal-Haeger, Dundee, Illinois", 3 3/8" Dia. base x 7 1/8" T.,

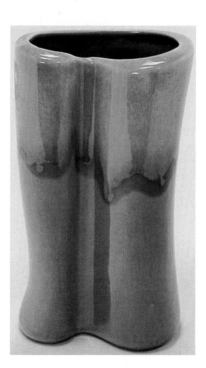

#R-979 Abstract Vase, "Chartreuse & Honey" colored, molded on bottom "Royal Haeger R979 U.S.A." 4 3/4" L x 3 1/2" W x 8 1/4" T.

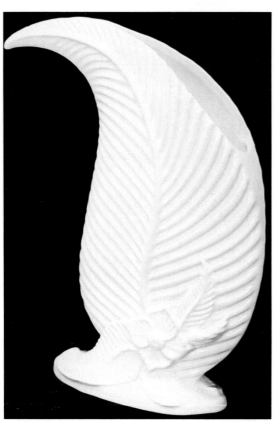

#D1021 Leaf Vase, white, molded on bottom "Royal Haeger - By - Royal Hickman - USA", 10 1/2" L x 3 1/4" W x 12 3/4" T.

#D-1028 Beehive Vase, "Green Briar" colored, molded on bottom "Royal Haeger U.S.A.", 3" Dia. base x 7 1/2" T.

#D-1001 Cylinder Vase, "Green Briar" colored, circa 1940's, molded on bottom "Royal Haeger USA", *(The rest is unreadable)* 2 3/4" Dia. base x 4" Dia. top x 7 1/2" T.

#714 Vase, "Green Briar" colored, circa 1959, stamped on bottom "Haeger USA", 5 1/8" Dia. base x 6 3/4" Dia. top x 11 1/4" T.

#R-501 Beehive Vase with applied floral relief, "Green Briar" colored with pink flowers, molded on bottom "Royal Haeger USA", 6" Dia. x 7 3/4" T.

#931 Vase, brown with green
accents, molded on bottom
"Haeger" *(the rest is unreadable)*.

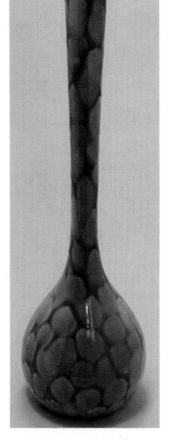

#R-251 Onion Jug Vase,
"Cloudy Blue" colored,
molded on bottom
"Royal Haeger U.S.A. R251",
4 1/8" Dia. base x 20 1/2" T.

#3273 Vase with wheat in relief,
"Green Briar" colored, no markings,
7 1/2" L x 3 5/8" W x 12" T.

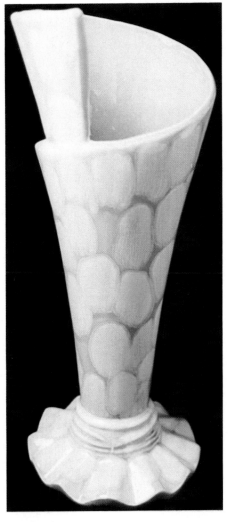

#R-456 Wrap-around Spiral Vase,
"Cloudy Blue" colored, marked on bottom
"Royal Haeger R456 U.S.A.",
5 1/4" Dia. base x 14" T.

#R-416 Urn, "French Grey with
Mallow" colored, molded on
bottom "Royal Haeger by
Royal Hickman R416",
3 1/2" Dia. base x 10" T.
*(This piece is missing a
lid with a bird finial).*

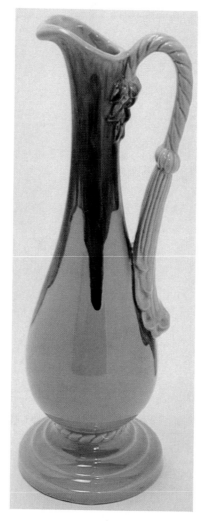

#R-419 Pitcher Vase, "French Grey with
Mallow" colored, molded on
bottom "Royal Haeger by
Royal Hickman R419 USA",
5" Dia. base x 14 3/8" T.

#R-417 Gourd Vase, "French Grey
with Mallow" colored, molded on
bottom "Royal Haeger by
Royal Hickman R417",
3 5/8" Dia. base x 12" T.

#R-1619-S Flower Pitcher,
"Ebony Cascade" colored,
molded on bottom "Royal Haeger
USA R1619-S",
6 7/8" Dia. base x 15 7/8" T.

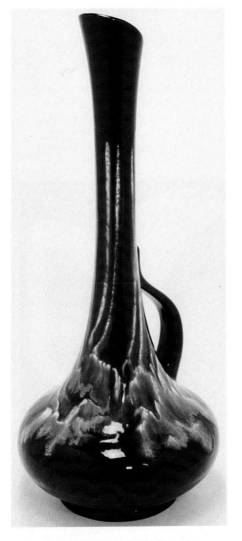

#408 Handled Pitcher,
"Ebony Cascade" colored, molded on
bottom "Royal Haeger 408 U.S.A.",
5" Dia. base x 18 1/2" T.

#R-1812-S Vase, "Ebony
Cascade" colored, molded on
bottom "Royal Haeger
U.S.A. R1812-S",
5" Dia. x 13 1/4" T.

#R-1752-W Eccentric Vase,
"Ebony Cascade" colored, molded on
bottom "Royal Haeger R-1752-W
U.S.A.", 7" Dia. x 16" T.

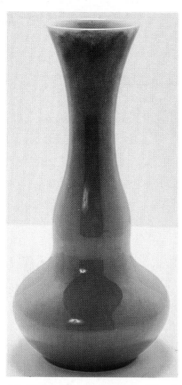

#R-1776 Vase, "Turquoise-Blue" color, marked on bottom "Royal Haeger - R1776 U.S.A.", 3 1/2" Dia. base x 3 3/8" Dia. top x 12" T.

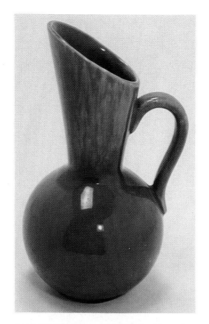

RG-82 Jug Vase, "Lilac" colored, molded on bottom "Royal Haeger USA RG82", 2 1/2" Dia. base x 9 1/8" T.

#413 Small Eccentric Vase, "Turquoise-Blue" color, molded on bottom "Royal Haeger 413 U.S.A.", 3 1/4" Dia. base x 9" T.

#4029-H Boutique Jar, "Etruscan Blue" colored, circa 1950's, molded on bottom, *(molding is unreadable)* 4 1/4" Dia. base x 5 1/2" T.

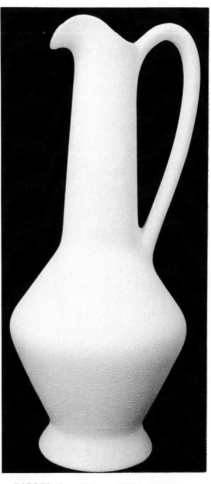

#456 Pitcher, "Cotton White & Turquoise" color, circa 1960's, molded on bottom "Royal Haeger © 456 U.S.A.", 5 1/8" Dia. base x 18 1/4" T.

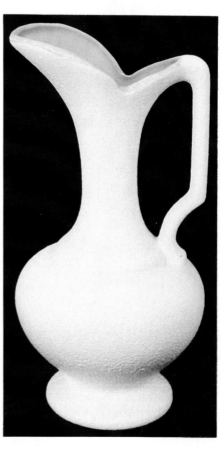

#8180 Pitcher Vase, "Cotton White & Chartreuse" colored, stamped on bottom "Haeger © - USA", 3 1/2" Dia. base x 10" T.

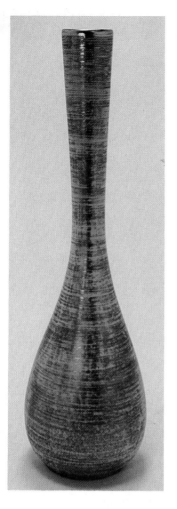

#R-1915 Onion Style Vase,
"Gold Tweed" colored, molded on
bottom "Royal Haeger R1915 U.S.A.",
3" Dia. base x 15 1/4" T.

#493 Vase, "Aqua Crystal" colored,
circa 1950's, molded on bottom
"Royal Haeger © 493 USA",
5" Dia. base x 4 3/8" Dia. top x 16 3/4" T.

#455 Flared Top Vase, green in color,
molded on bottom "Royal Haeger © #455
U.S.A." and a foil stamp that reads
"handcrafted Haeger",
5 1/2" Dia. base x 16 1/4" T.

#413 Small Eccentric Vase,
"Gold Tweed" colored, molded on
bottom "Royal Haeger 413 U.S.A.",
also marked with foil label "Haeger -
Gold Tweed Glaze - 22K Gold",
3 1/4" Dia. base x 9" T.

#RG-68 Bottle Vase, "Mandarin
Orange" colored, marked on
bottom "Royal Haeger, U.S.A.,
RG-68", 7 1/4" T.

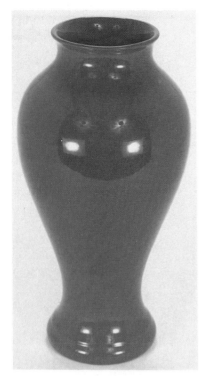

#4031 Vase, "Mandarin Orange"
colored, molded on bottom
"Royal Haeger © 4031, U.S.A." and
also a foil label "Haeger" in an 'H' logo,
9 1/8" x 3 3/4" Dia. base.

#478 Vase, "Mandarin Orange" colored,
marked with foil label "handcrafted
Haeger" and molded on bottom
"Royal Haeger 478 © U.S.A.",
4 1/8" x 4 1/8" x 12" T.

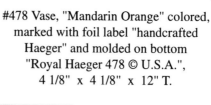

#R-1919 Bottle Vase,
"Mandarin Orange" colored,
molded on bottom
"Royal Haeger, R1919, U.S.A.",
10 1/4" T.

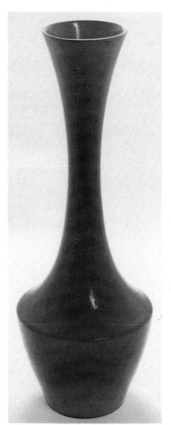

#4038 Classic Medium Vase,
"Mandarin Orange" colored,
marked on bottom "Royal
Haeger 4038 U.S.A.",
3 1/8" Dia. base x 14 1/4" T.

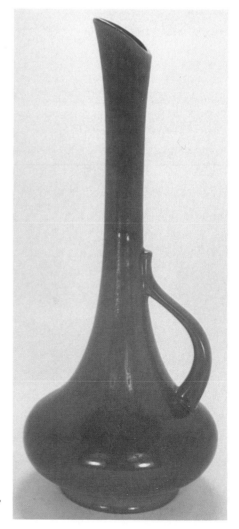

#408 Handled Pitcher Vase,
"Mandarin Orange" colored,
5" Dia. base x 18 1/2" T.

#483 "Cobra" Vase, "Mandarin Orange"
colored, marked on bottom
"Royal Haeger © 483 U.S.A.", 16" T.

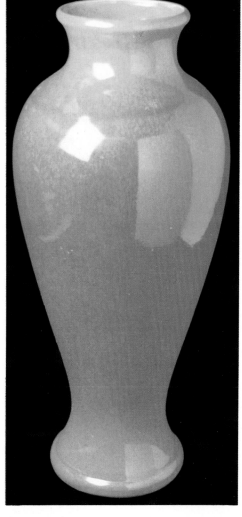

#493 Traditional Vase, "Mandarin Orange" colored,
marked on bottom "Royal Haeger © 493 U.S.A.",
5" Dia. base x 4 1/2" Dia. top x 17" T.

(*Note: these two photos show the
true color "Mandarin Orange")

#1-H Vase *(from the American*
Heritage Series) "Mandarin Orange"
colored, molded on bottom
"Haeger USA", 7" Dia. x 22" T.

#R-1919 Bottle Vase, "Bittersweet"
colored, marked on bottom
"Royal Haeger R1919 U.S.A.",
2 1/2" Dia. base x 10 1/4" T.

#R-1619-S Flower Pitcher Vase,
"Black Mistique" colored,
molded on bottom "Royal Haeger R1619-S",
also has a foil label "Haeger" in an H logo,
6 7/8" Dia. base x 16" T.

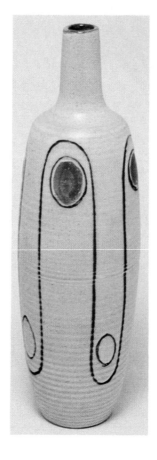

#2-H Bottle Styled Vase,
off white vase with blue and yellow
and brown, molded on bottom
"Haeger © USA 2-H",
3 1/4" Dia. x 14" T.

#R-1752 Eccentric Vase, "Pearl
Shell" colored, molded on bottom
"Royal Haeger R1752 U.S.A.",
4 1/2" Dia. base x 16 1/4" T.

#R-1444 Flat Sided Dented Vase,
"Pearl Shell" colored, no markings,
6 1/2" L x 4 1/2" W x 15" T.

#2021 Vase with wheat design in relief, light blue matte, with foil label that reads "Haeger - Made in USA", 4 3/4" Dia. base x 3" Dia. top x 9 3/4" T.

#RG-14 Pillow Vase, (Flower-ware), pink in color, molded on bottom "Royal Haeger RG-14 U.S.A.", 6 1/4" L x 3 1/4" W x 9" T.

#RG-42 Medium Flower Pitcher, "Matte Black" colored, molded on bottom "Royal Haeger" it also has a sticker on outside that reads "Haeger Flower-ware", 4" Dia. x 10" T.

#S-400 Textured Vase, "Sunset Yellow" colored, marked with foil label "Studio Haeger", 10 1/4" T.

Pictured at Left:
#RC-68 Bottle Vase, "Marigold
Agate" colored, molded on bottom
"Royal Haeger", 3" Dia. x 7 1/2" T.

#483 "Cobra" Vase, "Marigold Agate"
colored, marked on bottom
"Royal Haeger © 483 U.S.A.", 16" T.

#R-895 Vase, "Briar Agate" colored,
molded on bottom
"Royal-Haeger - R895 USA",
4" Dia. base x 11 1/4" T.

#4183 Tapered Vase,
"White Earth Graphic Wrap",
with paper label that reads
"Haeger - Style - 4183 - Price",
7 5/8" Dia. base x
4 5/8" Dia. top x 11 1/8" T.

#4200 Vase, "Brown Earth
Graphic Wrap", no markings,
2 1/2" Dia. base x
4 1/4" Dia. top x 5 3/8" T.

#4162X Cylinder Vase, "Fern
Agate Earth Graphic Wrap",
stamped on bottom "Royal-Haeger
- USA ©", 3 1/2" Dia. base x
3 1/2" Dia. top x 7" T.

#4244 Vase "Brown Earth
Graphic Wrap",
4 1/2" x 12 1/2"

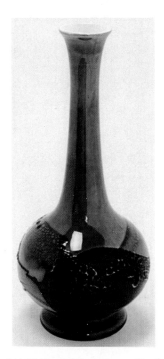

#4171 Vase,
"Brown Earth Graphic Wrap",
7" Dia. x 14 1/2" T.

#4132 Vase, "Fern Agate Earth
Graphic Wrap", stamped on
bottom "Royal-Haeger - USA ©",
3" Dia. base x
1 3/4" Dia. top x 10" T.

#4202 Vase,
"Brown Earth Graphic Wrap",
5 1/2" Dia. x 10" T.

#4161X Vase, "Fern Agate Earth Graphic Wrap", marked on bottom of felt "Royal Haeger ® U.S.A. The Haeger Potteries Inc. © Dundee, ILL.", 4" Dia. x 10 1/2" T.

#4238X Vase "Fern Agate Earth Graphic Wrap", marked on bottom of felt "Royal Haeger ® - Dundee, ILL.", 4" Dia. base x 5 1/4" Dia. top x 12" T.

#4248 Vase, "Marigold Agate Earth Graphic Wrap", stamped on bottom "Royal-Haeger - USA ©", 3 1/4" Dia. base x 2 1/2" Dia. top x 10 3/4" T.

#4160X Cylinder Vase, "Fern Agate Earth Graphic Wrap", marked on bottom of felt "Royal Haeger ® - U.S.A. – The Haeger Potteries Inc. © - Dundee, ILL.", 4 5/8" Dia. base and top x 12" T.

#4233X Vase, "Fern Agate Earth Graphic Wrap", stamped on bottom "Royal - Haeger USA ©", 4 7/8" Dia. base x 5" Dia. top x 11" T.

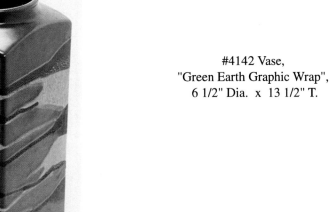

#4142 Vase,
"Green Earth Graphic Wrap",
6 1/2" Dia. x 13 1/2" T.

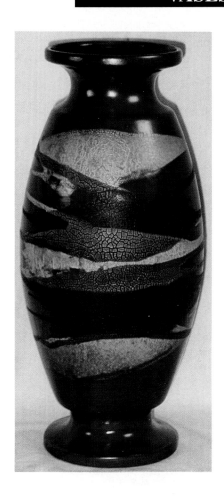

#4174 Vase, "Green Earth Graphic Wrap", marked
on bottom of felt "Royal Haeger ® - U.S.A. – The
Haeger Potteries Inc. © – Dundee, ILL.", paper label
"Haeger - Style - USA - 4174 - Price", 3 5/8" Dia.
base x 3 1/4" Dia. top x 9 3/4" T.

#4231X Vase, "Marigold Agate
Earth Graphic Wrap",
stamped on bottom
"Royal - Haeger - U.S.A. ©",
3 1/8" Dia. base x
3 1/8" Dia. top x 11" T.

#4181 Vase, "Green Earth Graphic Wrap",
8" Dia. x 13" T.

Pictured at Left:
#4106 Vase, "Marigold Agate Earth Graphic Wrap", marked on bottom of felt "Royal Haeger ® - U.S.A. – The Haeger Potteries Inc. © - Dundee, ILL.", 4 3/4" Dia. base x 5" Dia. top x 16" T.

Pictured at Right:
#4182 Handled Vase, "Earth Graphic Wrap", no markings, 4 7/8" Dia. base x 8" Dia. top x 12" T.

#4143 Vase, "Earth Graphic Wrap", no markings, 3" Dia. base x 2 3/8" Dia. top x 9 1/4" T.

Vase, "Earth Graphic Wrap", 7" Dia. x 14 1/2" T.

#4070 Pitcher Vase,
"Peasant Flame" with gold accents,
ink stamped on bottom
"Haeger USA", 17 1/2" T.

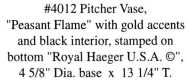

#4012 Pitcher Vase,
"Peasant Flame" with gold accents
and black interior, stamped on
bottom "Royal Haeger U.S.A. ©",
4 5/8" Dia. base x 13 1/4" T.

#S447 Oblong Vase, "Peasant Flame" colored, circa 1952,
ink stamped on bottom "Haeger © USA", and also has the
Haeger label that reads "Craftsman for a Century",
6" L x 4" W x 8" T.

#4002 Hexagon Vase, "Peasant Olive"
colored, molded on bottom
"Royal Haeger © 4002",
4 1/2" Dia. x 10 1/4" T.

#4205 Vase, "Peasant Olive" with black interior, stamped on bottom "Royal Haeger USA ©", 5 3/8" Dia. base x 6 1/2" Dia. top x 12" T.

#8097 Pitcher Vase, "Peasant Blue" colored, molded on bottom "Haeger", 8 1/2" Dia. x 18" T.

#4131 Vase, "Peasant Olive" colored, ink stamped "Haeger USA ©", 3 1/2" Dia. x 7" T.

#4103 Pitcher Vase with floral relief, "Peasant Yellow" colored, molded on bottom "Haeger © - 4103 - U.S.A.", 4 5/8" Dia. base x 18" T.

336

#451 Vase, "Nutmeg Textured",
molded on bottom
"Royal Haeger 451 USA",
3 1/2" Dia. base x 11" T.

#4144 Vase, "Bennington
Brown Foam" colored,
stamped on bottom
"Royal Haeger © USA",
3 3/4" Dia. base x 3" top
x 9 1/2" T.

#4141 Pitcher Vase, pearlescent tan & orange color,
stamped on bottom "Royal Haeger USA ©",
3 1/2" Dia. base x 11" T.

#303 Vase, brown and tan glossy
& matte colored, stamped on
bottom "Haeger © - USA - #303",
4 1/8" Dia. base x 5" Dia. top
x 9 1/8" T.

#RG-92 Vase with handle, brown in
color, ink stamped on bottom
"Haeger USA ©",
4" Dia. base x 7" T.

#4256 Vase, brown and tan matte &
glossy, stamped on bottom "Royal
Haeger USA ©", 4 1/2" Dia. base x
4 5/8" Dia. top x 12" T.

337

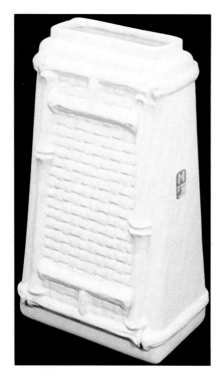

#4194 Bamboo Shoots Vase, cream
colored, with foil label that reads
"Haeger - Craftsmen for a Century"
and stamped on bottom "Royal
Haeger USA ©", also a
paper label that reads
"Haeger - Style 4194 - Price $6.50",
6 1/4" L x 4 1/4" W x 10 3/4" T.

#4243 Vase,
brown and tan colored,
stamped on bottom
"Royal Haeger USA ©",
2 1/8" Dia. base x 9 5/8" T.

#4162X Cylinder Vase,
tan and brown in color, stamped on bottom
"Haeger © USA" and a foil label reads
"Haeger - Craftsmen for a Century",
3 5/8" Dia. x 7 1/8" T.

#4411 Vase, blue and white in color, paper label reads "Haeger ® -
American Made - 4411" *(the rest of label missing)*,
6" Dia. base x 3 3/4" Dia. top x 10" T.

#517 Pair of Wall Pockets, yellow colored glaze,
circa 1936, 4" L x 2 1/2" W x 7 1/2" T.

#R-1135 Flower Wall
Pocket, grey in color,
molded "Royal Haeger
R1135 USA".

#R-16275 Fish Wall Pocket,
"Antique" colored, marked with a
crown label "Royal Haeger ©",
13 1/4" L x 6 1/2" x 3 1/4".

#R-745 Grape Vine Wall Pocket,
purple and green in color,
molded "Royal Haeger R-745 USA".

#917A Rocking Cradle Wall Pocket,
white, circa 1939, marked with label
"Haeger Pottery, Dundee, ILL.",
5" L x 3 1/2" W x 3" T.

#126 Red Wall Pocket
with white spots,
circa 1914, no markings,
10" L x 2 1/2" x 3 7/8" W.

#R-725 Wall Pocket, green in color,
marked on back "Haeger 725 U.S.A.", and a
paper label "Royal Haeger",
6 1/2" x 2 3/4" x 5 1/8" T.

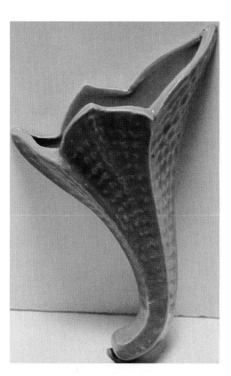

#3112 Wall Pocket, blue colored
glaze, circa 1941,
molded on back "Haeger USA",
6" L x 3" W x 7 1/2" T.

2069	Ashtray	White Earth Graphic Wrap	1970's	175
2084	Ashtray	White Earth Graphic Wrap	1970's	175
2085	Ashtray	White Earth Graphic Wrap	1970's	175
2124	Ashtray	Brown Earth Graphic Wrap	1970's	175
2125X	Ashtray	Fern Agate Earth Graphic Wrap	1970's	175
R1095	Ashtray (Lincoln)	Sesquicentennial Piece - brown	1968	176
	Ashtray (Commemorative)	1871-1971 Craftsmen for a Century	1971	176
	Ashtray (elephant)	1934, A Century of Progress - blue	1934	176
	Ashtray (advertising)	1934, A Century of Progress - brown	1934	176
	Ashtray (advertising)	A Century of Progress, 1934 - green	1934	176
	Ashtray (advertising)	A Century of Progress, 1934 - brown	1934	176
	Ashtray (advertising)	A Century of Progress, 1933-34 - green	1933-34	177
128	Ashtray	Gold Tweed		177
127	Ashtray	Gold Tweed		177
109S	Ashtray	Gold Tweed		177
1016S	Ashtray (convex Long John)	Mandarin Orange		177
128	Ashtray	Mandarin Orange		178
1045	Ashtray	Mandarin Orange		178
720S	Ashtray & Cigarette Holder	Mandarin Orange		178
1030	Ashtray	Mandarin Orange	1950's	178
153	Ashtray	Mandarin Orange		178
702	Ashtray & Cigarette Holder	Mandarin Orange		178
135	Ashtray	Mandarin Orange		179
	Ashtray (Stanley Snuffer)	green		179
2009	Ashtray	green/brown/white		179
2115	Ashtray	green		179
2145	Ashtray (leaf shaped with acorns)	green	1976	179
R873	Ashtray (freeform)	Green Agate		179
2105	Ashtray	Yellow Boco		180
R1894	Ashtray	transparent white glaze over red clay		180
134	Ashtray (palm leaf)	Green Agate		180
175	Ashtray (Sands of Time)	green		180
R125	Ashtray	Cotton White		180
153	Ashtray	Cotton White		180
162	Ashtray	Cotton White		181
2155	Ashtray	tan		181
1016S	Ashtray (convex Long John)	Pumpkin		181
R1718	Ashtray (boomerang)	orange		181
R1787	Ashbowl (egg shaped)	Pearl Shell		182
110H	Ashbowl (leaf)	Jade Crackle		182
R125	Ashtray	Briar Agate		182
R811	Ashtray (palette)	Pearl Grey Drip		182
135	Ashtray	Briar Agate		182
R1602	Ashtray (horseshoe)	Ebony		183
HJ8	Ashtray	green and blue		183
138	Ashtray	Turquoise and Blue		183
130	Ashtray	Turquoise		183
135	Ashtray	Purple Jewel Tone		183
153	Ashtray	purple	1960's-70's	184
2070	Ashtray	tan with black streaks		184
130	Ashtray	Haeger Red		184
113	Ashtray	Haeger Red		184
R1755	Ashtray (executive)	Haeger Red		185
SP12	Ashtray (palette)	Ebony Cascade		185
177	Ashtray (leaf)	Mandarin Orange	1950's	186
R449	Ashtray (leaf)	Mauve Agate		186
2057	Ashbowl	Brown Earth Graphic Wrap		213
	Bank (Harley Davidson Piggy Bank)	black with gold trim	1982	254
8034	Bank (dog)	white transparent		255
5015H	Basket (owl hanging)	Bennington Brown Foam		279
R575	Basket (rose of sharon)	Chartreuse with red flowers	1948	287
R1639S	Basket	green		290
R1640S	Basket	Turquoise-Blue		290
8229	Bean Pot	blue/white/brownish-green		265
	Bell (Sears Advertising)	yellow		262

6	Bird	white	1933	225
R359	Birds (two figural flower frogs)	Cloudy Blue	1940's	243
R186	Bird of Paradise	Cloudy Blue		298
3622	Bookends (planters)	Chartreuse		187
R132	Bookend (ram figure)	mint with blue and brown spots		187
R641	Bookend (stallion planter)	Chartreuse		187
R178	Bookends (ram head)	Oxblood		187
R1144	Bookends (water lily)	green with white flowers	1952	188
R638	Bookends (panther planters)	Ebony	1950's	188
R475	Bookends (calla lily)	Amber		188
648	Booties	light blue		240
4029H	Boutique Jar	Etruscan Blue	1950's	324
R282	Bowl (oblong, part of a console set)	Pearl Grey Drip	1950's	228
R309	Bowl (ruching)	peach/blue/cream		189
R333	Bowl	Lilac		189
R370	Bowl (dutch cup)	Green Agate		189
R759	Bowl	purple with white and light blue		190
RG56	Bowl Compote	Black Mistique		190
R614	Bowl (scroll)	Green Agate	1947	190
352	Bowl	Black Mistique		190
364H	Bowl (lily)	yellow-orange		191
R466	Bowl	Briar Agate		191
R309	Bowl (ruching)	Cloudy Blue	1946	191
H740	Bowl (footed)	Green Agate		192
R1494	Bowl (three legged low)	pink and black		192
334	Bowl (scalloped, also #R-357)	white		192
R358	Bowl (footed)	Mallow and Ebony		192
R1338	Bowl	Chartreuse and Ebony		192
329H	Bowl (pheasant)	Gold Tweed		193
364H	Bowl (lily)	Gold Tweed		193
373H	Bowl	Mandarin Orange		193
R484	Bowl (garden)	Chartreuse and Ebony		193
47	Bowl	Chartreuse	1938	194
362	Bowl	Mandarin Orange		194
W2005	Bowl (garden)	pink and white		194
3177	Bowl	white/yellow/orange/brown		195
3169	Bowl (two handled)	White Earth Graphic Wrap		195
R297	Bowl (shell shaped)	Chartreuse and Silver Spray		195
S552	Bowl	white/orange		196
101	Bowl	green		196
R466	Bowl	light blue and white		196
R442	Bowl	Mauve Agate		197
314	Bowl (compote)	green and white Boco		197
R373	Bowl with applied flowers	Cloudy Blue and white	1950's	197
R476	Bowl (beaded)	Mauve Agate		197
R1195	Bowl (abstract fish)	pink with white spots		198
R421	Bowl	Silver Spray and Chartreuse		198
R421	Bowl	Green Agate and Chartreuse		198
R328	Bowl (oval with plume base)	Mauve Agate/cream color center		198
R290	Bowl	Mauve Agate		199
8172	Bowl (planter)	Roman Bronze		199
60	Bowl (planter	Green Agate	1936	199
R877	Bowl (open leaf)	Ebony and Chartreuse	1951	199
342	Bowl	Lilac		200
106	Bowl (planter)	brown and purple	1930	200
3122	Bowl (ribbed)	green		200
R1729	Bowl (footed)	beige and gold (rough surface)		200
R112	Bowl (leaf edged)	Green Agate		200
R224	Bowl (daisy)	Chartreuse		201
450	Bowl	Gold Tweed		201
25	Bowl (three footed)	dark and light blue	1914	201
63	Bowl (planter)	blue with light blue and green	1918	201
4195	Bowl	White Earth Graphic Wrap		201
811	Bowl (planter	Briar Agate		202
33	Bowl	Briar Agate		202
863	Bowl (round diamond pattern)	tan and white interior		202

834	Bowl (octagon planter)	Peasant Red and white		202
RG37	Bowl (triangular)	green with black specks (Flower-Ware)		211
343	Bowl	Cotton White and Turquoise		214
R372	Bowl (fluted)	Mauve Agate		213
R467	Bowl (beaded)	Chartreuse and Silver Spray		217
R557	Bowl	Chartreuse and Silver Spray		217
R371	Bowl	Cloudy Blue		218
345S	Bowl	Lilac		218
R967	Bowl (starfish)	Pearl Grey Drip		218
318H	Bowl	Amethyst Crackle		219
845	Bowl Planter	green and lighter green cascade		258
R1402C	Bowl (bird)	Ebony Cascade		273
R1220	Bowl (gazelle)	Chartreuse and Honey		276
3532	Bowl (flower girl)	brown/cream		282
R460	Bowl (leaf)	light green		286
	Bowl (planter)	green/aqua		294
838	Boy Head	Gold Tweed		241
R424	Bucking Bronco	Amber	1940's	235
5190	Bucking Bronco Lamp	Amber		245
R1510	Bull	Mandarin Orange		238
R1510	Bull	Haeger Red		238
R379	Bull	Mallow	1941	237
502H	Bull Fighter (planter)	Haeger Red		237
34	Candle Holder	mint green	1910's-20's	203
120	Candlesticks (also #3044)	yellow	1917	203
R220	Candle Holder (birds)	Mauve Agate	1939	203
R203	Candle Holder (fish)	Mauve Agate		203
R579	Candle Holder (double tier)	Green Briar		203
243	Candle Holder (twisted stem)	Peach Agate	1927	203
R304	Candle Holder (fish)	Mauve Agate		204
R312	Candle Holders (cornucopia)	Chartreuse and one is Silver Spray		204
R1285	Candle Holders (lily)	Turquoise and Blue		204
R312	Candle Holder (cornucopia)	Green Briar	1949	204
R1728	Candle Holder (Roman)	Sable		204
R516	Candle Holder (Swan)	Mauve Agate		205
R433	Candle Holder (three plumes)	Mauve Agate		205
R418	Candle Holder	Cloudy Blue		205
R220	Candle Holders (birds)	Cloudy Blue		205
R437	Candle Holders (leaves)	Ebony		205
815H	Candle Holder Compote	Gold Tweed	1961	206
R473	Candle Holder	blue and white		206
8487	Candle Holder	blue and dark brown "Studio Haeger"		206
HT46	Candle Holder (pair of females)	blue/black and white "Haeger Maglio"		206
R485	Candle Holder (planter)	Chartreuse	1946	206
R185	Candle Holder	light blue and green accents		207
3004	Candle Holder	Blue Crackle		207
3004	Candle Holder	Peacock		207
3068	Candle Holder and dish (holds 3)'	brown with white accents		208
1552S	Candle Holders	Turquoise and Blue		208
R1354	Candle Holders (edged)	Ebony		208
	Candle Holder and planter (leaves)	Silver Spray		208
3142	Candle Holder (large)	Brown Earth Graphic Wrap		208
R312	Candle Holders (cornucopia)	Mauve Agate		212
3187X	Candle Holder	White Earth Graphic Wrap		213
3277	Candle Holder (bow)	blue	1947	215
336	Candle Holder	Blue Crackle with hints of green		215
3045	Candle Holder	Ebony and Amber		212
3232	Candle Holder (double branch)	Chartreuse		217
R438	Candle Holders (rosebud)	Cloudy Blue		218
R1746	Candle Holders	Lilac		218
R968	Candle Holders (starfish)	Pearl Grey Drip		218
R7285	Candle Holders (leaves, later #R7465)	Green Briar		219
R431	Candy Bowl (lily on lid)	Mallow and aqua lily		209
R431	Candy Bowl (lily on lid)	Chartreuse and Yellow		210
R459	Candy Dish (fish in middle of shells)	blue	1946	209
R459	Candy Dish (triple leaf)	Mauve Agate		210
R457	Candy Dish (triple leaf)	Mauve Agate		210

8044H	Candy Dish (with gold handle)	Mandarin Orange		210
R1730	Candy Jar	Mandarin Orange		209
726H	Cannister (horse)	Rust Brown	1967	221
8061 & 8062	Cannisters	blue and white		267
R1824	Centerpiece (palm leaf bowl)	Pearl Shell		189
R631	Cigarette Box (leopard)	Amber	1940's	182
R685	Cigarette Box (horse head)	Green Agate		180
	Clock, shelf (clock face done by Kingswood)			254
	Clock (pagoda)	Silver Spray and Chartreuse	1948	254
3910	Clown Jack-in-the-Box	pink		282
7	Cockatoo	pink	1933	226
R777	Cocker Spaniel	brown	1950's	233
R1585S	Coffee Pot	Turquoise	1957	268
R1265	Colt	Amber		235
R235	Colt Flower Holder	Green Briar		236
R875	Colt Lamp Base Planter	Ebony Cascade		245
R1170	Comedy/Tragedy Masks (planters)	Green Agate		222
3003	Compote	Cotton White and Turquoise		191
5	Compote (three footed)	blue	1914	201
RT63	Compote	Green Gold Tweed	1960	202
335	Compote	Blue Crackle with hints of green		215
R321	Conch Shell	Cloudy Blue	1947	287
	Cookie Jar (fire hydrant)	red with gold trim		223
8198	Cookie Jar (Gleep)	yellow-orange		223
	Cookie Jar (Keebler Treehouse)	green and brown		223
R188	Cookie Jar (shell base and finial)	rose and blue		223
8170	Covered Dish (rooster on lid)	Roman Bronze		209
707S	Covered Dish	Blue Crackle		210
9H	Covered Dish	Mandarin Orange		220
R1582S	Cream Pitcher	Turquoise	1957	268
	Cup	green	1910	266
R975	Deer	Ebony		234
3235	Deer	white		236
R277	Dish (spiral plume)	Peach Agate	1942	190
3961	Dish	blue with black specks	1967-68	195
746	Dish	Brown Earth Graphic Wrap		200
3170	Dish (handled)	green - Boco texture		220
3296	Donkey and Cart	blue	1943	236
F3	Ducks (pair)	white	1941	225
873H	Egg Serving Plate (chicken shaped)	Reseda Yellow		266
616	Egyptian Cat	Mandarin Orange	1950's	229
R784	Elephant	Chartreuse and Honey		239
R320	Elm Leaf	Mauve Agate	1947	305
R412	Fawn (standing)	pink	1950's	233
R413	Fawn (sitting)	brown	1949	233
	Fawn	green glaze	1960	260
R482	Feather Plume	Mallow		299
R248	Feather Plume	white		299
3225	Feather Plume	blue		299
284	Fish	tan and brown		239
R360	Fish	Pearl Grey Drip	1941	243
	Floral Frog (has one of the earliest mark)	brown and green	1930's	258
	Flower Frog (has one of the earliest marks)	brown and green		258
R138	Flying Fish	teal and yellow		239
R838	Frog (figural flower block)	Chartreuse		243
R484	Garden Bowl	Chartreuse and Ebony		244
837	Girl Head	Gold Tweed		241
3928	Goblet	Gold	1962-69	221
	Gondola Planter	pink/white		259
R166	Greyhound (head down)	Gun Metal	1940's	234
R167	Greyhound (head up)	Gun Metal	1940's	234
R1224	Gypsy Girl	brown and green		242
613	Hen	red/green/black		224
613	Hen	Burnt Sienna	1973	224
R434	Hen Pheasant	Mauve Agate		227
R709	Horn of Plenty	Chartreuse and brown		289
R103	Horse	Green Briar		219

R402	Horse	Mallow	1942	236
	Horse	red		257
	Horse Head	Desert Red and Ebony base	1930's	257
8142	Jar (floral relief)	Peasant Orange		216
	Jug	Ebony and Amber	1967	212
RG82	Jug Vase	Lilac		324
812	Lady Head	white	1936	240
R1782	Lamb	White Stone Lace		240
141	Lamp Base	purple	1914	245
R455	Lamp Base (bow)	Mauve Agate		245
6204	Lamp (stallion head)	Oxblood and white		245
1138	Lamp with horse (cylinder style)	Oxblood		246
5240	Lamp (horse head wall)	Ebony	1947	246
5353	Lamp (petal louvre reflector)	Walnut and Ebony	1954	246
R1262	Lamp (TV, prancing horse)	Chartreuse and Honey		246
R869	Lamp (gazelle planter)	Ebony Cascade		247
5195	Lamp (fawn table)	Ebony		247
5473	Lamp (TV deer abstract)	Oxblood and white		247
R115	Lamp (gazelle)	Ebony		247
6051TV	Lamp (TV panther)	Ebony and Turquoise		248
6140	Lamp (TV Sailfish)	Silver Spray		248
5202	Lamp Base (parrot on tree)	Green Agate and Yellow Decorated	1947	248
5237	Lamp (elephant head wall lamp)	white	1947	248
5401	Lamp (Tree of Life)	Green Agate with Chartreuse		249
6424STV	Lamp (TV angel fish)	Antique		249
5344	Lamp	Chartreuse and Honey		249
	Lamp (fish riding on a wave)	yellow		249
3003	Lamp Base (lady head)	green/brown		250
4172	Lamp (cabbage rose)	Mauve Agate	1941	250
5362	Lamp, table, with finial (ginger jar)	Yellow Crackle		250
5100	Lamps (modern man & lady head)	Ebony		251
5398	Lamp Base (mermaid)	Green Agate and grey		251
5205	Lamp, table (girl on turtle)	turquoise		251
5051	Lamp, table (toadstool)	Amber		252
5483	Lamp Base (modern)	Mallow and Ebony		252
	Lamp/Planter (panther)	Chartreuse/Ebony		259
	Lamp (giraffe table)	Amber		261
	Lamp (scottish terrier dogs)	Cloudy Blue		262
	Lamp Base	Brown Earth Graphic Wrap		263
R1504 and R1505	Lavabo (Lion's head, top & bottom)	Turquoise/Blue		253
R1506 and R1507	Lavabo (top and bottom)	matte pink		253
8186 and 8187	Lavabo (top and bottom)	cream and brown		253
R1131	Leopard	Chartreuse		231
813H	Lighter (tall)	Mandarin Orange		185
8167	Lighter	tan with black streaks		184
813H	Lighter (tall)	Marigold Agate		185
8167	Lighter	blue		186
8054	Lighter (boot)	Rust Brown	1967	221
	Lighter (Alladin lamp)	Gold Tweed		260
889	Lighter (ribbed)	Mandarin Orange	1950's-60's	177
812H	Lighter (fish)	Jade Crackle	1960's	186
R1253	Little Sister	black/white	1952	281
R1254	Little Brother	green/white	1952	281
6343	Matador	Haeger Red		238
R451	Mare and Foal	Amber	1943	235
514	Mermaid with bowl	Gold Tweed		241
86	Mermaid with child	green matte		244
	Mermaid Figure	Gold Tweed		255
650	Mourning Dove	rustish-brown	1973	226
649	Mourning Dove	white	1973	226
	Mug	orange and white		267
R364	Nude with seal (flower block)	Green Briar	1946	244
77	Nude Bathing (flower frog)	white	1927	244
R189	Nude (sitting flower frog)	Mauve Agate	1930'-40's	244
R1919	Onion Vase	orange and yellow		212
R1919	Onion Vase	Amethyst		219
R649	Panther (lying)	Oxblood		231

683	Panther	tan/cream	1950's	231
495	Panther	Ebony		232
315	Panther	Ebony	1994	232
R648	Panther (sitting on pedestal)	Ebony	1950's	231
	Panther on base	Ebony with brown and dark spots		259
	Paperweight (egg)	Green Agate	1950's	258
	Parker Pen and Ashtray Set	Midas Gold		255
R382	Peasant Man	Green Agate		242
R383	Peasant Woman	Green Agate		242
	Pen Holder (Haeger advertising)	white with gilded letters		255
649 & 650	Pigeons (Doves)	antique white/orange		225
R453	Planter (peacock)	Mauve Agate		213
R130	Pheasant	Green Agate		226
R165	Pheasant	Mauve Agate		228
8183X	Pitcher Vase	orange and yellow		212
8180	Pitcher Vase	orange and yellow		212
8183X	Pitcher Vase	brown glossy matte		221
4058 & 4060	Pitcher and Wash Basin	brown matte		264
8183	Pitcher Vase	Bennington Brown Foam		264
8188	Pitcher	Brown Earth Graphic Wrap		264
3182	Pitcher	Sunset		264
R698	Pitcher (Mexican Head)	Green Briar		265
R1679S	Pitcher	Turquoise-Blue		268
H608	Pitcher with Rooster Handle	Persian Blue		265
R1619S	Pitcher (flower)	Ebony Cascade		323
408	Pitcher (handled)	Ebony Cascade		323
456	Pitcher	Cotton White and Turquoise	1960's	324
8180	Pitcher Vase	Cotton White and Chartreuse		324
809	Planter (on pedestal)	brown/green/yellow/white	1966-72	216
3318	Planter (Colonial flower girl)	Chartreuse		217
616	Planter (Teddy Bear)	Chartreuse	1938	217
H72	Planters (two owls)	Green Marigold	1973-74	220
4200	Planter	brown glossy matte		221
3819	Planter on Pedestal	two shades of green		222
R282	Planter (centerpiece)	Amber		230
	Planter (panther sitting)	brown with dark spots/Ebony base		259
	Planter	light brown		257
	Planter (Pedestal)	green and lighter green cascade		258
	Planter (fish)	Chartreuse/ grey		260
	Planter	Briar Agate		261
	Planter (giraffe)	Ebony Cascade		261
	Planter (football)	Bennington Brown Foam	1951	262
	Planter (greyhound)	white		262
	Planter	brownish	1950's	263
14	Planter (fish)	yellow	1936	269
3314	Planter (horse)	white		269
618	Planter (elephant)	blue	1932	269
617	Planter (fawn)	yellow	1939	269
R754	Planter (donkey and cart)	blue	1943	270
B3107	Planter (lamb)	pink		270
3311	Planter (cat)	blue	1946	270
R540	Planter (turtle)	Green Agate		270
R766	Planter (Rudolph the Red Nosed Reindeer)	Desert Red Decorated	1949	270
R1844	Planter (duck)	Jade Crackle		271
B3322	Planter (stork and baby bed)	light pink		271
8008H	Planter (bird)	Blue Crackle		271
R334	Planter (fan tail pouter pigeon)	Mauve Agate	1934	271
R1747	Planter (rabbit)	grey		271
R182L	Planter (swan)	Peach Agate		272
R515	Planter (swan)	Mauve Agate		272
R453	Planter (peacock)	Cloudy Blue		272
R31	Planter (peacock)	Mauve Agate		272
R430	Planter (swan)	Mauve Agate		273
R108	Planter (pouter pigeon)	Mauve Agate	1938	273
R1226	Planter (horse)	brown		274
R1761	Planter (turkey)	red and black		274
508	Planter (donkey)	red transparent		274
R1146	Planter (deer)	Cotton White		275

R869	Planter (gazelle)	Antique		275
3511	Planter (panther)	Ebony/Chartreuse		275
	Planter (deer border)	Oxblood	1938	276
R1734	Planter (goat)	Sable		276
R1913	Planter (Bambi deer)	green		276
R1191	Planter Bowl (sailfish)	Briar Agate		277
R284	Planter (trout)	blue/white/green	1942	277
R284	Planter (trout)	pearl carnival with gold fins		277
R271	Planter (sailfish)	Peach Agate		278
R271	Planter (sailfish)	green/light blue		278
5051	Planter (koala bear)	Bennington Brown Foam		279
5084	Planter (squirrel)	Bennington Brown Foam		279
5072	Planter (Cats)	Bennington Brown Foam		279
5070	Planter (hippo)	Bennington Brown Foam		279
5033	Planter (lion)	Bennington Brown Foam		280
5080	Planter (hound puppy/shoe)	Bennington Brown Foam		280
5073	Planter (racoon with bucket)	Bennington Brown Foam		280
5025	Planter (playful critters elephant)	Bennington Brown Foam		280
3054	Planter (Southern Belle)	pink		281
RG98 & RG99	Planter (Dutch boy & girl)	matte white	1958	281
3947	Planter (boy and girl tricycle)	yellow/green/white	1950-51	282
R859	Planter (nude woman cornucopia)	Silver Spray/Chartreuse		282
RG132	Planter (Madonna)	white	1962	283
3427AM	Planter (musical Madonna)	white		283
990	Planter (Madonna)	white		283
RG118	Planter (colonial woman basket)	pink		283
RG18	Planter (Madonna)	matte white	1946	284
	Planter (Madonna)	white	1938	284
3932L	Planter (boy holding)	white		284
3264	Planter (Madonna with cherub child)	white		284
3855	Planter (Little Bo Peep)	pink	1959	284
368	Planter (sea shell)	green	1936	285
3280B	Planter (buggy)	pink	1942	285
3244	Planter (cornucopia/seashell base)	blue	1946	285
3061	Planter (cornucopia)	white		285
R483	Planter (shell)	Mallow	1947	286
R223	Planter (lily)	white-lavender		287
R293	Planter (violin bowl)	Mallow		287
R525	Planter (tulip)	Mallow and white	1947	288
3212	Planter (cornucopia)	Green Briar	1946	288
R657	Planter (gondolier)	Green Agate and white		288
R1293	Planter (acanthus)	Green Agate		289
394	Planter (pilgrim hat)	light brown		289
338	Planter (cowboy hat)	brown		289
R1462	Planter (wheelbarrow)	Briar Agate	1964	289
R1446	Planter (basket)	Turquoise-Blue		290
3292	Planter	aqua		290
3752	Planter	green		290
3175	Planter	Fern Agate Earth Graphic Wrap		290
3174XH	Planter (hanging)	White Earth Graphic Wrap		291
3172	Planter	Marigold Agate Earth Graphic Wrap		291
5000	Planter	Earth Graphic Wrap		291
4185X	Planter	Brown Earth Graphic Wrap		291
8207H	Planter (hanging)	Brown Earth Graphic Wrap		291
R843	Planter	Mauve Agate		292
776	Planter (goblet shaped)	Aqua Tweed		292
3085	Planter	pink/rose	1940's	292
R510	Planter (fish in relief)	white/blue		292
3130	Planter (pedestaled)	White Earth Graphic Wrap		293
R936	Planter	Pearl Grey Drip		293
R852	Plante (triple ball)	Oxblood		293
503	Planter	Ebony	1927	293
5040	Planter	Bennington Brown Sand		293
3880	Planter	green with black specks		294
	Planter	green and black speckled		294
167	Planter	yellow		295
667	Planter	yellow		295

	Planter	rose		295
4020	Planter	grey		295
8443	Planter	blue		295
36	Planter (leaf)	white		301
3053	Planter (donkey)	white		302
1076H	Plate (horse)	Rust Brown	1967	221
	Plate, cup and saucer	Peach Agate	1927	256
3207S	Plate	orange and white		267
R376A	Polar Bear (small standing)	grey-white	1942	240
R375A	Polar Bear (small sitting)	grey-white	1942	240
R375B	Polar Bear (large sitting)	grey-white	1942	240
R479	Prospector	Amber		235
3248	Rabbit	blue	1940's	239
R435	Rooster Pheasant	Mauve Agate		228
612	Rooster figure	red/green/black		224
612	Rooster	Burnt Sienna	1973	224
R1762	Rooster	dark brown/white	1973	225
R318	Russian Wolfhound	Green Briar	1940's	234
3201	Salt and Pepper Shakers	orange and white		267
R481	Seashell on base	Silver Spray and Chartreuse		199
R701	Sea Shell	Silver Spray	1949	309
878H	Serving Tray	Mandarin Orange	1950's	194
	Sign (display for Haeger)	tan		296
	Sign (crown display)	aqua		296
	Sign (gardenhouse display)	green		296
	Sign (Haeger logo)	brown		296
	Sign (advertising /shelf)	brown		296
920	Soap Dish/Toothbrush Holder	blue		265
R281	Sphere with three feather plumes	Mauve Agate		292
R772	Stag (flower block)	Chartreuse		244
	Stein World's Fair	yellow-brown	1933	255
	Sugar and Creamer Set	Mauve Agate		266
575	Sugar and Creamer Set	white	1936	267
57	Swan (flower frog)	green/white/beige	1918	243
8011 & 8010	Tiered Chip 'n Dip Tray	Misty Mint		266
314	Tigress (part of a console set)	Pearl Grey Drip	1950's	228
R313	Tiger (part of a console set)	Pearl Grey Drip	1950's	228
R313	Tiger	Amber		230
R314	Tigress	Amber		230
R313	Tiger	Amber		231
8300	Toe Tapper with flute	brown textured		211
8296	Toe Tapper with violin	brown textured		211
8295	Toe Tapper with french horn	brown textured		211
8297	Toe Tapper with banjo	brown textured		211
8299	Toe Tapper with cymbals	brown textured		211
8294	Toe Tapper with accordion	brown textured		211
R449	Trays (leaf design, set of four)	Cloudy Blue		258
	TV Lamp (gazelle)	green and white		233
6202	TVLamp /Planter (Greyhound)	brown		274
4150	Urn	Peasant Green		268
R416	Urn	French Grey with Mallow		322
RG68	Vase (bottle shaped)	green with black specks (Flower-Ware)		211
R284	Vase (trout)	Mauve Agate		212
4233X	Vase	Brown Earth Graphic Wrap		213
4232X	Vase	White Earth Graphic Wrap		213
4161X	Vase (cylinder style)	White Earth Graphic Wrap		213
R1752W	Vase (eccentric)	Cotton White and Turquoise		214
4011	Vase (chalice)	Cotton White and Turquoise		214
489	Vase (sculpted)	Cotton White and Turquoise		214
4034	Vase (boutique)	Cerulean Gold	1955	215
4035	Vase (boutique)	Cerulean Gold	1955	215
4027	Vessel (boutique)	Cerulean Gold	1955	215
R455	Vase (bow)	white with blue	1936	215
257	Vase	Brair Agate		216
4165	Vase	Peasant Orange		216
4131 and 4132 and 4133 Vases		Peasant Orange		216
R321	Vase (shell)	Chartreuse		217

R527	Vase (pillow)	Chartreuse and Silver Spray		217
R891	Vases (stem style)	Green Briar		219
R1915	Vase (stem styled)	Mandarin Orange		220
4132X	Vase	lime green - Boco texture		220
4001	Vase	Green Marigold		220
4149	Vase (leaves in relief)	Green Marigold		220
3968A	Vase	Gold	1969-75	221
4131	Vase	brown glossy matte		221
R1121	Vase	Green Agate		222
827	Vase	Green Agate		222
3108	Vase (two deer abstract)	white	1942	233
	Vase	green		256
	Vase	Peach Agate		256
	Vase	Peach Agate		256
	Vase (flower styled)	brown/rust	1930's	257
	Vase	yellow-green	1930's	263
	Vase	black		263
3106	Vase - oblong	Chartreuse		285
R298	Vase (cornucopia shell)	Boco white and pink	1948	286
R1460	Vase (leaf)	Antique		287
3296	Vase (swan)	white matte glaze	1946	297
3220	Vase (rooster)	white		297
R36	Vase (swan)	light blue		297
R182	Vase (swan)	blue-green crackle	1950's	297
R285	Vase (swan)	Green Briar	1947	298
R888	Vase with Bird on Branch	tan		298
3270	Vase (leaf)	blue		299
R301	Vase (leaf)	blue		300
R355	Vase (leaf)	Mallow		300
R138	Vase (leaf)	Green Briar		300
R826	Vase	brown with white interior		300
R320	Vase (elm)	Green Briar	1947	301
33	Vase (leaf)	Peach Agate		301
3240	Vases (two leaf styles)	green		301
R427	Vase (horse)	tan and white		302
R857	Vase (gazelle head)	Amber		302
R393	Vase (horse head - Pegasus)	blue		302
3386	Vase (Gazelle)	white		303
R647	Vase (sunflower)	green		303
R706	Vase (deer running)	Amber Crystal		303
R707	Vase (deer standing)	Ebony		303
186	Vase (lily)	green	1936	303
186	Vase (lily)	Peach Agate	1936	304
R455	Vase (bow)	Mauve Agate		304
R303	Vase (laurel wreath bow)	Mauve Agate		304
R446	Vase (lily)	blue	1943	304
R441	Vase (deco styled circular)	Mauve Agate	1940's	305
R441	Vase (deco styled circular)	Peach Agate		305
R131	Vases (basket style with fruit)	Peach Agate		306
R386	Vase (basket)	Mauve Agate	1943	306
3528	Vase (double flower)	grey		307
R452	Vase (morning glory)	Mauve Agate		307
3531	Vase (dancer with lily)	Chartreuse and white		307
332A	Vase (cornucopia)	Cloudy Blue		308
R426	Vase (cornucopia with nude)	Mauve Agate		308
R426	Vase (cornucopia with nude)	Chartreuse with white interior		308
332B	Vase (cornucopia)	Peach Agate		308
R523	Vase (fan)	Green Briar		309
3227	Vase (double shell)	Green Agate		309
R228	Vase (cornucopia)	Green Briar		310
R422	Vase (butterfly)	Mauve Agate	1940	310
R228	Vase (cornucopia)	Mauve Agate	1939	311
R246	Vase (double cornucopia)	Mauve Agate	1939	311
R332B	Vase (cornucopia)	Mauve Agate		311
R299	Vase (snail)	Cloudy Blue		311
R299	Vase (snail)	blue and white		311
3105	Vase (dancing girl)	green		312

3208	Vase (fish)	white		312
R322	Vase (conch shell)	Green Briar		312
1	Vase	Ebony	1914	313
141	Vase	dark blue-black	1914	313
1037	Vase	blue	1940's	313
19A	Vases	blue and light blue	1918	313
47	Vase	dark and light green	1938	313
39	Vase	rose	1918	313
628	Vases (pair of two handled)	blue	1938	314
43	Vase (three handled)	blue and red	1927	314
39	Vase (two handled)	blue and red	1918	314
182	Vase	blue and red	1936	314
8237	Vase	dark and light green		314
186	Vase (leaf design)	blue and white	1939	315
3015	Vase	green	1946	315
1018	Vase	pink	1941	315
607	Vase	mint-blue	1938	315
463	Vase (floral relief)	green	1930	315
136	Vase	white	1935	316
R337	Vase	charcoal grey and white	1942	316
R454	Vase (chinese)	Ebony with textured white	1936	316
R504	Vase (bee hive)	white/pink	1947	316
2908	Vase	yellow	1930's	317
R580	Vase (rose of sharon)	yellow with decorated flowers	1949	317
R456	Vase (wrap-around spiral)	Yellow Drip		317
3059	Vase	blue with sterling overlay	1930's	317
R441	Vase (circle)	blue with sterling overlay	1930's	317
R1123	Vases (two with leaves in relief)	peach/tan/cream		318
3617	Vase (rectangle)	grey/pink	1952-1966	318
R893	Vase (tulip)	Oxblood/white		318
R833	Vase (flat sided scroll)	Oxblood/white		318
4044	Vase (pitcher)	Green Agate		318
R651	Vase Pillow	Green Agate		319
W2002 & R490	Vase (triangular)	Chartreuse		319
R900	Vase (modern scroll)	Chartreuse and Honey		319
R830	Vase (wave styled)	Green Agate and Chartreuse		319
R1235	Vase (classic bud)	Chartreuse and Honey		319
R979	Vase (abstract)	Chartreuse and Honey		319
D1021	Vase (leaf)	white		320
D1028	Vase (beehive)	Green Briar		320
D1001	Vase (cylinder)	Green Briar	1940's	320
714	Vase	Green Briar	1959	320
R501	Vase (beehive applied floral relief)	Green Briar		320
931	Vase	brown and green		321
R251	Vase (onion jug)	Cloudy Blue		321
R456	Vase (wrap-around spiral)	Cloudy Blue		321
3273	Vase (wheat in relief)	Green Briar		321
R419	Vase (pitcher)	French Grey with Mallow		322
R417	Vase (gourd)	French Grey with Mallow		322
R1812S	Vase	Ebony Cascade		323
R1752W	Vase (eccentric)	Ebony Cascade		323
R1776	Vase	Turquoise-Blue		324
413	Vase	Turquoise-Blue		324
R1915	Vase (onion style)	Gold Tweed		325
455	Vase (flared top)	green		325
493	Vase	Aqua Crystal	1950's	325
413	Vase (eccentric, small)	Gold Tweed		325
RG68	Vase (bottle)	Mandarin Orange		325
4031	Vase	Mandarin Orange		326
478	Vase	Mandarin Orange		326
R1919	Vase (bottle)	Mandarin Orange		326
4038	Vase (classic medium)	Mandarin Orange		326
408	Vase (pitcher handled)	Mandarin Orange		326
483	Vase (cobra)	Mandarin Orange		327
493	Vase (traditional)	Mandarin Orange		327
R1919	Vase (bottle)	Bittersweet		327
1H	Vase	Mandarin Orange		327

R1752	Vase (eccentric)	Pearl Shell		328
R1619S	Vase (flower pitcher)	Black Mistique		328
2H	Vase (bottle styled)	white/blue/yellow/brown		328
R1444	Vase (flat sided dented)	Pearl Shell		328
2021	Vase (with wheat design in relief)	blue matte		329
RG14	Vase (pillow, Flower-ware)	pink		329
RG42	Pitcher (flower, medium)	Matte Black		329
S400	Vase (textured)	Sunset Yellow		329
RC68	Vase (bottle)	Marigold Agate		330
483	Vase (cobra)	Marigold Agate		330
R895	Vase	Briar Agate		330
4183	Vase (tapered)	White Earth Graphic Wrap		330
4244	Vase	Brown Earth Graphic Wrap		331
4200	Vase	Brown Earth Graphic Wrap		331
4162X	Vase (cylinder)	Fern Agate Earth Graphic Wrap		331
4171	Vase	Brown Earth Graphic Wrap		331
4202	Vase	Brown Earth Graphic Wrap		331
4132	Vase	Fern Agate Earth Graphic Wrap		331
4161X	Vase	Fern Agate Earth Graphic Wrap		332
4238X	Vase	Fern Agate Earth Graphic Wrap		332
4248	Vase	Marigold Agate Earth Graphic Wrap		332
4160X	Vase (cylinder)	Fern Agate Earth Graphic Wrap		332
4233X	Vase	Fern Agate Earth Graphic Wrap		332
4174	Vase	Green Earth Graphic Wrap		333
4142	Vase	Green Earth Graphic Wrap		333
4231X	Vase	Marigold Agate Earth Graphic Wrap		333
4181	Vase	Green Earth Graphic Wrap		333
4106	Vase	Marigold Agate Earth Graphic Wrap		334
4182	Vase (handled)	Earth Graphic Wrap		334
4143	Vase	Earth Graphic Wrap		334
	Vase	Earth Graphic Wrap		334
4070	Vase (pitcher)	Peasant Flame		335
4012	Vase (pitcher)	Peasant Flame with gold		335
S447	Vase (oblong)	Peasant Flame	1952	335
4002	Vase (hexagon)	Peasant Olive		335
4205	Vase	Peasant Olive		336
8097	Vase (pitcher)	Peasant Blue		336
4131	Vase	Peasant Olive		336
4103	Vase (pitcher, floral relief)	Peasant Yellow		336
451	Vase	Nutmeg Textured		337
4144	Vase	Bennington Brown Foam		337
4141	Vase (pitcher)	pearlescent tan and orange		337
303	Vase	brown and tan glossy-matte		337
RG92	Vase with handle	brown		337
4256	Vase	brown and tan matte-glossy		337
4194	Vase (bamboo shoot)	cream		338
4243	Vase	brown and tan		338
4162X	Vase (cylinder)	tan and brown		338
4411	Vase	blue/white		338
725	Wall Pocket	green	1952	222
517	Wall Pockets	yellow		339
R1135	Wall Pocket (flower)	grey		339
R16275	Wall Pocket (fish)	Antique		339
R745	Wall Pocket (grape vine)	purple and green		339
917A	Wall Pocket (rocking cradle)	white	1939	340
126	Wall Pocket	red and white		340
R725	Wall Pocket	green		340
3112	Wall Pocket	blue	1941	340
R531	Wall Shelf	Mallow	1947	260
8182	Water Pitcher	Peasant Green		268
F17	Wild Goose	white matte glaze	1941	226
R363	Woman riding a fish (flower block)	grey/green/white		243
R363	Woman riding a fish (flower block)	Green Agate		243
R287	Wren House	Mauve Agate	1949	227
R287	Wren House	Mauve Agate		227

All values in this guide are for items in very good condition. Pieces that are stained, with holes, chipped or cracked are worth much less. Items in mint condition may bring a higher dollar amount. Items in common shapes, but with hard to find glazes may also bring more. Glazes like Peacock, Black Mistique, Gold Tweed, Aztec Gold, Florentine Gold, Multi-Directional, Peacock Stoneware and Sunset Stoneware, Mirror Chrome and Mirror Gold bring a higher dollar amount. Some pages will be priced accordingly to the glaze and will be noted before the pricing on that page. Remember, this is only a guide. L-W Books nor Haeger Potteries nor the author assumes any liability because of loss or gain in using these prices. Prices may vary from region to region depending on availability, so keep in mind this is only a guide.

Page 21

Left Side

4	$20.00+
8	$15.00+
9	$10.00+
11	$10.00+
12	$10.00+
14	$20.00+
29a	$20.00+
46x	$15.00+
81	$15.00+
106a	$10.00+
566	$15.00+
601	$15.00+
607	$15.00+
608	$10.00+
609	$15.00+
614	$15.00+
615	$15.00+
641	$15.00+
642	$15.00+
646	$10.00+
647	$10.00+
709a	$10.00+
741a	$15.00+
841	$10.00+
850a	$15.00+
871a	$15.00+
884	$20.00+
893	$20.00+
905a	$15.00+
915	$15.00+
945a	$20.00+
946	$20.00+
948	$15.00+
950b	$10.00+
1607	$10.00+
1608	$10.00+
1610	$10.00+
1741	$10.00+
1904	$10.00+
1905	$15.00+
1935	$10.00+

Right Side

3	$25.00+
31	$50.00+
57	$40.00+
63a	$30.00+
367a	$10.00+
503b	$40.00+
517a	$45.00+
575	$35.00+set
610b	$10.00+
616	$15.00+
617	$15.00+
618	$15.00+
622	$10.00+
643	$15.00+
644	$15.00+
645	$20.00+
877	$20.00+set
883	$20.00+
972a	$25.00+
980	$10.00+
997	$10.00+

Page 22

6	$20.00+
10	$25.00+
49	$35.00+
223c	$40.00+
317	$15.00+
337b	$15.00+
367c	$10.00+
474c	$15.00+
474d	$20.00+
580	$15.00+
597d	$25.00+
611	$15.00+
624	$20.00+
625	$20.00+
626	$15.00+
628	$25.00+
633	$25.00+
634	$35.00+
635	$35.00+
650	$20.00+
651	$15.00+
739e	$75.00+
741c	$10.00+
741d	$15.00+
760e	$25.00+
770	$15.00+
792c	$25.00+
840c	$25.00+
867	$10.00+
879	$20.00+
880	$25.00+
906d	$25.00+
908b	$10.00+
923	$15.00+
945c	$25.00+
951	$15.00+
952a	$10.00+
952b	$15.00+
953	$25.00+
954	$15.00+
956	$25.00+
957	$25.00+
958	$20.00+
972b	$15.00+
987a	$15.00+

Page 23

47a/243	$60.00+ set
851	$40.00+ set
883	$50.00+ set

Page 24

8	$15.00+
11	$10.00+
31	$50.00+
46a	$10.00+
46x	$10.00+
237	$15.00+
367a	$10.00+
368	$10.00+
392b	$15.00+
395a	$10.00+
395b	$15.00+
456	$15.00+
517	$45.00+
566	$15.00+
575	$35.00+ set
601	$15.00+
602	$15.00+
607	$15.00+
608	$10.00+
609	$15.00+
610b	$10.00+
614	$15.00+
615	$15.00+
616	$15.00+
617	$15.00+
618	$15.00+
619	$15.00+
621	$15.00+
709z	$10.00+
741a	$15.00+
841	$10.00+
850a	$15.00+
855a	$15.00+
871a	$15.00+
884	$20.00+
885	$15.00+
889	$15.00+
891	$10.00+
893	$20.00+
905a	$15.00+
915	$15.00+
917a	$10.00+
918	$10.00+
924	$15.00+
945	$15.00+
946	$20.00+
947	$15.00+
948	$15.00+
950b	$10.00+
964	$15.00+
970	$10.00+
972a	$15.00+
997	$10.00+
1741	$10.00+
1792	$15.00+
1904	$10.00+
1905	$15.00+
1931	$10.00+
1935	$10.00+
1936	$10.00+

Page 25

21	$50.00+
39	$50.00+
223	$40.00+
367c	$10.00+
474c	$15.00+
604	$15.00+
610c	$15.00+
611	$15.00+
623	$20.00+
624	$20.00+
625	$20.00+
626	$15.00+
627	$15.00+
628	$25.00+
730c	$25.00+
741c	$10.00+
770	$15.00+
792	$20.00+
840	$25.00+
855c	$15.00+
904	$25.00+
908	$15.00+
923	$15.00+
941	$20.00+
942	$10.00+
950c	$20.00+
951	$15.00+
952	$15.00+
954	$15.00+
990	$20.00+
998	$20.00+

Page 26

95	$50.00+
605	$25.00+
634	$35.00+
635	$35.00+
636	$30.00+
741d	$15.00+
871e	$25.00+
906	$25.00+
953	$25.00+
956	$25.00+
957	$25.00+
958	$20.00+
981	$150.00+
987	$25.00+

Page 27

47	$60.00+ set
129	$60.00+ set
337	$35.00+ set
364	$50.00+ set
416	$40.00+ set
503	$40.00+ set

606 .... $40.00+ set
851 .... $40.00+ set
852 (3" to 6") .... $10.00+
852 (7" to 8") .... $15.00+
860 .... $40.00+ set
883 .... $50.00+ set
907 (10" to 12") ..... $15.00+
907 (7" to 8") .... $10.00+

Page 28

Top Section
D-1000 .... $150.00+
D-1021 .... $300.00+
D-1022 .... $80.00+
R-33 .... $75.00+
R-36 .... $100.00+
R-101 .... $125.00+
R-102 .... $125.00+
R-113 .... $150.00+
R-114 .... $100.00+
R-137 .... $50.00+
R-138 .... $50.00+
R-182 .... $25.00+
R-195 .... $125.00+
R-196 .... $100.00+
R-225 .... $125.00+
R-229 .... $200.00+
R-241 .... $250.00+
R-243 .... $100.00+
R-246 .... $50.00+

Bottom Section
R-31 .... $75.00+
R-107 .... $150.00+
R-115 .... $50.00+
R-117 .... $100.00+
R-131 .... $75.00+
R-144 .... $300.00+
R-177 .... $75.00+
R-187 .... $150.00+
R-190 .... $100.00+
R-193 .... $75.00+
R-194 .... $75.00+
R-228 .... $35.00+
R-231 .... $350.00+
R-238 .... $175.00+
R-345 .... $150.00+
R-347 .... $250.00+

Page 29

Top Section
R-116 .... $100.00+
R-188 .... $250.00+
R-198 .... $100.00+
R-200 .... $100.00+
R-209 .... $150.00+
R-251 .... $100.00+

Bottom Section
D-1001 .... $60.00+
D-1004 .... $100.00+
D-1006 .... $250.00+
D-1009 .... $100.00+
D-1011 .... $100.00+
D-1017 .... $125.00+
D-1018 .... $75.00+
D-1019 .... $75.00+
D-1020 .... $250.00+
D-1023 .... $200.00+
R-184 .... $40.00+
R-235 .... $80.00+

Page 30

Top Section
R-158 .... $75.00+
R-159 .... $75.00+
R-160 .... $75.00+
R-161 .... $125.00+
R-162 .... $175.00+
R-168 .... $500.00+
R-180 .... $200.00+
R-192 .... $150.00+
R-208 .... $150.00+
R-218 .... $175.00+
R-218-B .... $200.00+
R-237 .... $200.00+

Bottom Section
R-34 .... $100.00+
R-100 .... Not Pictured $200+
R-103 .... $60.00+
R-132 .... $150.00+ pair
R-138 .... $100.00+
R-157 .... $150.00+
R-164 .... $100.00+
R-165 .... $100.00+
R-166 .... $150.00+
R-167 .... $150.00+
R-171 .... $60.00+
R-172 .... $60.00+
R-178 .... $100.00+
R-178-D .... $100.00+
R-233 .... $200.00+ pair
R-234 .... Not Pictured $200+

Page 31

Top Section
R-110 .... $150.00+
R-155 .... $75.00+
R-156 .... $100.00+
R-157 .... $125.00+
R-179 .... $150.00+
R-199 .... $750.00+
R-205 .... $65.00+
R-206 .... $75.00+
R-230 .... $20.00+
R-247 .... $125.00+
R-248 .... $35.00+
R-252 .... $20.00+

Bottom Section
D-1007 .... $150.00+
R-134 .... $80.00+
R-181 .... $500.00+
R-210 .... $75.00+
R-221 .... $200.00+
R-222 .... $250.00+
R-223 .... $100.00+
R-226 .... $75.00+
R-227 .... $150.00+
R-232 .... $150.00+
R-242 .... $250.00+

Page 32

Top Section
8 .... $15.00+
9 .... $10.00+
11 .... $10.00+
12 .... $10.00+
46X .... $10.00+
81 .... $15.00+
395A .... $10.00+
395B .... $15.00+
566 .... $15.00+
581A .... $15.00+
601 .... $15.00+

614 .... $15.00+
615 .... $15.00+
622A .... $10.00+
641 .... $15.00+
642 .... $15.00+
841 .... $10.00+
853 .... $10.00+
856A .... $10.00+
915 .... $15.00+
970A .... $10.00+
970B .... $15.00+
1000A .... $10.00+
1608 .... $10.00+
1741 .... $10.00+
1904 .... $10.00+
1935 .... $10.00+

Bottom Section
1 .... $25.00+
2 .... $25.00+
3 .... $25.00+
29A .... $20.00+
63/57 .... $75.00+ set
93A .... $20.00+
276 .... $25.00+
351A .... $20.00+
367A .... $10.00+
517a .... $45.00+
581 .... $10.00+
602 .... $20.00+
607 .... $15.00+
608 .... $10.00+
609 .... $15.00+
610B .... $15.00+
622 .... $10.00+
648 .... $10.00+
709A .... $10.00+
891 .... $10.00+
901 .... $10.00+
917A .... $10.00+
945A .... $15.00+
1000B .... $10.00+
1006 .... $20.00+
2001 .... $20.00+
2002 .... $20.00+
2004 .... $25.00+
2007 .... $45.00+
2025B .... $15.00+

Page 33

Top Section
4 .... $20.00+
6-A .... $5.00+
7-A .... $5.00+
106A .... $10.00+
416x .... $10.00+
456 .... $15.00+
616 .... $15.00+
617 .... $15.00+
618 .... $15.00+
643 .... $15.00+
644 .... $15.00+
645 .... $20.00+
646 .... $10.00+
647 .... $10.00+
649 .... $15.00+
883 .... $15.00+
902 .... $15.00+
972A .... $15.00+
980 .... $10.00+
997 .... $10.00+
2003-A .... $25.00+
2009 .... $15.00+

2010 .... $10.00+
2011 .... $20.00+
2012 .... $20.00+

Bottom Section
150 .... $40.00+
151 .... $40.00+
152 .... $40.00+
153 .... $40.00+
154 .... $40.00+
155 .... $40.00+
1005 .... $20.00+
2029 .... $25.00+

Page 34

8010 .... $500.00+
8015 .... $600.00+
8020 .... $500.00+

Page 35

Top Section
15 .... $30.00+ set
41 .... $10.00+
42 .... $10.00+
43 .... $15.00+
44 .... $15.00+
106-B .... $25.00+
972-A .... $15.00+
1001-B .... $10.00+
1792 .... $15.00+
1850 .... $20.00+
3002 .... $10.00+
3047 .... $10.00+

Bottom Section
39 .... $35.00+
40 .... $35.00+
506 .... $100.00+

Page 36

Top Section
644 .... $15.00+
648 .... $10.00+
917-A .... $10.00+
917-C .... $10.00+
1005 .... $20.00+
3054 .... $75.00+

Bottom Section
855-A .... $15.00+
855-C .... $20.00+
3045 .... $25.00+
3057 .... $45.00+

Page 37

Top Section
618 .... $15.00+
3053 .... $125.00+
3055 .... $125.00+

Bottom Section
635 .... $35.00+
952-A .... $10.00+
3022 .... $20.00+
3023 .... $20.00+
3025 .... $25.00+
3026 .... $40.00+
3030 .... $20.00+

Page 38

Top Section
851 .... $40.00+ set
851 .... $15.00
3063 .... $40.00+ set
3068 .... $45.00+

Page 38
3069 .... $35.00+
Bottom Section
129 .... $75.00+ set
129 .... $35.00+
130 .... $15.00+ each
364/130 .... $50.00+ set
364 .... $15.00+
3004 .... $65.00+ set
3004 .... $30.00+

Page 39
50-A .... $75.00+
67 .... $30.00+
150 .... $40.00+
367-A .... $10.00+
502 .... $25.00+
860-B .... $40.00+
945-C .... $15.00+
972-A .... $15.00+
3033 .... $15.00+
3105 .... $15.00+
3112 .... $40.00+ each
F-6 .... $45.00+
F-7 .... $45.00+
F-16 .... $15.00+

Page 40
63-A .... $30.00+
68 .... $15.00+
69 .... $75.00+
152 .... $40.00+
351-A .... $20.00+
517-A .... $45.00+
645 .... $20.00+
952-A .... $10.00+
980 .... $10.00+
1020 .... $15.00+
2010 .... $10.00+
3106 .... $15.00+
R-410 .... $65.00+

Page 41
709-A .... $10.00+
1018 .... $20.00+
1019 .... $20.00+
2026 .... $15.00+
2027 .... $15.00+
3047 .... $10.00+
3089 .... $10.00+
3094 .... $15.00+
3104 .... $20.00+
3111 .... $10.00+
3116 .... $10.00+
F-2 .... $15.00+
F-3 .... $10.00+
F-4 .... $15.00+
F-5 .... $20.00+
F-9 .... $15.00+
F-10 .... $15.00+
F-11 .... $20.00+
F-17 .... $15.00+
R-310 .... $60.00+

Page 42
R-169B .... $125.00+
R-335 .... $30.00+
R-361 .... $125.00+
R-363 .... $125.00+
R-364 .... $125.00+
R-390 .... $300.00+
R-391 .... $300.00+

Page 42
R-392 .... $350.00+
R-400 .... $40.00+
R-401 .... $40.00+
R-402 .... $110.00+
R-403 .... $300.00+
R-404 .... $300.00+
R-427 .... $250.00+

Page 43
646 .... $10.00+
3020 .... $20.00+
3201 .... $25.00+
3215 .... $45.00+
3226 .... $30.00+
3235 .... $30.00+
3237 .... $30.00+
3239 .... $15.00+
3245 .... $10.00+
3247 .... $10.00+
3248 .... $20.00+
3253 .... $15.00+
F-12 .... $25.00+
R-369 .... $125.00+
R-425 .... $300.00+

Page 44
3220 .... $95.00+
R-117 .... $100.00+
R-241 .... $250.00+
R-281 .... $100.00+
R-290 .... $75.00+
R-303 .... $75.00+
R-326 .... $50.00+
R-327 .... $250.00+
R-397 .... $30.00+
R-408 .... $225.00+
R-409 .... $75.00+
R-416 .... $150.00+

Page 45
391-A .... $10.00+
391-B .... $10.00+
3061 .... $60.00+
3205-A .... $40.00+
3205-B .... $75.00+
D-1011 .... $100.00+
F-5 .... $25.00+
R-271 .... $45.00+
R-305 .... $300.00+
R-306 .... $75.00+
R-406 .... $250.00+

Page 46
Top Section
R-286 .... $25.00+
R-432 .... $20.00+
R-436 .... $20.00+
R-439 .... $40.00+
R-440 .... $15.00+ each
R-443 .... $50.00+
R-445 .... $15.00+ each
Bottom Section
R-295 .... $25.00+ each
R-248 .... $35.00+
R-458 .... $35.00+
R-457 .... $50.00+
R-459 .... $50.00+
R-433 .... $25.00+ each
R-438 .... $25.00+ pair
R-371 .... $20.00+

Page 46
R-437 .... $30.00+ pair
R-460 .... $50.00+
R-453 .... $75.00+

Page 47
Top Section
R-373 .... $75.00+
R-375A .... $50.00+
R-375B .... $100.00+
R-376A .... $50.00+
R-376B .... $150.00+
R-418 .... $75.00+ pair
R-421 .... $50.00+
R-442 .... $75.00+
Bottom Section
R-122 .... $100.00+
R-126A .... $25.00+
R-126 .... $50.00+
R-132 .... $150.00+ pair
R-441 .... $100.00+

Page 48
Top Section
R-230 .... $20.00+
R-252 .... $20.00+
R-422 .... $60.00+
R-431 .... $75.00+
R-444 .... $25.00+
R-451 .... $225.00+
Bottom Section
R-140 .... $50.00+
R-304 .... $60.00+ pair
R-322 .... $50.00+
R-337 .... $150.00+
R-357 .... $30.00+

Page 49
Top Section
3266 .... $15.00+
3280 .... $15.00+
3282 .... $15.00+
3285 .... $15.00+
3286 .... $15.00+
3289 .... $15.00+
Bottom Section
3261 .... $30.00+
3262 .... $40.00+
3274P .... $150.00+
3277 .... $60.00+ pair
3278 .... $45.00+
3287 .... $20.00+
3291 .... $10.00+

Page 50
Top Section
R-210 .... $75.00+
R-220 .... $25.00+ each
R-281 .... $100.00+
R-437 .... $30.00+ pair
R-453 .... $75.00+
R-460 .... $50.00+
Bottom Section
R-351 .... $65.00+
R-358 .... $40.00+
R-387 .... $100.00+
R-436 .... $20.00+
R-443 .... $50.00+
R-445 .... $15.00+ each
R-446 .... $75.00+

Page 51
Top Section
R-132 .... $150.00+ pair
R-393 .... $135.00+
R-402 .... $40.00+
R-489 .... $45.00+
R-497 .... $65.00+
Bottom Section
R-36 .... $100.00+
R-115 .... $50.00+
R-373 .... $75.00+
R-499 .... $75.00+

Page 52
Top Section
R-297 .... $30.00+
R-450 .... $100.00+
R-454 .... $150.00+
R-455 .... $75.00+
R-456 .... $50.00+
Bottom Section
A-230 .... $20.00+
R-252 .... $20.00+
R-279 .... $300.00+
R-286 .... $25.00+
R-335 .... $30.00+
R-363 .... $125.00+

Page 53
Top Section
D-1001 .... $40.00+
R-285 .... $25.00+
R-323 .... $60.00+
R-397 .... $30.00+ each
R-409 .... $75.00+
R-475 .... $75.00+ pair
Bottom Section
R-208 .... $80.00+
R-248 .... $35.00+
R-287 .... $75.00+
R-295 .... $25.00+ each
R-320 .... $30.00+

Page 54
Top Section
R-322 .... $50.00+
R-414 .... $125.00+
R-432 .... $20.00+
R-434 .... $50.00+
R-435 .... $50.00+
R-441 .... $100.00+
R-472 .... $150.00+
Bottom Section
A-332B .... $60.00+
R-277 .... $20.00+
R-278 .... $25.00+
R-332A .... $15.00+
R-447 .... $10.00+
R-448 .... $10.00+
R-449 .... $10.00+
R-452 .... $100.00+
R-492 .... $175.00+

Page 55
Top Section
R-103 .... $60.00+
R-140 .... $50.00+
R-284 .... $60.00+
R-293 .... $60.00+
R-359 .... $125.00+
R-360 .... $125.00+
R-364 .... $125.00+

Page 55

Bottom Section

R-33 .... $75.00+
R-271 .... $45.00+
R-386 .... $65.00+
R-418 .... $75.00+ pair
R-421 .... $50.00+
R-476 .... $25.00+

Page 56

Top Section

R-203 .... $40.00+ each
R-298 .... $60.00+
R-303 .... $75.00+
R-363 .... $125.00+
R-407 .... $45.00+
R-442 .... $75.00+
R-473 .... $40.00+ each
R-474 .... $65.00+

Bottom Section

R-484 .... $15.00+
R-485 .... $25.00+ each
R-491 .... $150.00+
R-493 .... $150.00+
R-494 .... $150.00+
R-496 .... $20.00+
R-498 .... $125.00+
R-500 .... $100.00+

Page 57

Top Section

R-479 .... $150.00+
R-483 .... $75.00+
R-486 .... $25.00+
R-488 .... $40.00+
R-490 .... $150.00+
R-501 .... $100.00+

Bottom Section

R-477 .... $200.00+
R-481 .... $75.00+
R-482 .... $75.00+
R-495 .... $250.00+ with
stretched out tail

Page 58

Top Section

517-A .... $45.00+
3200 .... $30.00+ pair
3208 .... $25.00+
3223 .... $15.00+
3256 .... $15.00+
3295 .... $20.00+
3296 .... $15.00+

Bottom Section

1005 .... $15.00+
1018 .... $25.00+
3005 .... $15.00+
3280 .... $15.00+
3282 .... $15.00+
3307 .... $20.00+
3319 .... $25.00+

Page 59

Top Section

823 .... $10.00+
3075 .... $15.00+
3234 .... $20.00+
3254 .... $35.00+ set
3257 .... $10.00+
3288 .... $25.00+
3291 .... $10.00+
3315 .... $30.00+

Page 59

3318 .... $20.00+

Bottom Section

1013 .... $25.00+
3084 .... $15.00+
3266 .... $25.00+
3270 .... $20.00+
3284 .... $35.00+
3289 .... $20.00+

Page 60

Top Section

1014 .... $15.00+
2012 .... $20.00+
3047 .... $10.00+
3085 .... $10.00+
3290 .... $25.00+
3306 .... $45.00+ each
3311 .... $25.00+

Bottom Section

741-C .... $15.00+
741-D .... $20.00+
3015 .... $20.00+
3213 .... $25.00+
3231 .... $20.00+
3314 .... $30.00+
3317 .... $25.00+
3321 .... $45.00+
3322 .... $20.00+

Page 61

Top Section

444-A .... $15.00+
2030 .... $20.00+
3202 .... $50.00+
3217 .... $15.00+
3292 .... $15.00+

Bottom Section

3104 .... $20.00+
3105 .... $15.00+
3118 .... $50.00+
3224 .... $20.00+
3309 .... $40.00+
3313 .... $25.00+

Page 62

Top Section

47 .... $15.00+
1037 .... $20.00+
2021 .... $25.00+
3049 .... $25.00+
3265 .... $30.00+

Bottom Section

130 .... $15.00+ each
364 .... $15.00+
364/130 .... $50.00+ set
1028 .... $30.00+
3020 .... $20.00+
3088 .... $25.00+

Page 63

Left Side

R-31 .... $75.00+
R-36 .... $100.00+
R-182 (L & R) ...... $25.00+ each
R-186 .... $75.00+
R-301 .... $25.00+
R-430 .... $35.00+
R-446 .... $75.00+
R-452 .... $100.00+
R-453 .... $75.00+
R-456 .... $50.00+

Page 63

R-691 .... $100.00+
R-693 .... $75.00+

Right Side

R-309 .... $30.00+
R-312 .... $30.00+ set
R-360 .... $125.00+
R-397 .... $30.00+ each
R-476 .... $25.00+
R-486 .... $25.00+
R-561 .... $100.00+
R-571 .... $125.00+
R-621 .... $20.00+
R-622 .... $40.00+ set
R-627 .... $15.00+
R-628 .... $20.00+
R-629 .... $20.00+
R-679 .... $45.00+
R-680 .... $30.00+ set
R-681 .... $20.00+
R-682 .... $30.00+ set
R-692 .... $30.00+
R-692A .... $10.00+
R-692B .... $45.00+

Page 64

Left Side

R-431 .... $75.00+
R-526 .... $20.00+
R-527 .... $25.00+
R-534 .... $25.00+
R-567 .... $15.00+
R-575 .... $75.00+
R-577 .... $45.00+
R-580 .... $50.00+
R-583 .... $50.00+
R-584 .... $15.00+
R-585 .... $15.00+
R-586 .... $15.00+
R-590 .... $75.00+
R-594 .... $25.00+
R-625 .... $75.00+
R-664 .... $75.00+
R-668 .... $35.00+
R-698 .... $50.00+
R-699 .... $20.00+

Right Side

R-115 .... $50.00+
R-271 .... $45.00+
R-287 .... $75.00+
R-299 .... $40.00+
R-320 .... $30.00+
R-321 .... $25.00+
R-386 .... $65.00+
R-407 .... $45.00+
R-426 .... $45.00+
R-647 .... $40.00+
R-651 .... $20.00+
R-652 .... $20.00+
R-653 .... $35.00+
R-658 .... $150.00+
R-659 .... $150.00+
R-660 .... $150.00+
R-701 .... $60.00+

Page 65

Left Side

R-103 .... $60.00+
R-132 .... $150.00+ pair
R-424 .... $200.00+
R-451 .... $225.00+
R-479 .... $150.00+
R-495 .... $250.00+ with

Page 65

stretched out tail

R-539 .... $75.00+
R-563 .... $75.00+
R-596 .... $300.00+
R-624 .... $150.00+
R-683 .... $150.00+ with
stretched out tail
R-694 .... $50.00+
R-702 .... $175.00+

Right Side

R-230 .... $20.00+
R-252 .... $20.00+
R-447 .... $10.00+
R-449 .... $10.00+
R-541 .... $25.00+
R-559 .... $15.00+
R-560 .... $25.00+
R-631 .... $75.00+
R-632 .... $60.00+
R-663 .... $45.00+
R-669 .... $45.00+
R-670 .... $15.00+
R-684 .... $60.00+
R-685 .... $75.00+
R-686 .... $15.00+
R-687 .... $50.00+
R-688 .... $10.00+
R-688X .... $75.00+ set

Page 66

Left Side

R-140 .... $50.00+
R-223 .... $100.00+
R-297 .... $30.00+
R-358 .... $40.00+
R-373 .... $75.00+
R-562 .... $45.00+
R-568 .... $150.00+
R-689 .... $30.00+

Right Side

R-363 .... $120.00+
R-475 .... $75.00+ pair
R-540 .... $45.00+
R-570 .... $150.00+
R-633 .... $150.00+
R-634 .... $150.00+
R-641 .... $50.00+ pair
R-655 .... $75.00+w/globe
R-656 .... $75.00+w/globe
R-657 .... $75.00+
R-672 .... $100.00+
R-673 .... $100.00+
R-700 .... $125.00+ pair

Page 67

Left Side

R-126 .... $50.00+
R-126A .... $25.00+
R-286 .... $25.00+
R-555 .... $100.00+
R-611 .... $25.00+
R-612 .... $75.00+
R-613 .... $15.00+
R-614 .... $100.00+
R-635 .... $65.00+
R-638 .... $150.00+ pair
R-639 .... $400.00+
R-654 .... $50.00+
R-665 .... $50.00+
R-666 .... $20.00+
R-667 .... $60.00+
R-801 .... $40.00+

R-804 .... $15.00+
R-805 .... $30.00+
Right Side
R-224 .... $40.00+
R-284 .... $60.00+
R-372 .... $30.00+
R-402 .... $40.00+
R-421 .... $50.00+
R-444 .... $25.00+
R-460 .... $50.00+
R-466 .... $20.00+
R-473 .... $40.00+ each
R-483 .... $75.00+
R-496 .... $20.00+
R-573 .... $15.00+
R-595 .... $50.00+

Page 68
Left Side
R-224 .... $40.00+
R-228 .... $35.00+
R-282 .... $60.00+
R-309 .... $30.00+
R-312 .... $30.00+ pair
R-313 .... $75.00+
R-314 .... $75.00+
R-360 .... $125.00+
R-363 .... $125.00+
R-397 .... $30.00+ each
R-437 .... $30.00+
R-484 .... $15.00+
R-485 .... $25.00+ each
R-486 .... $25.00+
R-597 .... $10.00+
R-598 .... $20.00+ pair
R-599 .... $40.00+
Right Side
R-727S .... $50.00+ set
R-728S .... $60.00+ set
R-731 .... $40.00+ set
R-737S .... $50.00+ set
R-746S .... $60.00+ set
R-749 .... $20.00+
R-755S .... $40.00+ set

Page 69
Left Side
F-16 .... $15.00+
F-17 .... $15.00+
R-371 .... $20.00+
R-438 .... $25.00+ pair
R-573 .... $15.00+
R-621 .... $20.00+
R-622 .... $40.00+ pair
R-648 .... $45.00+
R-649 .... $45.00+
R-650 .... $15.00+
R-689 .... $30.00+
R-690 .... $30.00+ pair
R-711 .... $65.00+
Right Side
R-140 .... $50.00+
R-373 .... $75.00+
R-418 .... $75.00+ pair
R-421 .... $50.00+
R-437 .... $30.00+ pair
R-466 .... $20.00+
R-473 .... $40.00+ each
R-476 .... $25.00+
R-522 .... $15.00+
R-562 .... $45.00+
R-681 .... $20.00+

R-682 .... $30.00+ pair
R-692B .... $45.00+

Page 70
Left Side
R-769 .... $60.00+
R-789 .... $75.00+
R-773 .... $50.00+
R-775 .... $40.00+
R-786 .... $75.00+
R-790 .... $85.00+
R-791 .... $85.00+
R-808 .... $400.00+
R-809 .... $150.00+
Right Side
R-31 .... $75.00+
R-36 .... $10.00+
R-115 .... $50.00+
R-182 .... $25.00+
R-186 .... $75.00+
R-271 .... $45.00+
R-284 .... $60.00+
R-426 .... $45.00+
R-430 .... $35.00+
R-453 .... $75.00+
R-708 .... $40.00+
R-712 .... $35.00+
R-742 .... $125.00+
R-744 .... $50.00+
R-750 .... $20.00+
R-751 .... $25.00+
R-752 .... $30.00+

Page 71
Left Side
R-407 .... $45.00+
R-647 .... $40.00+
R-651 .... $20.00+
R-652 .... $20.00+
R-697 .... $35.00+
R-705 .... $40.00+
R-706 .... $50.00+
R-707 .... $50.00+
R-709 .... $15.00+
R-713 .... $30.00+
R-714 .... $25.00+
R-723 .... $30.00+
Right Side
R-287 .... $75.00+
R-299 .... $40.00+
R-321 .... $25.00+
R-456 .... $50.00+
R-483 .... $75.00+
R-521 .... $50.00+
R-534 .... $25.00+
R-555 .... $100.00+
R-665 .... $50.00+
R-666 .... $20.00+
R-667 .... $60.00+
R-691 .... $100.00+
R-693 .... $75.00+
R-701 .... $60.00+
R-743 .... $25.00+

Page 72
Left Side
R-33 .... $75.00+
R-138 .... $100.00+
R-301 .... $25.00+
R-320 .... $30.00+
R-386 .... $65.00+
R-444 .... $25.00+

R-446 .... $75.00+
R-496 .... $20.00+
R-526 .... $20.00+
R-527 .... $25.00+
R-716 .... $15.00+
R-732 .... $25.00+
Right Side
R-770 .... $40.00+
R-771 .... $15.00+
R-772 .... $100.00+
R-787 .... $20.00+
R-788 .... $150.00+
R-792 .... $40.00+
R-793 .... $25.00+ pair
R-796 .... $15.00+
R-797 .... $15.00+
R-798 .... $15.00+
R-799 .... $15.00+
R-807 .... $15.00+
R-813 .... $20.00+

Page 73
Left Side
R-103 .... $60.00+
R-402 .... $40.00+
R-412 .... $40.00+
R-413 .... $30.00+
R-424 .... $200.00+
R-451 .... $225.00+
R-624 .... $150.00+
R-683 .... $150.00+
R-694 .... $50.00+
R-695 .... $500.00+
R-720 .... $200.00+
R-721 .... $500.00+
R-739 .... $175.00+
R-740 .... $225.00+
Right Side
R-758 .... $125.00+
R-759 .... $150.00+
R-774 .... $40.00+
R-783 .... $45.00+
R-784 .... $40.00+
R-785 .... $35.00+
R-794 .... $50.00+ pair
R-795 .... $50.00+ pair
R-811 .... $10.00+
R-812 .... $15.00+

Page 74
Left Side
R-724 .... $50.00+
R-725 .... $20.00+ each
R-745 .... $75.00+
R-748 .... $20.00+
R-753 .... $100.00+
R-762 .... $30.00+
R-763 .... $30.00+
R-764 .... $30.00+
R-765 .... $30.00+
Right Side
R-126A .... $25.00+
R-126X .... $45.00+
R-132 .... $150.00+ pair
R-175 .... $75.00+
R-286 .... $25.00+
R-431 .... $75.00+
R-475 .... $75.00+ pair
R-586 .... $15.00+
R-638 .... $150.00+ pair
R-641 .... $50.00+ pair
R-718 .... $75.00+ pair
R-741 .... $75.00+ pair

Page 75
Left Side
R-479 .... $150.00+
R-540 .... $45.00+
R-563 .... $75.00+
R-635 .... $65.00+
R-655 .... $75.00+w/globe
R-656 .... $75.00+w/globe
R-657 .... $75.00+
R-663 .... $45.00+
R-719 .... $60.00+
R-722 .... $200.00+
R-754 .... $20.00+
R-760 .... $150.00+
Right Side
R-230 .... $20.00+
R-252 .... $20.00+
R-447 .... $10.00+
R-449 .... $10.00+
R-520 .... $10.00+
R-541 .... $25.00+
R-567 .... $15.00+
R-625 .... $75.00+
R-631 .... $75.00+
R-632 .... $60.00+
R-668 .... $35.00+
R-669 .... $45.00+
R-670 .... $15.00+
R-684 .... $60.00+
R-685 .... $75.00+
R-686 .... $15.00+

Page 76
Left Side
739-E .... $75.00+
3221-X .... $20.00+
3353-X .... $35.00+
3395-X .... $60.00+
3418-X .... $60.00+
3422-Z .... $40.00+
3425-X .... $20.00+
3450 .... $50.00+
Right Side
334-BY .... $40.00+
337-X .... $15.00+
474-CX .... $15.00+
923-Z .... $15.00+
2021-Y .... $20.00+
3034-Y .... $20.00+
3049-Y .... $30.00+
3217-Y .... $15.00+
3264 .... $20.00+
3275-X .... $15.00+
3276-Z .... $20.00+
3409-Y .... $15.00+
3411-Z .... $20.00+
3434-Z .... $50.00+
3442 .... $30.00+ set
B-3321 .... $25.00+

Page 77
Left Side
R-132 .... $150.00+ pair
R-475 .... $75.00+ pair
R-641 .... $50.00+ pair
R-1144 .... $75.00+ pair
R-1162 .... $20.00+
R-1163 .... $20.00+
R-1198 .... $85.00+
R-1199 .... $85.00+
R-1240 .... $150.00+ pair
R-1266 .... $75.00+ pair

Right Side

R-657 .... $75.00+
R-709 .... $15.00+
R-869 .... $75.00+
R-875 .... $150.00+
R-1170 .... $50.00+
R-1239 .... $150.00+
R-1257 .... $175.00+
R-1262 .... $50.00+

Page 78

Left Side

5383 .... $125.00+
5384 .... $60.00+
6144 .... $175.00+
6147 .... $150.00+
6174 .... $100.00+
6221 .... $150.00+
6232 .... $175.00+
6248 .... $110.00+
6282 .... $110.00+
ϭ283 .... $110.00+
6291 .... $125.00+
6297 .... $150.00+

Right Side

R-186 .... $75.00+
R-453 .... $75.00+
R-904 .... $35.00+
R-1168 .... $150.00+
R-1215 .... $50.00+
R-1216 .... $50.00+
R-1230 .... $100.00+

Page 79

Left Side

5205 .... $300.00+
5374 .... $125.00+
5398 .... $200.00+
6169 .... $400.00+
6195 .... $150.00+
6234 .... $500.00+
6262 .... $200.00+
6268 .... $225.00+
6278 .... $100.00+
6279 .... $200.00+
6281 .... $500.00+

Right Side

5353 .... $50.00+
6116 .... $50.00+
6198 .... $75.00+
6200 .... $75.00+
6202 .... $75.00+
6256 .... $75.00+
6263 .... $50.00+
6264 .... $75.00+
6289 .... $50.00+
6301 .... $75.00+
6302 .... $150.00+

Page 80

5353 .... $50.00+
6198 .... $75.00+
6234 .... $500.00+

Page 81

5398 .... $200.00+
6044 .... $50.00+
6193 .... $100.00+
6204 .... $250.00+

Page 82

5205 .... $300.00+
5383 .... $125.00+
6169 .... $400.00+
6195 .... $150.00+

Page 83

Left Side

R-670 .... $15.00+
R-811 .... $10.00+
R-860 .... $10.00+
R-873 .... $15.00+
R-1148 .... $15.00+
R-1287 .... $15.00+
R-1357 .... $15.00+
R-1359 .... $15.00+
R-1403 .... $15.00+
R-1408 .... $20.00+

Right Side

R-475 .... $75.00+ pair
R-641 .... $50.00+ pair
R-1198 .... $85.00+
R-1199 .... $85.00+
R-1316 .... $60.00+
R-1324 .... $125.00+
R-1325 .... $75.00+
R-1364 .... $50.00+ pair
R-1365 .... $150.00+ pair

Page 84

Left Side

R-1366 .... $75.00+
R-1378 .... $60.00+
R-1417 .... $50.00+
S-512 .... $50.00+
S-515 .... $50.00+
S-516 .... $50.00+

Right Side

R-224 .... $40.00+
R-309 .... $30.00+ pair
R-312 .... $30.00+ pair
R-363 .... $125.00+
R-437 .... $30.00+ pair
R-1268 .... $25.00+ pair
R-1269 .... $30.00+
R-1338 .... $20.00+ pair
R-1339 .... $15.00+
R-1353 .... $20.00+ pair
R-1354 .... $15.00+
R-1413 .... $15.00+ pair
R-1414 .... $10.00+

Page 85

Left Side

R-1376-C .... $20.00+
R-1382-C .... $10.00+
R-1391-C .... $15.00+
R-1392-C .... $60.00+
R-1412-C .... $25.00+

Right Side

R-1400-C .... $45.00+
R-1402-C .... $60.00+
R-1406-C .... $60.00+
R-1411-C .... $15.00+

Page 86

Left Side

A-1446 .... $15.00+
R-754 .... $20.00+
R-1220 .... $35.00+
R-1262 .... $50.00+
R-1293 .... $20.00+

R-1331 .... $65.00+
R-1332 .... $75.00+
R-1375 .... $20.00+
R-1421 .... $20.00+
R-1433B .... $20.00+
R-1462 .... $15.00+

Right Side

R-683 .... $150.00+
R-735 .... $50.00+
R-1296 .... $125.00+
R-1301 .... $150.00+
R-1368 .... $150.00+
R-1396 .... $60.00+
R-1407 .... $500.00+
R-1440 .... $50.00+
R-1442 .... $40.00+

Page 87

6373 .... $250.00+
6375 .... $250.00+
6376 .... $125.00+
6377 .... $125.00+
6378S .... $50.00+

Page 88

Left Side

6361 .... $60.00+
6362 .... $60.00+
6362X .... $60.00+
6371 .... $65.00+
6389 .... $150.00+
6390 .... $150.00+

Right Side

6360 .... $60.00+
6367 .... $60.00+
6369 .... $225.00+
6370 .... $125.00+
6372 .... $60.00+
6371X .... $65.00+

Page 89

Left Side

110-H .... $10.00+
125 .... $8.00+
127 .... $10.00+
138 .... $8.00+
144 .... $10.00+
155 .... $10.00+
164 .... $8.00+
165 .... $8.00+
170-S .... $10.00+
177 .... $8.00+
178 .... $8.00+
185S .... $10.00+
1002 .... $10.00+
1015 .... $10.00+
1020 .... $8.00+
1027 .... $8.00+
1028 .... $8.00+
1029 .... $8.00+
1030 .... $8.00+
R-1311 .... $15.00+
R-1723 .... $20.00+
R-1755 .... $20.00+
R-1894 .... $10.00+

Right Side

117 .... $10.00+
128 .... $10.00+
135 .... $10.00+
149 .... $10.00+
153 .... $10.00+
162 .... $20.00+
173 .... $10.00+

192 .... $15.00+
1001S .... $15.00+
1003 .... $15.00+
1004 .... $20.00+
1005 .... $15.00+
1006 .... $15.00+
1008 .... $10.00+
1009 .... $10.00+
1014 .... $10.00+
1016-S .... $20.00+
1017-S .... $20.00+
1019 .... $8.00+
1021 .... $10.00+
1022 .... $10.00+
R-1735 .... $20.00+
R-1836 .... $10.00+
SP-12 .... $8.00+

Page 90

Left Side

1029 .... $8.00+
1029/39/40 .... $30.00+ set
1031 .... $10.00+
1032 .... $10.00+
1033-H .... $15.00+
1034-H .... $25.00+
1035-H .... $20.00+
1036-H .... $20.00+
1037-H .... $15.00+
1038-H .... $15.00+
1039 .... $15.00+
1040 .... $5.00+
1041 .... $15.00+
1042-S .... $10.00+
1042/43 .... $30.00+ set
1043-S .... $8.00+
3018 .... $20.00+
8008-H .... $20.00+
8009-H .... $20.00+
8021-B .... $25.00+
8022-B .... $30.00+
8023-B .... $25.00+
8024-B .... $25.00+

Right Side

1-H .... $150.00+
9-H .... $40.00+
13-H .... $35.00+
25-H .... $75.00+
26-H .... $75.00+
144 .... $10.00+
153 .... $10.00+
627 .... $125.00+
1762 .... $150.00+
1810 .... $30.00+
1811 .... $30.00+
3017 .... $25.00+
4012 .... $25.00+
4040 .... $35.00+
4041 .... $50.00+
4042 .... $50.00+
4043 .... $25.00+
4044 .... $20.00+
4045 .... $60.00+
4046 .... $30.00+
8008-H .... $20.00+
8009-H .... $20.00+

Page 91

Left Side

335 .... $25.00+
336 .... $20.00+ pair
707-S .... $20.00+

889	$15.00+
1035-H	$20.00+
1037-H	$15.00+
1743	$100.00+
1915	$30.00+
1919	$20.00+
3020-Z	$45.00+
3021-Z	$40.00+
4034	$40.00+
4035	$35.00+
4043	$25.00+
8012	$25.00+
8013	$20.00+
8014	$20.00+
8017	$100.00+
8018	$100.00+
8019	$100.00+
RG-68-X	$10.00+

Right Side

1035-H	$20.00+
1038-H	$15.00+
3022-2	$50.00
3023	$20.00+
4040	$35.00+
4041	$50.00+
4047-H	$50.00+
8010/11	$20.00+
8012	$25.00+
8013	$20.00+
8014	$20.00+
8015/16	$75.00+ set
8020	$200.00+
8025-S	$15.00+
8026-S	$35.00+

Page 92

Left Side

306	$15.00+
413	$15.00+
436	$50.00+
455	$45.00+
499-S	$30.00+
709	$15.00+
842/843	$75.00+
885	$350.00+
1504/05	$75.00+
4000-S	$35.00+
4012	$25.00+
4030	$35.00+
4031	$25.00+
R-1285	$15.00+ pair
R-1752	$40.00+
R-1915	$30.00+
R-1919	$20.00+
RG-68-X	$10.00+
RG-82-X	$15.00+

Right Side

1025	$10.00+
1026	$10.00+
4025-H	$40.00+
4026-H	$35.00+
4027-H	$45.00+
4028-H	$40.00+
4029-H	$25.00+
4033-H	$75.00+
4034	$40.00+
4035	$35.00+

Page 93

Left Side

382	$150.00+
489	$50.00+
518	$75.00+

612	$50.00+
613	$50.00+
633	$60.00+
634	$60.00+
879-H/880-H	$25.00+
1018	$20.00+
1024	$20.00+
3000	$35.00+
3008-H	$45.00+
3014-Z	$15.00+
4017	$75.00+
4018	$60.00+
4019	$25.00+
4022	$75.00+
4023	$45.00+
4024	$25.00+
R-31	$75.00+
R-1224	$75.00+
R-1913	$20.00+

Right Side

407	$75.00+
411-H	$125.00+
828	$50.00+
828-W	$60.00+
857	$150.00+
857-W	$150.00+
896	$100.00+
896-W	$100.00+
899	$100.00+
900	$125.00+
8001	$100.00+
8002	$100.00+
8005-Z	$150.00+
RG-90	$25.00+
RG-90-W	$35.00+
RG-91	$40.00+
RG-91-W	$50.00+

Page 94

Left Side

6314	$75.00+
6314X	$85.00+
6315	$60.00+
6315X	$70.00+
6322	$250.00+
6332S	$50.00+
6336S	$75.00+
6338S	$75.00+
6339	$50.00+
6345S	$60.00+
6353S	$75.00+

Right Side

R-657	$75.00+
R-683	$50.00+
R-1479	$25.00+
R-1490	$75.00+
R-1491	$50.00+
R-1492	$35.00+
R-1493	$30.00+ pair
R-1494	$25.00+

Page 95

Left Side - Reference Only
Right Side

R-1311	$15.00+
R-1601	$10.00+
R-1602	$15.00+
R-1608	$15.00+
R-1618	$25.00+
R-1634S	$10.00+
R-1663	$15.00+
R-1665	$25.00+

R-1673/74/75	$35.00+ set
R-1688S	$20.00+
R-1714S	$15.00+
R-1718/19/20	$35.00+ set
R-1723	$20.00+
R-1731	$20.00+
R-1735	$20.00+
R-1737S	$20.00+
R-1738S	$15.00+

Page 96

Left Side

RG-37	$10.00+
RG-42	$10.00+
RG-53	$20.00+ pair
RG-56	$10.00+
RG-60	$20.00+
RG-61	$20.00+
RG-63	$15.00+
RG-64	$10.00+
RG-65	$8.00+
RG-68	$10.00+
RG-72	$10.00+
RG-73	$10.00+
RG-74	$8.00+
RG-75	$40.00+
RG-76	$15.00+
RG-77	$10.00+

Right Side

R-1661B	$25.00+
R-1714S	$20.00+
R-1715S	$15.00+
R-1718	$15.00+
R-1724	$35.00+
R-1725	$30.00+
R-1726	$15.00+ each
R-1731	$10.00+
R-1738S	$15.00+
R-1739S	$15.00+
R-1740S	$20.00+ pair

Page 97

Left Side

R-1696	$30.00+
R-1701	$20.00+
R-1702	$55.00+
R-1704	$20.00+
R-1705	$15.00+
R-1708	$75.00+
R-1711S	$85.00+
R-1712S	$60.00+
R-1716S	$50.00+
R-1717S	$35.00+
R-1722	$20.00+
R-1725	$30.00+
R-1726	$15.00+ each
R-1727	$30.00+
R-1728	$15.00+
R-1730	$15.00+
R-1732	$25.00+
R-1733	$35.00+
R-1742	$125.00+

Right Side

R-1582S	$15.00+
R-1583S	$15.00+
R-1584S	$40.00+
R-1585S	$35.00+
R-1588S	$30.00+
R-1657	$75.00+
R-1683S	$20.00+
R-1699	$75.00+

Page 98

Left Side

6343	$50.00+
R-495	$60.00+
R-683	$50.00+
R-1396	$60.00+
R-1440	$50.00+
R-1442	$40.00+
R-1510	$100.00+
R-1693	$90.00+
R-1694	$90.00+
R-1695	$90.00+

Right Side

6356-TV	$75.00+
6357-TV	$75.00+
6478-TV	$100.00+
6479-TV	$100.00+
6480-TV	$125.00+

Page 99

Left Side

6462	$50.00+
6466	$100.00+
6470	$225.00+
6487	$125.00+
6488	$125.00+

Right Side

6409-TV	$40.00+ each
6492-TV	$100.00+
6514-TV	$100.00+
6518	$30.00+

Page 100

Left Side

6413S-TV	$60.00+
6414-TV	$85.00+
6415-TV	$75.00+
6472-TV	$150.00+
6473-TV	$150.00+
6474-TV	$100.00+

Right Side

6051-TV	$45.00+
6424S-TV	$125.00+
6475-TV	$225.00+
6477-TV	$225.00+

Page 101

Left Side

R-1706	$75.00+
R-1752W	$40.00+
R-1754	$15.00+
R-1755H	$20.00+
R-1759F	$30.00+
R-1760F	$25.00+ pair
R-1766S-H	$40.00+
R-1772S	$20.00+
R-1774S	$15.00+
R-1775S	$35.00+ pair
R-1776	$35.00+
R-1777	$20.00+
R-1779	$25.00+
R-1780	$20.00+
R-1782	$100.00+
R-1784	$10.00+
R-1785	$10.00+

Right Side

R-437	$30.00+ pair
R-1751	$50.00+
R-1753	$65.00+
R-1763	$50.00+
R-1764	$20.00+

R-1765 .... $20.00+ pair
R-1768S .... $40.00+
R-1769S .... $60.00+
R-1770S .... $35.00+
R-1771S .... $25.00+
R-1772S .... $20.00+
R-1773S .... $25.00+
R-1775S .... $35.00+ pair
R-1778 .... $20.00+
R-1783 .... $75.00+

Page 102
Left Side
R-1744 .... $80.00+
R-1757 .... $80.00+
R-1758 .... $80.00+
R-1761 .... $200.00+
R-1762 .... $150.00+
Right Side
110-H .... $10.00+
144 .... $10.00+
145 .... $40.00+
149 .... $10.00+
155 .... $10.00+
157 .... $15.00+
163-S .... $20.00+
335 .... $25.00+
336 .... $20.00+ pair
352 .... $25.00+
353 .... $25.00+ pair
452 .... $60.00+
454-H .... $60.00+
455 .... $45.00+
457 .... $20.00+
470 .... $25.00+
471 .... $25.00+
614 .... $300.00+
702 .... $20.00+
707-S .... $20.00+
709 .... $15.00+
710 .... $35.00+
830 .... $25.00+
839 .... $15.00+
840 .... $10.00+
841 .... $10.00+
R-1233 .... $15.00+
R-1920 .... $30.00+

Page 103
Left Side
6522 .... $80.00+
6523 .... $125.00+
6524 .... $100.00+
6525 .... $125.00+
6526 .... $100.00+
6538 .... $100.00+
Right Side
RG-26 .... $20.00+
RG-78 .... $10.00+
RG-79 .... $10.00+
RG-80 .... $20.00+
RG-81 .... $45.00+
RG-82 .... $15.00+
RG-83 .... $15.00+
RG-84 .... $25.00+
RG-85 .... $20.00+ pair

Page 104
Left Side - Reference Only
Right Side
R-1618B-G .... $20.00+

R-1714S-G .... $20.00+
R-1743 .... $100.00+
R-1774S .... $15.00+
R-1782 .... $100.00+
R-1796 .... $15.00+
R-1798 .... $25.00+
R-1799 .... $25.00+
R-1806 .... $175.00+
R-1808 .... $60.00+
R-1810 .... $30.00+
R-1811 .... $30.00+
R-1812S .... $60.00+
R-1815 .... $50.00+
R-1817S .... $20.00+ pair
R-1818S .... $20.00+
R-1822 .... $35.00+
R-1829 .... $45.00+

Page 105
Left Side
R-1285 .... $15.00+ pair
R-1776W .... $40.00+
R-1781 .... $300.00+
R-1794 .... $25.00+
R-1795 .... $20.00+ pair
R-1796 .... $15.00+
R-1800 .... $20.00+
R-1804 .... $65.00+
R-1805 .... $65.00+
R-1807 .... $125.00+
R-1809 .... $25.00+
R-1813S .... $45.00+
R-1814S .... $50.00+
R-1816S .... $25.00+
R-1817S .... $20.00+ pair
R-1824 .... $30.00+
R-1826 .... $35.00+
R-1827 .... $15.00+
R-1828 .... $90.00+
Right Side
R-1224 .... $75.00+
R-1692 .... $250.00+
R-1697 .... $100.00+
R-1698 .... $200.00+
R-1709 .... $125.00+
R-1741 .... $175.00+
R-1742 .... $125.00+
R-1761 .... $200.00+
R-1762 .... $150.00+

Page 106
Left Side
RG-1 .... $20.00+
RG-25 .... $25.00+
RG-26 .... $20.00+
RG-28 .... $10.00+
RG-41 .... $20.00+
RG-42 .... $10.00+
RG-56 .... $10.00+
RG-60 .... $20.00+
RG-63 .... $15.00+
RG-65 .... $8.00+
RG-68 .... $10.00+
RG-72 .... $10.00+
RG-78 .... $10.00+
RG-79 .... $10.00+
RG-80 .... $20.00+
RG-85 .... $20.00+ pair
RG-86 .... $30.00+
RG-87 .... $30.00+
RG-89 .... $10.00+
RG-90 .... $25.00+

Right Side
6554 .... $50.00+
6555 .... $50.00+
6558 .... $75.00+
6562 .... $50.00+
6563 .... $50.00+

Page 107
Left Side
6550 .... $50.00+
6553 .... $50.00+
6557 .... $75.00+
6564 .... $50.00+
6565 .... $50.00+
Right Side
6051-TV .... $45.00+
6200-TV .... $75.00+
6475-TV .... $225.00+
6522 .... $80.00+
6523 .... $125.00+
6525 .... $125.00+

Page 108
Left Side
R-1311 .... $15.00+
R-1429/30/31 .... $40.00+ set
R-1607 .... $75.00+
R-1618H .... $30.00+
R-1665 .... $25.00+
R-1735 .... $20.00+
R-1754H .... $15.00+
R-1766S .... $40.00+
R-1786 .... $20.00+
R-1787 .... $20.00+
R-1788A .... $10.00+
R-1789A .... $30.00+
R-1790 .... $30.00+
R-1791 .... $25.00+
R-1819/20/21 .... $35.00+ set
R-1823 .... $15.00+
R-1827 .... $15.00+
Right Side
6472-TV .... $150.00+
6473-TV .... $150.00+
6474-TV .... $100.00+
6492-TV .... $100.00+
6514-TV .... $100.00+

Page 109
Left Side
R-873H .... $15.00+
R-1766 .... $40.00+
R-1828 .... $90.00+
R-1838 .... $25.00+
R-1839 .... $25.00+
R-1840 .... $30.00+
R-1841 .... $30.00+
R-1842 .... $20.00+
R-1843 .... $30.00+ pair
R-1844 .... $20.00+
R-1845 .... $20.00+
R-1846 .... $100.00+
R-1847 .... $25.00+
R-1848 .... $65.00+
R-1849 .... $10.00+
R-1850 .... $10.00+
R-1855 .... $50.00+
R-1866S .... $15.00+
R-1867S .... $20.00+ pair
R-1870S .... $20.00+
R-1872S .... $10.00+
R-1873S .... $15.00+

R-1879S .... $10.00+
Right Side
RG-92 .... $8.00+
RG-93 .... $15.00+
RG-94 .... $15.00+
RG-95 .... $15.00+
RG-97 .... $15.00+
RG-98 .... $25.00+
RG-99 .... $25.00+
RG-100 .... $30.00+
RG-101 .... $15.00+
RG-102 .... $20.00+
RG-103 .... $10.00+

Page 110
Left Side
R-1504 .... $75.00+
R-1506 .... $60.00+
R-1868S .... $50.00+
R-1876S .... $50.00+
R-1877S .... $40.00+
R-1878S .... $40.00+
R-1881S .... $40.00+
R-1882S .... $35.00+
R-1884S .... $40.00+
Right Side
R-1830 .... $20.00+
R-1856 .... $20.00+
R-1857 .... $20.00+
R-1858 .... $20.00+
R-1859-60 .... $100.00+
R-1892 .... $20.00+
R-1893 .... $20.00+

Page 111
Left Side
R-1896 .... $35.00+
R-1897 .... $75.00+
R-1912 .... $30.00+
R-1913 .... $20.00+
R-1914 .... $25.00+
R-1944 .... $30.00+
R-1945 .... $35.00+
R-1946 .... $45.00+
RG-84-X .... $25.00+
RG-87-X .... $30.00+
Right Side
R-1233 .... $15.00+
R-1898 .... $75.00+
R-1900 .... $30.00+
R-1901 .... $35.00+
R-1902 .... $35.00+
R-1904 .... $30.00+
R-1915 .... $30.00+
R-1916 .... $75.00+
R-1919 .... $20.00+
R-1920 .... $30.00+
R-1932S .... $40.00+
R-1933S .... $15.00+
R-1934S .... $20.00+ pair
R-1937S .... $75.00+
R-1938S .... $20.00+

Page 112
Left Side
6343 .... $50.00+
R-495 .... $60.00+
R-683 .... $50.00+
R-1224 .... $75.00+
R-1510 .... $100.00+
R-1742 .... $125.00+
R-1782 .... $100.00+

Page 112

R-1806 .... $175.00+
R-1807 .... $125.00+
R-1829 .... $45.00+
Right Side
R-1697 .... $100.00+
R-1709 .... $125.00+
R-1741 .... $175.00+
R-1762 .... $150.00+
R-1840 .... $30.00+
R-1841 .... $30.00+
R-1844 .... $20.00+
R-1845 .... $20.00+
R-1846 .... $100.00+
R-1848 .... $65.00+
R-1855 .... $50.00+

Page 113
Left Side
R-1810 .... $30.00+
R-1811 .... $30.00+
R-1822 .... $35.00+
R-1826 .... $35.00+
R-1851 .... $30.00+
R-1891S .... $100.00+
R-1931S .... $100.00+
R-1943 .... $50.00+
Right Side
R-1504 .... $75.00+
R-1506 .... $60.00+
R-1886S .... $60.00+
R-1887S .... $35.00+
R-1888S .... $25.00+
R-1905 .... $100.00+
R-1906 .... $125.00+

Page 114
Left Side
RG-104 .... $15.00+
RG-105 .... $15.00+
RG-106 .... $10.00+
RG-110 .... $15.00+
RG-111 .... $10.00+
RG-112 .... $15.00+
RG-113 .... $20.00+
RG-114 .... $15.00+
RG-115 .... $10.00+
RG-116 .... $15.00+
RG-117 .... $20.00+ pair
RG-118 .... $15.00+
Right Side
6602 .... $75.00+
6603 .... $50.00+
6607 .... $50.00+
6624S .... $50.00+
6634 .... $50.00+

Page 115
Left Side
6620S .... $50.00+
6622S .... $60.00+
6626S .... $50.00+
6627S .... $50.00+
Right Side
6608 .... $75.00+
6609 .... $60.00+
6610 .... $60.00+
6619 .... $75.00+

Page 116
Left Side
5353-TV .... $50.00+
6051-TV .... $45.00+

Page 116

6409-TV .... $40.00+ each
6475-TV .... $225.00+
6631-TV .... $75.00+
6632-TV .... $50.00+
Right Side
R-1665 .... $25.00+
R-1756 .... $15.00+
R-1836S .... $10.00+
R-1894 .... $10.00+
R-1899 .... $30.00+
R-1907 .... $15.00+
R-1909 .... $10.00+
R-1910 .... $20.00+
R-1911 .... $10.00+
R-1926 .... $40.00+
R-1929 .... $25.00+
R-1939S .... $10.00+
R-1940S .... $8.00+
R-1941S .... $10.00+
R-1942S .... $10.00+

Page 117
Left Side
101-H .... $25.00+
102-H .... $25.00+
104 .... $15.00+
107 .... $20.00+
301-H .... $75.00+
305 .... $20.00+
308 .... $20.00+
309 .... $20.00+ pair
312-H .... $75.00+
405 .... $75.00+
406 .... $60.00+
408 .... $25.00+
410-H .... $100.00+
R-1745 .... $20.00+
R-1746 .... $20.00+ pair
R-1945 .... $35.00+
SP-12 .... $8.00+
Right Side
301-H .... $75.00+
302-H .... $35.00+
305 .... $20.00+
306 .... $15.00+
307 .... $10.00+
310-H .... $20.00+
311 .... $20.00+ pair
807-H .... $75.00+
808-H .... $40.00+
R-1922 .... $30.00+
R-1923 .... $30.00+ pair
RG-101-X .... $15.00+

Page 118
Left Side
401-H .... $40.00+
401-H-X .... $25.00+
402-H .... $40.00+
403-H .... $75.00+
404-H .... $40.00+
501-H .... $175.00+
502-H .... $100.00+
503-H .... $250.00+
505 .... $125.00+
601-H .... $85.00+
Right Side
504-H .... $100.00+
801-H .... $125.00+
802-H .... $100.00+
804-H .... $150.00+
805-H .... $150.00+

Page 118

806-H .... $150.00+
R-1905 .... $125.00+
R-1906 .... $125.00+

Page 119
Left Side
927 .... $40.00+
928-H .... $150.00+
931-S .... $50.00+
935-S .... $60.00+
Right Side
RG-119 .... $30.00+
RG-120 .... $30.00+
RG-121 .... $25.00+
RG-122 .... $15.00+
RG-123 .... $15.00+
RG-124 .... $15.00+
RG-125 .... $8.00+
RG-126 .... $10.00+
RG-128 .... $30.00+
RG-129 .... $15.00+
RG-130 .... $15.00+
RG-131 .... $15.00+
RG-132 .... $15.00+

Page 120
Left Side - Reference Only
Right Side
118 .... $10.00+
118 (Gold Tweed) .... $10.00+
301-H .... $75.00+
301-H (Gold Tweed) .... $45.00+
306 .... $15.00+
306 (Gold Tweed) .... $15.00+
814-H .... $175.00+
814-H-X .... $225.00+
815-H .... $60.00+
815-H (Gold Tweed) .... $50.00+
816-H .... $500.00+
817-H .... $150.00+
818-817-H-X .... $400.00+ set
818-H .... $150.00+
R-1941-S .... $10.00+
R-1941-S (Gold Tweed) .... $10.00+

Page 121
Left Side
118 (Gold Tweed) .... $10.00+
301-H (Gold Tweed) .... $45.00+
306 (Gold Tweed) .... $10.00+
314 .... $20.00+
315 .... $20.00+ pair
316-H .... $35.00+
317-H .... $15.00+
317-H (Gold Tweed) .... $15.00+
318-H .... $35.00+
320 .... $20.00+
322-H .... $30.00+ pair
323 .... $20.00+
413 (Gold Tweed) .... $10.00+
425 .... $15.00+
815-H (Gold Tweed) .... $50.00+
R-1224 .... $75.00+
R-1285 .... $15.00+ pair
R-1285 .... $15.00+ pair
R-1714-S (Gold Tweed) .... $15.00+
R-1776 (Gold Tweed) .... $25.00+
R-1919 (Gold Tweed) .... $15.00+
R-1922 (Gold Tweed) .... $25.00+ pair
R-1923 (Gold Tweed) .... $25.00+ pair
R-1941-S (Gold Tweed) .... $10.00+
Right Side
302-H .... $35.00+

Page 121

312-H .... $75.00+
319-H .... $30.00+
319-H (Gold Tweed) .... $25.00+
418-H .... $60.00+
420-H .... $75.00+
R-534 .... $25.00+
R-709 .... $15.00+
R-1881-S .... $40.00+
R-1918 .... $50.00+

Page 122
Left Side
408-C .... $45.00+
R-1724-C .... $50.00+
R-1743-C .... $125.00+
R-1915-C .... $40.00+
R-1916-C .... $100.00+
R-1919-C .... $20.00+
RG-1-C .... $50.00+
RG-15-C .... $30.00+
RG-31-C .... $30.00+
RG-24-C .... $50.00+
RG-81-C .... $40.00+
RG-86-C .... $75.00+
RG-120-C .... $60.00+
Right Side
RG-68 .... $10.00+
RG-82 .... $15.00+
RG-111 .... $10.00+
RG-112 .... $15.00+
RG-133 .... $10.00+
RG-133-P .... $15.00+
RG-134 .... $15.00+
RG-134-P .... $20.00+
RG-135 .... $10.00+
RG-135-P .... $15.00+
RG-136 .... $15.00+ pair
RG-137 .... $40.00+
RG-138 .... $40.00+
RG-139 .... $20.00+
RG-142 .... $15.00+
RG-143 .... $10.00+
RG-144 .... $20.00+
RG-145 .... $10.00+

Page 123
Left Side
949 .... $40.00+
950 .... $40.00+
951 .... $75.00+
6459 .... $40.00+
6460 .... $50.00+
6513 .... $50.00+
6603 .... $50.00+
Right Side
991-HF (Triple) .... $125.00+
995-HF (Triple) .... $150.00+

Page 124
Left Side
991-HF (Single) .... $60.00+
992-HF (Single) .... $60.00+
992-HF (Triple) .... $125.00+
994-HF (Single) .... $60.00+
994-HF (Triple) .... $100.00+
995-HF (Single) .... $75.00+
Right Side
107 .... $20.00+
108-H .... $25.00+
109-S .... $10.00+
109-S (Gold Tweed) .... $10.00+
110-H .... $10.00+

Page 124

111-H	$15.00+
112	$8.00+
113	$8.00+
113 (Gold Tweed)	$8.00+
114	$15.00+
115	$10.00+
116	$15.00+
118	$15.00+
118 (Gold Tweed)	$10.00+
119	$15.00+
702	$20.00+
811-H	$20.00+
811-H (Gold Tweed)	$15.00+
812-H	$30.00+
813-H	$15.00+
R-1894	$10.00+
R-1907	$15.00+
117	$10.00+
112/115/116	$40.00+ set

Page 125

Left Side - Reference Only
Right Side

109-S	$10.00+
324-S	$45.00+
325-H	$20.00
329-H	$40.00+
330	$20.00+
410-H	$100.00+
426-S	$35.00+
430-H	$45.00+
R-1285	$15.00+ pair
R-1406	$45.00+
R-1702	$55.00+
R-1724	$35.00+
R-1743	$100.00+
R-1752	$40.00+
R-1776	$35.00+
R-1915	$30.00+
R-1916	$75.00+
R-1919	$20.00+
R-1920	$30.00+
RG-68-X	$10.00+
RG-82-X	$15.00+
RG-87-X	$30.00+
RG-114-X	$15.00+
RG-131-X	$15.00+
RG-136-X	$20.00+ pair
RG-137-X	$40.00+
RG-138-X	$40.00+
RG-145-X	$10.00+

Page 126

Left Side - All prices on this side are priced as being in Gold Tweeds.

109-S	$10.00+
113	$8.00+
113-W	$40.00+ set
114	$15.00+
120	$15.00+
121	$15.00+
121-WF	$40.00+
125	$8.00+
317-H	$15.00+
318-H	$35.00+
319-H	$30.00+
322-H	$30.00+ pair
324-S	$45.00+
325-H	$20.00+
329-H	$40.00+
414	$40.00+
424	$30.00+
426-S	$35.00+
429-S	$50.00+

Page 126

430-H	$45.00+
431-S	$40.00+
510-H	$100.00+
702	$20.00+
811-H	$20.00+
813-H	$15.00+
R-1285	$15.00+ pair
R-1504/05	$75.00+
R-1724	$35.00+
R-1730	$15.00+
R-1752	$40.00+
R-1899	$30.00+
R-1916	$35.00+
R-1920	$30.00+
RG-63-X	$15.00+
RG-68-X	$10.00+
RG-114-X	$15.00+
RG-115-X	$10.00+
RG-145-X	$10.00+

Right Side

105	$15.00+
106	$20.00+
107	$20.00+
113	$8.00+
113-W	$40.00+ set
114	$15.00+
117	$10.00+
120	$15.00+
122	$20.00+
123-S	$15.00+
124-S	$15.00+
125	$8.00+
126	$15.00+
701	$40.00+
702	$20.00+
703	$40.00+
811-H	$20.00+
813-H	$15.00+
R-1311	$15.00+
R-1663	$15.00+
R-1665	$25.00+
R-1718	$15.00+
R-1718/19/20	$35.00+ set
R-1719	$10.00+
R-1720	$8.00+
R-1723	$20.00+
R-1735	$20.00+
R-1755	$20.00+
R-1756	$15.00+
R-1836	$10.00+
R-1894	$10.00+
R-1899	$30.00+
R-1941-S	$10.00+
SP-12	$8.00+

Page 127

Left Side

976-H	$75.00+
6001	$60.00+
6002	$60.00+
6002	$60.00+
6015-H	$60.00+
6015-H (Gold Tweed)	$50.00+
6594-SC	$75.00+
6596-SC	$90.00+

Right Side

409-JC	$100.00+
948-JC (Double)	$150.00+
948-JC (Single)	$100.00+
967-JC	$90.00+
1943-JC	$100.00+
6594-SC/6459-JC	$300.00+ set

Page 127

6594-SC/973-JC	$150.00+ set
6594-SCJC	$100.00+

Page 128

Left Side - Reference Only
Right Side - All prices on this side are priced as being in Gold Tweeds.

109-S	$10.00+
121	$15.00+
121-WF	$40.00+ set
125	$8.00+
127	$10.00+
128	$10.00+
132	$20.00+
134	$15.00+
137-S	$10.00+
140-H	$10.00+
141-H	$10.00+
328-S	$20.00+
340	$25.00+
405	$75.00+
419	$60.00+
436	$40.00+
438	$60.00+
450	$15.00+
702	$20.00+
813-H	$15.00+
827-H	$15.00+
R-1714-S	$20.00+
R-1941-S	$10.00+
RG-82-X	$15.00+
RG-145-X	$10.00+
RG-150-X	$15.00+

Page 129

Left Side - Top Section

A. (19-H)	$50.00+
B. (18-H)	$15.00+
C. (16-H)	$75.00+
D. (15-H)	$50.00+
E. (6-H)	$30.00+
F. (17-S)	$40.00+
G. (7-H)	$15.00+

Left Side - Bottom Section
All pieces priced on Page 102, (Right Side)
Right Side

316-H	$35.00+
331-S	$20.00+
332	$20.00+
333	$20.00+
334	$20.00+ pair
335	$25.00+
336	$20.00+ pair
337	$15.00+
337	$15.00+
339	$15.00+
408	$25.00+
413	$15.00+
436	$50.00+
438	$75.00+
439	$40.00+
441-S	$50.00+
445-H	$50.00+
449	$60.00+
451	$40.00+
452	$60.00+
453	$60.00+
R-1233	$15.00+
R-1285	$15.00+ pair
R-1745	$20.00+
R-1746	$20.00+ pair

Page 130

Left Side

113	$8.00+
117	$10.00+
128	$10.00+
129	$10.00+
138	$8.00+
139	$15.00+
318-H	$35.00+
322-H	$30.00+ pair
331-S	$20.00+
332	$20.00+
335	$25.00+
336	$20.00+ pair
337	$15.00+
339	$15.00+
439	$40.00+
441-S	$50.00+
446	$40.00+
447	$35.00+
449	$60.00+
450	$15.00+
451	$40.00+
452	$60.00+
702	$20.00+
706	$25.00+
809-H	$45.00+
813-H	$15.00+
825-H	$35.00+
829	$60.00+
R-1311	$15.00+
R-1714-S	$20.00+
R-1752	$40.00+
R-1755	$20.00+
R-1759	$30.00+
R-1760	$25.00+ pair
R-1891	$100.00+
R-1915	$30.00+
R-1920	$30.00+
RG-81-X	$45.00+
SP-12	$8.00+

Right Side

306 (Gold Tweed)	$15.00+
323	$20.00+
330	$15.00+
415	$15.00+
421	$100.00+
426-S	$50.00+
443-H	$25.00+
444-H	$60.00+
445-H	$50.00+
450	$15.00+
612	$50.00+
613	$50.00+
706	$25.00+
807-H	$75.00+
3660	$75.00+
R-466	$20.00+
R-1285	$15.00+ pair
R-1702	$55.00+
R-1730	$15.00+
R-1824	$30.00+
R-1944	$30.00+
R-1946	$45.00+

Page 131

Left Side

112	$8.00+
113	$8.00+
115	$10.00+
117	$10.00+
125	$8.00+

Page 131

128 .... $10.00+
129 .... $10.00+
130 .... $15.00+
133 .... $20.00+
135 .... $10.00+
138 .... $8.00+
702 .... $20.00+
813-H .... $15.00+
R-1311 .... $15.00+
R-1665 .... $25.00+
R-1718/19/20 .... $35.00+ set
R-1720 .... $8.00+
R-1723 .... $20.00+
R-1735 .... $20.00+
R-1755 .... $20.00+
R-1836 .... $10.00+
R-1894 .... $10.00+
R-1941-S .... $10.00+
SP-12 .... $8.00+

Right Side
105 .... $15.00+
106 .... $20.00+
107 .... $20.00+
109-S .... $10.00+
110-H .... $10.00+
113-W .... $40.00+ set
116 .... $15.00+
116/115/112 .... $35.00+ set
119 .... $15.00+
122 .... $20.00+
123-S .... $15.00+
127 .... $10.00+
129 .... $10.00+
131 .... $15.00+
134 .... $15.00+
136-S .... $20.00+
139 .... $15.00+
140-H .... $10.00+
R-1663 .... $15.00+
R-1714-S .... $20.00+
R-1718 .... $15.00+
R-1719 .... $10.00+
R-1735 .... $20.00+

Page 132

Left Side - Reference Only
Right Side
306 .... $15.00+
318 .... $35.00+
322-H .... $30.00+ pair
325-H .... $20.00+
329-H .... $40.00+
346 .... $40.00+
350-H .... $75.00+
354-S .... $20.00+
359 .... $30.00+
413 .... $15.00+
424 .... $30.00+
430-H .... $45.00+
439 .... $40.00+
458 .... $15.00+
459 .... $15.00+
461 .... $15.00+
465 .... $85.00+
467-S .... $30.00+
815-H .... $60.00+
R-31 .... $75.00+
R-1224 .... $75.00+
R-1730 .... $15.00+
R-1752 .... $40.00+
R-1776 .... $35.00+

R-1919 .... $20.00+
R-1920 .... $30.00+
RG-68-X .... $10.00+
RG-114-X .... $15.00+
RG-115-X .... $10.00+

Page 133

Left Side
332 .... $20.00+
333 .... $20.00+
334 .... $20.00+ pair
335 .... $25.00+
336 .... $20.00+ pair
337 .... $15.00+
349-H .... $15.00+
359 .... $30.00+
408 .... $25.00+
438 .... $75.00+
439 .... $40.00+
449 .... $60.00+
450 .... $15.00+
452 .... $60.00+
467-S .... $30.00+
472 .... $50.00+
473 .... $50.00+
711-S .... $25.00+
R-31 .... $75.00+
R-1233 .... $15.00+
R-1285 .... $15.00+ pair
R-1702 .... $55.00+
R-1730 .... $15.00+
R-1743 .... $100.00+
R-1745 .... $20.00+
R-1746 .... $20.00+ pair
R-1919 .... $20.00+
RG-81-X .... $45.00+
RG-82-X .... $15.00+
RG-86-X .... $30.00+
RG-114-X .... $15.00+

Right Side
339 .... $15.00+
350-H .... $75.00+
351 .... $20.00+
352 .... $25.00+
353 .... $25.00+ pair
354-S .... $20.00+
358 .... $60.00+ pair
436 .... $50.00+
458 .... $15.00+
459 .... $15.00+
461 .... $15.00+
463-H .... $40.00+
464 .... $20.00+
465 .... $85.00+
468-S .... $45.00+
469 .... $45.00+
472 .... $50.00+
706 .... $25.00+
711-S .... $25.00+
R-709 .... $15.00+
R-1730 .... $15.00+
RG-63-X .... $15.00+
RG-178-X .... $15.00+
RG-179-X .... $15.00+

Page 134

Left Side
113 .... $8.00+
117 .... $10.00+
125 .... $8.00+
128 .... $10.00+
129 .... $10.00+

130 .... $15.00+
133 .... $20.00+
135 .... $10.00+
138 .... $8.00+
153 .... $10.00+
154 .... $10.00+
156 .... $15.00+
158 .... $20.00+
160 .... $15.00+
162 .... $20.00+
R-1311 .... $15.00+
R-1723 .... $20.00+
R-1755 .... $20.00+
R-1894 .... $10.00+
SP-12 .... $8.00+

Right Side
105 .... $15.00+
107 .... $20.00+
110-H .... $10.00+
113-W .... $40.00+ set
119 .... $15.00+
127 .... $10.00+
134 .... $15.00+
144 .... $10.00+
146-S .... $10.00+
148-S .... $10.00+
149 .... $10.00+
150 .... $10.00+
151 .... $8.00+
152 .... $8.00+
155 .... $10.00+
157 .... $15.00+
159 .... $10.00+
163-S .... $20.00+
R-1718 .... $15.00+
R-1718/19/20 .... $35.00+ set
R-1719 .... $10.00+
R-1720 .... $8.00+
R-1735 .... $20.00+
R-1836 .... $10.00+

Page 135

Left Side
3-H .... $45.00+
5-H .... $20.00+
7-H .... $15.00+
10-H .... $40.00+
13-H .... $35.00+
20-H .... $25.00+
21-H .... $75.00+
22-H .... $40.00+
23-H .... $75.00+
833 .... $15.00+
RG-170 .... $15.00+
RG-171 .... $15.00+
RG-172 .... $15.00+
RG-173 .... $15.00+
RG-175/176 .... $25.00+ set
RG-178 .... $10.00+
RG-179 .... $10.00+
RG-180 .... $8.00+
RG-181 .... $10.00+
RG-183 .... $25.00+
RG-184 .... $8.00+
RG-185 .... $8.00+
RG-186 .... $8.00+
RG-187 .... $8.00+

Right Side
145 .... $20.00+
702 .... $20.00+
708 .... $30.00+
710 .... $35.00+

Page 135

813-H .... $15.00+
827-H .... $15.00+
839 .... $15.00+
839/840/841 .... $35.00+ set
840 .... $10.00+
841 .... $10.00+

Bottom Section
109-S .... $10.00+
125 .... $8.00+
127 .... $10.00+
128 .... $20.00+
132 .... $20.00+
134 .... $15.00+
137-S .... $10.00+
155 .... $10.00+
156 .... $15.00+
157 .... $15.00+
702 .... $20.00+
710 .... $35.00+
813-H .... $15.00+
827-H .... $15.00+
839 .... $15.00+
839/840/841 .... $35.00+ set
840 .... $10.00+
841 .... $10.00+

Page 136

323 .... $20.00+
325-H .... $20.00+
331-S .... $20.00+
359 .... $30.00+
361 .... $80.00+ pair
408 .... $25.00+
411-H .... $125.00+
835 .... $200.00+
836 .... $50.00+
837 .... $75.00+
838 .... $75.00+
R-1619-S .... $25.00+
RG-68-X .... $10.00+
RG-137-X .... $40.00+

Page 137

Left Side
512 .... $40.00+
513 .... $40.00+
515/16/17 .... $60.00+ set
516/517 .... $50.00+ set
842 .... $35.00+
842/843 .... $75.00+
842/843 (Gold Tweed) ..... $50.00+
843 .... $25.00+
858 .... $50.00+
859 .... $60.00+
864-S .... $25.00+
865-S .... $50.00+

Right Side
454-H .... $60.00+
495 .... $40.00+
612 .... $50.00+
613 .... $50.00+
6343 .... $50.00+
R-1510 .... $100.00+
R-1762 .... $150.00+
R-1810 .... $30.00+
R-1811 .... $30.00+

Page 138

Left Side
Top Section - All prices on this section are priced as being in Aztec Gold.

363

Page 138

1-H	$200.00+
2-H	$100.00+
13-H	$50.00+
125	$15.00+
191	$25.00+
1311	$30.00+
4001	$25.00+
5600	$250.00+
R-1915	$50.00+
R-1919	$40.00+

Middle Section - All prices on this section are priced as being in Florentine Gold.

382	$150.00+
385	$20.00+
411-H	$125.00+
449	$60.00+
518	$75.00+
519-H	$60.00+
711-S	$25.00+
868 R & L	$50.00+
4002	$30.00+
4003	$50.00+
R-1224	$75.00+
R-1510	$200.00+
R-1915	$30.00+
R-1919	$20.00+

Bottom Section - All prices on this section are priced as being in Black/White Lava or Gold Tweed.

1-H	$200.00+
27-H	$25.00+
157	$25.00+
165	$15.00+
185-S	$8.00+
190	$10.00+
386	$15.00+ pair
411-H	$200.00+
413	$30.00+
514	$50.00+
864-S	$25.00+
4003	$100.00+
R-1730	$40.00+
R-1919	$40.00+

Right Side

505	$125.00+
514	$50.00+
518	$75.00+
519-H	$60.00+
624	$125.00+
625	$125.00+
626	$125.00+
627	$85.00+
868	$50.00+

Page 139

Left Side - All prices on this side are priced as being in Black Mistique.

1-H	$250.00+
2-H	$100.00+
8-H	$50.00+
9-H	$60.00+
13-H	$50.00+
16-H	$125.00+
25-H	$100.00+
26-H	$100.00+
117	$20.00+
125	$15.00+
127	$20.00+
149	$20.00+
153	$20.00+
170-S	$20.00+
173	$20.00+

Page 139

183-F	$25.00+
183-F/184-F	$50.00+ set
184-F	$15.00+
352	$60.00+
353	$45.00+ pair
358	$75.00+ pair
388	$75.00+
390	$100.00+
408	$75.00+
493	$125.00+
715	$50.00+
813	$30.00+
857	$250.00+
889	$25.00+
1000	$25.00+
1008	$20.00+
1014	$20.00+
1016-S	$35.00+
1017-S	$35.00+
4004	$75.00+
4005	$150.00+
4006	$90.00+
4011	$125.00+
R-1311	$30.00+
R-1730	$60.00+
R-1836	$20.00+
R-1915	$60.00+
R-1919	$40.00+
RG-56-X	$25.00+
RG-68-X	$25.00+
RG-114-X	$25.00+
RG-170-X	$45.00+

Right Side

117	$10.00+
125	$8.00+
129	$10.00+
130	$15.00+
148-S	$10.00+
149	$10.00+
164	$8.00+
170-S	$10.00+
183-F	$15.00+
183-F/184-F	$30.00+ set
184-F	$8.00+
188-S	$10.00+
191	$15.00+
192	$15.00+
382	$150.00+
386	$15.00+
393	$25.00+
394	$30.00+
395	$35.00+
396	$30.00+
612	$50.00+
613	$50.00+
631	$150.00+
702	$20.00+
718	$25.00+
813	$15.00+
889	$15.00+
894	$150.00+
1002	$10.00+
1004	$20.00+
1011	$10.00+
1011/1012	$20.00+
1012	$8.00+
1013	$25.00+
1014	$10.00+
1016-S	$20.00+
4003	$50.00+
4012	$25.00+
4013	$35.00+

Page 139

4015	$100.00+
4020	$15.00+
4021	$15.00+
6343	$50.00+
R-1510	$100.00+
R-1723	$20.00+
R-1730	$15.00+
R-1743	$100.00+
R-1755	$20.00+
R-1762	$150.00+
R-1915	$30.00+
R-1919	$20.00+

Page 140

Left Side

125	$8.00+
128	$10.00+
144	$10.00+
165	$8.00+
185-S	$10.00+
335	$25.00+
336	$20.00+ pair
379	$30.00+
384-S	$20.00+
397	$20.00+
413	$15.00+
430-H	$45.00+
482	$75.00+
483	$60.00+
491-H	$45.00+
612	$50.00+
613	$50.00+
707-S	$20.00+
709	$15.00+
711-S	$25.00+
716	$20.00+
717	$25.00+
718	$25.00+
878-H	$25.00+
889	$15.00+
895	$30.00+
1003	$15.00+
1011	$10.00+
1011/1012	$20.00+ set
1012	$8.00+
1013	$25.00+
1014	$10.00+
1017-S	$20.00+
1019	$20.00+
4000-S	$35.00+
4007	$60.00+
4008	$45.00+
4012	$25.00+
4019	$25.00+
4020	$15.00+
4021	$15.00+
R-1233	$15.00+
R-1285	$15.00+ pair
R-1810	$30.00+
R-1811	$30.00+
R-1894	$10.00+
R-1915	$30.00+
R-1919	$20.00+
RG-25-X	$25.00+
RG-68-X	$10.00+
RG-124-X	$20.00+
RG-137-X	$40.00+
SP-12	$8.00+

Right Side

110-H	$10.00+
127	$10.00+

128	$10.00+
135	$10.00+
138	$8.00+
144	$15.00+
164	$8.00+
188-S	$10.00+
306	$30.00+
343	$15.00+
345-S	$20.00+
384-S	$30.00+
392	$20.00+ pair
396	$30.00+
397	$30.00+
399	$40.00+
455	$45.00+
472	$40.00+
477	$75.00+
491-H	$45.00+
499-S	$30.00+
514	$100.00+
612	$50.00+
613	$50.00+
716	$30.00+
717	$40.00+
718	$20.00+
848-H	$40.00+
849-H	$10.00+
849-H/850-H	$25.00+ set
850-H	$15.00+
854-H	$40.00+
856-H	$30.00+
862-H	$50.00+
873-H	$75.00+
878-H	$20.00+
879-H	$15.00+
879/880	$40.00+ set
880-H	$15.00+
890	$15.00+
891	$30.00+
895	$30.00+
1005	$20.00+
1009	$10.00+
1018	$35.00+
1019	$20.00+
3000	$30.00+
3660	$75.00+
4000-S	$35.00+
4011	$50.00+
4017	$45.00+
4018	$45.00+
4019	$25.00+
4022	$40.00+
4023	$30.00+
4024	$25.00+
R-1233	$30.00+
R-1285	$15.00+ pair
R-1619-S	$55.00+
R-1735	$15.00+
R-1755	$20.00+
R-1759	$30.00+
R-1760	$20.00+ pair
R-1810	$35.00+
R-1811	$35.00+
R-1844	$30.00+
R-1845	$30.00+

Page 141

Left Side

HT-30	$100.00+
HT-31	$50.00+
HT-32	$100.00+
HT-33	$60.00+
HT-34	$20.00+

HT-35 ...... $100.00+
HT-36 ...... $50.00+
HT-37 ...... $20.00+
HT-38 ...... $50.00+
HT-39 ...... $40.00+
HT-40 ...... $75.00+
Right Side
128 ...... $10.00+
138 ...... $8.00+
183-F ...... $15.00+
184-F ...... $8.00+
183-F/184-F ...... $25.00+
188-S ...... $10.00+
813 ...... $15.00+
1006 ...... $20.00+
1008 ...... $10.00+
1009 ...... $10.00+
1011 ...... $15.00+
1011/1012 ...... $20.00+
1012 ...... $8.00+
1013 ...... $25.00+
1014 ...... $10.00+
1015 ...... $10.00+
1017-S ...... $20.00+
1019 ...... $20.00+

Page 142
Left Side
523 ...... $50.00+
724 ...... $60.00+
723 ...... $50.00+
3028 ...... $35.00+
Right Side: This glaze can bring 2-3 times the shape value
408 ...... $25.00+
493 ...... $40.00+
1074 ...... $15.00+
1915 ...... $30.00+
1919 ...... $20.00+
3051 ...... $20.00+
3052 ...... $15.00+
4034 ...... $40.00+
4068 ...... $50.00+
4069 ...... $50.00+
4071 ...... $40.00+
4073 ...... $30.00+
4075 ...... $40.00+

Page 143
Left Side
722 ...... $30.00+
890 ...... $15.00+
1056 ...... $10.00+
1068 ...... $10.00+
1072 ...... $40.00+
1075 ...... $15.00+
3051 ...... $20.00+
3052 ...... $15.00+
3053 ...... $15.00+
3053/54 ...... $40.00+ set
3054 ...... $20.00+ pair
4068 ...... $50.00+
4070 ...... $75.00+
4071 ...... $40.00+
4073 ...... $30.00+
4075 ...... $40.00+
Right Side
155 ...... $10.00+
165 ...... $8.00+
183 ...... $15.00+
184 ...... $8.00+
325 ...... $40.00+

335 ...... $25.00+
336 ...... $20.00+ pair
364 ...... $25.00+
382 ...... $150.00+
707 ...... $20.00+
813 ...... $15.00+
1046 ...... $15.00+
1058 ...... $10.00+
1059 ...... $10.00+
1894 ...... $15.00+
1915 ...... $30.00+
1919 ...... $20.00+
4012 ...... $25.00+
4040 ...... $35.00+
4043 ...... $25.00+
4044 ...... $20.00+
4050 ...... $50.00+
4054 ...... $40.00+
4055 ...... $60.00+
4056 ...... $25.00+
4063 ...... $45.00+
4064 ...... $35.00+
RG-68-X ...... $10.00+

Page 144
Left Side
155 ...... $10.00+
165 ...... $8.00+
173 ...... $10.00+
183 ...... $15.00+
183/184 ...... $25.00+ set
184 ...... $8.00+
325 ...... $40.00+
335 ...... $25.00+
335/336 ...... $50.00+ set
336 ...... $20.00+ pair
364 ...... $25.00+
382 ...... $150.00+
707 ...... $20.00+
721 ...... $20.00+
813 ...... $15.00+
896 ...... $100.00+
896W ...... $100.00+
1045 ...... $10.00+
1046 ...... $15.00+
1058 ...... $10.00+
1059 ...... $10.00+
1063 ...... $10.00+
1066 ...... $10.00+
1894 ...... $15.00+
1915 ...... $30.00+
1919 ...... $20.00+
3040 ...... $20.00+
3041 ...... $25.00+
3045 ...... $20.00+ pair
3045/48 ...... $40.00+ set
3048 ...... $20.00+
4012 ...... $25.00+
4040 ...... $35.00+
4042 ...... $50.00+
4043 ...... $25.00+
4044 ...... $20.00+
4050 ...... $50.00+
4054 ...... $40.00+
4055 ...... $60.00+
4056 ...... $25.00+
4063 ...... $45.00+
4064 ...... $35.00+
4065 ...... $30.00+
RG-68-X ...... $10.00+
Right Side
153 ...... $10.00+

155 ...... $10.00+
165 ...... $8.00+
173 ...... $10.00+
335 ...... $25.00+
336 ...... $20.00+ pair
436 ...... $50.00+
455 ...... $45.00+
491 ...... $45.00+
518 ...... $75.00+
709 ...... $15.00+
813 ...... $15.00+
842/43 ...... $75.00+ set
1045 ...... $10.00+
1054 ...... $10.00+
1056 ...... $10.00+
1063 ...... $10.00+
1072 ...... $40.00+
1233 ...... $15.00+
1504/5 ...... $75.00+
1810 ...... $30.00+
1811 ...... $30.00+
1894 ...... $15.00+
3034 ...... $40.00+
3040 ...... $20.00+
3041 ...... $25.00+
3043 ...... $60.00+
4043 ...... $25.00+
4044 ...... $20.00+
4054 ...... $40.00+
4055 ...... $60.00+
4056 ...... $25.00+
RG-60-X ...... $20.00+

Page 145
Left Side
8030 ...... $150.00+
8031 ...... $150.00+
HT-45 ...... $90.00+
HT-51 ...... $25.00+
HT-52 ...... $25.00+
HT-57 ...... $65.00+
HT-58 ...... $70.00+
HT-59 ...... $85.00+
Right Side
HT-44 ...... $150.00+
HT-45 ...... $90.00+
HT-46 ...... $75.00+
HT-47 ...... $150.00+
HT-51 ...... $25.00+
HT-52 ...... $25.00+
HT-57 ...... $65.00+
HT-58 ...... $75.00+
HT-59 ...... $85.00+

Page 146
Left Side
721 ...... $20.00+
722 ...... $30.00+
724 ...... $50.00+
725 ...... $25.00+
727 ...... $20.00+
1066 ...... $10.00+
1068 ...... $10.00+
1072 ...... $40.00+
1073 ...... $20.00+
3058 ...... $20.00+
4063 ...... $45.00+
8056 ...... $10.00+
8057 ...... $10.00+
Right Side
117 ...... $10.00+
125 ...... $8.00+

135 ...... $10.00+
138 ...... $8.00+
153 ...... $10.00+
165 ...... $8.00+
1008 ...... $10.00+
1014 ...... $10.00+
1027 ...... $8.00+
1028 ...... $8.00+
1029 ...... $8.00+
1030 ...... $8.00+
1044 ...... $8.00+
1046 ...... $15.00+
1054 ...... $10.00+
1056 ...... $10.00+
1057 ...... $15.00+
1058 ...... $10.00+
1061 ...... $10.00+
1062 ...... $10.00+
1063 ...... $10.00+
1064 ...... $10.00+
1066 ...... $10.00+
1068 ...... $10.00+
1076 ...... $15.00+
1078 ...... $8.00+
1079 ...... $10.00+
1836 ...... $15.00+
1894 ...... $15.00+
SP-12 ...... $8.00+
SP-42 ...... $10.00+

Page 147
Left Side
127 ...... $10.00+
128 ...... $10.00+
149 ...... $10.00+
155 ...... $10.00+
162 ...... $20.00+
813 ...... $15.00+
1002 ...... $10.00+
1004 ...... $20.00+
1005 ...... $20.00+
1006 ...... $20.00+
1016 ...... $20.00+
1021 ...... $10.00+
1039 ...... $15.00+
1041 ...... $15.00+
1059 ...... $40.00+
1072 ...... $40.00+
1073 ...... $25.00+
1074 ...... $15.00+
1075 ...... $15.00+
1311 ...... $15.00+
1723 ...... $20.00+
1735 ...... $15.00+
1755 ...... $20.00+
Right Side
125 (Gold Tweed) ...... $8.00+
128 (Gold Tweed) ...... $10.00+
144 ...... $10.00+
165 (Gold Tweed) ...... $8.00+
173 (Gold Tweed) ...... $10.00+
184 ...... $8.00+
720 (Gold Tweed) ...... $15.00+
722 ...... $30.00+
726 (Gold Tweed) ...... $40.00+
726/8054/1076 ...... $65.00+ set
727 (Gold Tweed) ...... $20.00+
813 ...... $15.00+
1006 ...... $20.00+
1044 (Gold Tweed) ...... $10.00+
1046 ...... $15.00+
1054 ...... $10.00+

1056 .... $10.00+
1058 .... $10.00+
1063 .... $10.00+
1066 (Gold Tweed) .... $10.00+
1068 (Gold Tweed) .... $10.00+
1076 (Gold Tweed) .... $15.00+
1080 .... $20.00+
1311 .... $15.00+
8054 (Gold Tweed) .... $15.00+

Page 148
Left Side
183/184 .... $25.00+ set
702 .... $20.00+
720 .... $15.00+
722 .... $30.00+
726 .... $40.00+
813 .... $15.00+
890 .... $15.00+
1029/39/40 .... $30.00+ set
1044 .... $8.00+
1076 .... $15.00+
8054 .... $15.00+
Boot Set .... $65.00+
Right Side
1-H .... $150.00+
9-H .... $40.00+
26 .... $100.00+
345 .... $20.00+
408 .... $25.00+
456 .... $75.00+
477 .... $60.00+
483 .... $60.00+
493 .... $40.00+
616 .... $60.00+
702 .... $20.00+
707 .... $20.00+
720 .... $15.00+
722 .... $30.00+
813 .... $15.00+
879 .... $8.00+
890 .... $15.00+
1029 .... $8.00+
1029/39/40 .... $30.00+ set
1039 .... $15.00+
1040 .... $5.00+
1044 .... $8.00+
1285 .... $20.00+ pair
1730 .... $30.00+
3001 .... $15.00+
3003 .... $15.00+
3003/4 .... $40.00+ set
3004 .... $15.00+ pair
3027 .... $15.00+
3044 .... $40.00+ pair
4064 .... $35.00+
RG-42-X .... $15.00+
RG-56-X .... $10.00+
RG-68-X .... $10.00+
RG-92-X .... $8.00+
RG-124-X .... $15.00+
SP-41/42/43 .... $40.00+ set

Page 149
Left Side
1-H .... $150.00+
26-H .... $75.00+
408 .... $25.00+
493 .... $40.00+
813 .... $15.00+
857-W .... $150.00+
1008 .... $10.00+

1014 .... $10.00+
1054 .... $10.00+
1066 .... $10.00+
1730 .... $30.00+
1743 .... $100.00+
1915 .... $30.00+
1919 .... $20.00+
4001 .... $15.00+
4030 .... $35.00+
4031 .... $25.00+
4038 .... $35.00+
RG-56-X .... $10.00+
RG-68-X .... $10.00+
RG-92-X .... $8.00+
RG-114-X .... $15.00+
SP-42 .... $10.00+
Right Side
1-H .... $150.00+
9-H .... $40.00+
26-H .... $75.00+
117 .... $10.00+
125 .... $8.00+
127 .... $10.00+
128 .... $10.00+
135 .... $10.00+
138 .... $8.00+
149 .... $10.00+
153 .... $10.00+
183 .... $15.00+
183/84 .... $25.00+ set
408 .... $25.00+
493 .... $40.00+
720 .... $15.00+
813 .... $15.00+
857 .... $150.00+
857-W .... $150.00+
1004 .... $20.00+
1008 .... $10.00+
1014 .... $10.00+
1016 .... $20.00+
1028 .... $8.00+
1029 .... $8.00+
1029/39/40 .... $30.00+ set
1039 .... $15.00+
1040 .... $5.00+
1044 .... $8.00+
1046 .... $15.00+
1054 .... $10.00+
1056 .... $10.00+
1058 .... $10.00+
1059 .... $10.00+
1061 .... $10.00+
1066 .... $10.00+
1311 .... $15.00+
1723 .... $20.00+
1730 .... $30.00+
1743 .... $100.00+
1755 .... $20.00+
1836 .... $15.00+
1915 .... $30.00+
1919 .... $20.00+
3034 .... $40.00+
3038 .... $60.00+
3039 .... $50.00+
4001 .... $15.00+
4011 .... $60.00+
4030 .... $35.00+
4031 .... $25.00+
4034 .... $40.00+
4038 .... $35.00+
4050 .... $50.00+
RG-56-X .... $10.00+

RG-68-X .... $10.00+
RG-92-X .... $8.00+
RG-114-X .... $15.00+
SP-41/42/43 .... $40.00+ set

Page 150
Left Side - Reference Only
Right Side
2022 .... $10.00+
4134 .... $35.00+
4135 .... $30.00+
4136 .... $20.00+
8113 .... $15.00+

Page 151
Left Side
526 .... $65.00+
527 .... $110.00+
744 .... $40.00+
745 .... $50.00+
2062 .... $60.00+
2063 .... $25.00+
2065 .... $25.00+
2066 .... $60.00+
3135 .... $125.00+
3136 .... $60.00+
8169 .... $50.00+
8170 .... $75.00+
8171 .... $75.00+
8172 .... $75.00+
8175 .... $200.00+
8176 .... $250.00+
Lamp .... $300.00+
Right Side
2055 .... $15.00+
2056 .... $20.00+
2057 .... $20.00+
3129 .... $25.00+
3130 .... $40.00+
4141 .... $75.00+
4142 .... $75.00+
4143 .... $60.00+
8161 .... $30.00+
8163 .... $75.00+
8164 .... $50.00+
8165/66 .... $100.00+ set
8166 .... $20.00+
Note: Peasant glazes bring much less.

Page 152
Left Side
709 .... $15.00+
721 .... $20.00+
1915 .... $30.00+
1919 .... $20.00+
2043 .... $8.00+
2045 .... $8.00+
2051 .... $8.00+
3045 .... $20.00+ pair
3057 .... $45.00+
3076 .... $10.00+
3082 .... $8.00+
3108 .... $8.00+
3126 .... $15.00+
3127 .... $15.00+
4012 .... $25.00+
4106 .... $30.00+
4138 .... $15.00+
8118 .... $15.00+
Owl Lighter .... $10.00+
RG-68-X .... $10.00+
Right Side
721 .... $20.00+

728 .... $25.00+ set
1068 .... $10.00+
1086 .... $8.00+
2006 .... $8.00+
2025 .... $8.00+
2043 .... $8.00+
2045 .... $8.00+
3074 .... $10.00+
3075 .... $15.00+
3088 .... $10.00+
3102 .... $10.00+
4103 .... $15.00+
8084 .... $40.00+ set
8084 .... $10.00+
8085 .... $10.00+
8086 .... $10.00+
8088 .... $20.00+
8092 .... $10.00+
8097 .... $15.00+

Page 153
Left Side
491 .... $45.00+
612 .... $50.00+
613 .... $50.00+
1233 .... $15.00+
2043 .... $8.00+
2045 .... $8.00+
2051 .... $8.00+
3086 .... $10.00+
3126 .... $15.00+
3127 .... $15.00+
4088 .... $15.00+
4131 .... $8.00+
4132 .... $10.00+
4133 .... $15.00+
4138 .... $15.00+
4140 .... $30.00+
8089 .... $20.00+
8090 .... $20.00+
SP-42 .... $10.00+
Right Side
491 .... $45.00+
1915 .... $30.00+
1919 .... $20.00+
4012 .... $25.00+
4054 .... $40.00+
4056 .... $25.00+
4070 .... $75.00+
4103 .... $15.00+
4106 .... $30.00+
4127 .... $20.00+
4128 .... $20.00+
4131 .... $8.00+
4132 .... $10.00+
4133 .... $15.00+
4138 .... $15.00+
4140 .... $30.00+
8097 .... $20.00+
RG-68-X .... $10.00+

Page 154
Left Side
520 .... $30.00+
735 .... $15.00+
736 .... $15.00+
2006 .... $8.00+
2034 .... $8.00+
2051 .... $8.00+
3074 .... $10.00+
3075 .... $15.00+
3126 .... $15.00+

3127 .... $15.00+
4070 .... $75.00+
4103-X .... $15.00+
4122 .... $15.00+
4123 .... $15.00+
4127 .... $20.00+
4128 .... $20.00+
4138 .... $15.00+
4140 .... $30.00+
8097 .... $20.00+
8134 .... $20.00+
8141 .... $10.00+
8141 (4-piece set) . $40.00+ set
8142 .... $10.00+
8145 .... $10.00+

Right Side
628 .... $45.00+
660 .... $45.00+
661 .... $65.00+
709 .... $15.00+
1068 .... $10.00+
1233/3108 .... $25.00+ set
1510 .... $100.00+
3044/3077 .... $40.00+ set
3045/3076 .... $25.00+ set
3057 .... $45.00+
3082 .... $8.00+
3086 .... $8.00+
3088 .... $10.00+
3093 .... $8.00+
3102 .... $10.00+
3103 .... $8.00+

Page 155

Left Side - All prices on this side are priced as being in Mirror Chrome & Mirror Gold.
738 .... $15.00+
2057 .... $20.00+
3096 .... $8.00+
3097 .... $10.00+
3103 .... $10.00+
3112 .... $20.00+
3113 .... $45.00+ set
3120 .... $15.00+
4118 .... $35.00+
4121 .... $20.00+
4143 .... $60.00+
4144 .... $20.00+
4145 .... $20.00+
6707P .... $75.00+
7003P .... $75.00+
7021 .... $75.00+
8113 .... $15.00+
8139 .... $8.00+
8140 .... $15.00+
8167 .... $10.00+
C-7021 .... $100.00+
Right Side - All priced on left side.

Page 156

738 .... $15.00+
1066 .... $10.00+
1311 .... $15.00+
2009 .... $5.00+
2022 .... $10.00+
2023 .... $5.00+
2025 .... $8.00+
2032 .... $5.00+
2033 .... $8.00+
2048 .... $10.00+
2049 .... $5.00+

2050 .... $8.00+
3074 .... $10.00+
3075 .... $15.00+
3096 .... $8.00+
3097 .... $10.00+
3102 .... $10.00+
3109 .... $8.00+
3111 .... $8.00+
3112 .... $20.00+
3113 .... $8.00+ each
3113 .... $45.00+ set
3118 .... $10.00+
3120 .... $15.00+
3121 .... $15.00+
3123 .... $5.00+
3125 .... $10.00+
4117 .... $40.00+
4118 .... $35.00+
4121 .... $20.00+
8056 .... $40.00+ set
8056 .... $10.00+
8057 .... $10.00+
8058 .... $10.00+
8091 .... $15.00+
8109/10 .... $15.00+ set
8113 .... $15.00+
8133 .... $15.00+
8135 .... $60.00+ set
8135C .... $15.00+
8136C .... $10.00+
8137C .... $10.00+
8138C .... $10.00+
8139 .... $8.00+
8140 .... $15.00+

Page 157

Left Side
721 .... $20.00+
1066 .... $10.00+
2009 .... $8.00+
2032 .... $8.00+
3045 .... $20.00+ pair
3055/4074 .... $20.00+ set
3057 .... $45.00+
3058 .... $20.00+
3074 .... $10.00+
3075 .... $15.00+
3087 .... $8.00+
3109 .... $5.00+
3111 .... $5.00+
3118 .... $10.00+
3125 .... $10.00+
4058/60 .... $40.00+ set
4126 .... $25.00+
8056 .... $20.00+
8057 .... $25.00+
8058 .... $10.00+
8063 .... $15.00+
8067 .... $45.00+ set
8079 .... $8.00+
8080 .... $10.00+
8081 .... $10.00+
8087 .... $25.00+ set
8091 .... $15.00+
8109 .... $10.00+
8109/10 .... $15.00+ set
8110 .... $10.00+
8113 .... $15.00+
8118 .... $15.00+
8133 .... $15.00+
8146 .... $45.00+ set
Right Side

153 .... $10.00+
408 .... $25.00+
707 .... $20.00+
728 .... $25.00+ set
741X .... $15.00+
890 .... $15.00+
1054 .... $10.00+
1058 .... $10.00+
1066 .... $10.00+
1091 .... $10.00+
1092 .... $10.00+
1093 .... $10.00+
1311 .... $15.00+
1723 .... $20.00+
1735 .... $15.00+
1752 .... $40.00+
1755 .... $20.00+
1919 .... $20.00+
2011 .... $8.00+
2027 .... $8.00+
2028 .... $8.00+
2044 .... $8.00+
2046X .... $8.00+
2052 .... $10.00+
2053 .... $10.00+
3003/4 .... $40.00+ set
3116X .... $10.00+
3133 .... $20.00+
4030 .... $35.00+
4044 .... $20.00+
4104 .... $35.00+
4107 .... $40.00+
4123 .... $15.00+
4126 .... $25.00+
4131 .... $8.00+
4132 .... $10.00+
4133 .... $15.00+
4140 .... $30.00+
4144 .... $20.00+
4145 .... $20.00+
8156X .... $10.00+
RG-68-X .... $10.00+

Page 158

Left Side
153 .... $10.00+
408 .... $25.00+
707 .... $20.00+
736 .... $15.00+
890 .... $15.00+
1058 .... $10.00+
1066 .... $10.00+
1092 .... $10.00+
1093 .... $10.00+
1915 .... $30.00+
1919 .... $20.00+
2011 .... $8.00+
2027 .... $8.00+
2028 .... $8.00+
2044 .... $8.00+
2052 .... $10.00+
2053 .... $10.00+
3003/4 .... $40.00+ set
3058 .... $20.00+
3133 .... $20.00+
4044 .... $20.00+
4070 .... $75.00+
4104 .... $35.00+
4123 .... $15.00+
4126 .... $25.00+
4131 .... $8.00+
4132 .... $10.00+

4133 .... $15.00+
4140 .... $20.00+
4144 .... $20.00+
4145 .... $20.00+
RG-68-X .... $10.00+
Right Side
612 .... $50.00+
612X .... $50.00+
613 .... $50.00+
613X .... $50.00+
642X .... $30.00+
644 .... $25.00+
644X .... $25.00+
649 .... $15.00+
650 .... $15.00+
655 .... $20.00+
656 .... $20.00+
1762 .... $150.00+
3071 .... $25.00+
8036 .... $30.00+
8100 L/R .... $25.00+ pair
Owl Lighter .... $10.00+

Page 159

Left Side
709 .... $15.00+
3057 .... $45.00+
3074 .... $10.00+
3075 .... $15.00+
3082 .... $8.00+
3086 .... $8.00+
3088 .... $10.00+
3093 .... $8.00+
3102 .... $10.00+
3103 .... $8.00+
3107 .... $8.00+
3108 .... $8.00+
8134 .... $20.00+
Right Side
693 .... $50.00+
695 .... $50.00+
696 .... $50.00+
697 .... $50.00+
698 .... $50.00+
700 .... $50.00+

Page 160

Left Side
746 .... $25.00+
2057 .... $20.00+
2085X .... $10.00+
3130 .... $40.00+
3139 .... $40.00+
3142 .... $20.00+
3144 .... $150.00+
4131X .... $8.00+
4132X .... $10.00+
4152 .... $50.00+
4187 .... $75.00+
8167 .... $15.00+
8188 .... $40.00+
Right Side
746 .... $25.00+
746 (w/out cover) .... $15.00+
2057 .... $20.00+
2085X .... $10.00+
2094X .... $10.00+
3130 .... $40.00+
4131X .... $8.00+
4132X .... $10.00+
4142 .... $75.00+
4143 .... $60.00+

4160X .... $60.00+
4161X .... $50.00+
4162X .... $30.00+
4179 .... $75.00+
4181 .... $75.00+
4182 .... $75.00+
4183 .... $75.00+
4185 .... $50.00+
8167 .... $15.00+
8201 .... $75.00+
8202 .... $65.00+

Page 161
Left Side
2069X .... $10.00+
2070X .... $10.00+
2083X .... $10.00+
2084X .... $10.00+
2094X .... $10.00+
2095X .... $10.00+
4131X .... $8.00+
4132X .... $10.00+
4142 .... $75.00+
4143 .... $60.00+
4160X .... $60.00+
4161X .... $50.00+
4162X .... $30.00+
4179 .... $75.00+
4180 .... $75.00+
4182 .... $75.00+
4183 .... $75.00+
4184 .... $60.00+
4185 .... $50.00+
4186 .... $75.00+
4188 .... $75.00+

Right Side
408X .... $25.00+
738X .... $15.00+
1058X .... $10.00+
1066X .... $10.00+
1093X .... $10.00+
1311X .... $15.00+
1752X .... $40.00+
1915X .... $30.00+
1919X .... $20.00+
2046X .... $8.00+
2073X .... $10.00+
2094X .... $10.00+
3139 .... $40.00+
3142 .... $20.00+
4044X .... $20.00+
4106X .... $30.00+
4144X .... $20.00+
4145X .... $20.00+
4178X .... $50.00+
4189 .... $75.00+
8140X .... $15.00+
8156X .... $10.00+
8181X .... $15.00+
8183X .... $15.00+
RG-68-X .... $10.00+

Page 162
Left Side
408 .... $25.00+
707 .... $20.00+
748 .... $25.00+
890 .... $15.00+
1054 .... $10.00+
1058 .... $10.00+
1092 .... $10.00+
1311 .... $15.00+

1752 .... $40.00+
1755 .... $20.00+
2011 .... $8.00+
2027 .... $8.00+
2043 .... $8.00+
2046 .... $8.00+
2095 .... $8.00+
2096 .... $8.00+
3103 .... $8.00+
4044 .... $20.00+
4070 .... $75.00+
4104 .... $35.00+
4131 .... $8.00+
4133 .... $15.00+
4140 .... $30.00+
4142 .... $75.00+
4144 .... $20.00+
4145 .... $20.00+
4159 .... $45.00+
4168 .... $60.00+
8190 .... $45.00+
8196 .... $40.00+
8200 .... $50.00+
Right Side
68X .... $10.00+
153 .... $10.00+
408 .... $25.00+
707 .... $20.00+
890 .... $15.00+
1091 .... $10.00+
1311 .... $15.00+
1735 .... $15.00+
1752 .... $40.00+
1755 .... $20.00+
1915 .... $30.00+
1919 .... $20.00+
2043 .... $8.00+
2045 .... $8.00+
2072 .... $8.00+
2073 .... $10.00+
4044 .... $20.00+
4070 .... $75.00+
4104 .... $35.00+
4122 .... $15.00+
4131 .... $8.00+
4133 .... $15.00+
4140 .... $30.00+
4144 .... $20.00+
4145 .... $20.00+
4147 .... $20.00+
4148 .... $25.00+
4149 .... $15.00+
4150 .... $30.00+
4166 .... $25.00+
4167 .... $25.00+
8156 .... $10.00+
8181 .... $15.00+
8182 .... $20.00+
8183 .... $20.00+

Page 163
Left Side - All prices on this side are priced as being in Multi Directional.
746 .... $50.00+
2057 .... $20.00+
2069X .... $15.00+
2070X .... $15.00+
2083X .... $15.00+
2084X .... $15.00+
3074X .... $20.00+
3075X .... $25.00+
3130 .... $50.00+

3142 .... $25.00+
3144 .... $150.00+
3157 .... $45.00+
4141 .... $75.00+
4142 .... $75.00+
4143 .... $60.00+
4152 .... $50.00+
4161X .... $50.00+
4162X .... $40.00+
8167 .... $15.00+
8188 .... $50.00+
Right Side
3139H (Multi-Directional) $60.00+
4185H .... $60.00+
8193H .... $60.00+
8207XH .... $60.00+
8215 .... $125.00+
8216 .... $125.00+

Page 164
Left Side
4185H .... $60.00+
4185H .... $60.00+
4199 .... $30.00+
4199H .... $50.00+
5000 .... $50.00+
5001 .... $50.00+
5002 .... $50.00+
5003H .... $60.00+
5004H .... $60.00+
5005H .... $30.00+
8207H .... $60.00+
8215 .... $125.00+
8216 .... $125.00
8219H .... $40.00+
8225 .... $30.00+
8226 .... $30.00+
8228H .... $60.00+
Right Side
2105 .... $8.00+
2109 .... $8.00+
3168 .... $20.00+
3169 .... $25.00+
3170 .... $25.00+
3171 .... $15.00+
3172 .... $20.00+
3173 .... $25.00+
3174 .... $20.00+
4106X .... $30.00+
4131X .... $8.00+
4132X .... $10.00+
4133X .... $15.00+
4170 .... $30.00+
4171 .... $40.00+
4174 .... $40.00+
4196 .... $25.00+
4197 .... $35.00+
4200 .... $15.00+
8207H .... $60.00+

Page 165
Left Side
2105 .... $8.00+
2109 .... $8.00+
3169 .... $25.00+
3172 .... $20.00+
3173 .... $25.00+
3174 .... $20.00+
4106X .... $30.00+
4131X .... $8.00+
4132X .... $10.00+
4133X .... $15.00+

4170 .... $30.00+
4171 .... $40.00+
4172 .... $50.00+
4185 .... $50.00+
4195 .... $20.00+
4200 .... $15.00+
4202 .... $30.00+
Right Side
612X .... $50.00+
613X .... $50.00+
649 .... $15.00+
650 .... $15.00+
748 .... $25.00+
1068 .... $10.00+
1762 .... $150.00+
2043 .... $8.00+
2067 .... $8.00+
2100 .... $15.00+
3045/3076 .... $25.00+ set
3071 .... $25.00+
3074 .... $10.00+
3075 .... $15.00+
3160 .... $10.00+
4070 .... $75.00+
4131 .... $8.00+
4132 .... $15.00+
4133 .... $15.00+
4140 .... $30.00+
4147 .... $20.00+
4148 .... $25.00+
4149 .... $15.00+
4158 .... $40.00+
4159 .... $45.00+
4168 .... $60.00+
4190 .... $20.00+
4193 .... $15.00+
4203 .... $20.00+
4205 .... $15.00+
4206 .... $20.00+
5006H .... $60.00+
8097 .... $20.00+
8182 .... $20.00+
8186/87 .... $50.00+ set
8205H .... $60.00+
8208 .... $20.00+

Page 166
Left Side
520 .... $30.00+
642X .... $30.00+
709 .... $15.00+
721 .... $20.00+
1086 .... $8.00+
1233 .... $15.00+
2034 .... $8.00+
2045 .... $8.00+
2092 .... $8.00+
3057 .... $45.00+
3153 .... $10.00+
3160 .... $10.00+
3161 .... $10.00+
3162 .... $10.00+
3166 .... $10.00+
4012 .... $25.00+
4088 .... $15.00+
4122 .... $15.00+
4128 .... $20.00+
4150 .... $30.00+
4165 .... $20.00+
4175 .... $25.00+
4176 .... $15.00+
4204 .... $15.00+

8134 .... $20.00+
8141 .... $40.00+ set
8141 .... $10.00+
8142 .... $10.00+
8145 .... $10.00+
8190 .... $45.00+
8190H .... $60.00+
8191 .... $20.00+
8191 .... $20.00+
8193 .... $15.00+
8193H .... $60.00+
8200 .... $50.00+
SP-42 .... $25.00+
Right Side
153 .... $10.00+
408 .... $25.00+
1054 .... $10.00+
1091 .... $10.00+
2043 .... $8.00+
2044 .... $8.00+
2045 .... $8.00+
2070 .... $10.00+
2071 .... $8.00+
2072 .... $8.00+
2099 .... $10.00+
2103 .... $8.00+
2104 .... $8.00+
2106 .... $8.00+
4070 .... $75.00+
4103 .... $15.00+
4159 .... $45.00+
4203 .... $20.00+
4204 .... $15.00+
4205 .... $15.00+
4206 .... $20.00+
8097 .... $20.00+

Page 167
Left Side
3174XH .... $45.00+
4185X .... $30.00+
4195X .... $30.00+
5000 .... $50.00+
5005H .... $30.00+
5006H .... $60.00+
5007 .... $30.00+
8190 .... $45.00+
8193H .... $60.00+
8207H .... $60.00+
8215 .... $125.00+
8216 .... $125.00+
Right Side
612 .... $50.00+
612X .... $50.00+
613 .... $50.00+
613X .... $50.00+
628 (with base) ..... $45.00+
628X .... $45.00+
642X .... $30.00+
649 .... $15.00+
650 .... $15.00+
5022 .... $30.00+
5023 .... $30.00+
5024 .... $30.00+
5025 .... $30.00+
5026 .... $25.00+
5027 .... $35.00+
5028 .... $35.00+

Page 168
Left Side
2057 .... $20.00+

2069X .... $10.00+
2070X .... $10.00+
2094X .... $10.00+
2094X .... $10.00+
2105 .... $8.00+
2109 .... $8.00+
2113X .... $10.00+
2115X .... $8.00+
2124X .... $10.00+
2125X .... $10.00+
2126X .... $15.00+
3173XH .... $60.00+
4160X .... $60.00+
4161X .... $50.00+
4162X .... $30.00+
4201X .... $50.00+
4202 .... $30.00+
4231X .... $30.00+
4232X .... $30.00+
4233X .... $30.00+
8167X .... $10.00+
8188 .... $40.00+
8207H .... $60.00+
Right Side
3178H (Sunset) ..... $175.00+
3183XH (Peacock) $175.00+
5005H .... $30.00+
5015H .... $60.00+
5016H .... $60.00+
5017H .... $60.00+
Iron Stand .... $200.00+

Page 169
Left Side
746 .... $25.00+
2057 .... $20.00+
2069X .... $10.00+
2070X .... $10.00+
2085X .... $10.00+
2094X .... $10.00+
2105 .... $8.00+
2109 .... $8.00+
2113X .... $10.00+
2114X .... $15.00+
3170 .... $40.00+
3171X .... $15.00+
3172X .... $15.00+
3172XH .... $40.00+
3173X .... $25.00+
3174X .... $20.00+
3175X .... $15.00+
3187X .... $20.00+
4131X .... $8.00+
4132X .... $10.00+
4141 .... $75.00+
4143X .... $60.00+
4152X .... $40.00+
4160X .... $60.00+
4161X .... $50.00+
4162X .... $30.00+
4170X .... $30.00+
4171 .... $40.00+
4172X .... $20.00+
4184 .... $60.00+
4185X .... $50.00+
4195X .... $20.00+
4200X .... $15.00+
4202 .... $30.00+
8167X .... $10.00+
8188 .... $40.00+
8207 .... $45.00+
Right Side

2069X .... $10.00+
3175X .... $15.00+
3187X .... $20.00+
4131X .... $8.00+
4132X .... $10.00+
4172X .... $20.00+
4184 .... $60.00+
4185X .... $50.00+
4185XH .... $60.00+
4195X .... $20.00+
4200X .... $15.00+
5000H (w/hanger) .... $75.00+
5000H (w/o hanger) ...... $50.00+
8167X .... $10.00+

Page 170
Left Side - All prices on this side are priced as being in Stoneware Peacock.
746 .... $75.00+
1915X .... $100.00+
1919X .... $65.00+
2109 .... $25.00+
2111X .... $30.00+
2113X .... $30.00+
2115X .... $25.00+
3177 .... $85.00+
3178 .... $175.00+
3179H .... $300.00+
3180 .... $100.00+
3182 .... $200.00+
3183H .... $175.00+
3184 .... $80.00+
4160X .... $125.00+
4161X .... $100.00+
4162X .... $75.00+
4170X .... $150.00+
4200X .... $60.00+
4202 .... $100.00+
4207 .... $225.00+
4208X .... $250.00+
8167X .... $40.00+
Right Side - All prices on this side are priced as being in Stoneware Sunset.
1919X .... $55.00+
2111X .... $25.00+
2115X .... $20.00+
3178 .... $150.00+
3182 .... $125.00+
3183H .... $150.00+
3184 .... $70.00+
4160X .... $100.00+
4161X .... $75.00+
4162X .... $50.00+
4170X .... $110.00+
4202 .... $75.00+
4207 .... $200.00+
4208X .... $225.00+
RG-68-XX .... $45.00+

Page 171
Reference Only

Page 172
Reference Only

Page 173
Reference Only

Page 174
Reference Only

Page 175
2069 .... $10.00+
2084 .... $10.00+
2085 .... $10.00+
2124 .... $10.00+
2125X .... $10.00+

Page 176
R-1095 .... $15.00+
Top Right .... $20.00+
Middle Left .... $50.00+ w/label
Middle Right .... $30.00+
Bottom Left .... $30.00+
Bottom Right .... $30.00+

Page 177
Top Left .... $30.00+
128 (Gold Tweed) .... $10.00+
127 (Gold Tweed) .... $10.00+
109-S (Gold Tweed) .... $10.00+
1016-S .... $20.00+
889 .... $15.00+

Page 178
128 .... $10.00+
1045 .... $10.00+
720-S .... $15.00+
1030 .... $8.00+
153 .... $10.00+
702 .... $20.00+

Page 179
135 .... $10.00+
Top Right .... $15.00+
2009 .... $8.00+
2115 .... $8.00+
2145 .... $10.00+
R-873 .... $15.00+

Page 180
R-685 .... $75.00+
2105 .... $8.00+
R-1894 .... $10.00+
134 .... $15.00+
175 .... $15.00+
R-125 .... $8.00+
153 .... $10.00+
Page 181
162 .... $20.00+
2155 .... $8.00+
1016-S .... $20.00+
R-1718 .... $15.00+

Page 182
R-1787 .... $20.00+
110-H .... $10.00+
R-125 .... $8.00+
R-631 .... $75.00+
R-811 .... $10.00+
135 .... $10.00+

Page 183
R-1602 .... $15.00+
HJ-8 .... $15.00+
138 .... $8.00+
130 .... $15.00+
135 (Purple Jewel Tone) ..... $20.00+

Page 184
153 .... $10.00+

2070	$10.00+
8167	$15.00+
130	$15.00+
113	$8.00+ each

Page 185
813-H	$15.00+
R-1755	$20.00+
SP-12	$8.00+
813-H	$15.00+

Page 186
177	$8.00+
812-H	$30.00+
8167	$15.00+
R-449	$10.00+ each

Page 187
3622	$35.00+ pair
R-132	$150.00+ pair
R-641	$50.00+ pair
R-718	$75.00+ pair

Page 188
R-1144	$75.00+ pair
R-638	$150.00+ pair
R-475	$75.00+ pair

Page 189
R-309	$30.00+
R-1824	$30.00+
R-333	$20.00+
R-370	$40.00+

Page 190
R-759	$25.00+
RG-56 (Black Mistique)	$25.00+
R-277	$20.00+
R-614	$100.00+
352 (Black Mistique)	$60.00+

Page 191
364-H	$30.00+
R-466	$20.00+
R-309	$30.00+
3003	$15.00+

Page 192
H-740	$20.00+
R-1494	$25.00+
334	$20.00+
R-358	$40.00+
R-1338	$20.00+

Page 193
329-H (Gold Tweed)	$40.00+
364-H (Gold Tweed)	$20.00+
373-H	$20.00+
R-484	$15.00+

Page 194
47	$15.00+
362	$20.00+
W-2005	$15.00+
878-H	$25.00+

Page 195
3177	$25.00+
3961	$8.00+
3169	$25.00+

Page 196
S-552	$10.00+
101	$8.00+
R-466	$20.00+

Page 197
R-442	$75.00+
314	$20.00+
R-373	$75.00+
R-476	$25.00+

Page 198
R-1195	$25.00+
R-421	$50.00+
R-421	$50.00+
R-328	$75.00+

Page 199
R-290	$75.00+
R-481	$75.00+
8172	$75.00+
60	$30.00+
R-877	$20.00+

Page 200
342	$15.00+
106	$30.00+
3122-A	$8.00+
R-1729	$20.00+
R-112	$75.00+
746 (w/o lid)	$10.00+

Page 201
R-224	$40.00+
450 (Gold Tweed)	$15.00+
25	$75.00+
5	$35.00+
63	$40.00+
4195	$30.00+

Page 202
RT-63 (Green Gold Tweed)	$15.00+
811	$5.00+
33	$5.00+
863	$8.00+
834	$8.00+

Page 203
34	$30.00+ each
120	$60.00+ pair
R-220	$25.00+ each
R-203	$40.00+ each
R-579	$20.00+ each
R-397	$30.00+ each
243	$50.00+ each

Page 204
R-304	$60.00+ pair
R-312	$30.00+ pair
R-1285	$15.00+ pair
R-312	$30.00+ pair
R-1728	$15.00+ pair

Page 205
R-516	$150.00+ pair
R-433	$25.00+ each
R-418	$75.00+ pair
R-220	$50.00+ pair

Page 206
815-H (Gold Tweed)	$50.00+
R-473	$40.00+ each
HT-46	$75.00+ each
8487	$50.00+ pair
R-485	$25.00+ each

Page 207
R-185	$75.00+ pair
3004	$15.00+ pair
3004 (Peacock)	$25.00+ pair

Page 208
3068	$45.00+
1552-S	$20.00+ pair
R-1354	$15.00+ pair
Bottom Left	$15.00+
3142	$20.00+

Page 209
R-431	$75.00+
R-1730	$15.00+
8170	$75.00+
R-459	$50.00+

Page 210
R-459	$50.00+
R-457	$50.00+
707-S	$20.00+
R-431	$75.00+
8004-H	$15.00+

Page 211
8300	$75.00+
8296	$75.00+
8295	$75.00+
8297	$75.00+
8299	$75.00+
8294	$75.00+
RG-68	$10.00+
RG-37	$10.00+

Page 212
3045	reference
Top Left (Jug)	reference
8183-X	$15.00+
R-1919	$20.00+
8180	$15.00+
R-312	$30.00+ pair
R-284	$60.00+

Page 213
4233-X	$30.00+
2057	$20.00+
4232-X	$30.00+
3187-X	$20.00+
4161-X	$50.00+
R-453	$75.00+
R-372	$30.00+

Page 214
R-1752W	$40.00+
4011	$60.00+
343	$15.00+
489	$50.00+

Page 215
| 4034 (Cerulean Gold) | $80.00+ |

4035 (Cerulean Gold)	$70.00+
4027 (Cerulean Gold)	$100.00+
R-455	$75.00+
3277	$60.00+
336	$20.00+ pair
335	$25.00+
336/335	$50.00+ set

Page 216
257	$15.00+
809	$10.00+
4131	$8.00+
4132	$10.00+
4133	$15.00+
4165	$20.00+
8142 (w/lid)	$10.00+
8142 (w/o lid)	$8.00+

Page 217
R-321	$25.00+
R-476	$25.00+
R-557	$25.00+
R-527	$25.00+
3318	$20.00+
3232	$15.00+
616	$15.00+

Page 218
R-371	$25.00+
R-438	$25.00+ each
345-S	$20.00+
R-1746	$20.00+ pair
R-967	$60.00+
R-968	$50.00+ pair

Page 219
R-891	$40.00+ pair
R-7285	$30.00+ pair
R-103	$60.00+
318-H	$35.00+
R-1919	$20.00+

Page 220
4132-X	$10.00+
3170	$40.00+
4001	$15.00+
H-72	$30.00+
4149	$15.00+
9-H	$40.00+
R-1915	$30.00+

Page 221
726-H	$40.00+
1076-H	$15.00+
8054	$15.00+
3928	$15.00+
3968A	$15.00+
8183-X	$15.00+
4131	$8.00+
4200	$15.00+

Page 222
3819	$10.00+
725	$25.00+
R-1121	$20.00+
R-1170	$50.00+
827	$15.00+

Page 223
| Top Left | $200.00+ |
| 8189 | $200.00+ |

Bottom Left .... $125.00+
R-188 .... $250.00+

Page 224
612 .... $50.00+
613 .... $50.00+

Page 225
R-1762 .... $150.00+
F-3 .... $10.00+ each
6 .... $20.00+
649 .... $15.00+
650 .... $15.00+

Page 226
F-17 .... $15.00+
R-130 .... $15.00+
7 .... $20.00+
650 .... $15.00+
649 .... $15.00+

Page 227
R-287 (Hickman) .... $75.00+
R-287 .... $75.00+
R-434 .... $50.00+

Page 228
R-435 .... $50.00+
R-165 .... $100.00+
R-313 .... $75.00+
R-282 .... $60.00+
R-313 .... $75.00+

Page 229
616 .... $60.00+

Page 230
R-313 .... $75.00+
R-282 .... $60.00+
R-314 .... $75.00+

Page 231
R-648 .... $45.00+
R-313 .... $75.00+
R-1131 .... $500.00+
R-649 .... $45.00+
683 .... $150.00+

Page 232
495 .... $40.00+
315 .... $30.00+

Page 233
R-412 .... $40.00+
3108 .... $8.00+
R-777 .... $40.00+
Bot. Left (Phil-Mar) ... $60.00+
R-413 .... $30.00+

Page 234
R-318 .... $100.00+
R-166 .... $150.00+
R-167 .... $150.00+
R-975 .... $50.00+

Page 235
R-424 .... $200.00+
R-451 .... $225.00+
R-1265 .... $50.00+

R-479 .... $150.00+

Page 236
3235 .... $30.00+
3296 .... $15.00+
R-235 .... $80.00+
R-402 .... $40.00+

Page 237
502-H .... $100.00+
R-379 .... $500.00+
R-379 (with base) .... $400.00+

Page 238
6343 .... $50.00+
R-1510 (Mandarin Orange) .. $150.00+
R-1510 .... $100.00+

Page 239
R-138 .... $100.00+
R-284 .... $60.00+
3248 .... $20.00+
R-784 .... $40.00+

Page 240
648 .... $10.00+
R-1782 .... $100.00+
R-376A .... $50.00+
R-375A .... $50.00+
R-375B .... $150.00+
812 .... $75.00+

Page 241
514 .... $50.00+
837 .... $75.00+
838 .... $75.00+

Page 242
R-1224 .... $75.00+
R-382 .... $75.00+
R-383 .... $75.00+

Page 243
R-363 .... $125.00+
R-838 .... $75.00+
57 .... $40.00+
R-360 .... $125.00+
R-359 .... $150.00+

Page 244
86 .... $200.00+
R-772 .... $100.00+
R-484 .... $15.00+
R-364 .... $125.00+
77 .... $75.00+
R-189 .... $200.00+

Page 245
R-875 .... $150.00+
141 .... $75.00+
5190 .... $250.00+
R-455 .... $75.00+
6204 .... $250.00+

Page 246
1138 .... $150.00+
5240 .... $150.00+
5353 .... $50.00+
R-1262 .... $50.00+

Page 247
R-869 .... $75.00+
5195 .... $75.00+
5473 .... $200.00+
R-115 .... $50.00+

Page 248
6051-TV .... $45.00+
6140 .... $50.00+
5202 .... $225.00+
5237 .... $200.00+

Page 249
5401 .... $50.00+
6424S-TV .... $125.00+
5344 .... $50.00+
Bottom Right .... $125.00+

Page 250
3003 .... $250.00+
4172 .... $150.00+
5362 .... $75.00+

Page 251
5100 .... $100.00+ each
5398 .... $200.00+
5205 .... $300.00+

Page 252
5051 .... $300.00+
5483 .... $75.00+

Page 253
R-1504/R-1505 ..... $75.00+ set
R-1506/R-1507 ..... $50.00+ set
8186/8187 .... $50.00+ set

Page 254
Top Left .... reference only
Top Right .... $150.00+
Bottom Left .... $75.00+

Page 255
Top Left .... $75.00+
Top Right .... $150.00+
8034 .... $40.00+
Haeger Pen Holder $100.0+
Parker Pen Holder . $75.00+

Page 256
Top Left .... $40.00+
Top Middle .... $25.00+
Top Right .... $200.00+
Bottom (Plate) ...... $20.00+
Bottom (Saucer) .... $10.00+
Bottom (Cup) .... $15.00+

Page 257
Top Left .... $250.00+
Top Right .... $20.00+
Bottom Left .... $35.00+
Bottom Right .... $150.00+

Page 258
Top Left .... $20.00+
845 .... $35.00+
Middle Left .... $20.00+
Middle Right .... $35.00+
Bottom Left .... $40.00+
R-449 .... $10.00+ each

Page 259
Top Left .... $150.00+
Top Right .... $75.00+
Middle .... $15.00+
Bottom .... $125.00+

Page 260
Top Left .... $15.00+
Top Right .... $75.00+
R-531 .... $75.00+
Bottom Right .... $40.00+

Page 261
Top .... $20.00+
Bottom Left .... $250.00+
Bottom Right .... $200.00+

Page 262
Top Left .... $40.00+
Top Right .... $25.00+
Middle .... $60.00+ each
Bottom Left .... $225.00+
Bottom Right .... $50.00+

Page 263
Top Left .... $65.00+
Top Right .... $10.00+
Bottom Left .... $125.00+
Bottom Right .... $10.00+

Page 264
4058/4060 .... $25.00+ set
8183 .... $20.00+
8188 .... $40.00+
3182 (Sunset) .... $125.00+

Page 265
R-698 .... $50.00+
8229 .... $30.00+
H-608 .... $40.00+
920 .... $8.00+

Page 266
8011/8010 .... $20.00+
Top Left .... reference only
Middle .... $50.00+ pair
873-H .... $40.00+

Page 267
575 .... $35.00+ set
Middle (Cup) .... $5.00+
3207-S .... $10.00+
3201 .... $25.00+ set
8061 .... $20.00+
8062 .... $30.00+

Page 268
R-1679-S .... $50.00+
4150 .... $30.00+
8182 .... $20.00+
R-1582-S .... $15.00+
R-1585-S .... $40.00+
R-1584-S .... $40.00+
R-1583-S .... $15.00+

Page 269
14 .... $15.00+
3314 .... $30.00+
618 .... $15.00+
617 .... $15.00+

Page 270
R-754 .... $20.00+
B-3107 .... $15.00+
3311 .... $25.00+
R-540 .... $45.00+
R-766 .... $85.00+

Page 271
R-1844 .... $20.00+
B-3322 .... $20.00+
8008-H .... $20.00+
R-334 .... $150.00+
R-1747 .... $20.00+

Page 272
R-182L .... $35.00+
R-515 .... $125.00+
R-453 .... $75.00+
R-31 .... $75.00+

Page 273
R-1402-C .... $60.00+
R-430 .... $35.00+
R-108 .... $100.00+

Page 274
R-1226 .... $45.00+
R-1761 .... $200.00+
508 .... $45.00+
6202 .... $75.00+

Page 275
R-1146 .... $50.00+
R-869 .... $75.00+
3511 .... $45.00+

Page 276
R-1220 .... $35.00+
Top Right .... $250.00+
R-1734 .... $75.00+
R-1913 .... $20.00+

Page 277
R-1191 .... $45.00+
R-284 .... $60.00+
R-284 .... $60.00+

Page 278
R-271 .... $45.00+
R-271 .... $45.00+

Page 279
5051 .... $40.00+
5084 .... $40.00+
5015-H .... $60.00+
5072 .... $40.00+
5070 .... $50.00+

Page 280
5033 .... $55.00+
5080 .... $40.00+
5073 .... $40.00+
5025 .... $30.00+

Page 281
3054 .... $20.00+
R-1253 .... $45.00+
R-1254 .... $45.00+
RG-98 .... $25.00+
RG-99 .... $25.00+

Page 282
3947 .... $30.00+
3532 .... $30.00+
R-859 .... $50.00+
3910 .... $15.00+

Page 283
RG-132 .... $15.00+
3427-AM .... $40.00+
990 .... $20.00+
RG-118 .... $15.00+

Page 284
Top Left .... $15.00+
RG-18 .... $15.00+
3264 .... $20.00+
3932 .... $20.00+
3855 .... $15.00+

Page 285
368 .... $10.00+
3280-B .... $10.00+
3244 .... $10.00+
3106 .... $15.00+
3061 .... $60.00+

Page 286
R-460 .... $50.00+
R-483 .... $75.00+
R-298 .... $60.00+

Page 287
R-1460 .... $20.00+
R-575 .... $75.00+
R-321 .... $25.00+
R-223 .... $100.00+
R-293 .... $60.00+

Page 288
R-525 .... $75.00+
3212 .... $40.00+
R-657 .... $75.00+

Page 289
R-1293 .... $20.00+
R-709 .... $15.00+
394 .... $15.00+
338 .... $15.00+
R-1462 .... $15.00+

Page 290
R-1446 .... $15.00+
3292 .... $15.00+
3752 .... $10.00+
R-1639-S .... $35.00+
3175 .... $15.00+
R-1640-S .... $25.00+

Page 291
3174-XH .... $20.00+
3172 .... $20.00+
5000 .... $50.00+
4185-X .... $50.00+
8207-H .... $60.00+

Page 292
R-843 .... $60.00+
R-281 .... $100.00+
776 (Aqua Tweed) .... $15.00+
3085 .... $10.00+

R-510 .... $50.00+

Page 293
3130 .... $40.00+
R-936 .... $20.00+
R-852 .... $20.00+
503 .... $40.00+
5040 .... $25.00+

Page 294
Top .... $8.00+
3880 .... $10.00+
Bottom .... $8.00+

Page 295
167 .... $10.00+
667 .... $8.00+
Middle .... $8.00+
4020 .... $15.00+
8443 .... $8.00+

Page 296
Top Left .... $35.00+
Top Right .... $500.00+
Middle Left .... $25.00+
Middle Right .... $25.00+
Bottom .... $75.00+

Page 297
3276 .... $20.00+
3220 .... $95.00+
R-36 .... $100.00+
R-182 .... $25.00+

Page 298
R-285 .... $25.00+
R-186 .... $75.00+
R-888 .... $30.00+

Page 299
R-482 .... $75.00+
R-248 .... $35.00+
3225 .... $10.00+
3270 .... $20.00+

Page 300
R-301 .... $25.00+
R-355 .... $40.00+
R-138 .... $100.00+
R-826 .... $20.00+

Page 301
R-320 .... $30.00+
33 .... $75.00+
3240 .... $8.00+ each
36 .... $45.00+

Page 302
3053 .... $75.00+
R-427 .... $250.00+
R-857 .... $50.00+
R-393 .... $125.00+

Page 303
3386 .... $20.00+
R-647 .... $40.00+
R-706 .... $50.00+
R-707 .... $50.00+
186 .... $35.00+

Page 304
186 .... $35.00+
R-455 .... $75.00+
R-303 .... $75.00+
R-446 .... $75.00+

Page 305
R-441 .... $100.00+
R-320 .... $30.00+
R-441 .... $100.00+

Page 306
R-131 .... $75.00+
R-386 .... $65.00+

Page 307
3528 .... $15.00+
R-452 .... $100.00+
3531 .... $25.00+

Page 308
332A .... $25.00+
R-426 .... $45.00+
R-426 .... $45.00+
332B .... $35.00+

Page 309
R-701 .... $60.00+
R-523 .... $60.00+
3227 .... $75.00+

Page 310
R-228 .... $35.00+
R-422 .... $60.00+

Page 311
R-228 .... $35.00+
R-246 .... $50.00+
R-332B .... $35.00+ each
R-299 .... $40.00+
R-299 .... $40.00+

Page 312
3105 .... $15.00+
3208 .... $25.00+
R-322 .... $35.00+

Page 313
Top Left (Original-1914) $75.00+
141 .... $85.00+
1037 .... $20.00+
19A .... $45.00+ each
47 .... $75.00+
39 .... $50.00+

Page 314
628 .... $25.00+ each
43 .... $75.00+
39 .... $50.00+
182 .... $100.00+
8237 .... $100.00+

Page 315
186 .... $150.00+
1018 .... $20.00+
3015 .... $20.00+
607 .... $15.00+
463 .... $45.00+

Page 316
136 .... $20.00+
R-337 .... $150.00+
R-454 .... $150.00+
R-504 .... $50.00+

Page 317
2908 .... $35.00+
R-580 .... $50.00+
R-456 .... $50.00+
R-441 (Silver Overlay) . $200.00+
3059 .... $75.00+

Page 318
R-1123 .... $35.00+ each
3617 .... $15.00+
R-893 .... $40.00+
R-833 .... $60.00+
4044 .... $20.00+

Page 319
R-651 .... $20.00+
W-2002 .... $150.00+
R-490 .... $150.00+
R-900 .... $20.00+
R-830 .... $85.00+
R-1235 .... $20.00+
R-979 .... $20.00+

Page 320
D-1021 .... $60.00+
D-1028 .... $50.00+
D-1001 .... $60.00+
714 .... $20.00+
R-501 .... $100.00+

Page 321
931 .... $35.00+
R-251 .... $100.00+
3273 .... $35.00+
R-456 .... $50.00+

Page 322
R-416 (w/lid) .... $150.00+
R-416 (w/o lid) .... $75.00+
R-419 .... $75.00+
R-417 .... $75.00+

Page 323
R-1619-S .... $25.00+
408 .... $25.00+
R-1812-S .... $60.00+
R-1752-W .... $40.00+

Page 324
R-1776 .... $35.00+
RG-82 .... $15.00+
413 .... $15.00+
4029-H .... $25.00+
456 .... $75.00+
8180 .... $15.00+

Page 325
R-1915 .... $30.00+
455 .... $45.00+
493 .... $150.00+
413 (Gold Tweed) .... $10.00+
RG-68 .... $10.00+

Page 326
4031 .... $25.00+
478 .... $25.00+
R-1919 .... $20.00+
4038 .... $35.00+
408 .... $25.00+

Page 327
483 .... $60.00+
493 .... $150.00
R-1919 .... $20.00+
1-H .... $150.00+

Page 328
R-1619-S .... $100.00+
2-H .... $100.00+
R-1752 .... $40.00+
R-1444 .... $75.00+

Page 329
2021 .... $20.00+
RG-14 .... $10.00+
RG-42 .... $10.00+
S-400 .... $75.00+

Page 330
RG-68 .... $10.00+
483 .... $60.00+
R-895 .... $45.00+
4183 .... $75.00+

Page 331
4244 .... $65.00+
4200 .... $15.00+
4162-X .... $30.00+
4202 .... $30.00+
4171 .... $40.00+
4132 .... $10.00+

Page 332
4161-X .... $50.00+
4248 .... $30.00+
4238-X .... $60.00+
4160-X .... $60.00+
4233-X .... $30.00+

Page 333
4174 .... $40.00+
4142 .... $75.00+
4181 .... $75.00+
4231-X .... $30.00+

Page 334
4106 .... $50.00+
4182 .... $75.00+
4143 .... $60.00+
Bottom Right .... $65.00+

Page 335
4070 .... $20.00+
4012 .... $15.00+
S-447 .... $15.00+
4002 .... $15.00+

Page 336
4205 .... $15.00+
8097 .... $20.00+
4131 .... $8.00+
4103 .... $15.00+

Page 337
451 .... $40.00+
4144 .... $20.00+
4141 .... $75.00+
303 .... $15.00+
RG-92 .... $8.00+
4256 .... $15.00+

Page 338
4194 .... $30.00+
4243 .... $20.00+
4162-X .... $30.00+
4411 .... $75.00+

Page 339
517 .... $45.00+ each
R-1135 .... $50.00+
R-16275 .... $75.00+
R-745 .... $75.00+
R-1627-S .... $

Page 340
917A .... $10.00+
126 .... $65.00+
R-725 .... $20.00+
3112 .... $20.00+